THE LANGUAGE OF THE HEART

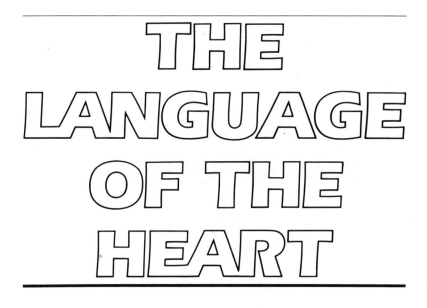

THE LANGUAGE OF THE HEART

Bill W.'s Grapevine Writings

The AA Grapevine, Inc.
New York

Several of Bill W.'s Grapevine articles (or excerpts from them) appear in AA Conference-approved pamphlets. "Problems Other Than Alcohol" has been reprinted as a pamphlet, and excerpts from the same article have also been published as a flyer. All the articles in the pamphlet "AA Tradition: How It Developed" were originally published in the Grapevine, and appear in Part One of this volume.

Copyright © 1988 by the AA Grapevine, Inc., PO Box 1980, Grand Central Station, New York, NY 10163-1980
All Rights Reserved.

Eighth printing 2004

Grateful acknowledgment is made for permission to reprint the following:

Letter to William Wilson from C. G. Jung, January 30, 1961. Copyright © 1963 by Princeton University Press, Princeton, NJ. Reprinted by permission.

Excerpts from *AA Comes of Age* (copyright © 1985) and *Twelve Concepts for World Service* (copyright © 1985) are reprinted with the permission of AA World Services, Inc.

Library of Congress Catalog Card No. 88-71930

ISBN 0-933685-16-5

Printed in the United States of America

CONTENTS

PART ONE: 1944-1950

Segment 1: The Shaping of the Traditions

Segment 2: Additional Writings from This Period

PART TWO: 1950-1958

Segment 1: AA Grows to Maturity

Segment 2: Let's Be Friendly with Our Friends

Segment 3: Additional Writings from This Period

PART THREE: 1958-1970

Segment 1: In All Our Affairs

Segment 2: Looking Toward the Future

Segment 3: Additional Writings from This Period

Memorial Articles

Articles About the Grapevine

FOREWORD

Dear Friends,

As you may know, Bill wrote quite extensively for the <u>Grapevine</u> over many years. It was a way for him to share his experience, strength and hope with the entire Fellowship.

I think it is wonderful that so much of this work will now be available again -- especially for the countless A.A.s who have come into the Fellowship since these articles were first published.

I hope they will find them useful.

Gratefully,

Lois

INTRODUCTION

Publication of *The Language of the Heart* brings together for the first time virtually every article written for the AA Grapevine by Bill W., co-founder of Alcoholics Anonymous. Though several of his articles are available in reprint form, whether as pamphlets, AA books, or in later issues of the magazine, they have never before been published in one volume.

In June 1944, the Grapevine was established as a local newsletter through the individual efforts of six New York City AAs who were concerned about what seemed to be "a lack of understanding" among groups in the metropolitan area. Mailed by the six editors to all known groups in the U.S. and Canada, and sent free to AAs in the World War II armed forces, the Grapevine soon caught on nationally. In 1945, by vote of the groups, it became the principal journal of the Fellowship as a whole, and since the January 1949 issue it has been known as the international journal of Alcoholics Anonymous.

From the first issue of the eight-page newsletter, Bill W. was a prolific contributor, an enthusiastic advocate, and for many years a consulting editor. In spite of a grueling travel schedule and a copious correspondence, Bill could never find enough time to respond to all the many and varied demands of a Fellowship that was still in the process of formation, and in the Grapevine he discovered an ideal vehicle of communication with the members and groups who clamored for his insights and experience. In more than 150 articles, written over a span of twenty-six years, Bill documented the painstaking process of trial and error that resulted in AA's spiritual principles of Recovery, Unity, and Service, and articulated his vision of what the Fellowship could become.

When the current Grapevine editors began to consider ways of grouping Bill's articles in logical segments, it seemed at first a Herculean task — yet in the end it was not. Largely because of Bill's own highly focused way of thinking and working, the articles virtually fell into place. They are arranged chronologically in three Parts, according to the primary AA concerns Bill was thinking and writing about during each period of time. They are further subdivided by major and minor subject matter within each Part. Brief introductions to Parts One, Two, and Three outline the major events and trends in AA that impelled Bill to emphasize a particular aspect of AA life, and in a few cases, an introductory sentence or two sets the context for a specific article. Toward the end appear a group of memorial articles (written in appreciation for several nonalcoholic friends of AA, as well as for Dr. Bob and for Bill D., AA Number Three), and an Appendix containing seven articles in which Bill reflected on the Grapevine itself.

While the intent is to make available the whole body of Bill's Grapevine writings, a few omissions have been made because of length. His series of articles on the Traditions, written in 1952 and 1953 and later reprinted in the book *Twelve Steps and Twelve Traditions*, is readily accessible in that book and thus is not repeated here: similarly, two excerpts from *AA Comes of Age* that were reprinted as Grapevine articles have not been included, and one article that appeared twice in the Grapevine appears only once here. All of Bill's very brief (about half a page each) Christmas and Thanksgiving greetings to the Fellowship have been cut, with the exception of the December 1970 Christmas message, his last Grapevine piece. And finally, a few brief items (short memorial tributes to General Service Office staff and an announcement that the General Service Office was moving to a new location) have also been omitted.

Since this collection is by its nature an historical document, several characteristics should be mentioned. First, repetition: The articles appeared originally in a periodical publication, and Bill could never be sure that any reader had seen a previous one. Thus, he often repeated ideas or illustrations, and those repetitions have been retained to assure the integrity of Bill's work. Second, some material has become outdated; for example, a few ideas that were articulated in very early articles about the Traditions proved unworkable in the light of later experience, but for the sake of historical accuracy, earlier versions have not been edited. And last, Bill was a man of his times, and some readers may find unfamiliar idioms and terminology, or may be taken aback by phraseology that would be considered inappropriate today. Once again, the original language (with a few changes that necessitated no rewriting) has been re-tained, because any tampering with phraseology might also have tam-pered with the meaning.

Bill W.'s most-quoted description of the Grapevine appears in *AA Comes of Age*: "The Grapevine is the mirror of AA thought and action, worldwide. It is a sort of magic carpet on which all of us can travel from one distant AA outpost to another, and it has become a wonderful ex-change medium of our current thought and experience." It is the hope of the Grapevine editors that Bill W.'s timeless insights, written in the 1940s, '50s, and '60s, will serve as a mirror for AA members in the 1980s and beyond, reminding us of what it used to be like, documenting what happened and why it happened, and illuminating the present with the wisdom of AA's experience in its first thirty years.

PART

ONE

1944 - 1950

In the summer of 1944, Alcoholics Anonymous was experiencing phenomenal growth. AA's leadership still lay primarily in the hands of its founding members, and from one tiny office in New York City, Bill W. and a few others sought to keep up with a nearly overwhelming surge in membership. The Jack Alexander article, published in the *Saturday Evening Post* in 1941, had caused AA's numbers to grow from 2,000 to 8,000 by the end of that year. By 1950, the membership would swell to more than 96,000, and the number of groups would jump from about 500 in 1944 to 3,500 in 1950. In tandem with this upsurge within the Fellowship, many nonalcoholics in medicine, religion, and the media were becoming aware of AA as a solution for seemingly hopeless alcoholics, and were clamoring for information and answers about AA's policies.

The flood of letters pouring into AA's small Headquarters office, along with the experience gleaned from visits to groups all over North America, clarified for Bill and the other founding members the principles that seemed to enhance group unity, as well as those that often led to conflict. Faced with growth and challenges from within and without, Bill was fully aware that the new Fellowship could easily founder under the weight of its own success — unless a common body of guiding principles and an effective policy for relating to the general public could be formulated.

In the articles in Part One, Bill described the accumulated experience and suggested for the Fellowship's consideration a set of practical guiding principles. These landmark articles reached a climax in the April 1946 issue with "Twelve Suggested Points for AA Tradition," now the long form of the Twelve Traditions.

Segment

1

The Shaping
of the Traditions

Modesty One Plank
for Good Public Relations

August 1945

During its brief few years in the public eye, Alcoholics Anonymous has received hundreds of thousands of words of newspaper and magazine publicity. These channels have been augmented recently by radio commentators and, here and there, AA-sponsored radio broadcasts. Hardly a word of criticism or ridicule has ever been uttered about us. While our publicity has sometimes lacked a certain dignity, we can scarcely complain of that. After all, drinking is not such a dignified business!

We surely have reason for great gratitude that multitudes of writers, editors, clergy, doctors — friends of every description — have continued so sympathetically and so enthusiastically to urge our cause. As a direct result of their efforts thousands of alcoholics have come to AA. It is a good record. Providentially good, when one considers how many mistakes we might have made; how deeply, had other policies been followed, we might now be involved. In the "wet-dry" controversy, for example. Conceivably we might even have fallen out with our good friends, religion and medicine. None of these things have happened. We have been unbelievably fortunate, thank God.

While this makes fine success story reading, it is not, to our way of thinking, any reason for self-congratulation. Older AAs who know the record are unanimous in their feeling that an intelligence greater than ours has surely been at work, else we could never have avoided so many pitfalls, could never have been so happily related to our millions of friends in the outside world.

Yet history records the rise and, let us not forget, the fall of any number of promising and benign undertakings — political, religious, and social. While some did outlive their usefulness the greater part died prematurely. Something wrong or unsound within them always became apparent without. Their public relations suffered, they grew no more; they bogged down to a dead level or fell apart.

Personal glorification, overweening pride, consuming ambition, exhibitionism, intolerant smugness, money or power madness, refusal to admit mistakes and learn from them, self-satisfaction, lazy complacency — these and many more are the garden varieties of ills which so often beset movements as well as individuals.

While we AAs, as individuals, have suffered much from just such defects, and must daily admit and deal with them in our personal lives if we are to stay sober and useful, it is nevertheless true that such attitudes have seldom crept into our public relations. But someday they might. Let us never say, "It can't happen here."

Those who read the July Grapevine were startled, then sobered, by the account which it carried of the Washingtonian movement. It was hard for us to believe that a hundred years ago the newspapers of this country were carrying enthusiastic accounts about a hundred thousand alcoholics who were helping each other stay sober; that today the influence of this good work has so completely disappeared that few of us had ever heard of it.

Let's cast our eyes over the Grapevine piece about the Washingtonians and excerpt a few sentences: "Mass meeting in 1841, at City Hall Park, New York City, attracted 4,000 listeners. Speakers stood on upturned rum kegs." "Triumphal parades in Boston. Historic Faneuil Hall jammed." (Overdone self-advertising — exhibitionism? Anyhow, it sounds very alcoholic, doesn't it!) "Politicians looked hungrily at the swelling membership...helped wreck local groups through their efforts to line up votes." (Looks like personal ambition again, also unnecessary group participation in controversial issues; the hot political issue was then abolition of slavery.) "The Washingtonians were confident...they scorned old methods." (Too cocksure, maybe. Couldn't learn from others and became competitive, instead of cooperative, with other organizations in their field.)

Like AA, the Washingtonians originally had but one object: "Was concerned only with the reclamation of drunkards and held that it was none of its affair if others used alcohol who seemed little harmed by it." But later on came this development: "There was division among the older local organizations — some wanted wines and beers — some clamored for legislation to outlaw alcohol — in its zeal for new members many intemperate drinkers, not necessarily alcoholic, were pledged." (The original strong and simple group purpose was thus dissipated in fruitless controversy and divergent aims.)

And again, "Some [of the Washingtonian local groups] dipped into their treasuries to finance their own publications. There was no overall editorial policy. Editors of local papers got into squabbles with editors of temperance papers." (Apparently the difficulty was not necessarily the fact they had local publications. It was more the refusal of the Washingtonians to stick to their original purpose and so refrain from fighting anybody; also the obvious fact that they had no national public relations policy or tradition which all members were willing to follow.)

We are sure that if the original Washingtonians could return to this planet they would be glad to see us learning from their mistakes. They would not regard our observations as aimless criticism. Had we lived in their day we might have made the same errors. Perhaps we are beginning to make some of them now.

So we need to constantly scrutinize ourselves carefully, in order to make everlastingly certain that we shall always be strong enough and single-purposed enough from within, to relate ourselves rightly to the world without.

Now then, does AA have a public relations policy? Is it good enough? Are its main principles clear? Can it meet changing conditions over the years to come?

Now that we are growing so rapidly into public view, many AAs are becoming acutely conscious of these questions. In the September Grapevine I'll try to briefly outline what our present public relations practices are, how they developed, and where, in the judgment of most older AA members, they could perhaps be improved to better cope with our new and more pressing problems.

May we always be willing to learn from experience!

'Rules' Dangerous but Unity Vital

September 1945

D oes Alcoholics Anonymous have a public relations policy? Is it adequate to meet our present and future needs?

Though it has never been definitely formulated or precisely stated, we certainly have a partly formed public relations policy. Like everything else in AA, it has grown up out of trial and error. Nobody invented it. Nobody has ever laid down a set of rules or regulations to cover it, and I hope no one ever will. This is because rules and regulations seem to be little good for us. They seldom work well.

Were we to proceed by rules, somebody would have to make them and, more difficult still, somebody would have to enforce them. Rule-making has often been tried. It usually results in controversy among the rule-makers as to what the rules should be. And when it comes to enforcing an edict — well, you all know the answer. When we try to enforce rules and regulations, however reasonable, we almost always get in so "dutch" that our authority disappears. A cry goes up: "Down with the dictators, off with their heads!" Hurt and astonished control committee after control committee, "leader" after "leader," makes the discovery that *human authority,* be it ever so impartial or benign, seldom works long or well in our affairs. Alcoholics (no matter if ragged) are yet the most rugged of individualists, true anarchists at heart.

Of course, nobody claims this trait of ours to be a sterling virtue. During his first AA years every AA has had plenty of the urge to revolt against authority. I know I did, and can't claim to be over it yet. I've also served my time as a maker of rules, a regulator of other people's conduct. I, too, have spent sleepless nights nursing my "wounded" ego, wondering how others whose lives I sought to manage could be so unreasonable, so thoughtless of "poor me." I can now look back upon such experiences with much amusement. And gratitude as well. They taught me that the very quality which prompted me to govern other people was the identical egocentricity which boiled up in my fellow AAs when they themselves refused to be governed!

A non-AA reader can be heard to exclaim: "This looks very serious for the future of these people. No organization, no rules, no authority? It's anarchy; it's dynamite; it's 'atomic' and bound to blow up. Public relations indeed! If there is no authority how can they have any public relations policy at all? That's the very defect which ruined the Washingtonian alcoholics a hundred years ago. They mushroomed to a hundred thousand members, then collapsed. No effective policy or authority. Quarreled among themselves, so finally got a black eye with the public. Aren't these AAs just the same kind of drunks, the same kind of anarchists? How can they expect to succeed where the Washingtonians failed?"

Good questions, these. Have we the answers? While we must never be too sure, there is reason to hope that we have, because forces seem to be at work in AA that were little evident among our fellow alcoholics of the 1840s.

For one thing, our AA program is spiritually centered. Most of us have found enough humility to believe in and depend upon God. We have found that humility by facing the fact that alcoholism is a fatal malady over which we are individually powerless. The Washingtonians, on the contrary, thought drinking to be just another strong habit which could be broken by willpower as expressed in pledges, plus the sustaining force of mutual aid through an understanding society of ex-drunks. Apparently they thought little of personality change, and nothing at all of spiritual conversion.

Mutual aid plus pledges did do a lot for them, but it wasn't enough; their individual egos still ran riot in every channel save alcohol. Self-serving forces having no real humility, having little appreciation that the penalty for too much self-will is death to the alcoholic, having no greater power to serve, finally destroyed the Washingtonians.

When, therefore, we AAs look to the future, we must always be asking ourselves if the *spirit* which now binds us together in our common cause will always be stronger than those personal ambitions and desires which tend to drive us apart. So long as the positive forces are greater we cannot fail. Happily, so far, the ties that bind us have been much stronger than those that might break us. Though the individual AA is under no human coercion, is at almost perfect personal liberty, we have, nevertheless, achieved a wonderful unity on vital essentials.

For example, the Twelve Steps of our AA program are not crammed down anybody's throat. They are not sustained by any human authority. Yet we powerfully unite around them because the truth they contain has saved our lives, has opened the door to a new world. Our experience tells us these universal truths work. The anarchy of the individual yields to their persuasion. He sobers up and is led, little by little, to complete agreement with our simple fundamentals.

Ultimately, these truths govern his life and he comes to live under their authority, the most powerful authority known, *the authority of his full consent, willingly given.* He is ruled, not by people, but by principles, by truths and, as most of us would say, by God.

Now some might ask, "What has all this got to do with an AA public relations policy?" An older AA would say, "Plenty." While experience shows that in AA no policy can be created and announced full-blown, much less effectively enforced by human authority, we are nevertheless faced with the problem of developing a public relations policy and securing for it the only authority we know — that of common understanding and widespread, if not universal, consent. When this consent is secured we can then be sure of ourselves. AAs will everywhere put the policy into effect as a matter of course, automatically. But we must at first be clear on certain basic principles. And these must have been well tried and tested in our crucible of experience.

In forthcoming articles I shall therefore try to trace the development of our public relations from the very first day we came to public notice. This will show what our experience has already taught us. Then every AA can have a real background for constructive thinking on this terribly vital matter — a matter on which we dare not make grave mistakes; upon which, over the years, we cannot afford to become unsound.

One qualification, however. A policy isn't quite like a fixed truth. A policy is something which can change to meet variable conditions, even though the basic underlying truths upon which it is founded do not change at all. Our policy might, for example, rest upon our Twelve Steps for its underlying truths, yet remain reasonably flexible so far as the means or method of its application is concerned.

Hence I earnestly hope thousands of AAs start thinking a great deal about these policy matters which are now becoming so important to us. It is out of our discussions, our differences of opinion, our daily experiences, and our general consent that the true answers must finally come.

As an older member I may be able to marshal the facts and help analyze what has happened so far. Perhaps I can even make some suggestions of value for the future. But that is all. Whether we are going to have a clear-cut workable public relations policy will finally be determined by all of us together — not by me alone!

The Book Is Born

October 1945

In recent Grapevine articles attention has been drawn to the fact that AA is still in the process of forming a public relations policy, that failure to crystallize a sound policy could seriously cripple us.

During the first three years of AA no one gave a thought to public relations. It was a time of "flying blind," when we feverishly sought the principles upon which we might stay sober and assist the few alcoholics who came around wanting to do likewise. We were entirely preoccupied with the life-and-death question of personal recovery. It was strictly a man-to-man affair. We hadn't even agreed upon a name for our movement. There was no literature.

By the fall of 1937 we could count what looked like forty recovered members. One of us had been sober three years, another two and a half, and a fair number had a year or more behind them. As all of us had been hopeless cases, this amount of time elapsed began to be significant. The realization that we "had found something" began to take hold of us. No longer were we a dubious experiment. *Alcoholics could stay sober. Great numbers, perhaps!* While some of us had always clung to this possibility, the dream now had real substance. If forty alcoholics could recover, why not four hundred, four thousand — even forty thousand?

Once this spectacular notion gripped us, our thinking underwent a sudden change. Our alcoholic imaginations certainly had a field day. By temperament most of us are salesmen, promoters. So we began talking very big. Mere boxcar numbers wouldn't do. We went astronomical. Undoubtedly, we said, this was the beginning of one of the greatest medical, religious, and social developments of all time. We would show the medical profession and the sky pilots where they got off! A million alcoholics in America; more millions all over the world! Why, we only had to sober up all these boys and girls (and sell them God), whereupon they would revolutionize society. A brand-new world with ex-drunks running it. Just think of that, folks!

Publicity? Why of course! Millions of words! Money? Sure! It would take millions, naturally. The matter of money and publicity would be a cinch — just a campaign of high-powered selling directed at our American tycoons and editors would quickly settle that question. How could they resist when they saw what we had? Just watch us drunks. Actually, a few of us were pretty nearly as bad as that! No circus barker was ever so enthusiastic or extravagant in his cries as were some of us in the fall of 1937. In fact, I can recall having done a great deal of the barking myself!

Now suppose the promoters of those pioneering days had not been slowed down. Suppose that our public relations policy had been left fully in their hands. Suppose they had been able to raise millions, to flood the country with AA propaganda and wild claims. We would not only have fallen out with our best friends, religion and medicine, we would surely have been discredited among the very people we wished most to reach — alcoholic men and women. Much money would have meant a large staff of professional AA therapists or "do-gooders," and promoters plus money would surely have meant ballyhoo on every subject under the sun from prohibition to communist Russia. Internally, if we still existed at all, we would have been torn apart by political controversy, religious dissension. It happened to the Washingtonians. Who, then, has saved us thus far?

The people who did the saving job then, and who have continued to save us much trouble since, are a class of individuals with whom most AAs are impatient. *These people are the conservatives.* They are the "go slow," "think it over," "let's not do that" type. Not many of them are to be found among us alcoholics, but it's certainly providential that we have always had a few such around. Often accused of being a drag on progress (as they sometimes are), they are nevertheless a priceless asset. They bring the rest of us down out of the clouds; they make us face the realities of experience; they foresee dangers which most of us would blithely ignore. Sometimes their conservatism is overdone; they needlessly "view with alarm for the good of the movement." Knowing that mere change is not necessarily progress, they instinctively resist change. They never wish to take an irrevocable step; they often shrink from those final decisions from which there is no retreat. They keep out of trouble by making sure never to get into it.

The first discussion of our public relations in 1937 at Akron will always live in my memory. The promoters could think of nothing but getting the glad news of our recoveries to a million alcoholics, overnight if possible. If this were done, God would do the rest, they said. But the conservatives did not think God did business that way.

The conservatives then proceeded, with terrific impact, to make the point that the man of Galilee had no press agent, no newspapers, no pamphlets, no books — nothing but word of mouth to carry the spirit from person to person, from group to group. Why should we deviate from his example? Were we about to substitute ballyhoo for personal demonstration? Were we to favor personal glorification in public in place of quietness, humility, and anonymity?

These were good questions; they made us promoters stop and think. Though obliged to concede much to the conservatives on principle, we still felt their counsel was that of perfection. It wasn't practical. The conservatives retorted that while promoters had built many a successful enterprise they almost always bankrupted what they had built if they were left long enough in charge. We promoters (and I was one of them) came back with this: How, we inquired, could the "go slow boys" sleep nights when they reflected that after three long years we had produced but three small groups; that America had a million alcoholics dying like flies; that within gunshot of where we sat there were perhaps hundreds who could get well if they only knew what we knew? And did alcoholics in California have to wait for relief to get there by word of mouth only? And wasn't there grave danger of our successful methods being badly distorted unless reduced to writing and put in book form? And if we made no written record of what we had found, might not columnists get funny and start deadly ridicule? Caution, we agreed, ought to be observed by all means, but still didn't we need a book of our own, some publicity?

Such was the gist of the discussion out of which came the decision to publish the book *Alcoholics Anonymous*. This led to publicity, to the establishment of our Board of Trustees (The Alcoholic Foundation), and to the creation of the Central Office [now the General Service Office] at New York where alcoholics and their families can write for literature and direct help. Our rapid and seemingly healthy growth the past few years has pretty well demonstrated the wisdom of these early decisions.

The point is obvious. If these vital matters had been left entirely to the promoters like me, we would surely have gone hog-wild and spoiled everything. Had these affairs been left exclusively to the conservatives, it is probable that few of our present membership would yet have heard of AA. Thousands would have remained miserable. Many would have been dead.

So it seems clear that sound policy can only be made by rubbing the conservatives and the promoters together. Their discussions, if free from personal ambitions and resentment, can be depended upon to produce the right answers. For us, there is no other way.

Having now shown how our first step in public relations was taken, I would like, in forthcoming pieces, to tell more of our recent experiences in this field, with emphasis on the desirability of continued modesty, anonymity, and fidelity to one objective only: that of carrying AA to the alcoholic who wishes to recover.

A Tradition Born
of Our Anonymity

January 1946

I n the years that lie ahead the principle of anonymity will undoubtedly become a part of our vital Tradition. Even today, we sense its practical value. But more important still, we are beginning to feel that the word "anonymous" has for us an immense spiritual significance. Subtly but powerfully it reminds us that we are always to place principles before personalities; that we have renounced personal glorification in public; that our movement not only preaches, but actually practices a truly humble modesty. That the practice of anonymity in our public relations has already had a profound effect upon us, and upon our millions of friends in the outside world, there can hardly be doubt. Anonymity is already a cornerstone of our public relations policy.

How this idea first originated and subsequently took hold of us is an interesting bit of AA history. In the years before the publication of the book *Alcoholics Anonymous,* we had no name. Nameless, formless, our essential principles of recovery still under debate and test, we were just a group of drinkers groping our way along what we hoped would be the road to freedom. Once we became sure that our feet were set on the right track, we decided upon a book in which we could tell other alcoholics the good news. As the book took form we inscribed in it the essence of our experience. It was the product of thousands of hours of discussion. It truly represented the collective voice, heart, and conscience of those of us who had pioneered the first four years of AA.

As the day of publication approached we racked our brains to find a suitable name for the volume. We must have considered at least two hundred titles. Thinking up titles and voting upon them at meetings became one of our main activities. A great welter of discussion and argument finally narrowed our choice to a single pair of names. Should we call our new book *The Way Out* or should we call it *Alcoholics Anonymous*? That was the final question. A last-minute vote was taken by the Akron and New York groups. By a narrow majority the verdict was for naming our book *The Way Out*. Just before we went to print somebody suggested there might be other books having the same title. One of our early Lone Members (dear old Fitz M., who then lived in Washington) went over to the Library of Congress to investigate. He found exactly twelve books already titled *The Way Out*. When this information was passed around, we shivered at the possibility of being the "thirteenth Way Out." So *Alcoholics Anonymous* became first choice. That's how we got a name for our book of experience, a name for our movement and, as we are now beginning to see, a Tradition of the greatest spiritual import. God does move in mysterious ways his wonders to perform!

In the book *Alcoholics Anonymous* there are only three references to the principle of anonymity. The foreword of our first edition states: "Being mostly business or professional folk some of us could not carry on our occupations if known" and "When writing or speaking publicly about alcoholism, we urge each of our fellowship to omit his personal name, designating himself instead as 'a member of Alcoholics Anonymous,' " and then, "very earnestly we ask the press also to observe this request for otherwise we shall be greatly handicapped."

Since the publication of *Alcoholics Anonymous* in 1939, hundreds of AA groups have been formed. Every one of them asks these questions: "Just how anonymous are we supposed to be?" and "After all, what good is this principle of anonymity anyway?" To a great extent each group has settled upon its own interpretation. Naturally enough, wide differences of opinion remain among us. Just what our anonymity means and just how far it ought to go are unsettled questions.

Though we no longer fear the stigma of alcoholism as we once did, we still find individuals who are extremely sensitive about their connection with us. A few come in under assumed names. Others swear us to the deepest secrecy. They fear their connection with Alcoholics Anonymous may ruin their business or social position. At the other end of the scale of opinion we have the individual who declares that anonymity is a lot of childish nonsense. He feels it his bounden duty to cry his membership in Alcoholics Anonymous from the housetops. He points out that our AA Fellowship contains people of renown, some of national importance. Why, he asks, shouldn't we capitalize on their personal prestige just as any other organization would?

In between these extremes, the shades of opinion are legion. Some groups, especially newer ones, conduct themselves like secret societies. They do not wish their activities known even to friends. Nor do they propose to have preachers, doctors, or even their wives at any of their meetings. As for inviting in newspaper reporters — perish the thought!

Other groups feel that their communities should know all about Alcoholics Anonymous. Though they print no names, they do seize every opportunity to advertise the activities of their group. They occasionally hold public or semipublic meetings where AAs appear on the platform by name. Doctors, clergy, and public officials are frequently invited to speak at such gatherings. Here and there a few AAs have dropped their anonymity completely. Their names, pictures, and personal activities have appeared in the public prints. As AAs they have sometimes signed their names to articles telling of their membership.

So while it is quite evident that most of us believe in anonymity, our practice of the principle does vary a great deal.

Of course, it should be the privilege, even the right, of each individual or group to handle anonymity as they wish. But to do that intelligently we shall need to be convinced that the principle is a good one for practically all of us; indeed we must realize that the future safety and effectiveness of Alcoholics Anonymous may depend upon its preservation. Each individual will then have to decide where he ought to draw the line — how far he ought to carry the principle in his own affairs, how far he may go in dropping his own anonymity without injury to Alcoholics Anonymous as a whole.

The vital question is: Just where shall we fix this point where personalities fade out and anonymity begins?

As a matter of fact, few of us are anonymous so far as our daily contacts go. We have dropped anonymity at this level because we think our friends and associates ought to know about Alcoholics Anonymous and what it has done for us. We also wish to lose the fear of admitting that we are alcoholics. Though we earnestly request reporters not to disclose our identities, we frequently speak before semipublic gatherings under our right names. We wish to impress audiences that our alcoholism is a sickness we no longer fear to discuss before anyone. So far, so good. If, however, we venture beyond this limit we shall surely lose the principle of anonymity forever. If every AA felt free to publish his own name, picture, and story we would soon be launched upon a vast orgy of personal publicity which obviously could have no limit whatever. Isn't this where, by the strongest kind of attraction, we must draw the line?

If I were asked to outline a Tradition for anonymity it might run as follows:

1. It should be the privilege of each individual AA to cloak himself with as much personal anonymity as he desires. His fellow AAs should respect his wishes and help guard whatever status he wants to assume.

2. Conversely, the individual AA ought to respect the feeling of his

local group as to anonymity. If his group wishes to be more anonymous than he does, he ought to go along with them until they change their views.

3. With very rare exceptions it ought to be a national Tradition that no member of Alcoholics Anonymous shall ever feel free to publish his name or picture (in connection with his Alcoholics Anonymous activities) in any medium of public circulation, or by radio. Of course, this should not restrict the free use of his name in other public activities, provided he does not disclose his AA connection.

4. If for some extraordinary reason, for the good of AA as a whole, a member thinks it desirable to completely drop his anonymity, he should only do so after consulting the older members of his local group. If he is to make a nationwide public appearance as an AA the matter ought to be referred to our Central Office [GSO].

Of course, I am not for a moment thinking of these statements as rules or regulations; they merely suggest what would seem to be sound Tradition for the future. In the last analysis every AA will have to search his own conscience.

If we are going to evolve a clear-cut Tradition about anonymity we shall do it only through our usual process: trial and error, much discussion, collective judgment, and common consent.

To stimulate further discussion I would like, in an early issue of the Grapevine, to review our experience with anonymity. That we shall eventually come up with the right answers I can have no doubt.

Our Anonymity Is Both Inspiration and Safety

March 1946

D iscussing the subject of anonymity in a previous Grapevine article, I tried to make the following points: that anonymity has, for us AAs, an immense spiritual significance; that the principle ought to be preserved as part of our vital Tradition; that since we have as yet no sharply defined policy there is confusion in some quarters as to what anonymity ought to mean; that we need, therefore, a perfectly clear Tradition which all AAs would feel bound to respect. I also offered some suggestions which I hoped might become, after further discussion, the basis of a national policy on anonymity. These suggestions were:

1. It should be the privilege of each AA to cloak himself with as much personal anonymity as he desires. His fellow AAs should respect his wishes and help guard whatever status he wants to assume.

2. Conversely, the individual AA ought to respect the feeling of his local group about anonymity. If the group wishes to be less conspicuous in their locality than he does, he ought to go along with them until they change their views.

3. With very rare exceptions, it ought to be a national policy that no member of Alcoholics Anonymous shall ever feel free to publish, in connection with an AA activity, his name or picture in media of public circulation. This would not, however, restrict the use of his name in other public activities provided, of course, he does not disclose his AA membership.

4. If, for some extraordinary reason, a member thinks it desirable to drop his anonymity locally he should do so only after consulting his own group. If, as an AA, he is to make a nationwide public appearance the matter ought to be referred to national Headquarters.

If these suggestions, or variations of them, are to be adopted as a national policy, every AA will want to know more about our experience so far. He will surely wish to know how most of our older members are thinking on the subject of anonymity at the present time. It will be the purpose of this piece to bring everybody up to date on our collective experience.

First, I believe most of us would agree that the general idea of anonymity is sound, because it encourages alcoholics and the families of alcoholics to approach us for help. Still fearful of being stigmatized, they regard our anonymity as an assurance their problems will be kept confidential, that the alcoholic skeleton in the family closet will not wander in the streets.

Second, the policy of anonymity is a protection to our cause. It prevents our founders or leaders, so called, from becoming household names who might at any time get drunk and give AA a black eye. No one need say that couldn't happen here. It could.

Third, almost every newspaper reporter who covers us complains, at first, of the difficulty of writing his story without names. But he quickly forgets this difficulty when he realizes that here is a group of people who care nothing for personal gain. Probably it is the first time in his life he has ever reported an organization which wants no personal publicity. Cynic though he may be, this obvious sincerity instantly transforms him into a friend of AA. Therefore his piece is a friendly piece, never a routine job. It is enthusiastic writing because the reporter feels that way himself. People often ask how Alcoholics Anonymous has been able to secure such an incredible amount of excellent publicity. The answer seems to be that practically everyone who writes about us becomes an AA convert, sometimes a zealot. Is not our policy of anonymity mainly responsible for this phenomenon?

Fourth, why does the general public regard us so favorably? Is it simply because we are bringing recovery to lots of alcoholics? No, this can hardly be the whole story. However impressed he may be by our recoveries, John Q. Public is even more interested in our way of life. Weary of pressure selling, spectacular promotion, and shouting public characters, he is refreshed by our quietness, modesty, and anonymity. It well may be that he feels a great spiritual power is being generated on this account — that something new has come into his own life.

If anonymity has already done these things for us, we surely ought to continue it as a national policy. So very valuable to us now, it may become an incalculable asset for the future. *In a spiritual sense, anonymity amounts to the renunciation of personal prestige as an instrument of national policy.* I am confident that we shall do well to preserve this powerful principle; that we should resolve never to let go of it.

Now what about its application? Since we advertise anonymity to every newcomer, we ought, of course, to preserve a new member's anonymity so long as he wishes it preserved. Because, when he read our publicity and came to us, we contracted to do exactly that. And even if he wants to come in under an assumed name, we should assure him he can. If he wishes us to refrain from discussing his case with anyone, even other AA members, we ought to respect that wish too. While most newcomers do not care a rap who knows about their alcoholism, there are others who care very much. Let us guard them in every way until they get over that feeling.

Then comes the problem of the newcomer who wishes to drop his anonymity too fast. He rushes to all his friends with the glad news of AA. If his group does not caution him he may rush to a newspaper office or a microphone to tell the wide world all about himself. He is also likely to tell everyone the innermost details of his personal life, soon to find that, in this respect, he has altogether too much publicity! We ought to suggest to him that he take things easy; that he first get on his own feet before talking about AA to all and sundry; that no one thinks of publicizing AA without being sure of the approval of his own group.

Then there is the problem of group anonymity. Like the individual, it is probable that the group ought to feel its way along cautiously until it gains strength and experience. There should not be too much haste to bring in outsiders or to set up public meetings. Yet this early conservatism can be overdone. Some groups go on, year after year, shunning all publicity or any meetings except those for alcoholics only. Such groups are apt to grow slowly. They become stale because they are not taking in fresh blood fast enough. In their anxiety to maintain secrecy, they forget their obligation to other alcoholics in their communities who have not heard that AA has come to town. But this unreasonable caution eventually breaks down. Little by little some meetings are opened to families and close friends. Clergy and doctors may now and then be invited. Finally the group enlists the aid of the local newspaper.

In most places, but not all, it is customary for AAs to use their own names when speaking before public or semipublic gatherings. This is done to impress audiences that we no longer fear the stigma of alcoholism. If, however, newspaper reporters are present they are earnestly requested not to use the names of any of the alcoholic speakers on the program. This preserves the principle of anonymity so far as the general public is concerned and at the same time represents us as a group of alcoholics who no longer fear to let our friends know that we have been very sick people.

In practice, then, the principle of anonymity seems to come down to this: With one very important exception, the question of how far each individual or group shall go in dropping anonymity is left strictly to the individual or group concerned. The exception is: that all groups or individuals, when writing or speaking for publication as members of Alcoholics Anonymous, feel bound never to disclose their true names. Except for very rare cases, it is at this point of publication that nearly all of us feel we should draw the anonymity line. *We ought not disclose ourselves to the general public.*

In our whole history not more than a handful of AAs have ever dropped their anonymity so far as the general public is concerned. Some of these instances have been accidental, a few have been quite unnecessary, and one or two are apparently justified. Of course there must be few policies which cannot sometimes, in the general interest, be suspended. Yet any who would drop their anonymity must reflect that they may set a precedent which could eventually destroy a valuable principle. The exceptions will have to be few, far between, and most carefully considered. We must never let any immediate advantage shake us in our determination to hang on to such a really vital Tradition.

Great modesty and humility are needed by every AA for his own permanent recovery. If these virtues are such vital needs to the individual, so must they be to AA as a whole. This principle of anonymity before the general public can, if we take it seriously enough, guarantee the Alcoholics Anonymous movement these sterling attributes forever. Our public relations policy should mainly rest upon the principle of attraction and seldom, if ever, upon promotion.

Twelve Suggested Points
for AA Tradition

April 1946

Nobody invented Alcoholics Anonymous. It grew. Trial and error has produced a rich experience. Little by little we have been adopting the lessons of that experience, first as policy and then as Tradition. That process still goes on and we hope it never stops. Should we ever harden too much, the letter might crush the spirit. We could victimize ourselves by petty rules and prohibitions; we could imagine that we had said the last word. We might even be asking alcoholics to accept our rigid ideas or stay away. May we never stifle progress like that!

Yet the lessons of our experience count for a great deal — a very great deal, we are each convinced. The first written record of AA experience was the book *Alcoholics Anonymous*. It was addressed to the heart of our foremost problem — release from the alcohol obsession. It contained personal experiences of drinking and recovery and a statement of those divine but ancient principles which have brought us a miraculous regeneration. Since publication of *Alcoholics Anonymous* in 1939 we have grown from 100 to 24,000 members. Seven years have passed; seven years of vast experience with our next greatest undertaking — the problem of living and working together. This is today our main concern. If we can succeed in this adventure — and keep succeeding — then, and only then, will our future be secure.

Since personal calamity holds us in bondage no more, our most challenging concern has become the future of Alcoholics Anonymous; how to preserve among us AAs such a powerful unity that neither weakness of persons nor the strain and strife of these troubled times can harm our common cause. We know that Alcoholics Anonymous must continue to live. Else, save few exceptions, we and our fellow alcoholics throughout the world will surely resume the hopeless journey to oblivion.

Almost any AA can tell you what our group problems are. Fundamentally they have to do with our relations, one with the other, and with the world outside. They involve relations of the AA to the group, the relation of the group to Alcoholics Anonymous as a whole, and the place of Alcoholics Anonymous in that troubled sea called modern society, where all of humankind must presently shipwreck or find haven. Terribly relevant is the problem of our basic structure and our attitude toward those ever pressing questions of leadership, money, and authority. The future may well depend on how we feel and act about things that are controversial and how we regard our public relations. Our final destiny will surely hang upon what we presently decide to do with these danger-fraught issues!

Now comes the crux of our discussion. It is this: Have we yet acquired sufficient experience to state clear-cut policies on these, our chief concerns? Can we now declare general principles which could grow into vital Traditions — Traditions sustained in the heart of each AA by his own deep conviction and by the common consent of his fellows? That is the question. Though full answers to all our perplexities may never be found, I'm sure we have come at least to a vantage point whence we can discern the main outlines of a body of Tradition; which, God willing, can stand as an effective guard against all the ravages of time and circumstance.

Acting upon the persistent urge of old AA friends, and upon the conviction that general agreement and consent between our members is now possible, I shall venture to place in words these suggestions for an Alcoholics Anonymous Tradition of Relations — Twelve Points to Assure Our Future.

Our AA experience has taught us that:

1. Each member of Alcoholics Anonymous is but a small part of a great whole. AA must continue to live or most of us will surely die. Hence our common welfare comes first. But individual welfare follows close afterward.

2. For our group purpose there is but one ultimate authority — a loving God as he may express himself in our group conscience.

3. Our membership ought to include all who suffer alcoholism. Hence we may refuse none who wish to recover. Nor ought AA membership ever depend upon money or conformity. Any two or three alcoholics gathered together for sobriety may call themselves an AA group.

4. With respect to its own affairs, each AA group should be responsible to no other authority than its own conscience. But when its plans concern the welfare of neighboring groups also, those groups ought to be consulted. And no group, regional committee, or individual should ever take any action that might greatly affect AA as a whole without conferring with the trustees of the Alcoholic Foundation [now the General Service Board]. On such issues our common welfare is paramount.

5. Each Alcoholics Anonymous group ought to be a spiritual entity *having but one primary purpose* — that of carrying its message to the alcoholic who still suffers.

6. Problems of money, property, and authority may easily divert us from our primary spiritual aim. We think, therefore, that any considerable property of genuine use to AA should be separately incorporated and managed, thus dividing the material from the spiritual. An AA group, as such, should never go into business. Secondary aids to AA, such as clubs or hospitals which require much property or administration, ought to be so set apart that, if necessary, they can be freely discarded by the groups. The management of these special facilities should be the sole responsibility of those people, whether AAs or not, who financially support them. For our clubs, we prefer AA managers. But hospitals, as well as other places of recuperation, ought to be well outside AA — and medically supervised. An AA group may cooperate with anyone, but should bind itself to no one.

7. The AA groups themselves ought to be fully supported by the voluntary contributions of their own members. We think that each group should soon achieve this ideal; that any public solicitation of

funds using the name of Alcoholics Anonymous is highly dangerous; that acceptance of large gifts from any source or of contributions carrying any obligation whatever is usually unwise. Then, too, we view with much concern those AA treasuries which continue, beyond prudent reserves, to accumulate funds for no stated AA purpose. Experience has often warned us that nothing can so surely destroy our spiritual heritage as futile disputes over property, money, and authority.

8. Alcoholics Anonymous should remain forever nonprofessional. We define professionalism as the occupation of counseling alcoholics for fees or hire. But we may employ alcoholics where they are going to perform those full-time services for which we might otherwise have to engage nonalcoholics. Such special services may be well recompensed. But personal Twelfth Step work is never to be paid for.

9. Each AA group needs the least possible organization. Rotating leadership is usually the best. The small group may elect its secretary, the large group its rotating committee, and the groups of a large metropolitan area their central committee, which often employs a full-time secretary. The trustees of the Alcoholic Foundation are, in effect, our general service committee. They are the custodians of our AA Tradition and the receivers of voluntary AA contributions by which they maintain AA general Headquarters and our general secretary at New York. They are authorized by the groups to handle our overall public relations and they guarantee the integrity of our principal publication, the AA Grapevine. All such representatives are to be guided in the spirit of service, for true leaders in AA are but trusted and experienced servants of the whole. They derive no real authority from their titles. Universal respect is the key to their usefulness.

10. No AA group or member should ever, *in such a way as to implicate AA,* express any opinion on outside controversial issues — particularly those of politics, alcohol reform, or sectarian religion. The Alcoholics Anonymous groups oppose no one. Concerning such matters they can express no views whatever.

11. Our relations with the outside world should be characterized by modesty and anonymity. We think AA ought to avoid sensational advertising. Our public relations should be guided by the principle of attraction rather than promotion. There is never need to praise ourselves. We feel it better to let our friends recommend us.

12. And finally, we of Alcoholics Anonymous believe that the principle of anonymity has an immense spiritual significance. It reminds us that we are to place principles before personalities; that we are

actually to practice a truly humble modesty. This to the end that our great blessings may never spoil us; that we shall forever live in thankful contemplation of him who presides over us all.

May it be urged that while these principles have been stated in rather positive language they are still only suggestions for our future. We of Alcoholics Anonymous have never enthusiastically responded to any assumption of personal authority. Perhaps it is well for AA that this is true. So I offer these suggestions neither as one man's dictum nor as a creed of any kind, but rather as a first attempt to portray that group ideal toward which we have assuredly been led by a Higher Power these ten years past.

P.S. To help free discussion I would like to amplify the Twelve Points of Tradition in future Grapevine pieces.

Safe Use of Money

May 1946

In Alcoholics Anonymous, does money make the mare go or is it the root of all evil? We are in the process of solving that riddle. Nobody pretends to have the complete answer. Where the proper use of money ends — and its misuse begins — is the point in "spiritual space" we are all seeking. Few group problems are giving thoughtful AAs more concern than this. Every one is asking, "What shall be our attitude toward voluntary contributions, paid workers, professionalism, and outside donations?"

In the first years of AA we had no money problems. We met in homes where our wives made sandwiches and coffee. If an individual AA wished to grub stake a fellow alcoholic, he did so. It was purely his own affair. We had no group funds, hence no group money troubles. And it must be recorded that many an old-time AA wishes we could now return to those early days of halcyon simplicity. Knowing that quarrels over material things have crushed the spirit of many a good undertaking, it is often thought that too much money may prove an evil for us too.

It's small use yearning for the impossible. Money *has* entered our picture and we *are definitely committed* to its sparing use. No one would seriously think of abolishing our meeting places and clubs for the sake of avoiding money altogether. Experience has shown that we very much need these facilities, so we must accept whatever risk there is in them.

But how shall we keep these risks to a minimum; how shall we traditionally limit the use of money so that it may never topple the spiritual foundation upon which each AA life so completely depends? That is our real problem today. So let us look together at the main phases of our financial situation, seeking to discover what is essential, what is nonessential, what is legitimate and harmless, and what may be dangerous or unnecessary.

Suppose we begin with voluntary contributions. Each AA finds himself dropping money in "the hat" to pay the rent of a meeting place, a club, or the maintenance of his local or national headquarters. Though not all of us believe in clubs, and while a few AAs see no necessity for any local or national offices, it can be said fairly that the vast majority of us believe that these services are basically necessary. Provided such facilities are efficiently handled, and their funds properly accounted for, we are only too glad to pledge them our regular support, with the full understanding, of course, that such contributions are in no wise a condition of our AA membership. These particular uses of our money are now generally accepted and, with some qualifications, there is little worry of dire long-range consequences.

Yet some concern does remain, arising mostly in connection with our clubs, local offices, and the national headquarters. Because these places customarily employ paid workers, and because their operation implies a certain amount of business management, it is sometimes felt that we may get bogged down with a heavy officialdom or, still worse, a downright professionalization of AA. Though it must be said that these doubts are not always unreasonable, we have already had enough experience to relieve them in large part.

To begin with, it seems most certain that we need never be overwhelmed by our clubs, local offices, or the general headquarters at New York City. These are places of service; they cannot really control or govern AA. If any of them were to become inefficient or overbearing the remedy is simple enough. The average AA would stop his financial support until conditions were changed. As our *AA membership does not depend on fees or dues,* we can always "take our special facilities or leave them alone." These services must always serve us well or go out of business. Because no one is compelled to support them they can never dictate, nor can they stray from the main body of AA Tradition for very long.

In direct line with the principle of taking our facilities or leaving them alone there is an encouraging tendency to incorporate all such special functions separately if they involve any great amount of money, property, or management. More and more, the AA groups are realizing that they are spiritual entities, not business organizations. Of course the smaller clubrooms or meeting places often remain unincorporated because their business aspect is only nominal. But as large growth takes place it is usually found wise to incorporate and so set the club apart from surrounding groups. *Support of the club then becomes an individual matter rather than a group matter.* If, however, the club also provides a central office secretary serving the surrounding area it seems only fair that group treasuries in that area should shoulder this particular expense, because such a secretary serves all groups, even though the club itself may not. Our evolution in large AA centers is beginning to indicate most clearly that while it is a proper function of a cluster of groups, or their central committee, to support a paid secretary for their area, it is not a group or central committee function to support clubs financially. Not all AAs care for clubs. Therefore club support has to come mainly from those individual AAs who need or like clubs. Which, by the way, is the majority. But the majority ought not to try to coerce the minority into supporting clubs they do not want or need.

Of course, clubs also get a certain amount of help from meetings held in them. Where central meetings for an area take place in a club it is customary to divide the collections between the club and the central committee for the area, heavily favoring the club, of course, because the club is providing the meeting place. The same arrangement may be entered into between the club and any particular group which wishes to use the club whether for meeting or entertainment. Generally speaking, the board of directors of a club looks after the financial management and the social life of the place. But strictly AA matters remain the function of the surrounding groups themselves. This division of activity is by no means the rule everywhere. It is offered as a suggestion only, much in keeping, however, with the present trend.

A large club or central office usually means one or more paid workers. What about them — are they professionalizing AA? About this, there is a hot debate every time a club or central committee gets large enough to require paid help. On this subject we have all done a pile of fuzzy thinking. And I would be one of the first to plead guilty to that charge.

The reason for our fuzzy thinking is the usual one — it is fear. To each one of us, the ideal of AA, however short we may be of it personally, is a thing of beauty and perfection. It is a Power greater than ourselves which has lifted us out of the quicksand and set us safe on shore. The slightest thought of marring our ideal, much less bartering it for gold, is to most of us unthinkable. So we are constantly on the alert against the rise within AA of a paid class of practitioners or missionaries. In AA, where each of us is a goodwill practitioner and missionary in his own right, there is no need for anyone to be paid for simple Twelfth Step work — a purely spiritual undertaking. While I suppose fear of any kind ought to be deplored, I must confess that I am rather glad that we exercise such great vigilance in this critical matter.

Yet there is a principle upon which I believe we can honestly solve our dilemma. It is this: A janitor can sweep the floor, a cook can boil the beef, a steward can eject a troublesome drunk, a secretary can manage an office, an editor can get out a newspaper — all, I am sure, without professionalizing AA. If we didn't do these jobs ourselves we would have to hire nonalcoholics to do them for us. We would not ask any non-alcoholic to do these things full-time without pay. So why should some of us, who are earning good livings ourselves in the outside world, expect other AAs to be full-time caretakers, cooks, or secretaries? Why should these AAs work for nothing at jobs which the rest of us could not or would not attempt ourselves? Or why, for that matter, should they be any the less well paid than for similar labor elsewhere? And what difference should it make if, in the course of their duties, they do some Twelfth Step work besides? Clearly the principle seems to be that we may pay well for special services — but never for straight Twelfth Step work.

How, then, could AA be professionalized? Quite simply I might, for example, hire an office and hang on the door a sign reading: "Bill W. — Alcoholics Anonymous Therapist. Charges $10.00 per hour." That would be face-to-face treatment of alcoholism for a fee. And I would surely be trading on the name of Alcoholics Anonymous, a purely ama-teur organization, to enlarge my professional practice. That *would* be pro-fessionalizing AA — and how! It would be quite legal, but hardly ethical.

Now does this mean we should criticize therapists as a class — even AAs who might choose to go into that field? Not at all. The point is that no one ought to advertise himself as an AA therapist. As we are strictly amateur there could be no such thing. That would be a distortion of the facts which none of us could afford to try. As the tennis player has to drop his amateur status when he turns professional so should AAs who become therapists cease publishing their AA connection. While I doubt if many AAs ever go into the field of alcohol therapy, none ought to feel excluded, especially if they are trained social workers, psychologists, or psychiatrists. But they certainly ought never to use their AA connection publicly or in such a way as to make people feel that AA has such a special class within its own ranks. That is where we all must draw the line.

Policy on Gift Funds

June 1946

Discussing this topic in last month's Grapevine we made the following observations:

1. That the use of money in AA is a matter of the gravest importance. Where its use ends and its misuse begins is the point we should vigilantly watch.

2. That AA is already committed to a qualified use of money, because we would not think of abolishing our offices, meeting places, and clubs simply for the sake of avoiding finances altogether.

3. That our real problem today consists in setting intelligent and traditional limits upon our use of money, thus keeping its disruptive tendency at the minimum.

4. That the voluntary contributions or pledges of AA members should be our principal, and eventually, our sole support; that this kind of self-support would always prevent our clubs and offices from getting out of hand because their funds could readily be cut off whenever they failed to serve us well.

5. That we have found it generally wise to separately incorporate those special facilities which require much money or management; that

an AA group is a spiritual entity, not a business concern.

6. That we must, at all costs, avoid the professionalization of AA; that simple Twelfth Step work is never to be paid for; that AAs going into alcohol therapy should never trade on their AA connection; that there is not, and never can be, any such thing as an "AA therapist."

7. That AA members may, however, be employed by us as full-time workers provided they have legitimate duties over and beyond normal Twelfth Step work. We may, for example, surely engage secretaries, stewards, and cooks without making them professional AAs.

Continuing now the discussion of professionalism: AAs frequently consult local communities or the Alcoholic Foundation saying they have been offered positions in related fields. Hospitals want AA nurses and doctors, clinics ask for AAs who are social workers, universities ask for AAs to work in the field of alcohol education on a noncontroversial basis, and industry wants us to recommend AAs as personnel officers. Can we, acting as individuals, accept such offers? Most of us see no reason why we cannot.

It comes down to this. Have we AAs the right to deny society the benefit of our special knowledge of the alcohol problem? Are we to tell society, even though we might make superior nurses, doctors, social workers, or educators in the field of alcohol that we cannot undertake such missions for fear of professionalizing AA? That would certainly be far-fetched — even ridiculous. Surely no AA should be barred from such employment because of membership with us. He needs only to avoid "AA therapy" and any action or word which might hurt AA as a whole. Aside from this he ought to be just as employable as the nonalcoholic who would otherwise get the job and perhaps not do it half as well. In fact, I believe we still have a few AA bartenders. Though bartending, for obvious reasons, is not a specially recommended occupation, I have never heard anyone cry out that these few members are professionalizing AA on account of their very special knowledge of barrooms!

Years ago we used to think AA should have its own hospitals, rest homes, and farms. Nowadays we are equally convinced we should have nothing of the sort. Even our clubs, well inside AA, are somewhat set apart. And in the judgment of practically all, places of hospitalization or rest should be well outside AA — and medically supervised. Hospitalization is most definitely the job of the doctor backed, of course, by private or community aid. It is not a function of AA in the sense of management or ownership. Everywhere we cooperate with hospitals. Many afford us special privileges and working arrangements. Some consult us. Others employ AA nurses or attendants. Relationships such as these almost always work well. But none of these institutions are known as "AA hospitals."

We have also had some experience with farms and drying-out places which, though outside AA and medically supervised, have nevertheless been managed and financed by AA members. Some of these operations have done well, others very badly. And with one or two conspicuous exceptions, the worst possible set-up has been that in which AA groups, with group money and management, have gone into the "drying-out" business. Despite exceptions, these "AA hospitals" seem the least promising of all. The group which takes one on usually finds that it has contracted an unnecessary responsibility and a heartbreaking amount of dissension. Being a group project, it cannot be "taken or left alone." Either it has to be abandoned or it remains a raw sore on the body politic. These experiments have well demonstrated that the AA group will always have to be a spiritual entity, not a business concern. Better do one thing supremely well than two things badly!

Now what about donations or payments to AA from outside sources? There was a time, some years ago, when we desperately needed a little outside aid. This we received. And we shall never cease being grateful to those devoted friends whose contributions made possible the Alcoholic Foundation, the book *Alcoholics Anonymous,* and our Central Office. Heaven has surely reserved a special place for every one of them. They met a great need, for in those days we AAs were very few and very insolvent!

But times have changed. Alcoholics Anonymous now has more than 24,000 members, whose combined earnings this year ought to be many millions. Hence a very powerful feeling is spreading among us that AA ought to be self-supporting. Since most members feel they owe their very lives to the movement, they think we AAs ought to pay its very modest expenses. And isn't it, they ask, high time that we commenced to revise the prevalent idea that an alcoholic is *always* a person who must be helped — usually with money. Let us AAs, they say, be no longer takers from society. Instead, let us be givers. We are not helpless now. Neither are we penniless anymore. Were it possible to publish tomorrow that every AA group had become fully self-supporting, it is probable that nothing could create more goodwill for us than such a declaration. Let our generous public devote its funds to alcohol research, hospitalization, or education. Those fields really need money. But we do not. We are no longer poor. We can, and we should, pay our own way.

Of course, it can hardly be counted an exception to the principle of self-support if a nonalcoholic friend comes to a meeting and drops a dollar in the hat. It is doubtful, too, if we should refuse the relative who sends in his $5 mite, a token of appreciation for the recovery of someone close. Perhaps we would be ungracious to refuse his gift.

But it is not these small tokens of regard which concern us. It is the large contributions, especially those that may carry future obligations, which should give us pause. Then, too, there is evidence that wealthy people are setting aside sums for AA in their wills under the impression we could use a great deal of money if we had it. Shouldn't we discourage them? And already there have been a few alarming attempts at the public solicitation of money in the name of Alcoholics Anonymous. Few AAs will fail to imagine where such a course could lead us. Every now and then we are offered money from so-called "wet" or "dry" sources. Obviously dangerous, this. For we must stay out of that ill-starred controversy. Now and then the parents of an alcoholic, out of sheer gratitude, wish to donate heavily. Is this wise? Would it be good for the alcoholic himself? Perhaps a wealthy AA wishes to make a large gift. Would it be good for him, or for us, if he did so? Might we not feel in his debt and might he not, especially if a newcomer, begin to think he had bought a ticket to that happy destination, sobriety?

In no case have we ever been able to question the true generosity of these givers. But is it wise to take their gifts? Though there may be rare exceptions, I share the opinion of most older AAs that acceptance of large donations from any source is very questionable — almost always a hazardous policy. The struggling club may badly need a friendly gift or loan. Even so, it might be better in the long run to pay as we go. We must never let any immediate advantage, however attractive, blind us to the possibility that we may be creating a disastrous precedent for the future. Strife over money and property has too often wrecked better people than us temperamental alcoholics!

It is with the deepest gratitude and satisfaction that I can now tell you of a recent resolution passed by our general service committee, the trustees of the Alcoholic Foundation, who are the custodians of our national AA funds. As a matter of policy, they have just gone on record that they will decline all gifts carrying the slightest obligation, expressed or implied. And further, that the Alcoholic Foundation will accept no earnings which may be tendered from any commercial source. As many readers know, we have been approached of late by several motion picture concerns about the possibility of an AA film. Naturally money has been discussed. But our trustees, very rightly I think, will take the position that AA has nothing to sell; that we all wish to avoid even the suggestion of commerce, and that in any case AA, nationally speaking, is now self-supporting.

To my mind, this is a decision of enormous importance to our future — a very long step in the right direction. When such an attitude about money becomes universal throughout AA, we shall have finally steered clear of that golden, alluring, but ever treacherous reef called *materialism*.

In the years that lie just ahead Alcoholics Anonymous faces a supreme test — the great ordeal of its own prosperity and success. I think it will prove the greatest trial of all. Can we but weather that, the waves of time and circumstance may beat upon us in vain. Our destiny will be secure!

The Individual in Relation to AA as a Group

July 1946

It may be that Alcoholics Anonymous is a new form of human society. The first of our Twelve Points of AA Tradition states: "Each member of Alcoholics Anonymous is but a small part of a great whole. AA must continue to live or most of us will surely die. Hence our common welfare comes first. But individual welfare follows close afterward." This is a recognition, common in all forms of society, that the individual must sometimes place the welfare of his fellows ahead of his own uncontrolled desires. Were the individual to yield nothing to the common welfare there could be no society at all — only self-will run riot; anarchy in the worst sense of that word.

Yet point three in our AA Tradition looks like a wide-open

invitation to anarchy. Seemingly, it contradicts point one. It reads, "Our membership ought to include all who suffer alcoholism. Hence *we may refuse none* who wish to recover. Nor ought AA membership *ever depend on money or conformity. Any two or three alcoholics* gathered together for sobriety *may call themselves an AA group."* This clearly implies that an alcoholic is a member if *he* says so; that we can't deny him membership; that we can't demand from him a cent; that we can't force our beliefs or practices upon him; that he may flout everything we stand for and still be a member. In fact, our Tradition carries the principle of independence for the individual to such an apparently fantastic length that, so long as there is the slightest interest in sobriety, the most unmoral, the most antisocial, the most critical alcoholic may gather about him a few kindred spirits and announce to us that a new Alcoholics Anonymous group has been formed. Anti-God, anti-medicine, anti-our recovery program, even anti-each other — these rampant individuals are still an AA group if *they think so!*

Our nonalcoholic friends sometimes exclaim, "Did we hear you say that AA has a sound social structure? You must be joking. To us, your Tradition Three looks about as firmly grounded as the Tower of Babel. In your point one you plainly say that group welfare comes first. Then you evidently proceed, in point three, to tell every AA that nobody can stop him if he thinks and does exactly what he pleases! True enough, your second point speaks vaguely about an *ultimate authority,* 'A loving God as he may express himself in our group conscience.' With all deference to your views, that point does look just a little impractical to outsiders. After all, the whole world today is but the sad story of how most men have lost their conscience and so cannot find their way. Now come you alcoholics (unstable people, too, you'll admit) and you blandly tell us: 1) That AA is a beautiful socialism — most democratic. 2) That AA is also a dictatorship, its members subject to the benign rule of God. And finally, 3) That AA is so very individualistic that the organization cannot discipline its own members for misbehavior or unbelief.

"So," continue our friends, "within the Society of Alcoholics Anonymous it appears to us that you have a democracy, a dictatorship, and an anarchy, all functioning at once. Do these sleep quietly in the same bed — these same concepts whose conflict is tearing apart our world of today? Yet we know that AA works. So you people must have somehow become reconciled to these great forces. Tell us, if you can, what holds AA together? Why doesn't AA tear apart, too? If each AA has personal liberty which can amount to license, why doesn't your AA

Society blow up? It ought to, yet it doesn't."

Our friends of the world outside, so puzzled over this paradox, are apt to miss a most significant statement as they read our point one. It is this: "AA must continue to live or most of us will surely die."

That stark assertion carries a world of meaning for every member of Alcoholics Anonymous. While it is perfectly true that no AA group can possibly coerce an alcoholic to contribute money, to conform to the Twelve Steps of our recovery program or to the Twelve Points of AA Tradition, each AA member is, nevertheless, most powerfully compelled, in the long run, to do these very things. The truth is, that in the life of each AA member, there still lurks a tyrant. His name is alcohol. He is cunning, ruthless. And his weapons are misery, insanity, and death. No matter how long we may be sober, he always stands at each man's elbow, ever watchful of an opportunity to resume his destruction. Like an agent of the Gestapo he ever threatens each AA citizen with torture or extinction. Unless, of course, the AA citizen is willing to live unselfishly, often placing the welfare of AA as a whole ahead of his own personal plans and ambitions. Apparently no human being can force alcoholics to live happily and usefully together. But Mr. John Barleycorn can — and he often does!

A story will illustrate: Some time ago we made a long list of our seeming failures in the first years of AA. Every alcoholic on the list had been given a good exposure. Most of them had attended AA meetings for several months. After slipping and sliding around they had all disappeared. Some said they were not alcoholic. Others couldn't stand for our belief in God. Many had developed intense resentments toward their fellows. Anarchists at heart, they could not conform to our Society. And because our Society did not conform to them, they quit. *But only temporarily.* Over the years, most of these so-called failures have returned, often becoming magnificent members. We never ran after them; they returned of their own accord. Each time I spot one newly back, I ask him why he has rejoined our fold. Invariably his answer runs like this: "When I first contacted AA I learned that alcoholism is a disease: an obsession of the mind that compels us to drink, and a sensitivity of the body that condemns us to go mad or die if we keep on. I also learned that AA worked, at least for some alcoholics. But I then disliked AA methods, hated some of the alcoholics I met there, and I still toyed with the idea that I could do the job of quitting all by myself. After several more years of terrible drinking, which I found I was powerless to control, I gave up. I returned to AA because it was the only place left to go; I'd tried everything else. Arrived at this point, I knew that I must act quickly: that I must adopt the Twelve Steps of the AA recovery program; that I must cease hating my fellow alcoholics; that I must now take my place among them as a very small part of that great whole, the Society of Alcoholics Anonymous. It all boiled down to a simple question of 'do or die.' I had to conform to AA principles — or else. No more anarchy for me. So I'm back.''

This illustration shows why we of AA must hang together "or else hang separately." We are players at a stern drama where death is the prompter to those who falter. Could anyone imagine a more powerful restraint upon us than this?

Yet the history of uncontrolled drinking shows that fear alone has chastened but few alcoholics. Much more than fear is needed to bind us anarchists together. Several years ago, speaking at Baltimore, I ran on at a great rate about the terrible sufferings we alcoholics had endured. My talk must have had a strong flavor of self-pity and exhibitionism. I kept referring to our drinking experience as a great calamity, a terrible misfortune. After the meeting I was approached by a Catholic clergyman who genially remarked, "I heard you say you thought your drinking a great misfortune. But it seems to me that in your case it was your *great good fortune*. Was not this terrible experience the very thing which humbled you so completely that you were able to find God? Did not suffering open your eyes and your heart? All the opportunity you have today, all this wonderful experience you call AA, once had its beginnings in deep personal suffering. In your case that was actually no misfortune. It was your great good fortune. You AAs are a privileged people.''

That simple yet profound remark affected me deeply. It is a landmark in my life. It set me thinking as never before about my relationship to my fellow AAs. It caused me to question my own motives. Why had I come to Baltimore anyway? Had I come only to enjoy the applause and approval of my fellows? Was I there as a teacher or a preacher? Did I fancy myself a great moral crusader? On reflection, I shamefacedly admitted to myself that I had all these motives, that I had been taking a vicarious and rather self-centered enjoyment out of my visit. But was that all? Had I no better motive than my natural craving for prestige and applause? Had I come to Baltimore in response to no better or deeper need than that? Then followed a flash of realization. Underneath my shallow and childish vainglory, I saw Someone much greater than I at work! Someone who sought to transform me; who would, if I permitted, sweep away my less worthy desires and replace them with truer aspirations. In these I might, were I humble enough, find peace.

At that moment I saw ever so clearly why I really should have come to Baltimore. I should have journeyed there with the happy conviction that I needed the Baltimoreans even more than they needed me; that I needed to share with them both their burdens and their joys; that I needed to feel at one with them, merging myself into their society; that even if they did insist on thinking me their teacher, I should actually feel myself their pupil. I saw that I had been living too much alone, too much aloof from my fellows, and too deaf to that voice within. Instead of coming to Baltimore as a simple agent bearing the message of experience, I had come as a founder of Alcoholics Anonymous. And, like a salesman at a convention, I had been wearing my identification badge so that all might well see it. How much better it would have been had I felt *gratitude* rather than self-satisfaction — *gratitude* that I had once suffered the pains of alcoholism, *gratitude* that a miracle of recovery had been worked upon me from above, *gratitude* for the privilege of serving my fellow alcoholics, and *gratitude* for those fraternal ties which bound me ever closer to them in a comradeship such as few societies of men have ever known. Truly did the clergyman say, "Your misfortune has become your good fortune. You AAs are a privileged people."

My experience at Baltimore was not unique. Every AA has such spiritual landmarks in his life — moments of insight which draw him closer to his fellows and to his Maker. The cycle is ever the same. First, we turn to AA because we may die if we don't. Next, we depend upon its fellowship and philosophy to stop our drinking. Then, for a time, we tend once more to depend upon ourselves, seeking happiness through power and acclaim. Finally, some incident, perhaps a sharp reverse, opens our eyes still wider. Then, as we learn our new lesson and *really accept its teaching,* we enter a new level of better feeling and doing. Life takes on a finer meaning. We glimpse realities new to us; we apprehend the kind of love which assures us that it is more blessed to give than to receive. These are some of the reasons why we think that Alcoholics Anonymous may be a new form of society.

Each AA group is a safe haven. But it is always circumscribed by the tyrant alcohol. Like the men on Eddie Rickenbacker's raft, we who live in the haven of AA cling together with an intensity of purpose which the outside world seldom comprehends. The anarchy of the individual melts away. Self-love subsides and democracy becomes a reality. We begin to know true freedom of the spirit. The awareness grows that all is well; that each of us may implicitly trust in him who is our loving guide from within — and from above.

Who Is a Member of Alcoholics Anonymous?

August 1946

T he first edition of the book *Alcoholics Anonymous* makes this brief statement about membership: "The only requirement for membership is an honest desire to stop drinking. We are not allied with any particular faith, sect or denomination nor do we oppose anyone. We simply wish to be helpful to those who are afflicted." This expressed our feeling as of 1939, the year our book was published.

Since that day all kinds of experiments with membership have been tried. The number of membership rules which have been made (and mostly broken!) are legion. Two or three years ago the Central Office asked the groups to list their membership rules and send them in. After they arrived we set them all down. They took a great many sheets of paper. A little reflection upon these many rules brought us to an astonishing conclusion. If all of these edicts had been in force everywhere at once, it would have been practically impossible for any alcoholic to have ever joined Alcoholics Anonymous. About nine-tenths of our oldest and best members could never have got by!

In some cases we would have been too discouraged by the demands made upon us. Most of the early members of AA would have been thrown out because they slipped too much, because their morals were too bad, because they had mental as well as alcoholic difficulties. Or, believe it or not, because they did not come from the so-called better classes of society. We oldsters could have been excluded for our failure to read the book *Alcoholics Anonymous* or the refusal of our sponsor to vouch for us as a candidate. And so on ad infinitum. The way our "worthy" alcoholics have sometimes tried to judge the "less worthy" is, as we look back on it, rather comical. Imagine, if you can, one alcoholic judging another!

At one time or another most AA groups go on rule-making benders. Naturally enough, too, as a group commences to grow rapidly it is confronted with many alarming problems. Panhandlers begin to panhandle. Members get drunk and sometimes get others drunk with them. Those with mental difficulties throw depressions or break out into paranoid denunciations of fellow members. Gossips gossip, and righ-

teously denounce the local Wolves and Red Riding Hoods. Newcomers
argue that they aren't alcoholics at all, but keep coming around anyway.
"Slippers" trade on the fair name of AA in order to get themselves jobs.
Others refuse to accept all the Twelve Steps of the recovery program.
Some go still further, saying that the "God business" is bunk and quite
unnecessary. Under these conditions our conservative program-abiding
members get scared. These appalling conditions must be controlled, they
think, else AA will surely go to rack and ruin. They view with alarm for
the good of the movement!

At this point the group enters the rule and regulation phase. Charters, bylaws, and membership rules are excitedly passed and authority is
granted committees to filter out undesirables and discipline the evildoers. Then the group elders, now clothed with authority, commence to
get busy. Recalcitrants are cast into the outer darkness, respectable busy-
bodies throw stones at the sinners. As for the so-called sinners, they
either insist on staying around, or else they form a new group of their
own. Or maybe they join a more congenial and less intolerant crowd in
their neighborhood. The elders soon discover that the rules and regulations aren't working very well. Most attempts at enforcement generate
such waves of dissension and intolerance in the group that this condition
is presently recognized to be worse for the group life than the very worst
that the worst ever did.

After a time fear and intolerance subside. The group survives unscathed. Everybody has learned a great deal. So it is that few of us are
any longer afraid of what any newcomer can do to our AA reputation or
effectiveness. Those who slip, those who panhandle, those who scanda-
lize, those with mental twists, those who rebel at the program, those who
trade on the AA reputation — all such persons seldom harm an AA
group for long. Some of these have become our most respected and best
loved. Some have remained to try our patience, sober nevertheless.
Others have drifted away. We have begun to regard these ones not as
menaces, but rather as our teachers. They oblige us to cultivate patience,
tolerance, and humility. We finally see that they are only people sicker
than the rest of us, that we who condemn them are the Pharisees whose
false righteousness does our group the deeper spiritual damage.

Every older AA shudders when he remembers the names of persons
he once condemned; people he confidently predicted would never sober up;
persons he was sure ought to be thrown out of AA for the good of the
movement. Now that some of these very persons have been sober for years,

and may be numbered among his best friends, the old-timer thinks to himself, "What if everybody had judged these people as I once did? What if AA had slammed its door in their faces? Where would they be now?"

That is why we all judge the newcomer less and less. If alcohol is an uncontrollable problem to *him* and *he* wishes to do something about it, that is enough for us. We care not whether his case is severe or light, whether his morals are good or bad, whether he has other complications or not. Our AA door stands wide open, and if he passes through it and commences to do anything at all about his problem, he is considered a member of Alcoholics Anonymous. He signs nothing, agrees to nothing, promises nothing. We demand nothing. He joins us on his own say-so. Nowadays, in most groups, he doesn't even have to admit he is an alcoholic. He can join AA on the mere suspicion that he may be one, that he may already show the fatal symptoms of our malady.

Of course this is not the universal state of affairs throughout AA. Membership rules still exist. If a member persists in coming to meetings drunk he may be led outside; we may ask someone to take him away. But in most groups he can come back next day, if sober. Though he may be thrown out of a club, nobody thinks of throwing him out of AA. He is a member as long as he says he is. While this broad concept of AA membership is not yet unanimous, it does represent the main current of AA thought today. We do not wish to deny anyone his chance to recover from alcoholism. We wish to be just as inclusive as we can, never exclusive.

Perhaps this trend signifies something much deeper than a mere change of attitude on the question of membership. Perhaps it means that we are losing all fear of those violent emotional storms which sometimes cross our alcoholic world; perhaps it bespeaks our confidence that every storm will be followed by a calm; a calm which is more understanding, more compassionate, more tolerant than any we ever knew before.

Will AA Ever Have a Personal Government?

January 1947

T he answer to this question is almost surely "no." That is the clear verdict of our experience.

To begin with, each AA has been an individual who, because of his alcoholism, could seldom govern himself. Nor could any other human being govern the alcoholic's obsession to drink, his drive to have things his own way. Time out of mind, families, friends, employers, doctors, clergy, and judges have tried their hand at disciplining alcoholics. Almost without exception the failure to accomplish anything by coercion has been complete. Yet we alcoholics can be led, we can be inspired; coming into AA we can, and we gladly do, yield to the will of God. Hence it is not strange that the only real authority to be found in AA is that of spiritual principle. It is never personal authority.

Our unreasonable individualism (egocentricity if you like) was, of course, the main reason we all failed in life and betook ourselves to alcohol. When we couldn't coerce others into conformity with our own plans and desires, we drank. When others tried to coerce us, we also drank. Though now sober, we still have a strong hangover of these early traits which caused us to resist authority. Therein probably hangs a clue to our lack of personal government in AA: no fees, no dues, no rules and regulations, no demand that alcoholics conform to AA principles, no one set in personal authority over anyone else. Though no sterling virtue, our aversion to obedience does pretty well guarantee us freedom from personal domination of any kind.

Still, it is a fact that most of us do follow, in our personal lives, the Twelve suggested Steps to recovery. But we do this from choice. We prefer recovery to death. Then, little by little, we perceive that the spiritual basis of life is the best. We conform because we want to.

Likewise, most AA groups become willing to follow the "Twelve Points of Tradition to Assure Our Future." The groups are willing to avoid controversy over outside issues such as politics, reform, or religion; they stick to their single purpose of helping alcoholics to recover; they increasingly rely on self-support rather than outside charity. More and more do they insist on modesty and anonymity in their public relations. The AA groups follow these other traditional principles for the very same reason that the individual AA follows the Twelve Steps to recovery. Groups see they would disintegrate if they didn't and they soon discover that adherence to our Tradition and experience is the foundation for a happier and more effective group life.

Nowhere in AA is there to be seen any constituted human authority that can compel an AA group to do anything. Some AA groups, for example, elect their leaders. But even with such a mandate, each leader soon discovers that while he can always guide by example or persuasion he can never boss, else at election time he may find himself passed by.

The majority of AA groups do not even choose leaders. They prefer rotating committees to handle their simple affairs. These committees are invariably regarded as servants; they have only the authorization to serve, never to command. Each committee carries out what it believes to be the wishes of its group. That is all. Though AA committees used to try to discipline wayward members, though they have sometimes composed minute rules and regulations and now and then have set themselves up as judges of other people's personal morals, I know of no case where any of these seemingly worthy strivings had any lasting effect — except, perhaps, the election of a brand-new committee!

Surely I can make these assertions with the greatest of confidence. For in my own turn I, too, have tried a hand at governing AA. Each time I have strenuously tried it I have been shouted down; so loudly, in fact, that on several occasions it looked as though I was due for swift and certain excommunication!

Sitting at a desk in our Central Office I often watch the incoming floods of personal, group, and intergroup problems as they flow in. The tide has been rising so fast of late that each morning's mail brings us an avalanche invariably containing at least one very critical problem from some place or other in the world. The AA Central Office has became a hot spot; so hot, indeed, that a "crisis" a day is getting to be routine.

Once upon a time my temptation was to take a strong position on every one of these problems, to exert every bit of pressure and authority that I could bring to bear, to write hot letters telling erring groups or individuals where to head in. At such moments, I used to be convinced that AA needed a strong personal government — someone, for example, like myself!

After struggling a few years to run the AA movement I had to give it up — it simply didn't work. Heavy-handed assertion of my personal authority always created confusion and resistance. If I took sides in a controversy, I was joyfully quoted by some, while others murmured, "And just who does this dictator think he is?" If I sharply criticized, I usually got double criticism on the return bounce. Personal power always failed. I can see my older AA friends smiling. They are recalling those times when they, too, felt a mighty call to "save the AA movement" from something or other. But their days of playing "Pharisee" are now over. So those little maxims "Easy Does It" and "Live and Let Live" have come to be deeply meaningful and significant to them and to me. In such fashion each of us learns that, in AA, one can be a servant only.

Here at the Central Office we have long known that we can merely supply certain indispensable services. We can supply information and literature; we can usually tell how the majority of AAs feel about our current problems; we can assist new groups to start, giving advice if asked; we can look after the overall AA public relations, we can sometimes mediate difficulties. Similarly, the editors of our monthly journal, the AA Grapevine, believe themselves simply a mirror of current AA life and thought. Serving purely as such, they cannot rule or propagandize. So also, the trustees of the Alcoholic Foundation (our AA general service committee) know themselves to be simple custodians, custodians who guarantee the effectiveness of the AA Central Office and the AA Grapevine and who are the repository of our general funds and Traditions — caretakers only.

It is most clearly apparent that, even here at the very center of AA, there can only exist a center of service — custodians, editors, secretaries, and the like — each, to be sure, with a special vital function, but none of them with any authority to govern Alcoholics Anonymous.

That such centers of service — international, national, metropolitan area, or local — will be sufficient for the future, I can have no doubt. So long as we avoid any menacing accumulation of wealth or the growth of personal government at these centers, we cannot go astray. While wealth and authority lie at the foundation of many a noble institution, we of AA now apprehend, and thoroughly well, that these things are not for us. Have we not found that one man's meat is often another man's poison?

Shall we not do well if instead we can cling in some part to the brotherly ideals of the early Franciscans? Let all of us AAs, whether we be trustees, editors, secretaries, janitors, or cooks — or just members — ever recall the unimportance of wealth and authority as compared with the vast import of our brotherhood, love, and service.

Dangers in Linking AA to Other Projects

March 1947

⓪ ur AA experience has been raising the following set of important but as yet unresolved questions. First, should AA as a whole enter the outside fields of hospitalization, research, and noncontroversial alcohol education? Second, is an AA member, acting strictly as an individual, justified in bringing his special experience and knowledge into such enterprises? And third, if an AA member does take up these phases of the total alcohol problem, under what conditions should he work?

With respect to these questions, almost any opinion can be heard among our groups. Generally speaking, there are three schools of thought: the "do everything" school, the "do something" school, and the "do nothing" school.

We have AAs so fearful we may become entangled, or somehow exploited, that they would keep us a strictly closed corporation. They would exert the strongest possible pressure to prevent all AAs, whether as individuals or groups, from doing anything at all about the total alcohol problem, except of course their straight AA work. They see the specter of the Washingtonian movement among alcoholics of a hundred years ago, which fell into disunity partly because its members publicly took up cudgels for abolition, prohibition, and what-not. These AAs believe that we must preserve our isolation at any cost; that we must keep absolutely to ourselves if we would avoid like perils.

Then we have the AA who would have us "do everything" for the total alcohol problem — any time, any place, and any way! In his enthusiasm, he not only thinks his beloved AA a cure-all for drunks, but he also thinks we have the answer for everything and everybody touching alcohol. He strongly feels that AA ought to place its name and financial credit squarely behind any first-rate research, hospital, or educational project. Seeing that AA now makes the headlines, he argues that we should freely loan out our huge goodwill. Says he: "Why shouldn't we AAs stand right up in public and be counted? Millions could be raised easily for good works in alcohol." The judgment of this enthusiast is sometimes beclouded by the fact that he wants to make a career. But with most who enthuse so carelessly, I'm sure it's more often a case of sheer exuberance plus, in many instances, a deep sense of social responsibility.

So we have with us the enthusiasts and the ultracautious, the "do everythings" and the "do nothings." But the average AA is not so worried about these phenomena as he used to be. He knows that out of the heat and smoke there will soon come light. Presently there will issue an enlightened policy, palatable to everyone. Tested by time, that policy, if sound, will become AA Tradition.

Sometimes I've feared that AA would never bring forth a workable policy. Nor was my fear abated as my own views swung with complete inconsistency from one extreme to the other. But I should have had more faith. We are commencing to have enough of the strong light of experience to see more surely; to be able to say with more certainty what we can, and what we surely cannot, do about causes such as education, research, and the like.

For example, we can say quite emphatically that neither AA as a whole nor any AA group ought to enter any other activity than straight AA. As groups, we cannot endorse, finance, or form an alliance with any other cause, however good; we cannot link the AA name to other enterprises in the alcohol field to the extent that the public gets the impression we have abandoned our sole aim. We must discourage our members and our friends in these fields from stressing the AA name in their publicity or appeals for funds. To act otherwise will certainly imperil our unity, and to maintain our unity is surely our greatest obligation — to our brother alcoholics and the public at large. Experience, we think, has already made these principles self-evident.

Though we now come to more debatable ground, we must earnestly ask ourselves whether any of us, as individuals, ought to carry our special experience into other phases of the alcohol problem. Do we not owe this much to society, and can it be done without involving AA as a whole?

To my mind, the "do nothing" policy has become unthinkable, partly because I'm sure that our members can work in other noncontroversial alcohol activities without jeopardizing AA if they observe a few simple precautions, and partly because I have developed a deep conviction that to do less would be to deprive the whole of society of the immensely valuable contributions we could almost certainly make. Though we are AAs, and AA must come first, we are also citizens of the world. Besides, we are, like our good friends the physicians, honorbound to share what we know with all.

Therefore, it seems to me that some of us must heed the call from other fields. And those who do, need only remember first and last they are AAs; that in their new activities they are individuals only. This means that they will respect the principle of anonymity in the press; that if they do appear before the general public they will not describe themselves as AAs; that they will refrain from emphasizing their AA status in appeals for money or publicity.

These simple principles of conduct, if conscientiously applied, could soon dispel all fears, reasonable and unreasonable, which many AAs now entertain. On such a basis AA as a whole could remain uncommitted yet friendly to any noncontroversial cause seeking to write a brighter page in the dark annals of alcoholism.

A concluding word. Several years ago, I believed that we might, in a limited and cautious way, lend our name to selected outside ventures. One of these was a very promising educational project. I was asked by faculty members of Yale University sponsoring the National Committee for Education on Alcoholism whether they might hire an AA. And could that AA, for this special purpose, break anonymity? My answer was that of course an AA could be engaged; that such an engagement could not, by any imagination, be a professionalization of AA, as the work to be done would be in another field entirely; that if an AA could make a better educator, then why not? Though there has never been much question that this was sound enough policy, the same could not be said for my reply on the matter of dropping anonymity, to which, in this instance, I gave approval.

That course has since proved mistaken. A good AA friend of mine took this particular post and then dropped anonymity. The first effect was good. It brought AA a considerable amount of publicity and many members. On the educational side the public was made conscious as never before that alcoholism is a sickness and that something could be done about it. So far, very good.

But of late, some confusion has arisen. Because of the large amount of publicity linking the AA name and that of the educational project, the public tends to think AA as a whole has gone in for alcohol education. And when the AA name became associated in the public mind with a fund-raising campaign, there was still more confusion. Some givers were under the impression they were contributing to AA, only to be told by friends that AA did not solicit money. Hence a long-term liability of dropping anonymity is beginning to offset its short-term advantages. As experience makes this more clear, not only to me but to my friends of the university and of the educational committee, they agree perfectly and are now endeavoring to correct the situation.

Naturally, and most earnestly, I hope that none of those involved or the work of the committee will suffer to any degree from our mistake. Such, after all, is the purpose of the trial and error by which we all learn and grow.

Briefly summarizing, I'm rather sure our policy with respect to "outside" projects will turn out to be this: AA does not sponsor projects in other fields. But if these projects are constructive and noncontroversial in character, AA members are free to engage in them without criticism if they act as individuals only, and are careful of the AA name. Perhaps that's it. Shall we try it?

Clubs in AA

April 1947

The club idea has become part of AA life. Scores of these hospitable havens can report years of useful service; new ones are being started monthly. Were a vote taken tomorrow on the desirability of clubs, a sizable majority of AAs would record a resounding "yes." There would be thousands who would testify that they might have had a harder time staying sober in their first months of AA without clubs and that, in any case, they would always wish the easy contacts and warm friendships which clubs afford.

As the majority view, we might suppose that to be a blanket endorsement for clubs; we might think we couldn't get along without them. We might conceive them as a central AA institution — a sort of "thirteenth step" of our recovery program without which the other Twelve Steps wouldn't work. At times club enthusiasts will act as though they really believed we could handle our alcohol problems by club life alone. They are apt to depend upon clubs rather than upon the AA program.

But we have AAs, rather a strong minority, too, who want no part of clubs. Not only, they assert, does the social life of a club often divert the attention of members from the program, they claim that clubs are an actual drag on AA progress. They point to the danger of clubs degenerating into mere hangouts, even "joints"; they stress the bickerings that do arise over questions of money, management, and personal authority; they are afraid of "incidents" that might give us unfavorable publicity. In short, they "view with alarm." Thumbs down on clubs, they say.

For several years now, we have been feeling our way toward a middle ground. Despite alarms, it is quite settled that AAs who need and want clubs ought to have them. So the real concern is not whether we shall have clubs. It is how we shall enhance them as assets; how we may diminish their known liabilities; how we shall be sure, in the long future, that their liabilities do not exceed their assets.

Of our four largest AA centers, two are club-minded and two are not. I happen to live in one which is. The very first AA club of all was started in New York. Though our experience here may not have been the best, it is the one I know. So, by way of portraying the principles and problems we need to discuss, I shall use it, as an average illustration of club evolution rather than as a model set-up.

When AA was very young we met in homes. People came miles, not only for the AA meeting itself, but to sit hours afterward at coffee, cake, and eager intimate talk. Alcoholics and their families had been lonely too long.

Then homes became too small. We couldn't bear to break up into many little meetings, so we looked for a larger place. We lodged first in the workshop of a tailoring establishment, then in a rented room at Steinway Hall. This kept us together during the meeting hour. Afterward we held forth at a cafeteria, but something was missing. It was the home atmosphere; a restaurant didn't have enough of it. Let's have a club, someone said.

So we had a club. We took over an interesting place, the former Artists and Illustrators Club on West 24th Street. What excitement! A couple of our older members signed the lease. We painted and we scrubbed. We had a home. Wonderful memories of days and nights at that first club will always linger.

But, it must be admitted, not all those memories are ecstatic. Growth brought headaches; growing pains, we call them now. How serious they seemed then! "Dictators" ran amok; drunks fell on the floor or disturbed the meetings; "steering committees" tried to nominate their friends to succeed them and found to their dismay that even sober drunks couldn't be "steered." Sometimes we could scarcely get up the rent; card players were impervious to any suggestion that they talk to new people; secretaries got in each others' hair. A corporation was formed to take over the clubroom lease, so we then had "officials." Should these "directors" run the club or would it be the AA rotating committee?

Such were our problems. We found that the use of money, the need for a certain amount of club organization, and the crowded intimacy of the place created situations we hadn't anticipated. Club life still had great joys. But it had liabilities, too, that was for sure. Was it worth all the risk and trouble? The answer was "yes," for the 24th Street Club kept right on going, and is today occupied by the AA seamen. We have, besides, three more clubs in this area, and a fourth is contemplated.

Our first club was known, of course, as an "AA clubhouse." The corporation holding its lease was titled "Alcoholics Anonymous of New York, Inc." Only later did we realize we had incorporated the whole of New York State, a mistake recently rectified. Of course our incorporation should have covered 24th Street only. Throughout the country most clubs have started as ours did. At first we regard them as central AA institutions. But later experience invariably brings a shift in their status, a shift much to be desired, we now think.

For example, the early Manhattan AA Club had members from every section of the metropolitan area, including New Jersey. After a while dozens of groups sprang up in our suburban districts. They got themselves more convenient meeting places. Our Jersey friends secured a club of their own. So these outlying groups, originally spawned from the Manhattan clubhouse, began to acquire hundreds of members who were not tied to Manhattan either by convenience, inclination, or old-time sentiment. They had their own local AA friends, their own convenient gathering places. They weren't interested in Manhattan.

This irked us New Yorkers not a little. Since we had nurtured them, why shouldn't they be interested? We were puzzled why they refused to consider the Manhattan club the AA center for the metropolitan area. Wasn't the club running a central meeting with speakers from other groups? Didn't we maintain a paid secretary who sat in the New York clubhouse taking telephone calls for assistance and making hospital arrangements for all groups in the area? Of course, we thought, our out-lying groups ought financially to support the Manhattan club; dutiful children should look after their "parents." But our parental pleas were no use. Though many outlying AA members personally contributed to the 24th Street Club, nary a cent did their respective groups ever send in.

Then we took another tack. If the outlying groups would not support the club, they at least might want to pay the salary of its secre-tary. She was really doing an "area" job. Surely this was a reasonable request. But it never got anywhere. They just couldn't mentally separate the "area secretary" from the Manhattan club. So for a long time, our area needs, our common AA problems, and our club management were tied into a trying financial and psychological snarl.

This tangle slowly commenced to unravel, as we began to get the idea that clubs ought to be strictly the business of those individuals who specially want clubs, and who are willing to pay for them. We began to see that club management is a pure business proposition, which ought to be separately incorporated under another name such, for example, as Alano; that the directors of a club corporation ought to look after club business only; that an AA group, as such, should never get into active management of a business project. Hectic experience has since taught us that if an AA rotating committee tries to boss the club corporation or if the corporation tries to run the AA affairs of those groups who may meet at the club there is difficulty at once. The only way we have found to cure this is *to separate the material from the spiritual.* If an AA group wishes to use a given club let them pay rent or split the meeting take with the club management. To a small group opening its first clubroom, this procedure may seem silly, because for the moment the group members will also be club members. Nevertheless, separation by early incorpora-tion is recommended because it will save much confusion later on as other groups start forming in the area.

Questions are often asked: "Who elects the business directors of a club?" And "Does club membership differ from AA membership?" As practices vary we don't quite know the answers yet. The most reasonable suggestions seem these: Any AA member ought to feel free to enjoy the ordinary privileges of any AA club whether he makes a regular voluntary contribution or not. If he contributes regularly he should, in addition, be entitled to vote in the business meetings which elect the business directors of his club corporation. This would open all clubs to all AAs. But it would limit their business conduct to those interested enough to contribute regularly. In this connection we might remind ourselves that in AA we have no fees or compulsory dues. But it ought to be added, of course, that since clubs are becoming separate and private ventures they can be run on other lines if their members insist.

Club evolution is also telling us this: In none but small communities are clubs likely to remain the principal centers of AA activity. Originally starting as the main center of a city, many a club moves to larger and larger quarters, thinking to retain the central meeting for its area within its own walls. Finally, however, circumstances defeat this purpose.

Circumstance number one is that the growing AA will burst the walls of any clubhouse. Sooner or later the principal or central meeting has to be moved into a large auditorium. The club can't hold it. This is a fact which ought to be soberly contemplated whenever we think of buying or building large clubhouses. A second circumstance seems sure to leave most clubs in an "off center" position, especially in large cities. That is our strong tendency toward central or intergroup committee management of the common AA problems of metropolitan areas. Every area, sooner or later, realizes that such concerns as intergroup meetings, hospital arrangements, local public relations, a central office for interviews and information are things in which every AA is interested, whether he has any use for clubs or not. These being strictly AA matters, a central or intergroup committee has to be elected and financed to look after them. The groups of an area will usually support with group funds these truly central activities. Even though the club is still large enough for intergroup meetings and these meetings are still held, the center of gravity for the area will continue to shift to the intergroup committee and its central activities. The club is left definitely offside — where, in the opinion of many, it should be. Actively supported and managed by those who want clubs, they can be taken or left alone.

Should these principles be fully applied to our clubs, we shall have placed ourselves in a position to enjoy their warmth yet drop any that get too hot. We shall then realize that a club is but a valuable social aid. And, more important still, we shall always preserve the simple AA group as that primary spiritual entity whence issues our greatest strength.

Adequate Hospitalization: One Great Need

May 1947

D espite the general effectiveness of the AA program, we often need the help of friendly agencies outside AA. Nowhere is this more strikingly true than in the field of hospitalization. Most of us feel that ready access to hospitals and other places of rest and recuperation borders on absolute necessity. While many an alcoholic has somehow got over his bender without medical aid, and while a few of us hold the view that the hard "cold turkey" method is the best, the vast majority of AAs believe the newcomer whose case is at all serious has a much better chance of making the grade if well hospitalized at the outset. Indeed, we see many cases where recoveries without medical help would seem virtually impossible, mentally so beclouded have they become, even when temporarily sober.

The primary purpose of hospitalization is not to save our prospect the pain of getting sober; its real purpose is to place him in the state of greatest possible receptivity to our AA program. Medical treatment clears his brain, takes away his jitters, and if it is done at a hospital he is kept there under control so that everybody knows just where and when he can be visited. Moreover, the atmosphere of most hospitals is extremely conducive to a good first presentation of AA. The very fact that he has now landed in a hospital impresses the new man with the seriousness of his situation. If he has gone there voluntarily (which should be the case if at all possible), he usually regards hospitalization as the actual beginning of his sobriety. It puts, as it were, a "period" to his drinking. It is an admission that he needs help; that his drinking is out of control; that he cannot do the job alone. Often enough, hospitalization is the event that beautifully clears his path to acceptance of that all-important First Step: "We admitted we were powerless over alcohol — that our lives had become unmanageable."

With each passing year we increasingly realize the immense importance of adequately presenting the program to every new prospect who is in the least inclined to listen. Many of us feel this to be our greatest obligation to him and our failure to do so our greatest dereliction. The difference between a good approach and a bad one can mean life or death to those who seek our help. We have seen excellent prospects who received nothing but our brief and casual notice continue their stumbling journey to the undertaker, while seemingly impossible cases who had received careful and considerate attention recovered on the spot or later came back and found their sobriety.

This careful and considerate attention can nowhere be better given than in the confines of a hospital. More and more, AA groups are adopting the idea of "sponsorship." Each newcomer is assigned a reasonably stable AA member whose ward he becomes during his brief period of introduction to our way of life. The sponsor helps make hospital arrangements, takes his man there, visits him frequently, and sees that he is visited by other AAs whose experience might be specially helpful. Hence a prospect so handled has received a powerful shot of AA and a good preview of what our Society is like before he ever goes to a meeting. At the hospital he has time to soberly think through his situation, read our literature, and exchange impressions with other alcoholics who are going through the same process. Contrast this with the frequent situation in which, for lack of hospitalization, the sponsor has to try to "taper off" his prospect at home or drag him, half dazed, to an AA meeting where the new man proceeds to get a lot of confused impressions or unfounded prejudices. While many of us have made our first contact with AA under these unfavorable circumstances, and have stuck nevertheless, there are probably many who do not stick on such a poor contact; people who might have remained with us had they been properly hospitalized and sponsored.

So, out of what is now a huge experience, our conclusions are these: That hospitalization is imperative in many cases and because the hospital provides such a firm basis for good sponsorship it is desirable even in the less serious situations if the prospects are drinking or "foggy" when contacted. They definitely have a better chance if hospitalized.

Until recently, few hospitals have wanted us alcoholics. We almost never got really well; we were hard to manage and disturbed other patients; we were regarded as sinners more than as sick people and, as a class, we were financially irresponsible. The average hospital management has always said, and with good reason, "Why bother with drunks? We can scarcely handle the people who are legitimately sick, people we can really do something for. Sobering up drunks is a sheer waste of time and money."

Happily, this attitude is changing because it is now becoming clear to physicians and public alike that a true alcoholic is really sick, however lacking in character he may be. Hope has now taken the place of centuries of despair that anything much could be done for problem drinkers. AA and other agencies are now proving that recovery is possible to hundreds of thousands and that adequate hospital care can and must play a vital part in this process.

Though the trend is now in the right direction, it has not yet produced any large-scale result. Except the fortunate few, most AA groups are up against it. Reasonably priced or free hospital accommodation for alcoholics is still woefully scarce. Each group has to do the best it can.

Let's take stock, therefore, of what is generally available today and what kind of relations we can best cultivate with existing agencies. Let us also consider what part we ought to play in securing improved hospitalization.

Many AAs have been state asylum inmates. While our treatment at these institutions has been far better than many suppose, it is a fact that the average asylum superintendent still prefers to handle insane persons. The average mental case stays put for a while. Then, too, for mental cases an asylum could feel it was really doing something, by way of either custody or cure. But the average alcoholic, unless permanently insane, was a headache. Brought in temporarily balmy he would promptly recover his sanity, at least legally speaking, and would clamor to get out, only to return in days or weeks. No wonder the average institution disliked alcoholics.

Now that so many of us are coming out of asylums to stay, the authorities are everywhere becoming more cooperative. In many institutions the alcoholics able and willing to recover are placed in a ward of their own. They are no longer mingled with the insane. Visiting AAs are admitted, and meetings are held within the walls. While no asylum can, of course, be used as a simple sobering-up place only, it is true that asylum doctors are now often willing to take cases on less evidence of psychosis than formerly, provided they and the nearby AA group feel that a permanent recovery is possible. The doctors are also more willing to commit promising patients for much briefer periods and liberate earlier those who seem to be making good AA progress. So any AA group near an asylum which contains alcoholics capable of recovery can usually form these desirable relationships with the authorities, but they should *never* try to tell the doctors how to run the place! We must never blame any doctor who has not yet seen AA at work for his skepticism. Let us remember he probably has good reason to be that way!

Our experience with public hospitals in large cities has been varied.

Here we usually find much reluctance to keep our good prospects even a few days, unless, of course, they happen to be delirious, psychotic, or physically injured. These hospitals feel they have no right to use precious beds to sober up run-of-the-mill drunks. But as public hospitals become aware that we are bringing recovery to a substantial number of their regular habitues, they become more hopeful and cooperative. Visiting privileges are extended to us, and promising cases are kept several days. The development of these relations takes place slowly. The hospital has to be thoroughly convinced that we are bringing recovery to enough patients to justify any special consideration. Because public hospitals are mostly free or very moderate in their charges, we too often abuse our privileges. We are tempted to ask special treatment for slippers who have no present idea of stopping drinking; we often insist on visiting at all hours and in any numbers; we are likely to brag about AA as the only remedy for alcoholism, and thus incur the displeasure of hard-working nurses and doctors who might otherwise be glad to help us. But these natural mistakes are usually corrected, and we finally come up with a friendly, clear-cut relationship which is often handled in large AA centers through our intergroup central offices or hospital committees.

We enjoy fine privileges with many private sanitariums and drying-out places. Occasionally the reverse has been true. Here and there we have found some tendency to exploit alcoholics — too much sedative, too many "tapering off" drinks, too long and too expensive stays, an inclination to misuse the AA name for business purposes, etc. But these tendencies are disappearing. It is realized, even by those who might be tempted to take liberties with us, that cooperation with AA is more profitable in the long run than noncooperation. But it must always be remembered that on the whole our treatment at these places is good — some of them are staffed by the warmest friends we have. I cannot forget that the first physician ever to take a serious and helpful interest in us is still a staff member of a private hospital for alcoholics; that the first psychiatrist to see the possibilities of AA, and one who had the courage to go to bat for us before his profession, is the staff member of a sanitarium. When such excellent places offer us friendly cooperation we surely ought to return it in kind.

Many sanitariums and private hospitals are necessarily too high priced for the average alcoholic. Public hospitals being too few, asylums and religious institutions too seldom available, the average group has been hard put to find spots where prospective members can be hospitalized a few days at modest expense.

This urgency has tempted some AA groups to set up drying-out places of their own, hiring AA managers, nurses, and securing the services of a visiting physician. Where this has been done under the direct auspices of an AA group, it has almost always backfired. It has put the group into business, a kind of business about which few AAs know anything at all. Too many clashing personalities, too many cooks spoiling the broth, usually bring about the abandonment of such attempts. We have reluctantly been obliged to see that an AA group is primarily a spiritual entity; that, as a group, the less business it has to transact, the better. While on this theme it ought to be noted that practically all group schemes to finance or guarantee hospital bills for fellow members have failed also. Not only do many such loans go unpaid, there is always the controversial question in the group as to which prospects deserve them in the first place.

In still other instances, AA groups, driven by their acute need for medical aid, have started public money-raising campaigns to set up "AA hospitals" in their communities. These efforts almost invariably come to naught. Not only do these groups intend to go into the hospital business, they intend to finance their ventures by soliciting the public in the name of Alcoholics Anonymous. Instantly all sorts of doubts are generated; the projects bog down. Conservative AAs realize that business ventures or solicitations carrying the AA endorsement are truly dangerous to us all. Were this practice to become general, the lid would be off. Promoters, AA and otherwise, would have a field day.

This search for reasonably priced and understanding medical treatment has brought into being still another class of facilities. These are rest farms and drying-out places, operated by individual AAs under suitable medical supervision. These set-ups have proved far more satisfactory than group-directed projects. As might be expected, their success is in exact proportion to the managerial ability and good faith of the AA in charge. If he is able and conscientious, a very good result is possible; if neither, the place folds up. Not being a group project and not bearing the AA name, these ventures can be taken or left alone. The operation of such establishments is always beset with peculiar difficulties. It is difficult for the AA manager to charge high enough rates to make the venture include a fair living for himself. If he does, people are apt to say that he is professionalizing, or "making money out of AA." Nonsense though this may often be, it is a severe handicap nevertheless. Yet, in spite of the headaches encountered, a good number of these farms and sobering-up spots are in active operation and can seemingly continue just as long as they are tactfully managed, do not carry the AA name, and do not publicly solicit funds as AA enterprises. When a place has an AA in charge we sometimes do take thoughtless advantage of the fact. We dump alcoholics into it just to get them off our hands; we promise to pay bills and do not. Any AA who can successfully manage one of these "drunk emporiums" ought to be congratulated. It is a hard and often thankless job, though it may bring him deep spiritual satisfaction. Perhaps this is the reason so many AAs wish to try it!

The question often arises about what to do with a severe case when no hospital is available. First of all, we ought, if possible, to call a doctor. We should ascertain for the doctor's benefit how long our man has been drinking and particularly whether he has been taking much sedative. Under no circumstances should we laymen ever administer any sedatives. We must leave this strictly to the doctor.

In some places, AAs take turns sitting the clock around tapering off a man with a bad hangover. Though this can sometimes be done, the patient will usually insist on tapering himself "up" instead of "off." Now and then we have to adopt the desperate expedient of putting a man in jail, especially if violent. But when absolutely necessary, patience, persuasion, and a doctor's help will generally do the trick — if the patient will really try. If he won't, there is little to do but let him drink on until he has had enough.

Among AAs, one hears much discussion about the merits of the several treatments. Actually, our only concern about physical treatment is that of being satisfied that the physician in charge understands alcoholics.

Two other promising prospects for good and reasonably priced hospitalization are in view. These are the various general hospitals which continue to open their doors to us. Very early in AA history, Catholic hospitals in a few midwestern cities saw our need and took us in, regardless of denomination. Their example has led other religiously oriented institutions to do likewise, for which we are extremely grateful. Quite recently, other private and semiprivate general hospitals have begun to show great interest. Sometimes they go so far as setting apart wards for AA use, admitting alcoholics on our recommendation only, giving us generous visiting privileges and very reasonable rates. Arrangements of this sort already functioning have been so satisfactory to both hospitals and AA that many such set-ups should soon be active. In these situations we do not participate in hospital management. We are afforded special privileges in exchange for our cooperation.

It surely may be said that the future looks bright. Much more hospitalization, based on the certainty that we are a sick people and that plenty can be done about it, is now on the way. We ought gratefully to acknowledge the work of those agencies outside AA who are strenuously helping this life-redeeming trend along. State, county, and municipal governments, large universities are agitating our cause. They are being ably seconded by various hospital and other associations. While traditionally AA does not ever exert any political or promotional pressure, we can, as individuals, make our great need for sufficient hospitalization known to all who might be interested; emphasizing, of course, that though we believe hospitalization to be primarily a medical problem for communities and physicians to answer, we AAs would like to cooperate in every possible way.

Lack of Money Proved AA Boon

June 1947

Thousands of newer AAs inquire: "Just what is the Alcoholic Foundation, what is its place in AA, who set it up, why do we send it funds?"

Most members, because their groups are in frequent contact with our Headquarters in New York, understand that place to be a sort of general service to all AA. Reading the AA Grapevine each month, they know the Grapevine to be our principal monthly journal. But the history of the Alcoholic Foundation and its relation to these vital functions, and to AA as a whole, they scarcely understand at all.

Now for a bit of history. During its first years, Alcoholics Anonymous didn't even have that name. Anonymous, nameless indeed, we consisted by late 1937 of but three small clusters of alcoholics — Akron, Ohio, the first group; New York City, the second; and a few members at Cleveland, our third group to be. There were, I should guess, about fifty members in all three cities. The very early pioneering period had passed, Dr. Bob and I having first met at Akron in the spring of 1935. We were becoming sure we had something for those other thousands of alcoholics who didn't yet know any answer. How were we to let them know; just how could the good news be spread? That was the burning question.

Much discussion in a little meeting called by Dr. Bob and me at Akron in the fall of 1937 developed a plan. This plan later proved to be approximately one-third right and about two-thirds wrong — familiar process of trial and error. Because the development of the first groups had been such a slow, hard process we then supposed that none but seasoned pioneers could start new ones. Though we had misgivings, it seemed inevitable that about twenty of our solid members would have to lay aside their personal affairs and go to other cities to create new centers. Much as we disliked the idea, it appeared as if we must take on, temporarily at least, a squad of AA missionaries. Plainly, too, these missionaries and their families would have to eat. That would take money — quite a lot of it, we thought!

But that was not all. It was felt we needed AA hospitals at Akron and New York, these places being regarded as our twin "Meccas." There, excellent medical care and high-power spirituality could, we were sure, be sprayed on drunks who would flock from all corners of the nation once the magic word "cure" got around. Even as many newer AAs still have such fancies, we old-timers did dream these very dreams. Providentially, neither the AA hospital nor our wholesale missionary dreams came true. Had these then materialized, AA would surely have been ruined. We would have gone professional on the spot.

Then there was still a third dream. That was to prepare a book of experience — the one we know today as *Alcoholics Anonymous.* We were sure that unless our recovery experiences were put on paper, our principles and practices would soon be distorted. We might be ridiculed in the press. Besides, did we not owe at least a book to those alcoholics who couldn't get to our hospitals or who, perchance, weren't reached right away by our advancing missionaries! As everybody knows, the AA book dream did come true; the other dreams didn't.

But it surely looked, in 1937, as though we must have considerable money. Perhaps it was because I lived at New York, where there is supposed to be lots of it, that I was delegated to set about raising funds so our nameless movement might have its field workers, hospitals, and books. How simple it appeared. Did we not already have (in prideful imagination) the beginning of one of the greatest social, medical, and spiritual developments of all time? Weren't we drunks all salesmen? Hadn't I been a Wall Street man? How easy to raise money for such a cause as ours!

The awakening from that money dream was rude. It soon appeared that people with money had little interest in drunks. As for our grandiose scheme of banding alcoholics together in squads, platoons, and regiments — well, that was plainly fantastic, wasn't it? Drunks, people said, were difficult enough one at a time. Why present each American community with an organized regiment of them? Hadn't the donors better put their money into something constructive, like tuberculosis or cancer? Or why shouldn't they invest in the prevention of alcoholism? One more attempt to salvage hopeless drunks couldn't possibly succeed. Such were the answers to our plea for money.

Then one day, in the midst of discouragement, something momentous happened. It was another of those critical turning points in AA of which we have seen so many that no one can call them coincidence. At the office of my physician brother-in-law, I was bemoaning, in typical alcoholic fashion, how little we poor drunks were appreciated, especially by people of means. I was telling my relative for the tenth time how we had to have money soon — or else. Listening patiently, he suddenly said, "I've got an idea. I used to know a man by the name of Dick Richardson. He was somehow connected with the Rockefellers. But that was years ago. I wonder if he is still there. Let me call up and find out." On what little events our destinies sometimes turn! How could either of us know that a simple phone message was to open a new era in AA! That it was to inaugurate the Alcoholic Foundation, the book *Alcoholics Anonymous,* and our AA Central Office.

Two days after my brother-in-law's call, we sat in the Rockefeller offices talking to Willard ("Dick") Richardson. The most lovable of men, Dick was the first of that early series of nonalcoholic laymen who saw us through when the going was very hard, and without whose wisdom and devotion the Alcoholics Anonymous movement might never have been. When he had heard the story, our new friend showed instant understanding. He immediately translated understanding into action. He suggested that some of our alcoholic brotherhood meet with several of his own friends and himself.

Shortly afterward, on a winter's evening in 1937, this meeting took place at Rockefeller Center. Present were Dick Richardson, A. LeRoy

Chipman, since known as "Chip," Albert Scott, Frank Amos, and my brother-in-law, Leonard Strong. Dr. Bob and Paul S. came down from Akron. The New York ex-topers numbered half a dozen and were accompanied by Dr. William D. Silkworth, who, as the first physician ever to champion our cause, had already given us measureless help and encouragement. Of course, we alcoholics were delighted. Our money troubles, we thought, were over. If money was the answer, we had surely come to the right place!

Following introductions, each alcoholic told his own personal story, these accounts being enthusiastically confirmed by our ardent friend Dr. Silkworth. After which (with becoming reluctance!) we brought up the subject of money. As our hearers had seemed much impressed by our recovery stories, we made bold to expand on the urgent need for hospitals, field workers, and a book. We also made it clear that this would take money — quite a lot.

Then came one more turn in AA destiny. The chairman of the meeting, Albert Scott (now deceased), a man of large affairs and profoundly spiritual in his nature, said in substance: "I am deeply moved by what I have heard. I can see that your work, thus far, has been one of great goodwill — one alcoholic personally helping another for the love of the thing. That is first century Christianity in a beautiful form. But aren't you afraid that the introduction of hospitals and paid field workers might change all that? Shouldn't we be most careful *not to do anything* which might lead to a *professional* or *propertied* class within your ranks?"

These were great words for Alcoholics Anonymous. We alcoholics admitted their weight. Disappointed that our hope of substantial money help seemed to be fading, we confessed, nevertheless, that we had often had such misgivings. But, we persisted, what *are* we going to do? It has taken us three years to form three groups. We know we have a new life for those who die or go mad by thousands each year. Must our story wait while it is passed around by word of mouth only, becoming hopelessly garbled meanwhile? Finally, our friends agreed that something needed to be done. But they did continue to insist our movement ought never be professionalized. This struck the keynote of our relation to these men of goodwill for all the years since. Rightly enough, they have never secured us large sums of money. But each has given of himself to our cause, generously and continuously; how much, few AAs can ever know.

Seeing clearly that we must now spread the recovery message faster, they then suggested we might carefully experiment with a small rest home at Akron. This could be presided over by Dr. Bob who was, after all, a physician. Whereupon, early in 1938, Frank Amos, on his own time and with expenses paid by his associates, went to Akron to investigate. He returned most enthusiastic. He was inclined to the opinion that $30,000 ought to be invested in a center for alcoholics. Our friend, Dick Richardson, showed Frank's report to Mr. John D. Rockefeller, Jr., who at once manifested a warm interest. But Mr. Rockefeller also expressed anxiety about professionalizing us. Nevertheless, he gave us a sum, which turned out to be, however, about one-sixth of the amount Frank had suggested. His gift came in the spring of 1938 and its result was to help Dr. Bob and me through that very trying year. We could not have actively continued without it. Yet, money-wise, our budding movement of alcoholics was still left very much on its own — just where it should have been left, too, however difficult that seemed at the time. We still had no field staff, no hospital, and no book.

These were the events that led to the formation of the Alcoholic Foundation. The need for a volume describing our recovery experiences loomed larger than ever. Were such a book to appear, a great flow of inquiries from alcoholics and their families might start. Thousands, maybe. These appeals would certainly have to be cleared through some sort of central office. That was most evident.

For these saner purposes our friends suggested the formation of a foundation to which givers might make tax-free contributions. We alcoholics endlessly discussed this new project with them, consuming hours of their business time. Frank Amos and a friendly attorney, John E.F. Wood, put much effort on the original Foundation trust agreement. The lawyer had never seen anything like it. The new foundation should, we insisted, have two classes of trustees — alcoholics and nonalcoholics. But legally speaking, what *was* an alcoholic anyhow, he queried, and if an alcoholic had stopped drinking, was he an alcoholic anymore? Then, why two classes of trustees? That, said our attorney, was unheard of. We explained that we wanted our friends with us. And besides, we urged, suppose all of us alcoholics should get drunk at once, who then would hang on to the money! Surmounting many such obstacles, the Alcoholic Foundation was finally inaugurated. It had four nonalcoholic and three alcoholic trustees. They could appoint their own successors. It was chartered to do everything under the sun. So it had everything — except money!

Last Seven Years Have Made AA Self-Supporting

August 1947

H ow we ever got the book and our office through that summer of 1939 I shall never quite know. Had it not been for a truly sacrificial act on the part of Bert T., an early New York AA, I'm sure we couldn't have survived. Bert loaned the defunct Works Publishing Company $1,000, obtained by signing a note secured by his own business. This act of faith was followed by two more pieces of good fortune, which barely got us through the year. In the fall of 1939 *Liberty* magazine published a piece about us. This produced a flood of inquiries and some orders for the AA Book. Those few book receipts kept our little Central Office going. Then came a burst of articles in the Cleveland *Plain Dealer.* This started a prodigious growth of AA out there and created a little more demand for the AA Book.

Nor were our friends at Rockefeller Center idle. One day in February 1940, Dick Richardson reported that Mr. John D. Rockefeller, Jr. had been following our progress with intense interest; that he would like, for the inspiration of his guests and for the benefit of Alcoholics Anonymous, to give a dinner. We regarded this as a ten strike.

In March 1940, the dinner came off. Mr. R.'s friends turned out in force. An AA member was placed at each guest table. Dr. Harry Emerson Fosdick, who had superbly reviewed our book, spoke of AA from the spiritual viewpoint. Dr. Foster Kennedy, noted neurologist, gave his hearers the medical outlook. We alcoholics were asked to talk also. At the conclusion of the evening Mr. Nelson Rockefeller, explaining that his father had not been able to come because of illness, went on to say that few things more deeply affecting or promising than Alcoholics Anonymous had ever touched his father's life; that he wished his friends to share this experience with him.

Though great wealth was present at the dinner meeting that night, little was said about money. Hope was expressed that AA might soon become self-supporting. But the suggestion was made that until AA became self-supporting a little financial help might be needed. Following the dinner meeting Mr. Rockefeller wrote a personal letter to each guest, expressing his feeling about AA, and concluding with the observation that he was making us a modest gift. Accompanying each letter was a reprint of the talks given at the dinner and a copy of the book *Alcoholics Anonymous*. On receipt of Mr. Rockefeller's letter, many of his guests responded with donations to the Alcoholic Foundation.

This so-called "Rockefeller dinner list" has since been almost the only source of "outside" money gifts to the Alcoholic Foundation. These donations averaged around $3,000 annually and they were continued for about five years — 1940 to 1945. This income the Foundation divided between Dr. Bob and me to enable us to give AA a good part of our time during that critical period. Not long since, the Foundation trustees were able to write the original dinner contributors, with great thanks, that their help would no longer be needed; that the Alcoholic Foundation had become adequately supported by the AA groups and by income from the book *Alcoholics Anonymous;* that the personal needs of Dr. Bob and myself were being met out of book royalties.

The significant thing about Mr. Rockefeller's dinner, of course, was not only the money it raised. What we did need then, even as much, was favorable public recognition; we needed someone who would stand up and say what he thought and felt about Alcoholics Anonymous. Considering the fact that we were then few in number; that we were none too sure of ourselves; that not long since society had known us as common drunkards, I think Mr. Rockefeller's wisdom and courage were great indeed.

The effect of that dinner meeting was instantaneous; the news press wires all carried the story. Hundreds of alcoholics and their families rushed to buy the book. Our little Central Office was flooded with pleas for help. It soon had to be moved from New Jersey to Vesey Street, New York. Ruth Hock got her back pay and forthwith became our first national secretary. Enough books were sold to keep the office going. So passed 1940. Alcoholics Anonymous had made its national debut.

Just a year later, the *Saturday Evening Post* assigned Jack Alexander to do a story about us. Under the impetus of Mr. Rockefeller's dinner and the Cleveland *Plain Dealer* pieces, our membership had shot up to about 2,000. Our Clevelanders had just proved that even a small group could, if it must, successfully absorb great numbers of newcomers in a hurry. They had exploded the myth that AA must always grow slowly. From the Akron-Cleveland area we had begun to spread into other places — Chicago and Detroit in the Midwest. In the East, Philadelphia had taken fire. Washington and Baltimore were smoldering. Further west, Houston, Los Angeles, and San Francisco were taking spark. Growth continued at Akron and New York. We took special pride in Little Rock, Arkansas, which had sprung up with no personal contact with AA, having caught on through books and letters from the Central Office. Little Rock was the first of the so-called "mail order" groups now commonplace all over the world. Even then, we had started correspondence with many isolated alcoholics who were to form groups later on.

Despite this progress, the approaching *Saturday Evening Post* piece worried us. While our Cleveland experience had given assurance that our few established groups would survive the impact of heavy publicity, what could we possibly do with the thousands of burning appeals that would now swamp our little New York office, then staffed by Ruth Hock, a typist, and myself? How could three people handle the thousands of frantic inquiries we expected? The *Post* article would bring more book sales, but not enough to handle this emergency. We needed more office help — and quickly — or we must be prepared to throw heartbreaking appeals into the wastebasket.

We realized we must, for the first time, ask the AA groups for assistance. The Alcoholic Foundation still had no money save the $3,000 a year "dinner fund" which was helping to keep Dr. Bob and me afloat. Besides, some of the creditors and cash subscribers of Works Publishing (the AA book company) were getting anxious again.

Two of the alcoholic members of our Foundation traveled out among the AA groups to explain the need. They presented their listeners with these ideas: that support of our Central Office was a definite responsibility of the AA groups; that answering written inquiries was a necessary assistance to our Twelfth Step work; that we AAs ought to pay these office expenses ourselves and rely no further upon outside charity or insufficient book sales. The two trustees also suggested that the Alcoholic Foundation be made a regular depository for group funds; that the Foundation would earmark all group monies for Central Office expenses only; that each month the Central Office would bill the Foundation for the straight AA expenses of the place; that all group contributions ought to be entirely voluntary; that every AA group would receive equal service from the New York office, whether it contributed or not. It was estimated that if each group sent the Foundation a sum equal to $1 per member per year, this might eventually carry our office, without other assistance. Under this arrangement the office would ask the groups twice yearly for funds and render, at the same time, a statement of its expenses for the previous period.

Our two trustees, Horace C. and Bert T., did not come back empty handed. Now clearly understanding the situation, most groups began contributing to the Alcoholic Foundation for Central Office expenses, and have continued to do so ever since. In this practice the AA Tradition of self-support had a firm beginning. Thus we handled the *Saturday Evening Post* article for which thousands of AAs are today so grateful.

The enormous inpouring of fresh members quickly laid the foundation for hundreds of new AA groups, and they soon began to consult the Central Office about growing pains, thus confronting our service Headquarters with group problems as well as personal inquiries. The office then began to publish a list of all AA groups, and it furnished traveling AAs with lists of prospects in cities which had none. Out-of-towners we had never seen before began to visit us, so starting what is today the huge network of personal contact between our Central Service Office staff at New York and AA groups throughout the world.

The year 1941 was a great one for the growing AA. It was the beginning of the huge development to follow. Our Central Office got solid group backing; we began to abandon the idea of outside charitable help in favor of self-support. Last but not least, our Alcoholic Foundation really commenced to function. By this time linked to the AA Central Office because of its responsibility for the group funds being spent there, and to Works Publishing (the book *Alcoholics Anonymous*) by partial ownership, the trustees of our Alcoholic Foundation had already become, though they did not realize it, the custodians for Alcoholics Anonymous — both of money and of Tradition. Alcoholics Anonymous had become a national institution.

Quietly but effectively, the evolution of our Foundation has since continued. Several years ago the trustees had a certified audit made of the Alcoholic Foundation and Works Publishing from their very beginnings. A good bookkeeping system was installed and regular audits became an established custom.

About 1942 it became evident that the Foundation ought to complete its ownership of Works Publishing by calling in the stock of the outstanding cash subscribers of Works. Several thousand dollars were required to do this and, of course, group funds could not be used for this purpose.

So the trustees, spearheaded this time by our old friend Chip, turned again to Mr. Rockefeller and his "dinner list." These original donors most gladly made the Foundation the necessary loan which enabled the Foundation to acquire full ownership of our AA Book (Works Publishing, Inc.). Meanwhile, Works Publishing, being now partly relieved of supporting the Central Office, had been able to pay its own creditors in full. Later on, when out of AA Book income the trustees offered to pay off the Foundation debt, several of the lenders would take only a part payment — some none at all. At last we were in the clear. This event marked the end of our financial troubles.

The last few years of AA have been phenomenal. Nearly everybody in America knows about AA. Seemingly, the rest of the globe will soon learn as AA travelers go abroad and our literature is translated into other tongues. Today our general service Headquarters has a staff of twelve. Because of our prodigious growth and the continuous entry of AA into more foreign countries, the Headquarters will presently need twenty. Popularly known to thousands as "Bobbie," our AA general secretary now serves world AA. On the board of the Alcoholic Foundation three of the early trustees, whose contribution to AA is incalculable, remain. New faces are seen at the quarterly meetings, each as anxious to serve as the original group. The AA Grapevine, our national monthly periodical, which made its appearance three years ago, is now taking its place among our general Headquarters' services and is almost paying its own way already. Out of its Works Publishing income, the Foundation has accumulated a prudent financial reserve for the future. That reserve now stands at more than a full year's Headquarters expense, which still remains not much above the very low figure of $1 per AA member per year. Two years ago the trustees set aside, out of AA Book funds, a sum which enabled my wife and me to pay off the mortgage on our home and make some needed improvements. The Foundation also granted Dr. Bob and me each a royalty of 10 percent on the book *Alcoholics Anonymous,* our only income from AA sources. We are both very comfortable and deeply grateful.

This account of the stewardship of Alcoholics Anonymous during its infancy brings us to the present — the year 1947 — with continued AA growth and AA service the future's promise.

Traditions Stressed in Memphis Talk

October 1947

Urging all members of Alcoholics Anonymous to strive for humility before success and for unity before fame, Bill W., speaking before the third annual Southeastern Regional Convention in Memphis, Tennessee, on September 19, reviewed the Twelve suggested Traditions for the organization.

Pointing out that the success of AA could be "heady wine and a serious problem," Bill reminded members that as alcoholics "we are a people who could not exist at all except for the grace of God."

Here are the highlights of the talk as given to the AA Grapevine in advance of the Memphis meeting:

"Some years ago, Dr. Bob and I, among others, did a lot of traveling and speaking at AA groups the length and breadth of the country. Alcoholics Anonymous was just starting its astonishing growth. There was concern whether we could successfully expand so fast. Widely separated clusters of AAs were making their uncertain start, often too far from the original few groups to get much direct help. Many had to rely wholly on literature and letters.

"To meet this seeming emergency, the few of us who could do so got out among the new groups. We wanted to bring our experience and encouragement directly to the incoming thousands who were still unsure; we wanted them to feel a part of the growing whole; we wanted them to see that AA had nothing to do with geography; that it would work for them under any conditions whatever. We wished to foster a sound growth and the spirit of unity. So a few of us traveled much.

"Times have changed. As everyone knows, AA has since exceeded our wildest expectations. Speaking for Dr. Bob and myself, we feel that we oldsters need not take the prominent roles we once did. AA leadership is becoming, happily and healthily, a rotating matter. And besides, our literature, a generous press, and thousands of new travelers are carrying AA to every corner of the world.

"Yet there does remain a problem — a *serious* problem, in whose solution AAs will expect us oldsters to occasionally take a hand. That is the problem of *success* itself. Always a heady wine, success may sometimes cause us to forget that each of us lives on borrowed time; we may forget that we are a people who cannot exist at all, but for the grace of God. The wine of forgetfulness might make us dream that Alcoholics Anonymous was *our* success rather than *God's* will. The very malignancy which once tore us apart personally could again commence to rend us as groups. False pride might lead us to controversy, to claims of power and prestige, to bickerings over property, money, and personal authority. We would not be human if these illnesses didn't sometimes attack us.

"Therefore, many of us think today the main problem of Alcoholics Anonymous is this: How, as a movement, shall we maintain our humility — and so our unity — in the face of what the world calls a great triumph? Perhaps we need not look far afield for an answer. We need only adapt and apply to our group life those principles upon which each of us has founded his own recovery. If humility can expel the obsession to drink alcohol, then surely humility can be our antidote for that subtle wine called success."

Bill then went on to explain in detail the Twelve Points of Tradition, first printed in an article in the April 1946 issue of the AA Grapevine: "Two years ago my old friends urged that I try to sum up our experience of living and working together; that I try to state those definite principles of group conduct which had then quite clearly emerged from a decade of strenuous trial and error. In the spirit of our original Twelve Steps, and strictly within the ample proofs of our experience, I made the following tentative attempt: Twelve Points to Assure Our Future, an Alcoholics Anonymous Tradition of Relations (recently revised in the light of later experience).

"Our AA experience has taught us that:

"1. Each member of Alcoholics Anonymous is but a small part of a great whole. AA must continue to live or most of us will surely die. Hence our common welfare comes first. But individual welfare follows close afterward.

"2. For our group purpose there is but one ultimate authority — a loving God as he may express himself in our group conscience.

"3. Our membership ought to include all who suffer alcoholism. Hence we may refuse none who wish to recover. Nor ought AA membership ever depend upon money or conformity. Any two or three alcoholics gathered together for sobriety may call themselves an AA group, provided, of course, that, as a group, they have no other affiliation.

"4. With respect to its own affairs, each AA group should be responsible to no other authority than its own conscience. But when its plans concern the welfare of neighboring groups also, those groups ought to be consulted. And no group, regional committee, or individual should ever take any action that might greatly affect AA as a whole without conferring with the trustees of the Alcoholic Foundation. On such issues our common welfare is paramount.

"5. Each Alcoholics Anonymous group ought to be a spiritual entity *having but one primary purpose* — that of carrying its message to the alcoholic who still suffers.

"6. Problems of money, property, and authority may easily divert us from our primary spiritual aim. We think, therefore, that any considerable property of genuine use to AA should be separately incorporated and managed, thus dividing the material from the spiritual. An AA group, as such, should never go into business. Secondary aids to AA, such as clubs or hospitals which require much property or administration, ought to be incorporated and so set apart that, if necessary, they can be freely discarded by the groups. Hence, such facilities ought not to use the AA name. Their management should be the sole responsibility of those people who financially support them. For clubs, AA managers are usually preferred. But hospitals, as well as other places of recuperation, ought to be well outside AA — and medically supervised. While an AA group may cooperate with anyone, such cooperation ought never go so far as affiliation or endorsement, actual or implied. An AA group can bind itself to no one.

"7. AA groups themselves ought to be fully supported by the voluntary contributions of their own members. We think that each group should soon achieve this ideal; that any public solicitation of funds using the name of Alcoholics Anonymous is highly dangerous, whether by groups, clubs, hospitals, or other outside agencies; that acceptance of large gifts from any source or of contributions carrying any obligation whatever, is unwise. Then, too, we view with much concern those AA treasuries which continue, beyond prudent reserves, to accumulate funds for no stated AA purpose. Experience has often warned us that nothing can so surely destroy our spiritual heritage as futile disputes over property, money, and authority.

"8. Alcoholics Anonymous should remain forever nonprofessional. We define professionalism as the occupation of counseling alcoholics for fees or hire. But we may employ alcoholics where they are going to perform those services for which we might otherwise have to engage nonalcoholics. Such special services may be well recompensed. But our usual AA Twelfth Step work is never to be paid for.

"9. Each AA group needs the least possible organization. Rotating leadership is the best. The small group may elect its secretary, the large group its rotating committee, and the groups of a large metropolitan area their central or intergroup committee, which often employs a full-time secretary. The trustees of the Alcoholic Foundation are, in effect, our general service committee. They are the custodians of our AA Tradition and the receivers of voluntary AA contributions by which we maintain the AA General Service Office at New York. They are authorized by the groups to handle our overall public relations and they guarantee the integrity of our principal newspaper, the AA Grapevine. All such representatives are to be guided in the spirit of service, for true leaders in AA are but trusted and experienced servants of the whole. They derive no real authority from their titles; they do not govern. Universal respect is the key to their usefulness.

"10. No AA group or member should ever, in such a way as to implicate AA, express any opinion on outside controversial issues — particularly those of politics, alcohol reform, or sectarian religion. The Alcoholics Anonymous groups oppose no one. Concerning such matters they can express no views whatever.

"11. Our relations with the general public should be characterized by personal anonymity. We think AA ought to avoid sensational advertising. Our names and pictures as AA members ought not be broadcast, filmed, or publicly printed. Our public relations should be guided by the principle of attraction rather than promotion. There is never need to praise ourselves. We feel it better to let our friends recommend us.

"12. And finally, we of Alcoholics Anonymous believe that the principle of anonymity has an immense spiritual significance. It reminds us that we are to place principles before personalities; that we are actually to practice a genuine humility. This to the end that our great blessings may never spoil us; that we shall forever live in thankful contemplation of him who presides over us all.

"To sum up: For thousands of alcoholics yet to come, AA does have an answer. But there is one condition. We must, at all costs, preserve our essential unity; it must be made unbreakably secure. Without permanent unity there can be little lasting recovery for anyone.

Hence our future absolutely depends upon the creation and observance of a sound group Tradition. First things will always need to be first: *humility* before success, and *unity* before fame.''

Incorporations: Their Use and Misuse

November 1947

Many an AA group ruefully writes the New York office asking how to unscramble endless difficulties that have arisen over the incorporation and financing of clubs, drying-out places, educational projects, and the like. Most sincerely, *these groups wish that they had never gone into business.*

Once off to an awkward start, these difficulties are sometimes hard to cure. Still, if we intelligently use the experience we've already had, our newer groups ought easily avoid these growing pains. The purpose of this piece is to assemble and focus our experience on these particular problems.

First, let's review those parts of the Twelve Points of AA Tradition which bear directly on the status of incorporations and their financing:

Tradition Six states: "We think, therefore, that any considerable property of genuine use to AA should be *separately incorporated and managed,* thus dividing the material from the spiritual. . . An AA group, as such, should never go into business. . . . Clubs, hospitals, etc., ought to be incorporated. . . so set apart that they can be freely discarded by the groups. . . hence they ought not use the AA name. . . their management should be the sole responsibility of those who financially support them. . . . Hospitals or places of recuperation ought to be well *outside* AA and medically supervised. . . . An AA group may cooperate with anyone, but such cooperation ought never go so far as affiliation or endorsement, express or implied."

Tradition Seven states, after declaring for full financial self-support as soon as possible, "that any public solicitation of funds using the name 'Alcoholics Anonymous' is highly dangerous, whether by groups, clubs, hospitals, or other outside agencies — that acceptance of large gifts from any source, or of contributions carrying any obligations whatever, is unwise. . . that we view with concern those AA treasuries which continue, beyond prudent reserves, to accumulate funds for no stated purpose. . . that nothing can so surely destroy our spiritual heritage as futile disputes over property, money, and personal authority."

Being clear on these basic principles, it is next suggested that four of the articles in this book be carefully reread — [see pages 24, 46, 51, and 43 for] the ones on money, clubs, hospitals, and outside enterprises, which show our past experiences in these fields. They clearly reveal the fundamentals of our "money-management" Tradition. And in a general way, they quite clearly indicate what the corporate status of any useful or related enterprise ought to be.

Next, then, just what special type of incorporation is best, how should it be corporately named, what should be the limit of its scope, who should be its members (or stockholders), and how should it be financed? Many AAs write us asking for samples of model charters. As precise group purposes, local conditions, and state laws may vary much, it would probably be unwise for AA Headquarters to try to meet these requests. Any good attorney, once he is sure just what is needed and just what should be avoided, will do far better than we.

In response to the many group inquiries, we wish, however, to be as definite as possible. So here follows a set of typical questions that groups ask. To them we append definite answers. Of course, these answers aren't to be construed as final or perfect. Nor are they to be thought of as rules, regulations, or "musts." But they may help in perplexing situations.

1. *Should an AA group, as such, ever incorporate?*

No. Some have, but usually wish they hadn't.

2. *Should an AA group as such go into the business of running a club, a hospital, a research, educational, or rehabilitation venture?*

We think definitely not. Experience has been telling us to avoid this. The AA group ought to remain a spiritual entity.

3. *But how about clubs? Being so close to AA, shouldn't they be an exception; just why shouldn't they bear the AA name and be managed by the group itself?*

We used to think they should. When a group is small and merely hires a room, it is quite natural to call the place an "AA clubroom." Conversationally, most clubs are still called "AA clubs." But when an area contains many AAs, and perhaps several groups, not all the AA members will care for clubs. Hence the business management of the club (or clubs) in the area must become the function of those who individually contribute to their support, and the corporate title should omit "AA." The contributors ought to elect the business management. Then other AAs can take the club or leave it alone. Club corporations often adopt a related title, such as Alano or Alkanon. But more remote ventures, such as farms or drying-out places operated by individual AAs, ought not use these related titles.

4. *Our group* did *form a separate corporation for our club. We made every one of our AA group members a voting member of that corporation. Now the directors of the club corporation are at odds with our group rotating committee. The club directors try to run both the club and the group. The group committee also tries to run the club. What do we do about that?*

This is a natural difficulty. It can be corrected by a realization on the part of the club directors that theirs is the duty of providing a suitable club only — a pure business operation. They merely hold or rent the property, keep the place policed and swept out. They raise money from individual monthly pledges; they also receive rentals from the treasuries of such AA groups as may hold meetings in the club. This is usually a generous proportion of those funds which result from "passing the hat." Each AA group ought to have its own small treasury. Out of these funds the group pays for whatever use it may make of the local club. This avoids confusion between group monies and club corporation funds. Under these conditions the club has no special hold on the group, and vice versa. Pure AA matters are handled by the group committee. But jurisdiction over social activities in a club will vary; sometimes the club directors handle them, sometimes the group committee, sometimes a special committee.

There is often confusion between club membership and AA membership. In a limited sense, they are one and the same thing, as practically all clubs open their doors to every reasonably well-behaved AA who wishes to frequent them.

But when *club management* is involved, we are beginning to believe a distinction should be made between club privileges, club voting membership, and AA membership. Any AA interested in a club ought to be willing to contribute regularly to its support. Though he may not be able to contribute much, it will be something. Obviously, as a monthly contributor, he should be eligible to serve as a club officer or director and should vote at business meetings. While straight AA is free as air and most clubs are wide open to all, there seems no good reason why a persistent noncontributor should claim any right to vote at a club's business meeting. If he wants to help manage the club's money, he ought to contribute a little himself. So, when we come to distinguish clearly between club privileges, club voting membership, and AA membership itself, we shall have surmounted many current troubles.

5. *Our group is small. Every local AA member is a club enthusiast. Do you think we should incorporate just the same, even though AA membership and club membership are identical, and in our town everybody contributes to the club?*

If your club has to sign a lease, buy property, or have a sizable bank account, by all means incorporate. Establish this way of doing and thinking and you will avoid later complications. We suggest you be careful about mixing AA affairs with your club business meetings — business only there!

A clubroom may, of course, be so small and inexpensive, or its future so uncertain, that it would be premature to incorporate. That's a matter for sound judgment.

6. *Should a club corporation charter include other activities such as rehabilitation, hospitalization, education, research, etc.?*

We think definitely not. We suggest you limit corporation charters to one activity and one location only. To incorporate the whole world of alcohol and mix that up with AA almost invariably leads to confusion. A simple, sharply limited objective is best. Mixtures of several functions we have sometimes tried, but usually with poor results.

7. *May individual AAs organize foundations and raise money for research, education, rehabilitation, etc.?*

There can be no objection if they act as *individuals only* and *do not use the AA name in any way.* But experience shows that there is always a strong temptation to use the AA name. If that is done, the project will ultimately suffer because the surrounding AA groups will protest strongly — and rightly so, we think. The Alcoholic Foundation itself, though it unofficially represents AA as our General Service Board, has solicited no outside funds in recent years and it will soon abandon the title "Foundation."

8. *We want to build a clubhouse. Should we do so? And how shall*

we finance it?

Chances are that any club built will prove too small. Better lease if you can. A thickly populated AA area will eventually do better with several small leased clubs than a single costly one. If a club is big, expensive, and owned outright, it can later prove very difficult to take or leave alone.

It's always better for members to raise the money among themselves if they must build, supplemented if absolutely necessary by a friendly outside loan calling for easy but definite repayment. Our reputation for complete self-support is a valuable asset. Beware of loans or contributions with implied obligations, political entanglements, or controversial issues attached. And obviously, public solicitation using the AA name *is* dangerous.

9. *What about drying-out places — how ought they be handled?*

We feel that AA groups shouldn't go into these ventures. But individual AAs sometimes handle these situations very well if they avoid public solicitations and advertisements using the AA name. Places of recuperation ought to be private undertakings purely — and privately financed.

10. *What should be the attitude of an AA group toward "outside" ventures like education, research, and the like?*

No attitude at all. Participation in them is an individual mater. But individuals should not be discouraged from participation if they are careful of the AA name.

11. *We realize that our present club (or hospital) set-up is contrary, in some ways, to the general experience. But it hasn't yet given us much trouble. Shall we now change it to conform to the AA Tradition?*

That's entirely up to you. If your present set-up works very well, it may not be worth the trouble to change now. But if there is much serious objection locally, it may be well to try those principles best proved by our large general experience.

12. *Just what form of corporation structure is usually best?*

Most states and countries have special corporate forms variously called membership, charitable, eleemosynary, etc. Trust your lawyer to select the best. You might emphasize to him these points: If humanly possible, eliminate the name "Alcoholics Anonymous" from the corporate title. (This name ought to be the sole property of AA as a whole.) Limit the "purpose clause" to one simple objective only. Limit the activities of the corporation to one locality or address only. Don't try to incorporate a whole state or country; otherwise AAs in nearby places may well object.

This article has been written to help alleviate the many complications that have arisen throughout AA touching clubs, hospitals, and "outside ventures." There is nothing infallible about the principles set forth above. But they are, nevertheless, the distillation of much actual experience. It's very greatly hoped they will prove of especial assistance to our hundreds of new groups. They may be able to prevent many of the natural but painful mistakes we AA oldsters have so often made.

Tradition One

December 1947

Our whole AA program is securely founded on the principle of humility — that is to say, perspective. Which implies, among other things, that we relate ourselves rightly to God and to our fellows; that we each see ourselves as we really are — "a small part of a great whole." Seeing our fellows thus, we shall enjoy group harmony. That is why AA Tradition can confidently state, "Our common welfare comes first."

"Does this mean," some will ask, "that in AA the individual doesn't count too much? Is he to be swallowed up, dominated by the group?"

No, it doesn't seem to work out that way. Perhaps there is no society on earth more solicitous of personal welfare, more careful to grant the individual the greatest possible liberty of belief and action. Alcoholics Anonymous has no "musts." Few AA groups impose penalties on anyone for nonconformity. We do suggest, but we don't discipline. Instead, compliance or noncompliance with any principle of AA is a matter for the conscience of the individual; he is the judge of his own conduct. Those words of old time, "judge not," we observe most literally.

"But," some will argue, "if AA has no authority to govern its individual members or groups, how shall it ever be sure that the common welfare does come first? How is it possible to be governed without a government? If everyone can do as he pleases, how can you have aught but anarchy?''

The answer seems to be that we AAs cannot really do as we please, though there is no constituted human authority to restrain us. Actually, our common welfare is protected by powerful safeguards. The moment any action seriously threatens the common welfare, group opinion mobilizes to remind us; our conscience begins to complain. If one persists, he may become so disturbed as to get drunk; alcohol gives him a beating. Group opinion shows him that he is off the beam, his own conscience tells him that he is dead wrong, and, if he goes too far, Barleycorn brings him real conviction.

So it is we learn that in matters deeply affecting the group as a whole, "our common welfare comes first." Rebellion ceases and cooperation begins because it must: we have disciplined ourselves.

Eventually, of course, we cooperate because we really wish to; we see that without substantial unity there can be no AA, and that without AA there can be little lasting recovery for anyone. We gladly set aside personal ambitions whenever these might harm AA. We humbly confess that we are but "a small part of a great whole."

Tradition Two

January 1948

Sooner or later, every AA comes to depend upon a Power greater than himself. He finds that the God of his understanding is not only a source of strength, but also a source of *positive direction*. Realizing that some fraction of that infinite resource is now available, his life takes on an entirely different complexion. He experiences a new inner security together with such a sense of destiny and purpose as he has never known before. As each day passes, our AA reviews his mistakes and vicissitudes. He learns from daily experience what his remaining character defects are and becomes ever more willing that they be removed. In this fashion he improves his conscious contact with God.

Every AA group follows this same cycle of development. We are coming to realize that each group, as well as each individual, is a special entity, not quite like any other. Though AA groups are basically the same, each group does have its own special atmosphere, its own peculiar state of development. We believe that every AA group has a conscience. It is the collective conscience of its own membership. Daily experience informs and instructs this conscience. The group begins to recognize its own defects of character and, one by one, these are removed or lessened. As this process continues, the group becomes better able to receive right direction for its own affairs. Trial and error produces group experience, and out of corrected experience comes custom. When a customary way of doing things is definitely proved to be best, then that custom forms into AA Tradition. The Greater Power is then working through a clear group conscience.

We humbly hope and believe that our growing AA Tradition will prove to be the will of God for us.

Many people are coming to think that Alcoholics Anonymous is, to some extent, a new form of human society. In our discussion of the First Tradition, it was emphasized that we have, in AA, no coercive human authority. Because each AA, of necessity, has a sensitive and responsive conscience, and because alcohol will discipline him severely if he backslides, we are finding we have little need for manmade rules or regulations. Despite the fact that we do veer off at times on tangents, we are becoming more able to depend absolutely on the long-term stability of the AA group itself. With respect to its own affairs, the collective conscience of the group will, given time, almost surely demonstrate its perfect dependability. The group conscience will, in the end, prove a far more infallible guide for group affairs than the decision of any individual member, however good or wise he may be. This is a striking and almost unbelievable fact about Alcoholics Anonymous. Hence we can safely dispense with those exhortations and punishments seemingly so necessary to other societies. And we need not depend overmuch on inspired leaders. Because our active leadership of service can be truly rotating, we enjoy a kind of democracy rarely possible elsewhere. In this respect we may be, to a large degree, unique.

Therefore we of Alcoholics Anonymous are certain that there is but one ultimate authority, "a loving God as he may express himself in our group conscience."

Tradition Three

February 1948

T he Third Tradition is a sweeping statement indeed; it takes in a lot of territory. Some people might think it too idealistic to be practical. It tells every alcoholic in the world that he may become, and remain, a member of Alcoholics Anonymous *so long as he says so.* In short, Alcoholics Anonymous has no membership rule.

Why is this so? Our answer is simple and practical. Even in self-protection, we do not wish to erect the slightest barrier between ourselves and the fellow alcoholic who still suffers. We know that society has been demanding that he conform to its laws and conventions. But the essence of his alcoholic malady is the fact that he has been unable or unwilling to conform either to the laws of man or God. If he is anything, the sick alcoholic is a rebellious nonconformist. How well we understand that; every member of Alcoholics Anonymous was once a rebel himself. Hence we cannot offer to meet him at any halfway mark. We must enter the dark cave where he is and show him that we understand. We realize that he is altogether too weak and confused to jump hurdles. If we raise obstacles, he might stay away and perish. He might be denied his priceless opportunity.

So when he asks, "Are there any conditions?" we joyfully reply, "No, not a one." When skeptically he comes back saying, "But certainly there must be things that I have to do and believe," we quickly answer, "In Alcoholics Anonymous there are no *musts.*" Cynically, perhaps, he then inquires, "What is this all going to cost me?" We are able to laugh and say, "Nothing at all, there are no fees and dues." Thus, in a brief hour, is our friend disarmed of his suspicion and rebellion. His eyes begin to open on a new world of friendship and understanding. Bankrupt idealist that he has been, his ideal is no longer a dream. After years of lonely search it now stands revealed. The reality of Alcoholics Anonymous bursts upon him. For Alcoholics Anonymous is saying, "We have something priceless to give, if only you will receive." That is all. But to our new friend, it is everything. Without more ado, he becomes one of us.

Our membership Tradition does contain, however, one vitally important qualification. That qualification relates to the use of our name, Alcoholics Anonymous. We believe that any two or three alcoholics gathered together for sobriety may call themselves an AA group provided that, as a group, they have no other affiliation. Here our purpose is clear and unequivocal. For obvious reasons we wish the name Alcoholics Anonymous to be used only in connection with straight AA activities. One can think of no AA member who would like, for example, to see the formation of "dry" AA groups, "wet" AA groups, Republican AA groups, communist AA groups. Few, if any, would wish our groups to be designated by religious denominations. We cannot lend the AA name, even indirectly, to other activities, however worthy. If we do so we shall become hopelessly compromised and divided. We think that AA should offer its experience to the whole world for whatever use can be made of it. But not its name. Nothing could be more certain.

Let us of AA therefore resolve that we shall always be inclusive and never exclusive, offering all we have to all, save our title. May all barriers be thus leveled, may our unity thus be preserved. And may God grant us a long life — and a useful one!

Tradition Four

March 1948

Tradition Four is a specific application of general principles already outlined in Traditions One and Two. Tradition One states: "Each member of Alcoholics Anonymous is but a small part of a great whole. AA must continue to live or most of us will surely die. Hence our common welfare comes first. But individual welfare follows close afterward." Tradition Two states: "For our group purpose there is but one ultimate authority — a loving God as he may express himself in our group conscience."

With these concepts in mind, let us look more closely at Tradition Four. The first sentence guarantees each AA group local autonomy.

With respect to its own affairs, the group may make any decisions, adopt any attitudes that it likes. No overall or intergroup authority should challenge this primary privilege. We feel this ought to be so, even though the group might sometimes act with complete indifference to our Tradition. For example, an AA group could, if it wished, hire a paid preacher and support him out of the proceeds of a group nightclub. Though such an absurd procedure would be miles outside our Tradition, the group's "right to be wrong" would be held inviolate. We are sure that each group can be granted, and safely granted, these most extreme privileges. We know that our familiar process of trial and error would summarily eliminate both the preacher and the nightclub. Those severe growing pains which invariably follow any radical departure from AA Tradition can be absolutely relied upon to bring an erring group back into line. An AA group need not be coerced by any human government over and above its own members. Their own experience, plus AA opinion in surrounding groups, plus God's prompting in their group conscience would be sufficient. Much travail has already taught us this. Hence we may confidently say to each group, "You should be responsible to no other authority than your own conscience."

Yet please note one important qualification. It will be seen that such extreme liberty of thought and action applies only *to the group's own affairs.* Rightly enough, this Tradition goes on to say, "But when its plans concern the welfare of neighboring groups also, these groups ought to be consulted." Obviously, if any individual, group, or regional committee could take an action that might seriously affect the welfare of Alcoholics Anonymous as a whole or seriously disturb surrounding groups, that would not be liberty at all. It would be sheer license; it would be anarchy, not democracy.

Therefore, we AAs have universally adopted the principle of consultation. This means that if a single AA group wishes to take any action that might affect surrounding groups, it consults them. Or, it confers with the intergroup committee for the area, if there be one. Likewise, if a group or regional committee wishes to take any action that might affect AA as a whole, it consults the trustees of the Alcoholic Foundation, who are, in effect, our overall general service committee. For instance, no group or intergroup could feel free to initiate, without consultation, any publicity that might affect AA as a whole. Nor could it assume to represent the whole of Alcoholics Anonymous by printing and distributing anything purporting to be AA standard literature. This same principle would naturally apply to all similar situations. Though there is no formal compulsion to do so, all undertakings of this general character are customarily checked with our AA general Headquarters.

This idea is clearly summarized in the last sentence of Tradition Four, which observes, "On such issues our common welfare is paramount."

Tradition Five

April 1948

Says the old proverb, "Shoemaker, stick to thy last." Trite, yes. But very true for us of AA. How well we need to heed the principle that it is better to do one thing supremely well than many things badly.

Because it has now become plain enough that only a recovered alcoholic can do much for a sick alcoholic, a tremendous responsibility has descended upon us all, an obligation so great that it amounts to a sacred trust. For to our kind, those who suffer alcoholism, recovery is a matter of life or death. So the Society of Alcoholics Anonymous cannot, it dare not, ever be diverted from its primary purpose.

Temptations to do otherwise will come aplenty. Seeing fine works afoot in the field of alcohol, we shall be sorely tempted to loan out the name and credit of Alcoholics Anonymous to them; as a movement we shall be beset to finance and endorse other causes. Should our present success continue, people will commence to assert that AA is a brand-new way of life, maybe a new religion, capable of saving the world. We shall be told it is our bounden duty to show modern society how it ought to live.

Oh, how very attractive these projects and ideas can be! How flattering to imagine that we might be chosen to demonstrate that olden mystic promise: "The first shall be last and the last shall be first." Fantastic, you say. Yet some of our well-wishers have begun to say such things.

Fortunately, most of us are convinced that these are perilous speculations, alluring ingredients of that new heady wine we are now being offered, each bottle marked "Success"!

Of this subtle vintage may we never drink too deeply. May we never forget that we live by the grace of God — on borrowed time; that anonymity is better than acclaim; that for us as a movement poverty is better than wealth.

And may we reflect with ever deepening conviction, that we shall never be at our best except when we hew only to the primary spiritual aim of AA. That of carrying its message to the alcoholic who still suffers alcoholism.

Tradition Six

May 1948

T he sixth of our Twelve Points of AA Tradition is deemed so important that it states at length the relation of the AA movement to money and property.

This Tradition declares in substance that the accumulation of money, property, and the unwanted personal authority so often generated by material wealth comprise a cluster of serious hazards against which an AA group must ever be on guard.

Tradition Six also enjoins the group never to go into business nor ever to lend the AA name or money credit to any "outside" enterprise, no matter how good. Strongly expressed is the opinion that even clubs should not bear the AA name; that they ought to be separately incorporated and managed by those individual AAs who need or want clubs enough to financially support them.

We would thus divide the spiritual from the material, confine the AA movement to its sole aim, and ensure (however wealthy as individuals we may become) that AA itself shall always remain poor. We dare not risk the distractions of corporate wealth. Years of experience have proven these principles beyond doubt. They have become certainties, absolute verities for us.

Thank God, we AAs have never yet been caught in the kind of religious or political disputes which embroil the world of today. But we ought to face the fact that we have often quarreled violently about money, property, and the administration thereof. Money, in quantity, has always been a baleful influence in group life. Let a well-meaning donor present an AA group with a sizable sum and we break loose. Nor does trouble abate until that group, as such, somehow disposes of its bankroll. This experience is practically universal. "But," say our friends, "isn't this a confession of weakness? Other organizations do a lot of good with money. Why not AA?"

Of course, we of AA would be the first to say that many a fine enterprise does a lot of good with a lot of money. To these efforts, money is usually primary; it is their lifeblood. But money is *not* the lifeblood of AA. With us, it is very secondary. Even in small quantities, it is scarcely more than a necessary nuisance, something we wish we could do without entirely. Why is that so?

We explain this easily enough; we don't need money. The core of our AA procedure is one alcoholic talking to another, whether that be sitting on a curbstone, in a home, or at a meeting. It's the message, not the place; it's the talk, not the alms. That does our work. Just places to meet and talk, that's about all AA needs. Beyond these, a few small offices, a few secretaries at their desks, a few dollars apiece a year, easily met by voluntary contributions. Trivial indeed, *our* expenses!

Nowadays, the AA group answers its well-wishers saying: "Our expenses are trifling. As good earners, we can easily pay them. As we neither need nor want money, why risk its hazards? We'd rather stay poor. Thanks just the same!"

Tradition Seven

June 1948

(O)ur growth continuing, the combined income of Alcoholics Anonymous members will soon reach the astounding total of a quarter of a billion dollars yearly. This is the direct result of AA membership. Sober we now have it; drunk we would not.

By contrast, our overall AA expenses are trifling.

For instance, the AA General Service Office now costs us $1.50 per member a year. As a fact, the New York office asks the groups for this sum twice a year because not all of them contribute. Even so, the sum per member is exceedingly small. If an AA happens to live in a large metropolitan center where an intergroup office is absolutely essential to handle heavy inquiries and hospital arrangements, he contributes (or probably should contribute) about $5.00 annually. To pay the rent of his own group meeting place, and maybe coffee and doughnuts, he might drop $25.00 a year in the hat. Or if he belongs to a club, it could be $50.00. In case he takes the AA Grapevine, he squanders an extra $2.50!

So the AA member who really meets his group responsibilities finds himself liable for about $5.00 a month on the average. Yet his own personal income may be anywhere between $200 and $2,000 a month — the direct result of *not* drinking.

"But," some will contend, "our friends want to give us money to furnish that new clubhouse. We are a new small group. Most of us are still pretty broke. What then?"

I am sure that myriads of AA voices would now answer the new group saying: "Yes, we know just how you feel. We once solicited money ourselves. We even solicited publicly. We thought we could do a lot of good with other peoples' money. But we found that kind of money too hot to handle. It aroused unbelievable controversy. It simply wasn't worth it. Besides, it set a precedent which has tempted many people to use the valuable name of Alcoholics Anonymous for other than AA purposes. While there may be little harm in a small friendly loan which your group really means to repay, we really beg you to think hard before you ask the most willing friend to make a large donation. You can, and you soon will, pay your own way. For each of you these overhead expenses will never amount to more than the price of one bottle of good whiskey a month. You will be everlastingly thankful if you pay this small obligation yourselves."

When reflecting on these things, why should not each of us tell himself: "Yes, we AAs were once a burden on everybody. We were 'takers.' Now that we are sober, and by the grace of God have become responsible citizens of the world, why shouldn't we now about-face and become 'thankful givers'! Yes, it is high time we did!"

Tradition Eight

July 1948

T hroughout the world AAs are twelfth-stepping with thousands of new prospects a month. Between one and two thousand of these stick on our first presentation; past experience shows that most of the remainder will come back to us later on. Almost entirely unorganized, and completely nonprofessional, this mighty spiritual current is now flowing from alcoholics who are well to those who are sick. One alcoholic talking to another; that's all.

Could this vast and vital face-to-face effort ever be professionalized or even organized? Most emphatically, it could not. The few efforts to professionalize straight Twelfth Step work have always failed quickly. Today, no AA will tolerate the idea of paid "AA therapists" or "organizers." Nor does any AA like to be told just how he must handle that new prospect of his. No, this great life-giving stream can never be dammed up by paid do-gooders or professionals. Alcoholics Anonymous is never going to cut its own lifelines. To a man, we are sure of that.

But what about those who serve us full time in other capacities — are cooks, caretakers, and paid intergroup secretaries "AA professionals"?

Because our thinking about these people is still unclear, we often feel and act as though they were such. The impression of professionalism subtly attaches to them, so we frequently hear they are "making money out of AA" or that they are "professionalizing" AA. Seemingly, if they do take our AA dollars they don't quite belong with us AAs anymore. We sometimes go further; we underpay them on the theory they ought to be glad to "cook" for AA cheap.

Now isn't this carrying our fears of professionalism rather far? If these fears ever got too strong, none but a saint or an incompetent could work for Alcoholics Anonymous. Our supply of saints being quite small, we would certainly wind up with less competent workers than we need.

We are beginning to see that our few paid workers are performing only those service tasks that our volunteers cannot consistently handle. Primarily these folks are not doing Twelfth Step work. They are just making more and better Twelfth Step work possible. Secretaries at their desks are valuable points of contact, information, and public relations. That is what they are paid for, and nothing else. They help carry the good news of AA to the outside world and bring our prospects face to face with us. That's not "AA therapy"; it's just a lot of very necessary but often thankless work.

So, where needed, let's revise our attitude toward those who labor at our special services. Let us treat them as AA associates, and not as hired help; let's recompense them fairly and, above all, let's absolve them from the label of professionalism.

Let us also distinguish clearly between "organizing the AA movement" and setting up, in a reasonably businesslike manner, its few essential services of contact and propagation. Once we do that, all will be well. The million or so fellow alcoholics who are still sick will then continue to get the break we sixty thousand AAs have already had.

Let's give our "service desks" the hand they so well deserve.

Tradition Nine

August 1948

T he least possible organization, that's our universal ideal. No fees, no dues, no rules imposed on anybody, one alcoholic bringing recovery to the next; that's the substance of what we most desire, isn't it?

But how shall this simple ideal best be realized? Often a question, that.

We have, for example, the kind of AA who is for simplicity. Terrified of anything organized, he tells us that AA is getting too complicated. He thinks money only makes trouble, committees only make dissension, elections only make politics, paid workers only make professionals, and clubs only coddle slippers. Says he, let's get back to coffee and cakes by cozy firesides. If any alcoholics stray our way, let's look after them. But that's enough. Simplicity is our answer.

Quite opposed to such halcyon simplicity is the AA promoter. Left to himself, he would "bang the cannon and twang the lyre" at every crossroad of the world. Millions for drunks, great AA hospitals, batteries of paid organizers, and publicity experts wielding all the latest paraphernalia of sound and script; such would be our promoters dream. "Yes, sir," he would bark. "My two-year plan calls for one million AA members by 1950!"

For one, I'm glad we have both conservatives and enthusiasts. They teach us much. The conservative will surely see to it that the AA movement never gets overly organized. But the promoter will continue to remind us of our terrific obligation to the newcomer and to those hundreds of thousands of alcoholics still waiting all over the world to hear of AA.

We shall, naturally, take the firm and safe middle course. AA has always violently resisted the idea of any general organization. Yet, paradoxically, we have ever stoutly insisted upon organizing certain *special services;* mostly those absolutely necessary to effective and plentiful Twelfth Step work.

If, for instance, an AA group elects a secretary or rotating committee, if an area forms an intergroup committe, if we set up a foundation, a general office or a Grapevine, then we are organized for service. The AA book and pamphlets, our meeting places and clubs, our dinners and regional assemblies — these are services, too. Nor can we secure good hospital connections, properly sponsor new prospects, and obtain good public relations just by chance. People have to be appointed to look after these things, sometimes paid people. Special services are performed.

But by none of these special services has our spiritual or social activity, the great current of AA, ever been really organized or professionalized. Yet our recovery program has been enormously aided. While important, these service activities are very small by contrast with our main effort.

As such facts and distinctions become clear, we shall easily lay aside our fears of blighting organization or hazardous wealth. As a movement, we shall remain comfortably poor, for our service expenses are trifling.

With such assurances, we shall without doubt continue to improve and extend our vital lifelines of special service; to better carry our AA message to others; to make for ourselves a finer, greater Society, and, God willing, to assure Alcoholics Anonymous a long life and perfect unity.

Tradition Ten

September 1948

To most of us, Alcoholics Anonymous has become as solid as the Rock of Gibraltar. We like to believe that it will soon be as well known and just as enduring as that historic landmark. We enjoy this pleasant conviction because nothing has yet occurred to disturb it; we reason that we must hang together or die. Hence we take for granted our continued unity as a movement.

But should we? Though God has bestowed upon us great favors, and though we are bound by stronger ties of love and necessity than most societies, is it prudent to suppose that automatically these great gifts and attributes shall be ours forever? If we are worthy, we shall probably continue to enjoy them. So the real question is, how shall we always be worthy of our present blessings?

Seen from this point of view, our AA Traditions are those attitudes and practices by which we may deserve, as a movement, a long life and a useful one. To this end, none could be more vital than our Tenth Tradition, for it deals with the subject of controversy — serious controversy.

On the other side of the world, millions have died even recently in religious dissension. Other millions have died in political controversy. The end is not yet. Nearly everybody in the world has turned reformer. Each group, society, and nation is saying to the other, "You must do as we say, or else." Political controversy and reform by compulsion have reached an all-time high. And eternal, seemingly, are the flames of religious dissension.

Being like other men and women, how can we expect to remain forever immune from these perils? Probably we shall not. At length, we must meet them all. We cannot flee from them, nor ought we try. If these challenges do come, we shall, I am sure, go out to meet them gladly and unafraid. That will be the acid test of our worth.

Our best defense? This surely lies in the formation of a Tradition respecting serious controversy so powerful that neither the weakness of persons nor the strain and strife of our troubled times can harm Alcoholics Anonymous. We know that AA must continue to live, or else many of us and many of our fellow alcoholics throughout the world will surely resume the hopeless journey to oblivion. That must never be.

As though by some deep and compelling instinct, we have thus far avoided serious controversies. Save minor and healthy growing pains, we are at peace among ourselves. And because we have thus far adhered to our sole aim, the whole world regards us favorably.

May God grant us the wisdom and fortitude ever to sustain an unbreakable unity.

Tradition Eleven

October 1948

℗ rovidence has been looking after the public relations of Alcoholics Anonymous. It can scarcely have been otherwise. Though we are more than a dozen years old, hardly a syllable of criticism or ridicule has ever been spoken of AA. Somehow we have been spared all the pains of medical or religious controversy and we have good friends both wet and dry, right and left. Like most societies, we are sometimes scandalous — but never yet in public. From all over the world, naught comes but keen sympathy and downright admiration. Our friends of the press and radio have outdone themselves. Anyone can see that we are in a fair way to be spoiled. Our reputation is already so much better than our actual character!

Surely these phenomenal blessings must have a deep purpose. Who doubts that this purpose wishes to let every alcoholic in the world know that AA is truly for him, can he only want his liberation enough. Hence, our messages through public channels have never been seriously discolored, nor has the searing breath of prejudice ever issued from anywhere.

Good public relations are AA lifelines reaching out to the alcoholic who still does not know us. For years to come, our growth is sure to depend upon the strength and number of these lifelines. One serious public relations calamity could always turn thousands away from us to perish — a matter of life and death indeed!

The future poses no greater problem or challenge to AA than how best to preserve a friendly and vital relation to all the world about us. Success will rest heavily upon right principles, a wise vigilance, and the deepest personal responsibility on the part of every one of us. Nothing less will do. Else our brother may again turn his face to the wall because we did not care enough.

So the Eleventh Tradition stands sentinel over the lifelines, announcing that there is no need for self-praise, that it is better to let our friends recommend us, and that our whole public relations policy, contrary to usual customs, should be based upon the principle of *attraction* rather than promotion. Shot-in-the-arm methods are not for us — no press agents, no promotional devices, no big names. The hazards are too great. Immediate results will always be illusive because easy shortcuts to notoriety can generate permanent and smothering liabilities.

More and more, therefore, are we emphasizing the principle of personal anonymity as it applies to our public relations. We ask of each other the highest degree of personal responsibility in this respect. As a movement we have been, before now, tempted to exploit the names of our well-known public characters. We have rationalized that other societies, even the best, do the same. As individuals, we have sometimes believed that the public use of our names could demonstrate our personal courage in the face of stigma, so lending power and conviction to news stories and magazine articles.

But these are not the allures they once were. Vividly, we are becoming aware that no member ought to describe himself in full view of the general public as an AA, even for the most worthy purpose, lest a perilous precedent be set which would tempt others to do likewise for purposes not so worthy.

We see that on breaking anonymity by press, radio, or pictures, any one of us could easily transfer the valuable name of Alcoholics Anonymous over onto any enterprise or into the midst of any controversy.

So it is becoming our code that there are things that no AA ever does, lest he divert AA from its sole purpose and injure our public relations. And thereby the chances of those sick ones yet to come.

To the million alcoholics who have not yet heard our AA story, we should ever say, "Greetings and welcome. Be assured that we shall never weaken the lifelines which we float out to you. In our public relations, we shall, God willing, keep the faith."

Tradition Twelve

November 1948

One may say that anonymity is the spiritual base, the sure key to all the rest of our Traditions. It has come to stand for prudence and, most importantly, for self-effacement. True consideration for the new-comer if he desires to be nameless; vital protection against misuse of the name Alcoholics Anonymous at the public level; and to each of us a constant reminder that principles come before personal interest — such is the wide scope of this all-embracing principle. In it we see the cornerstone of our security as a movement; at a deeper spiritual level it points us to still greater self-renunciation.

A glance at the Twelve Traditions will instantly assure anyone that "giving up" is the essential idea of them all. In each Tradition, the individual or the group is asked to give up something for our general welfare. Tradition One asks us to place the common good ahead of personal desire. Tradition Two asks us to listen to God as he may speak in the group conscience. Tradition Three requires that we exclude *no* alcoholic from AA membership. Tradition Four implies that we abandon all idea of centralized human authority or government. But each group is enjoined to consult widely in matters affecting us all. Tradition Five restricts the AA group to a single purpose, carrying our message to other alcoholics.

Tradition Six points at the corroding influence of money, property, and personal authority; it begs that we keep these influences at a minimum by separate incorporation and management of our special services. It also warns against the natural temptation to make alliances or give endorsements. Tradition Seven states that we had best pay our own bills; that large contributions or those carrying obligations ought not be received; that public solicitation using the name Alcoholics Anonymous is positively dangerous. Tradition Eight forswears professionalizing our Twelfth Step work but it does guarantee our few paid service workers an unquestioned amateur status. Tradition Nine asks that we give up all idea of expensive organization; enough is needed to permit effective work by our special services — and no more. This Tradition breathes democracy; our leadership is one of service and it is rotating; our few titles never clothe their holders with arbitrary personal authority; they hold authorizations *to serve, never to govern.* Tradition Ten is an emphatic restraint of serious controversy; it implores each of us to take care against committing AA to the fires of reform, political or religious dissension. Tradition Eleven asks, in our public relations, that we be alert against sensationalism and it declares there is never need to praise ourselves. Personal anonymity at the level of press, radio, and film is urgently required, thus avoiding the pitfall of vanity, and the temptation through broken anonymity to link AA to other causes.

Tradition Twelve, in its mood of humble anonymity, plainly enough comprehends the preceding eleven. The Twelve Points of Tradition are little else than a specific application of the spirit of the Twelve Steps of recovery to our group life and to our relations with society in general. The recovery steps would make each individual AA whole and one with God; the Twelve Points of Tradition would make us one with each other and whole with the world about us. Unity is our aim.

Our AA Traditions are, we trust, securely anchored in those wise precepts: charity, gratitude, and humility. Nor have we forgotten *prudence.* May these virtues ever stand clear before us in our meditations; may Alcoholics Anonymous serve God in happy unison for so long as he may need us.

A Request and an Apology

December 1948

As an outcome of talks recently given, press reports carrying my full name have appeared.

Since two of the Twelve Points of AA Tradition emphasize the great importance of maintaining personal anonymity at the level of press and radio, I naturally feel uncommonly embarrassed and concerned at having been the subject of these anonymity breaks. Just how or why these lapses occurred, I have not yet learned; I had thought suitable precautions had been taken against them. Perhaps they were partly due to my own failure to caution reporters present at these particular meetings.

In any case, I feel that all AAs are entitled to this explanation and to my sincere apologies.

Everywhere the press has been uniformly cooperative on anonymity when it is explained as a vital protection to the Alcoholics Anonymous movement. May I therefore urgently request all AA groups to carefully cover my anonymity on any future appearances and I shall, of course, try to take far greater care myself.

Let us never let go of this vital principle.

A Suggestion for Thanksgiving

November 1949

The idea is in the air that AA might adopt Thanksgiving week as a time for meetings and meditation on the Traditions of Alcoholics Anonymous. The friend who hatched this notion tells you why he thinks the idea good. I heartily agree with what he says and hope you will too.

Pre-AA, we alkies could sometimes achieve that dubious state called "sobriety, period." How bleak and empty this alleged virtue is, only God or a dried-up drunk can fully testify. The reason? Of course every AA knows it: nothing has taken the place of the victim's grog; he's still a man of conflict and disunity. Come then the Twelve Steps of recovery, bringing to him a personality change. The shattered prospect feels reassembled; he now says he seems all one piece. We understand exactly what he means, for he describes the state of being at oneness; he is talking about personal unity. We know he must work to maintain it and that he can't stay alive without it.

Will not the same principle hold true for AA as a whole? Isn't it also a fact that the alcoholic is in no greater peril than when he takes sobriety for granted? If vigilant practice of sound principle is a matter of life and death for him, why isn't that equally so for the AA group, and for our far-flung Society itself?

Yet many of us still take the basic unity of Alcoholics Anonymous for granted. We seem to forget that the whole of modern society is on a dangerous and contagious "dry bender." We evidently assume we are so different from other men and women that disintegration can't hit us. Our unity appears as a gift of heaven; something to be perpetually enjoyed by us AAs quite without effort.

Criticism is not intended, because our present attitude is natural enough. It stems from the fact that no society in its infancy has ever enjoyed more providential protection against temptation and untoward happenings than has ours. Minor troubles we have had, but none serious enough to test our adult strength. It's not strange that we are a bit complacent and self-satisfied. Surely there need be no counsel of fear, nor lack of faith, in the prediction that a far greater time of trial may yet be ours. When we think our situation through, simple prudence and foresight will tell us that.

The Twelve Traditions of Alcoholics Anonymous are a distillate of our experience of living and working together. They apply the spirit of the Twelve recovery Steps to our group life and security. They deal with our relations with the world outside and with each other; they state our attitudes toward power and prestige, toward property and money. They would save us from tempting alliances and major controversies; they would elevate principles far above personal ambitions. And as a token of this last, they request that we maintain personal anonymity before the open public as a protection to AA and as proof of the fact that our Society intends to practice true humility.

For the information of the general public and for the instruction of new AA members, the Twelve Traditions have just been released in a much condensed "short form" which we hope will be as widely read and understood as the Twelve Steps of recovery. Should this happen, our current growing pains will be lessened and we shall commence to lay up a great store of insurance for the years ahead.

What then could be more appropriate than to set aside Thanksgiving week for discussion of the practical and spiritual values to be discovered in our Traditions? We could thus reinforce our faith in the future by these prudent works; we could show that we deserve to go on receiving that priceless gift of oneness which God in his wisdom has so freely given to us of Alcoholics Anonymous in the precious years of our infancy.

Segment

Additional Writings from This Period

Comments on Wylie Ideas

In an article entitled "Philip Wylie Jabs a Little Needle into Complacency," the noted writer said that he is an alcoholic who "quit solo." He went on to mention psychiatry and other scientific aids as the factors that kept him sober. Bill's reply follows.

September 1944

Philip Wylie's piece in this issue of the Grapevine will endear the man to every AA. And why? Because, of course, he's so very alcoholic! Neither can anyone miss the author's generous and self-sacrificing spirit.

Forgetting his own worldly importance, he snaps his fingers at what the public may think; he discards his *reputation* in order to share with us his *character.* A traveler who has felt his own way out of the night, he tells how he discovers haven. We could ask no better spirit of anyone. Mr. Wylie can be a member of AA the very day he says so!

It is tradition among us that the individual has the unlimited right to his own opinion on any subject under the sun. He is compelled to agree with no one; if he likes, he can disagree with everyone. And indeed, when on a "dry bender," many AAs do. Therefore, no AA should be disturbed if he cannot fully agree with all of Mr. Wylie's truly stimulating discourse. Rather shall we reflect that the roads to recovery are many; that any story or theory of recovery from one who has trod the highway is bound to contain much truth. Mr. Wylie's article is like an abundance of fresh fruit. Perhaps we should take the advice of the housewife who says, "We shall eat all we *can,* and then *can* what we can't."

What caught my attention most was his reference to the spiritual experience, "a la Jung," seemingly induced "by scientific psychological technique." What a boon that would be to us who wrestle every day with the agnostic newcomer. If only we could give him a straight dose of that "transcendent symbol" and have it over with! We wouldn't have to bother with that tedious business of waiting while our prospect batters himself into sufficient open-mindedness to accept the possibility of a Power greater than himself.

But, as Mr. Wylie broad-mindedly observes, it doesn't matter too much how the transforming spiritual experience is brought about so long as one gets one that works for him. Somehow the alcoholic must get enough objectivity about himself to abate his fears and collapse his false pride. If he can do all this through his intellect, and thereafter support his life structure upon a "transcendent symbol," more power to him! Most AAs, however, would think this design for living pretty inadequate. They would consider downright humility and faith in the power of the living God a much stronger medicine. AA draws frankly upon emotion and faith, while the scientific intellectual would avoid these resources as much as he can. Yet the more intellectual techniques do work sometimes, reaching those who might never be able to take the stronger dose. Besides, they remind us, when overly proud of our own accomplishment, that AA has no monopoly on reviving alcoholics.

In fact, it is already evident that the scientific world is becoming more appreciative of our methods than we are of theirs. In this respect they are commencing to teach *us* humility.

Listen again, as our friend Dr. Harry Tiebout, psychiatrist, closes his paper "Basic Techniques of Alcoholics Anonymous," before the American Psychiatric Association: "The lesson for psychiatrists is clear, it seems to me. Although we admittedly deal with emotional problems, we, as a group which tends to be intellectual, distrust emotions too much. We are self-conscious and a little ashamed when we are forced to use them, and always apologetic with our confreres if we suspect they have reason to think our methods are too emotional. In the meantime, others, less bound by tradition, go ahead to get results denied to us. It is highly imperative for us as presumably open-minded scientists to view wisely and long the efforts of others in our field of work. We may be wearing bigger blinders than we know." And again, as he says, "A religious, or spiritual experience, is *the act of giving up reliance on one's own omnipotence.*"

As we AAs are people who are *supposed* to have given up *all* our own "omnipotence," I'm sure that Mr. Wylie will be read with the attentive interest he deserves!

A Date with Destiny

S omebody once said, "As much as you may grow, as many recoveries as there may be, I think the eventual by-products of AA will be greater than AA itself."

Everywhere now, we hear such remarks. They come from all kinds of people. Doctors think of applying our methods to other neurotics; clergy wonder if our humble example may not vitalize their congregations; businesspeople find we make good personnel managers — they glimpse a new industrial democracy; educators see power in our noncontroversial way of presenting the truth; and our friends wistfully say, "We wish we were alcoholics — we need AA too."

Why these stirrings? They must all mean, I am sure, that we have suddenly become much more than recovered alcoholics, AA members only. Society has begun to hope that we are going to utilize, in every walk of life, that miraculous experience of our returning, almost overnight, from the fearsome land of Nowhere.

Yes, we are again citizens of the world. It is a distraught world, very tired, very uncertain. It has worshiped its own self-sufficiency — and that has failed. We AAs are a people who once did that very thing. That philosophy failed us, too. So perhaps, here and there, our example of recovery can help. As individuals, we have a responsibility, maybe a *double responsibility*. It may be that we have a date with destiny.

An example: Not long ago Dr. E. M. Jellinek, of Yale University, came to us. He said, "Yale, as you know, is sponsoring a program of public education on alcoholism, entirely noncontroversial in character. We need the cooperation of many AAs. To proceed on any education project concerning alcoholism without the goodwill, experience, and help of AA members would be unthinkable."

So, when the National Committee for Education on Alcoholism [now the National Council on Alcoholism] was formed, an AA member was made its executive director: Marty M., one of our oldest and finest. As a member of AA, she is just as much interested in us as before — AA is still her avocation. But as an officer of the Yale-sponsored National Committee, she is also interested in educating the general public on alcoholism. Her AA training has wonderfully fitted her for this post in a different field. Public education on alcoholism is to be her vocation.

Could an AA do such a job? At first, Marty herself wondered. She asked her AA friends, "Will I be regarded as a professional?" Her friends replied: "Had you come to us, Marty, proposing to be a therapist, to sell straight AA to alcoholics at so much a customer, we should certainly have branded that as professionalism. So would everybody else.

"But the National Committee for Education on Alcoholism is quite another matter. You will be taking your natural abilities and AA experience into a very different field. We don't see how that can affect your amateur status with us. Suppose you were to become a social worker, a personnel officer, the manager of a state farm for alcoholics, or even a minister of the gospel? Who could possibly say those activities would make you a professional AA? No one, of course."

They went on: "Yet we do hope that AA as a whole will never deviate from its sole purpose of helping other alcoholics. *As an organization, we should express no opinions save on the recovery of problem drinkers.*

That very sound national policy has kept us out of much useless trouble already, and will surely forestall untold complications in the future.

"Though AA as a whole," they continued, "should never have but one objective, we believe just as strongly that *for the individual there should be no limitations whatever, except his own conscience.* He should have the complete right to choose his own opinions and outside activities. If these are good, AAs everywhere will approve. Just so, Marty, do we think it will be in your case. While Yale is your actual sponsor, we feel sure that you are going to have the warm personal support of thousands of AAs wherever you go. We shall all be thinking how much better a break this new generation of potential alcoholic kids will have because of your work, how much it might have meant to us had our own mothers and fathers really understood alcoholism."

Personally I feel that Marty's friends have advised her wisely; that they have clearly distinguished between the limited scope of AA as a whole and the broad horizon of the individual AA acting on his own responsibility; that they have probably drawn a correct line between what we would regard as professional and amateur.

Letter to the Mother of an Alcoholic

December 1944

Dear Mother of "J.":

I cannot tell how poignantly I am stirred by the letter you wrote the Grapevine about your alcoholic son.

Just ten years ago my own mother, after years of frantic bewilderment, lost hope. Long a chronic problem drinker, I had come to the jumping-off place. A very good doctor had pronounced the grim sentence: "Obsessive drinker, deteriorating rapidly — hopeless." The doctor used to talk about my case somewhat like this: "Yes, Bill has underlying personality defects... great emotional sensitivity, childishness, and inferiority.

"This very real feeling of inferiority is magnified by his childish sensitivity and it is this state of affairs which generates in him that insatiable, abnormal craving for self-approval and success in the eyes of the world. Still a child, he cries for the moon. And the moon, it seems, won't have him!

"Discovering alcohol, he found much more in it than do normal folks. To him alcohol is no mere relaxation; it means release — release from inner conflict. It seems to set his troubled spirit free."

The doctor would then go on: "Seen this way, we normal people can picture how such a compulsive habit can become a real obsession; as indeed it has, in Bill's case. Once he arrives at the obsession point, alcohol overshadows all else. Hence he now appears utterly selfish. And immoral. He will lie, cheat, steal or what have you, to serve his drinking ends. Of course, those about him are shocked and dismayed because they think his actions are willful. But that's far from being so. The real picture of Bill is that of a bankrupt idealist: one who has gone broke on vain, childish dreams of perfection and power. Victimized now by his obsession, he is a little boy crying alone in a dark strange room; waiting agonized for mother — or God — to come and light a candle."

I must confess, Mother of "J.," that I may have put some of these words into the doctor's mouth. But that's the alcoholic's life as I have lived it.

Did I, an alcoholic, have a defective character? Of course I did. Was I, an alcoholic, also a sick man? Yes, very.

To what extent I was personally responsible for my drinking, I don't know. Yet I'm not one to take complete refuge in the idea that I was a sick man only. In earlier years I certainly had some degree of free will. That free will I used badly, to the great misery of my mother and countless others. I am deeply ashamed.

As one who knows me a little, you may have heard how, ten years ago, a friend, himself a liberated alcoholic, came to me bearing *the light* which finally led me out of the toils.

There will come a day like that for you and yours — I'm so confident!

As ever,
Bill W.

Those 'Goof Balls'

November 1945

Morphine, codeine, chloral hydrate, Luminal, Seconal, Nembutal, amytal, these and kindred drugs have killed many alcoholics. And I once nearly killed myself with chloral hydrate. Nor is my own observation and experience unique, for many an old-time AA can speak with force and fervor on the subject of "goof balls."

Excepting an infrequent suicide, nobody uses these drugs in the expectation of death. To many alcoholics, still in the drinking stage, they represent blessed relief from the agonies of a hangover.

Some of us, perfectly sober for months or years, contract the habit of using sedatives to cure insomnia or slight nervous irritability. I have the impression that some of us get away with it, too, year after year, just as we did when we first began to drink alcohol. Yet experience shows, all too often, that even the "controlled" pill-taker may get out of control. The same crazy rationalizations that once characterized his drinking begin to blight his existence. He thinks that if pills can cure insomnia so may they cure his worry.

Now a word about the use of morphine by physicians. Sometimes a general practitioner, not knowing his patient is already loaded with barbiturates, will give a morphine injection. A friend of mine died like that. Sober about three years, he got into an emotional jam. Pills led to alcohol and this combination to still more pills. His doctor found an excited heart. Out came the needle and a few hours later out went a very good friend. Another close friend, sober three years, also fell on evil days — pills and liquor. At the end of about three weeks of this diet he was placed one evening in a sanitarium. Nobody told the doctor there about the pills with which his system was already loaded. The patient was "eased" with a shot of codeine. Before daylight he was dead.

Near the end of my own drinking career I had an alarming experience. Chloral hydrate was prescribed for one of my terrible hangovers. The doctor warned me to stick rigidly to his dosage, but I kept possession of the bottle. While my wife slept quietly beside me, I reached under the mattress, took out the flask, and guzzled the whole business. I had a close shave. Moral: When a doctor gives a legitimate sedative prescription, don't let the alcoholic have the bottle.

As a matter of fact, our friends the doctors are seldom directly to blame for the dire results we so often experience. It is much too easy for alcoholics to buy these dangerous drugs, and once possessed of them the drinker is likely to use them without any judgment whatever. Sometimes his well-meaning friends, unable to see him suffer, hand him pills themselves. It's a very dangerous business.

It's even dangerous to give a suffering alcoholic a drink if he is already loaded with pills. Years ago, I had an experience of this sort. We had an "alkie" in tow whom I shall call Slim. He finally had consented to go to a hospital. On the way he had a few — but only a small quantity compared to his customary capacity. Just before we reached the hospital, Slim's speech suddenly got very thick and he passed out. I had to get a porter to help him to a cab. As he could usually manage a couple of bottles a day when active, I couldn't understand this performance at all. Arrived at the hospital, Slim was still slumped in his seat and I couldn't move him. Our good friend, Dr. Silkworth, came out and peered in the cab door. One look was apparently enough. Said he to me, "How is this man's heart?" Confidently I replied, "He's got a heart like an elephant. Told me so himself. But I don't see how he got drunk so fast. I gave him very little liquor." Out came the doctor's stethoscope. Turning then to me, he said, "Not much use bringing this man in here. He can't last long. What else has he been taking besides liquor?" Stunned, I replied, "Nothing, that I know of."

Very gingerly an attendant carried Slim inside. Out came the stethoscope again. The doctor shook his head, saying, "This poor chap has been loaded with barbiturates for days. When you gave him alcohol, even a little, it fired off the accumulated charge of sedative he had in him. See how blue he is? His heart isn't really working much. It's just jittering. I can't even count it."

The doctor rushed to the phone and called Slim's wife. To my horror she confirmed the fact that he had been taking heavy doses of amytal for about ten days. The doctor gently told her she had better hurry, else she might be too late. Then he called a famous heart specialist for consultation and told him to hurry too. They laid Slim on a bed upstairs. The great specialist came and drew out his stethoscope. At once he looked very serious and, motioning us out into the hall, he said he would leave a prescription but that he did not think my friend could possibly live through the night. Dr. Silkworth agreed.

During these proceedings I had been praying as I never had prayed before. After the two doctors had pronounced the death sentence on

Slim, I told them of my prayers and explained, cheerfully as I could, that I had been reading Dr. Alexis Carrel's book, *Man the Unknown,* in which prayer was described as effecting miraculous cures. The great specialist took his leave. Dr. Silkworth and I went downstairs to wait for the prescription to come in. A boy finally brought two capsules from the drugstore. The doctor looked at them, saying he hated to give them, they were so powerful. We went upstairs and as we stepped off the elevator we saw someone coming down the hall jauntily smoking a cigarette. "Hello, boys," roared Slim, "what am I supposed to be doing in here?"

Never, so long as I live, shall I forget the relief and astonishment which spread over the doctor's countenance as he quickly tested Slim's heart. Looking at me, he said, "This man's heart is now normal. Fifteen minutes ago I couldn't count it. I thought I knew these alcoholic hearts pretty well. But I've never seen anything like this — never. I can't understand it." What miracle saved Slim, no one can say. He left the hospital in a few days, without ill effects from his experience.

As for me — well, I guess I learned my lesson then and there. No more "goof balls" unless the doctor says so — not for me. No, thank you!

Book Publication Proved Discouraging Venture

July 1947

During the summer of 1938 we solicited the well-to-do for contributions to fill that grand new receptacle, our Alcoholic Foundation. Again we encountered a strange indifference to drunks. Nobody was interested. We didn't get a cent that I can remember. We were pretty discouraged; apparently Providence had deserted us. With the modest fund from Mr. Rockefeller running out, it looked like a lean winter ahead. There could be no book, no office. What good, we complained, was an Alcoholic Foundation without money!

By this time there had been roughed out what are now the first two chapters of the book now known as *Alcoholics Anonymous*. Our friend Frank referred us to a well-known publisher, who suggested the possibility of advancing royalties to me so the book could be finished. That made us feel fine until it was realized that if I ate up a lot of royalties while doing the book, there could be no more payments for a long time afterward. We saw, too, that my 10 percent royalty would never carry the office expense of answering the pleas for help that would surely follow publication. Nor might a commercial publisher, anxious for sales, advertise it as we would like.

These reflections led us straight into a typical alcoholic fantasy! Why not publish the book ourselves? Though told by almost everybody who knew anything of publishing that amateurs seldom produced anything but flops, we were not dismayed. This time, we said, it would be different. We had discovered that the bare printing cost of a book is but a fraction of its retail price, and a national magazine of huge circulation had offered to print an article about us when our book was finished. This was a clincher. How could we miss? We could see books selling by hundreds of thousands — money rolling in!

What a promotion it was! An AA friend and I hastily organized the Works Publishing Company. My friend Hank P. then bought a pad of stock certificates at a stationery store. He and I started selling them to fellow alcoholics and any who would buy at the bargain price of $25 a share. Our confidence must have been boundless. Not only were we selling common stock on a book to cure drunks — the book itself hadn't yet been written. Amazingly enough, we did sell that stock, $4,500 worth, to alcoholics in New York, New Jersey, and to their friends. No one of the original forty-nine subscribers put up over $300. Almost everybody paid on monthly installment, being too broke to do otherwise; save, of course, our good friends at Rockefeller Center.

Our agreement with the Works Publishing subscribers was that out of the first book income they were to get their money back; also that the Alcoholic Foundation was to receive the 10 percent royalty I might have had from a publisher. As for the shares of Works Publishing, the forty-nine cash subscribers were to have one-third, my friend Hank one-third, and I one-third. We also obtained a loan of $2,500 from Charles B. Towns, proprietor of a nationally known hospital for alcoholics. A friend indeed, he was to wait years to get his money back.

But, as anyone could then see, everything was all set — everything, of course, but writing and selling the book! Hope ran high. Out of the new financing we could keep a small office going at Newark, New

Jersey. There I began to dictate the text of *Alcoholics Anonymous* to Ruth Hock (our first national secretary). Rosily, we saw scads of money coming in, once the book was off the press. Still more, we expected the new book would turn right about and help finance our poverty-stricken Foundation — which, strangely enough, it really did years later.

Finally came April 1939. The book was done. Tales of recovery for its story section had been supplied by Dr. Bob and his Akron brethren. Others were supplied by New Yorkers, New Jerseyites. One came in from Cleveland and another from Maryland. Chapters had been read and discussed at meetings. I had thought myself the author of the text until I discovered I was just the umpire of the differences of opinion. After endless voting on a title for the new work, we had decided to call it *The Way Out*. But inquiry by Fitz M., our Maryland alcoholic, at the Library of Congress disclosed the fact that twelve books already bore that title. Surely we couldn't make our book the thirteenth. So we named it *Alcoholics Anonymous* instead! Though we didn't know it, our movement then got its name — a name which because of the implication of humility and modesty has given us our treasured spiritual principle of anonymity.

Five thousand copies of *Alcoholics Anonymous* lay in the printer's warehouse, except the few we joyously passed around. Each stockholder and each story writer got one free. The *New York Times* did a good review. We hastened to the national magazine to tell them we were ready for their promised article. We could see AA books going out in carload lots!

What a debacle! At the office of the great monthly periodical we were gently told they had entirely forgotten to let us know, nine months before, that they had decided to print nothing about us. The editors had concluded that drunks were too controversial a subject! This stunning announcement left us in a daze. The whole Alcoholics Anonymous movement could buy less than a hundred books, as it had only one hundred members. Besides, we had given away seventy-nine free ones! What were we to do with those other thousands of books? What could we say to the printer, whose bill wasn't half paid? What about that little loan of $2,500 and those forty-nine subscribers who had invested $4,500 in Works Publishing stock? How could we break the awful news to them? How could we tell them that since we had no publicity we could sell no books? Yes, that AA book venture was, I fear, very alcoholic!

Thus was the good book *Alcoholics Anonymous* born into bankruptcy. Some of the creditors got restive; the sheriff actually appeared at our Newark office. The promoters were very low — financially and otherwise. The house in which my wife and I had lived at Brooklyn was possibility. The widening conviction that active leadership ought to be transitory and rotating; that each AA group with respect to its own affairs need be accountable only to its own conscience; that our committees and boards are really servants, not officials; that we, as a movement, ought to remain poor, so avoiding the risks of disrupting wealth; that as individual members of AA we should remain anonymous before the general public — these are the signs and portents of a unique future. Such concepts certainly leave little room for a prestige-clothed leadership.

"But," some will say, "how shall we make such a vision actually work when most societies have to rely so greatly on management, money, and heavily publicized leadership exercising powerful personal suasion?" Yet, incredibly, we are beginning to see our vision come alive. Even though we persist in looking with misgiving on any large accumulation of money or personal prestige in the name of Alcoholics Anonymous, we do continue to grow despite the absence of those sometimes unstable factors upon which other human endeavors must so often depend.

Why is this possible? Is it because we are a superior people? Well, hardly! Far from being better than average, we are surely much more fallible. Strangely enough, our group strength seems to stem from our individual and ever-potential weakness. We are alcoholics. Even though now recovered, we are never too far removed from the possibility of fresh personal disaster. Each knows he must observe a high degree of honesty, humility, and tolerance, or else drink again. For us of AA to drink is to die; to love God and fellowman is to live.

Under such potent conditions the impossible has become possible. When each AA's life literally depends upon his unselfish service to others, when false pride, self-pity, or unhealthy self-seeking is almost certain to be unmercifully chastised by John Barleycorn, he needs but a minimum of man-made rules or inspired leaders to hold him on the right course. Nor for long is he apt to continue anything harmful to AA unity. He knows so well that we AAs shall have to hang together — or else hang separately! At first living the spiritual life because he must, he presently lives it because he wants to. Such is the truly providential circumstance in which we all find ourselves; that is why we are beginning to see new values in AA. We perceive in our midst *a spiritual realm,* which can be little disturbed by the distractions of wealth or self-serving egocentricity.

Against this background let's have another look at Dr. Bob and me. Seemingly, the larger AA grows, the more our particular part in its creation and continuance tends to be emphasized. Our status remains exceptional. Nearly all other early AAs have long since slipped over to the sidelines where, if they have retained the confidence of all, they are frequently consulted. By common consent they have become unofficial coaches, reservoirs of longer experience, to be sought out in the pinches. Their alma mater is now served by new teams. These too will have their day on the field, then finally retire. This is, we think, as it ought to be.

Dr. Bob and I feel this sound doctrine should apply to us as well. There seems no good reason to make an exception of "the founders." The more we early members continuously occupy the center of the AA stage, the more we shall set risky precedents for a highly personalized and permanent leadership. To insure well AA's future, is this not the very thing we should carefully avoid? Of course, Dr. Bob and I do not want to ignore any special responsibility remaining still upon us. Quite the contrary; our principal mission today is probably that of helping AA form a sound Tradition. But how, for example, can we advocate the traditional principle of rotating leadership if we allow the belief to grow that we ought to be permanent exceptions ourselves? Of course, we cannot.

Take, for instance, my own situation. It is known that my health is recently improved; that I'm going to a large regional conference. Instantly come warm but most urgent invitations to speak at gatherings all over North America. Most AAs being good salesmen, the pressure on me is truly enormous.

While it's a wonderful feeling to be so much wanted, these bids do leave me in the middle of an acute dilemma — a real heart-breaker. How, in fairness, can I speak at ten anniversary dinners and refuse ninety; how can I make special recordings or telephone talks for all these occasions? Or, again, how can I respond to all the mail I receive; how can I advise hundreds of individuals and groups about their special problems? It is a physical impossibility. Even though I could somehow accomplish all these things, and so remain in the center of AA affairs indefinitely, would that be best for AA in the long run? Surely you will agree it would not.

So the problem of Dr. Bob and me comes down to this: We shall somehow have to decide just what few things we are still specially fitted to do for AA and, within the limits of our health, set about them.

For my part, I feel I ought to do much more writing: more AA Grapevine pieces, more pamphlets, and possibly a new book dealing with the vital matter of AA unity. This material ought to be widely informative of our developing Traditions and of the little understood AA general service center. Occasionally, I would like to appear at the larger regional gatherings for the purpose of discussing these matters with as many AAs as possible.

Over the next two or three years, it will be desirable to broaden the base of our general service center here at New York so that it can include a yearly meeting of out-of-town AAs with the trustees of the Alcoholic Foundation, the AA General Office staff, and the AA Grapevine editors, this to be called the General Service Conference of Alcoholics Anonymous. To help construct such a Conference will be a real task which may eventually require us to visit a number of our large AA centers the country over.

For the good of AA as a whole these seem the things most needful to be done. If these projects are ever to be finished, I'm sure we can do little else. To succeed we shall need real freedom of decision and few diversions. Hence, we beg your whole-hearted cooperation.

Though these assignments are still before us, Dr. Bob and I are now going to confess a deep yearning. As private citizens of AA, we shall often wish to come and go among you like other people, without any special attention. And while we would like always to keep the wonderful satisfaction of having been among the originators, we hope you will begin to think of us as early AAs only, not as "founders."

So, can't we join AA, too?

As ever,
Bill

PART

1950 - 1958

The year 1950 brought two landmark events for Alcoholics Anonymous: The Twelve Traditions were adopted in July at the First International Convention in Cleveland. And four months later, on November 16, Dr. Bob died.

As the surviving co-founder, Bill concentrated his energies for the next five years primarily on AA's future, by consolidating its service structure. In 1950, he and Lois spent six weeks in Europe, visiting AA in several countries. European AA flourished, yet the discrepancies Bill found among AA practices in different countries strengthened his belief in the need for a structure that would enable the Fellowship to endure. He returned to North America convinced of the need to make literature available, to foster local leadership, and to expand AA services.

To that end, as Bill reported in *AA Comes of Age*, "fortified with the approval of the Trustees and of Dr. Bob, I stumped the country for the Third Legacy plan...." The first General Service Conference met in April 1951, beginning a five-year experimental period that ended in July 1955 when responsibility for AA's world services, until then performed by the founding members, was turned over to the Fellowship as a whole at the 20th Anniversary Convention in July 1955 at St. Louis.

Segment

1

AA Grows to Maturity

We Approach Maturity

October 1949

Alcoholics Anonymous is fourteen years old. Yet no one thinks we are just entering adolescence. On the contrary, we are approaching maturity. Therefore our problems and responsibilities as a Society are on the increase. It is becoming clear we cannot be forever immune from the fearful pressures that are tearing modern society apart. Like other societies of men and women, we shall no doubt be tempted to enter upon serious controversies. Perhaps some of us will seek fame and fortune at the expense of Alcoholics Anonymous. We shall be tempted to attack those who attack us; we shall yearn for alliances with powerful friends; we shall wish to write laws and so enter politics. It will be difficult to remain neutral in the science versus religion conflict; some might wish to see Alcoholics Anonymous divide on sectarian lines. And, as we become better known, we shall certainly be offered large grants of destruction in the form of money; we might forget our resolve to stay poor. These may well be the crucial problems of our maturity; even now one sees their outlines.

Yet, I am deeply, yes, fervently convinced that Alcoholics Anonymous will weather all adversities and every test of time for so long as God shall need us. My faith in our future rests upon certain facts of our experience:

First, we now humbly gaze upon 80,000 miracles of personal recovery; we see that each of us has been enabled by God's grace to achieve the impossible. In each life, unity has risen far above former chaos. This being God's grant to us personally, we may, if we are worthy, surely expect an equal unity for AA as a whole.

Second, we are sure there must be a million alcoholics who would join Alcoholics Anonymous tomorrow if only they knew what we do. We keenly realize that any fundamental disunity among us could instantly disillusion tens of thousands who would again turn their faces to the wall. Hence those disruptions common to great wealth, power, or controversy ought never be for us. Too many of the "million who don't yet know" would surely die.

Therefore our Fifth Tradition declares: "Each AA group ought to be a spiritual entity having *but one primary purpose* — that of carrying its message to the alcoholic who still suffers."

So long as we remain grateful for what has befallen us, and for so long as this Tradition of high and single purpose is indelibly emblazoned on our hearts, our destiny will be assured. We shall be worthy of God's Providence.

We Came of Age

September 1950

O n AA's 15th Anniversary everybody knew that we had grown up. There couldn't be any doubt about it. Members, families, and friends — seven thousand of them — spent three inspiring, almost awesome days with our good hosts at Cleveland.

The theme song of our Conference was gratitude; its keynote was the sure realization that we are now welded as one, the world over. As never before, we dedicated ourselves to the single purpose of carrying good news of AA to those millions who still don't know. And, as we affirmed the Traditions of Alcoholics Anonymous, we asked that we might remain in perfect unity under the grace of God for so long as he may need us.

Just what did we do? Well, we had meetings, lots of them. The medical meeting, for instance. Our first and great friend Dr. Silkworth couldn't get there. But his associate at Knickerbocker Hospital, New York, Dr. Meyer Texon, most ably filled the gap, telling how best the general hospital could relate itself to us. He clinched his points by a careful description of how, during the past four years at Knickerbocker, 5,000 drunks had been sponsored, processed, and turned loose in AA; and this to the great satisfaction of everybody concerned, including the hospital, whose board was delighted with the results and specially liked the fact that its modest charges were invariably paid, money on the line. Who had ever heard of 5,000 drunks who really paid their bills? Then Dr. Texon brought us up to the minute on the malady of alcoholism as they see it at Knickerbocker; he said it was a definite personality disorder hooked to a physical craving. That certainly made sense to most of us. Dr. Texon threw a heavy scare into prospective "slippers." It was that little matter of one's liver. This patient organ, he said, would surely develop hobnails or maybe galloping cirrhosis, if more guzzling went on. He had a brand-new one too, about salt water, claiming that every alcoholic on the loose had a big salt deficiency. Hence the craving for more drinks. Fill the victim with salt water, he said, and you'd quiet him right down. Of course we thought, "Why not put all drunks on salt water instead of gin? Then the world alcohol problem might be solved overnight." But that was our idea, not Dr. Texon's. To him, many thanks!

About the industrial meeting: Jake H., U.S. Steel, and Dave M., DuPont, both AAs, led it. Mr. Louis Seltzer, editor of the *Cleveland Press,* rounded out the session and brought down the house. Jake, as an officer of U.S. Steel, told what the company really thought about AA — and it was all good. Jake noted the huge collective earning power of somewhere between a quarter and a half billions of dollars annually. Instead of being a nerve-wracking drag on society's collective pocket book, we were now, for the most part, top grade employables who could contribute a yearly average of $4,000 apiece to our country's well-being. Dave M., personnel man at DuPont, who has a special eye to the company's alcohol problem, related what the "new look" on serious drinking had meant to DuPont and its workers of all grades. According to Dave, his company believes mightily in AA. By all odds the most stirring testimony at the industrial seminar was given by editor Louis Seltzer. Mr. Seltzer spoke to us from the viewpoint of an employer, citizen, and veteran newspaper man. It was about the most moving expression of utter confidence in Alcoholics Anonymous we had ever heard. It was almost too good; its implications brought us a little dismay. How could we fallible AAs ever measure up to Mr. Seltzer's high hope for our future? We began to wonder if the AA reputation wasn't getting far better than its actual character.

Next, came that wonderful session on prisons. Our great friend, Warden [Clinton] Duffy, told the startling story of our original group at San Quentin. His account of AA's five-year history there had a moving prelude. We heard a recording, soon for radio release, that thrillingly dramatized an actual incident of AA life within the walls. An alcoholic prisoner reacts bitterly to his confinement and develops amazing ingenuity in finding and drinking alcohol. Soon he becomes too ingenious. In the prison paint shop he discovers a promising fluid which he shares with his fellow alcoholics. It was deadly poison. Harrowing hours followed, during which several of them died. The whole prison was tense as the fatalities continued to mount. Nothing but quick blood transfusions could save those still living. The San Quentin AA Group volunteered instantly and spent the rest of that long night giving of themselves as they had never given before. AA hadn't been any too popular, but now prison morale hit an all-time high and stayed there. Many of the survivors joined up. The first prison group had made its mark; AA had come to San Quentin to stay.

Warden Duffy then spoke. Apparently we folks on the outside know nothing of prison sales resistance. The skepticism of San Quentin prisoners and keepers alike had been tremendous. They thought AA must be a racket. Or maybe a crackpot religion. Then, objected the prison board, why tempt Providence by freely mixing prisoners with outsiders, alcoholic women especially? Bedlam would be unloosed. But our friend the warden, somehow deeply convinced, insisted on AA. To this day, he said, not a single prison rule has ever been broken at an AA meeting, though hundreds of gatherings have been attended by hundreds of prisoners with almost no watching at all. Hardly needed is that solitary, sympathetic guard who sits in the back row.

The warden added that most prison authorities throughout the United States and Canada today share his views of Alcoholics Anonymous. Hitherto 80 percent of paroled alcoholic prisoners had to be scooped up and taken back to jail. Many institutions now report that this percentage has dropped to one-half, even one-third of what it used to be. Warden Duffy had traveled 2,000 miles to be with us at Cleveland. We soon saw why. He came because he is a great human being. Once again, we AAs sat and wondered how far our reputation had got ahead of our character.

Naturally we men folk couldn't go to the meeting of the alcoholic women. But we make no doubt they devised ways to combat the crushing stigma that still rests on those poor women who hit the bottle. Perhaps, too, our ladies had debated how to keep the occasional big bad wolf at a respectful distance. But no, the AA sister transcribing this piece crisply assures me nothing of the sort was discussed. A wonderfully constructive meeting, she says it was. And about 500 attended. Just think of it, AA was four years old before we could sober up even one. Life for the alcoholic woman is no sinecure.

Nor were other special sufferers overlooked, such as paid intergroup secretaries, plain everyday secretaries, our newspaper editors, and the wives and husbands of alcoholics, sometimes known as our "forgotten people." I'm sure the secretaries concluded that though sometimes unappreciated, they still loved every moment of their work. What the editors decided, I haven't learned. Judging from their telling efforts over the years, it is altogether probable they came up with many an ingenious idea.

Everybody agreed that the wives (and husbands) meeting was an eye-opener. Some recalled how Anne S., in the Akron early days, had been boon companion and adviser to distraught wives. She clearly saw alcoholism as a family problem. Meanwhile we AAs went all out on the work of sobering up incoming alkies by the thousands. Our good wives seemed entirely lost in that prodigious shuffle. Lots of the newer localities held closed meetings only; it looked like AA was going exclusive. But of late this trend has whipped about. More and more our partners have been taking the Twelve Steps into their own lives. As proof, witness the Twelfth Step work they are doing with the wives and husbands of newcomers, and note well those wives' meetings now springing up everywhere. At their Cleveland gathering they invited us alcoholics to listen. Many an AA skeptic left that session convinced that our "forgotten ones" really had something. As one alkie put it: "The deep understanding and spirituality I felt in that wives' meeting was something out of this world."

Far from it, the Cleveland Conference wasn't all meetings. Take that banquet, for example. Or should I say banquets? The original blue-print called for enough diners to fill the Rainbow Room of Hotel Carter. But the diners did much better. The banqueteers quickly overflowed the ballroom. Finally the Carter Coffee Shop and Petit Cafe had to be cleared for the surging celebrants. Two orchestras were drafted and our fine entertainers found they had to play their acts twice, both upstairs and down. Though nobody turned up tight, you should have heard those AAs sing. Slaphappy, they were, and why not? Yet a serious undertone crept in as we toasted the absent ones. We were first reminded of the absent by that AA from the Marshall Islands who, though all alone out there, still claimed his group had three members, to wit: "God, the book *Alcoholics Anonymous,* and me." The first leg of his 7,000 mile journey to Cleveland had finished at Hawaii whence with great care and refrigeration he had brought in a cluster of floral tributes, those leis for which the Islands are famous. One of these was sent by the AA lepers at Molokai — those isolated AAs who will always be of us, yet never with us.

We swallowed hard, too, when we thought of Dr. Bob, alone at home, gravely ill. One toast of the evening was to another AA who, more than anything, wanted to be at Cleveland when we came of age. Unhappily he never got to the Traditions meeting; he had been carried off by a heart attack the night before the Traditions meeting and the birthday banquet took place. But at length gaiety took over; we danced till midnight. We knew the absent ones would want it that way.

Several thousand of us crowded into the Cleveland Music Hall for the Traditions meeting, which was thought by most AAs to be the high point of our Conference. Six old-time stalwarts, coming from places far flung as Boston and San Diego, beautifully reviewed the years of AA experience which had led to the writing of our Traditions. Then I was asked to sum up, which I did, saying:

"That, touching all matters affecting AA unity, our common welfare should come first; that AA has no human authority — only God as he may speak in our group conscience; that our leaders are but trusted servants, they do not govern; that any alcoholic may become an AA member if he says so — we exclude no one; that every AA group may manage its own affairs as it likes, provided surrounding groups are not harmed thereby; that we AAs have but a single aim, the carrying of our message to the alcoholic who still suffers; that in consequence we cannot finance, endorse, or otherwise lend the name 'Alcoholics Anonymous' to any other enterprise, however worthy; that AA, as such, ought to remain poor, lest problems of property, management, and money divert us from our sole aim; that we ought to be self-supporting, gladly paying our small expenses ourselves; that AA should remain forever nonprofessional, ordinary Twelfth Step work never to be paid for; that, as a Fellowship, we should never be organized but may nevertheless create responsible service boards or committees to insure us better propagation and sponsorship and that these agencies may engage full-time workers for special tasks; that our public relations ought to proceed upon the principle of attraction rather than promotion, it being better to let our friends recommend us; that personal anonymity at the level of press, radio, and pictures ought to be strictly maintained as our best protection against the temptations of power or personal ambition; and finally, that anonymity before the general public is the spiritual key to all our Traditions, ever reminding us we are always to place principles before personalities, that we are actually to practice a genuine humility. This to the end that our great blessings may never spoil us; that we shall forever live in thankful contemplation of him who presides over us all."

So summing up, I then inquired if those present had any objections to the Twelve Traditions of Alcoholics Anonymous as they stood. Hearing none, I offered the AA Traditions for adoption. Impressively unanimous, the crowd stood up. So ended that fine hour in which we of Alcoholics Anonymous took our destiny by the hand.

On Sunday morning we listened to a panel of four AAs who portrayed the spiritual side of Alcoholics Anonymous — as they understood it. What with churchgoers and late-rising banqueteers, the Conference committee had never guessed this would be a heavy duty session. But churchgoers had already returned from their devotions and hardly a soul stayed abed. Hotel Cleveland's ballroom was filled an hour beforehand. Hundreds who couldn't get near the meeting packed its corridors and main lobby. People who have fear that AA is losing interest in things of the spirit should have been there.

A hush fell upon the crowd as we paused for a moment of silence. Then came the speakers, earnest and carefully prepared, all of them. I cannot recall an AA gathering where the attention was more complete, or the devotion deeper. Yet some thought that those truly excellent speakers had, in their enthusiasm, unintentionally created a bit of a problem. It was felt the meeting had gone overfar in the direction of religious comparison, philosophy, and interpretation, when by firm long-standing tradition we AAs had always left such questions strictly to the chosen faith of each individual. One member rose with a word of caution. As I heard him, I thought, "What a fortunate occurrence. How well we shall always remember that AA is never to be thought of as a religion. How firmly we shall insist that AA membership cannot depend upon any particular belief whatever; that our Twelve Steps contain no article of religious faith except faith in God — *as each of us understands him.* How carefully we shall thenceforth avoid any situation which could possibly lead us to debate matters of personal religious belief." It was, we felt, a great Sunday morning.

That afternoon we filed into the Cleveland Auditorium. The big event was the appearance of Dr. Bob. Earlier we thought he'd never make it, his illness had continued so severe. Seeing him once again was an experience we 7,000 shall always treasure. He spoke in a strong, sure voice for ten minutes, and he left us a great heritage, a heritage by which we AAs can surely grow. It was the legacy of one who had been sober since June 10, 1935, who saw our first group to success, and one who, in the fifteen years since, had given both medical help and vital AA to 4,000 of our afflicted ones at good St. Thomas Hospital in Akron, the birthplace of Alcoholics Anonymous. Simplicity, devotion, steadfastness, and loyalty; these, we remembered, were the hallmarks of that character which Dr. Bob had well implanted in so many of us. I, too, could gratefully recall that in all the years of our association there had never been an angry word between us. Such were our thoughts as we looked at Dr. Bob.

Then for an hour I tried to sum up. Yet how could one add much to what we had all seen, heard, and felt in those three wonderful days? With relief and certainty we had seen that AA could never become exhibitionistic or big business; that its early humility and simplicity is very much with us; that we are still mindful our beloved Fellowship is God's success, not ours.

As evidence I shared a vision of AA as Lois and I saw it unfold on a distant beachhead in far Norway. The vision began with one AA who listened to a voice in his conscience, and then sold all he had.

George, a Norwegian-American, came to us at Greenwich, Connecticut, five years ago. His parents back home hadn't heard from him in twenty. He began to send letters telling them of his new freedom. Back came very disquieting news. The family reported his only brother in desperate condition, about to lose all through alcohol. What could be done? The AA from Greenwich had a long talk with his wife. Together they took a decision to sell their little restaurant, all they had. They would go to Norway to help the brother. A few weeks later an airliner landed them at Oslo. They hastened from field to town and thence twenty-five miles down the fjord where the ailing brother lived. He was in a bad state all right. Unfortunately, though, everybody saw it but him. He'd have no AA, no American nonsense. He an alcoholic? Why certainly not! Of course the man from Greenwich had heard such objections before. But now this familiar argument was hard to take. Maybe he had sold all he had for no profit to anybody. George persisted every bit he dared, but finally surmised it was no use. Determined to start an AA group in Norway anyhow, he began a round of Oslo's clergy and physicians. Nothing happened, not one of them offered him a single prospect. Greatly cast down, he and his wife thought it high time they got back to Connecticut.

But Providence took a hand. The rebellious Norwegian obligingly tore off on one of his fantastic periodics. In the final anguish of his hangover he cried out to the man from Greenwich, "Tell me again of the 'Anonymous Alcoholics.' What, oh my brother, shall I do?" With perfect simplicity George retold the AA story. When he had done, he wrote out, in his all but forgotten Norwegian, a longhand translation of a little pamphlet published by the White Plains, N.Y. group. It contained, of course, our Twelve Steps of recovery. The family from Connecticut then flew away home. The Norwegian brother, himself a typesetter, commenced to place tiny ads in the Oslo newspapers. He explained he was a recovered alcoholic who wished to help others. At last a prospect appeared. When the newcomer was told the story and shown the White Plains pamphlet, he, too, sobered instantly. The founders-to-be then placed more ads.

Three years after, Lois and I alighted upon that same airfield. We then learned that Norway has hundreds of AAs. And good ones. The men of Oslo had already carried the life-giving news to other Norwegian cities and these beacons burned brightly. It had all been just as simple, but just as mysterious, as that.

In the final moments of our historic conference it seemed fitting to read from chapter eleven of *Alcoholics Anonymous*. These were the words we took home with us: "Abandon yourself to God as you understand God. Admit your faults to Him and your fellows. Clear away the wreckage of your past. Give freely of what you find, and join us. We shall be with you, in the Fellowship of the Spirit, and you will surely meet some of us as you trudge the Road of Happy Destiny. May God bless you and keep you — until then."

AA Is Not Big Business

November 1950

T hanksgiving is coming. And with it, Tradition Week. I never felt happier.

Our Traditions are set down on paper. But they were written first in our hearts. For each of us knows, instinctively I think, that AA is not ours to do with as we please. We are but caretakers to preserve the spiritual quality of our Fellowship; keep it whole for those who will come after us and have need of what has so generously been given to us.

We learned our lesson about money early. We feared organization lest we solidify and destroy ourselves as a *movement!* At the same time we faced the moral and humane obligation to make our program instantly available to all who asked for it. And they came in ever increasing numbers.

Yes, we've had need of money and we've had to provide services. But we've resolved never to allow either money or the management of our necessary affairs to obscure our spiritual aims. The same loving God whose divine wisdom has shown us that one desperate and shaky drunk, fumbling for a nickel to call for help, looms larger than any "organization" we shall ever have, or need!

At Cleveland, July last, 7,000 AAs set their approval to the Twelve Traditions of Alcoholics Anonymous. We took our destiny by the hand. Alcoholics Anonymous had grown up.

Three of those Traditions define the services of Alcoholics Anonymous and outline our collective responsibility for them — management responsibility and money responsibility. The Traditions also say that our trusted servants shall never govern; that they shall always be directly accountable to those they serve.

Last month I broadcast to you — the members of Alcoholics Anonymous — an urgent appeal. It was a plea that you take full money responsibility for your AA Headquarters — the Alcoholic Foundation and its AA General Service Office at New York. We who work in your Headquarters are delighted with the result. Groups who never helped before have now done so. New groups, very small groups, institutional groups not really under any obligation, have made sacrifices. If this keeps up, our deficit at Headquarters will be a thing of the past. Never have I been so encouraged about the future of our services. Your generous and responsible action makes a fitting setting for the news I am about to give you.

For twelve years, warmly aided by great friends, Dr. Bob and I have stood sentinel over your Headquarters. We have been holding these valuable assets in trust for you — your General Service Office, your book *Alcoholics Anonymous,* your principal magazine the AA Grapevine, your public relations, your common funds. We have never asked you to take any direct responsibility for them. But times have changed. Alcoholics Anonymous is now grown. Its founders are perishable. We cannot be your guardians always.

So the hour is come when you must take these things into your own keeping. We ask that you guard them well, for the future of Alcoholics Anonymous may much depend on how you maintain and support these life-giving arms of service.

Anticipating that you will happily accept this new responsibility, the trustees, Dr. Bob, and I propose the General Service Conference of Alcoholics Anonymous, a body of state and provincial representatives who will sit yearly with our Foundation trustees as their traditional guide. We have long considered and will soon present a detailed plan designed to bring this great change about.

Alcoholics Anonymous *has* come of age. It's a great Thanksgiving!

Your Third Legacy

A note preceding the original article read as follows: "This is a proposal to form 'The General Service Conference of Alcoholics Anonymous,' a small body of state and provincial AA delegates meeting yearly, who could assume direct responsiblity for the guidance of the AA general service Headquarters at New York City."

December 1950

We, who are the older members of AA, bequeath to you who are younger, these three Legacies — the Twelve Steps of recovery, the Twelve Traditions, and now the general services of Alcoholics Anonymous. Two of these Legacies have long been in your keeping. By the Twelve Steps we have recovered from alcoholism; by the Twelve Traditions we are achieving a fine unity.

Being someday perishable, Dr. Bob and I now wish to deliver to the members of AA their Third Legacy. Since 1938 we and our friends have been holding it in trust. This legacy is the general Headquarters services of Alcoholics Anonymous — the Alcoholic Foundation, the AA Book, the AA Grapevine, and the AA General Office. These are the principal services which have enabled our Society to function and to grow.

Acting on behalf of all, Dr. Bob and I ask that you — the members of AA — now assume guidance of these services and guard them well. The future growth, indeed the very survival, of Alcoholics Anonymous may one day depend on how prudently these arms of service are administered in years to come.

May we share with you a fragment of history? Twelve years ago, warmly aided by great friends, Dr. Bob and I established a Headquarters for our then obscure Fellowship. Soon thereafter we transferred this function to the Alcoholic Foundation, which was organized as a small board of trustees dedicated to serve our cause. This board was formed of alcoholics and nonalcoholic friends, who today number fifteen. When in the spring of 1938 our Foundation was born, AA was but three years old. We had only fifty members. The book *Alcoholics Anonymous* was just an idea. None could then guess the magnificence of the gift which Providence had begun to bestow.

In the twelve years since, those fifty early members have spawned

120,000 more. AA stretches worldwide. Religion and medicine have approvingly raised us out of that no man's land where we once foundered between them. We have no enemies; our friends are beyond count. Like gleaming coral islands our thousands of groups build themselves upward out of the alcohol sea. What a God-given miraculous circumstance!

Through our rather feverish infancy, the Alcoholic Foundation board, unseen by many, quietly played a great part in the formation and spread of our well-loved Society. Acting through our General Office, the book *Alcoholics Anonymous,* and latterly the Grapevine, the Foundation became directly responsible for half our growth and effectiveness — both in quality and quantity. There can be no question of that.

Suppose then, all these years, we had been without those services. Where would we be today minus the AA Book and our standard literature which now pours out of Headquarters at the rate of three tons a month? Suppose our public relations had been left to thoughtless chance? Suppose no one had been assigned to encourage good publicity and discourage the bad? Suppose no accurate information about AA had been available? Imagine our vital and delicate relations with medicine and religion left to pot luck. Then, too, where would thousands of AAs be today if the General Office hadn't answered their frantic letters and referred them to help? (Our New York office received and answered 28,000 letters of all kinds last year.) Or in what shape would hundreds of distant AA groups now be if that office hadn't started them by mail or directed travelers to them? How could we have managed without a world group directory? What about those foreign groups in twenty-eight countries clamoring for translations, proven experience and encouragement? Would we be publishing the AA Book at Oslo, Norway and London, England? What of those Lone Members on high seas or in far corners of the earth, those prisoners, those asylum inmates, those veterans in service or in hospitals? Where might we one day be if we never had the AA Grapevine, our mirror of AA life and principal forum of written expression? How grateful we are for those secretaries and those volunteer editors and those friendly trustees who have stood sentinel all these years over our principal affairs. Without all these things, where would we be? You must have guessed it. We'd be nowhere; that's sure.

So it is that by the Steps we have recovered, by the Traditions we have unified, and by our Headquarters services we have been able to function as a Society.

Yet some may still say, "Of course the Foundation should go on.

Certainly we'll pay that small expense. But why can't we leave its conduct to Dr. Bob and Bill and their friends, the trustees? We always have. Why do they now bother us with such business? Let's keep AA simple." Good questions, these. But today the answers are quite different than they once were.

Let's face these facts:

First: Dr. Bob and Bill are perishable; they can't last forever.

Second: Their friends, the trustees, are almost unknown to the AA movement.

Third: In future years our trustees couldn't possibly function without direct guidance from AA itself. Somebody must advise them. Somebody, or something, must take the place of Dr. Bob and Bill.

Fourth: Alcoholics Anonymous is out of its infancy. Grown up, adult now, it has full right and the plain duty to take direct responsibility for its own Headquarters.

Fifth: Clearly then, unless the Foundation is firmly anchored, through state and provincial representatives, to the movement it serves, a Headquarters breakdown will someday be inevitable. When its old-timers vanish, an isolated Foundation couldn't survive one grave mistake or serious controversy. Any storm could blow it down. Its revival wouldn't be simple. Possibly it could never be revived. Still isolated, there would be no means of doing that. Like a fine car without gasoline, it would be helpless.

Sixth: Another serious flaw: As a whole, the AA movement has never faced a grave crisis. But someday it will have to. Human affairs being what they are, we can't expect to remain untouched by the hour of serious trouble. With direct support unavailable, with no reliable cross section of AA opinion, how could our remote trustees handle a hazardous emergency? This gaping "open end" in our present setup could positively guarantee a debacle. Confidence in the Foundation would be lost. AAs would everywhere say: "By whose authority do the trustees speak for us? And how do they know they are right?" With AA's service lifelines tangled and severed, what then might happen to the millions who don't know. Thousands would continue to suffer on or die because we had forgotten the virtue of prudence. This should not come to pass.

That is why the trustees, Dr. Bob, and I now propose the General Service Conference of Alcoholics Anonymous. That is why we urgently need your direct help. Our principal services must go on living. We think the General Service Conference of Alcoholics Anonymous can be the agency to make that certain.

To Serve Is to Live

June 1951

Our first General Service Conference of Alcoholics Anonymous gathered at New York City in April, 1951. It was composed of thirty-seven U.S. and Canadian delegates plus AA's general service Headquarters staff and trustees. The single purpose of our Conference was to serve AA throughout the world.

This unexciting statement now carries a deep meaning for all who were there. We came to believe that AA's future had been made secure. We became certain that AA could live for so long as God might need us.

Why did each witness of the Conference feel so deeply about it? I think for two reasons: The group conscience of all Alcoholics Anonymous was heard to speak for the first time. And we realized, as never before, how perilous "faith without works" might really become. So it was, that AA's group conscience heard its first high call to service.

Making this plainer, let's look for a moment at a single AA member. Faith alone does not save him. He has to act, do something. He must *carry* his message to others, *practice* AA principles in all his affairs. Else he slips, he withers, and he dies. Look now at an AA group. Can pure faith, mere belief in right principle and sound tradition, make the group a going concern? Not in the least. Each AA group, as such, must also function, do something. It must serve its appointed purpose or it, too, withers and falls apart.

Now our Conference delegates were able to apply this principle to AA as a whole. The delegates could see far beyond the single AA and his particular group. In a flash, they took in the stark fact that AA *as a whole* must continue to function or else it might well suffer that common penalty of faith without works. Which is: disintegration. Gone was the comfortable illusion that should each AA group tend strictly to its own affairs God would then reward our shortsightedness by guarding AA as a whole entirely by himself — including our Headquarters, AA's public relations, and the welfare of the millions who still don't know. The delegates saw that this would spell faith without work and without responsibility. that could never be. Of course much work would always have to be done, much responsibility would have to be taken by many. To AA as a whole, every member would need to give a little.

Of age now, our Fellowship would have to begin looking after its own vital services; these couldn't be thoughtlessly left in the sole custody of our isolated, unknown, and unsupported board of trustees. The work of our Foundation and AA's "GHQ" would have to become widely understood and directly backed up by AA itself. Nothing was plainer, thought the delegates. When, therefore, you next see your local Conference member, you may find him talking something like this:

"Thanks for sending me to New York. I've just spent three days at AA's world Headquarters. Our trustees, General Office, and Grapevine people turned the place inside out so we delegates might vision its past, present, and future. What we saw and felt was startling.

"Very suddenly we got the feeling of AA as a whole. We looked out upon a Fellowship of surpassing unity, one on which the sun never sets, a world communion four thousand times larger than a single AA group.

"We then realized that this wonder had been made possible by the devoted service of a few; those Headquarters workers whose decade and more of labor had enabled us in distant fields to garner that great harvest of 120,000 fellow sufferers into the safety of our fold, and into the affectionate respect of the whole world. Our unseen servants at the Foundation had done all this because Dr. Bob and Bill had asked them to.

"But now they were saying to us delegates, 'Soon you must lend a hand. These are AA's arms of service, these are our Traditions. Come and help us administer them; times have changed, we oldsters are perishable. This is your Legacy of Service. Please accept it now and guard it well.' "

The Conference scene that Sunday afternoon we last met will always be a precious memory in the annals of AA. For in that historic assemblage we could all hear the voice of Alcoholics Anonymous. These were the words: "To serve AA is to live. We gladly accept our Third Legacy and may we guard it well and use it wisely. God grant that the Legacy of Service remain ever safe in our keeping."

In that fine hour the torch of Service did pass from the hands of us who are older to yours, which are younger; it passed to every oncoming generation of those children of the night whose darkness, God willing, shall be banished within the Society of Alcoholics Anonymous all through the bright years which destiny surely holds in store for us.

Services Make AA Tick

November 1951

A coffeepot simmers on the kitchen stove, a hospital sobers the stricken sufferer, general Headquarters broadcasts the AA message; our service lifelines span the seven seas. All these symbolize AA in action. For action is the magic word of Alcoholics Anonymous. So it is that every AA service daily proves that so-called "material activities" can lead to magnificent spiritual results.

Once upon a time, all AA meetings were held in homes. There weren't any committees and nobody put up a cent. We hadn't even a name and founders were unheard of. It was that simple.

Yet we did enjoy one "service" — a valuable one, too. Wives baked cakes and brewed strong coffee for us alkies huddling together in the front parlors, still terrified that our new program might not work after all. Those wifely dispensations of good cheer smoothed the way and so lightened our burden of doubt. Thus, from the very beginning, did such gracious service make AA tick.

By and by, meetings got big. Our front parlors couldn't hold them. We had to move into halls. Gathering places seldom came free so we must needs pay rent. Landlords weren't a particle interested in the spiritual advantages of group poverty. So someone passed the hat and we dropped money into it voluntarily. We knew we couldn't meet or function as a group unless we did. We grudgingly learned that rent was necessary to insure sobriety — our spiritual dividend, life itself.

This rent-paying process also produced the first AA "official." The gent we picked to pass the hat soon became our treasurer. Then phone calls had to be answered, letters written, literature ordered and distributed. The now familiar group secretary put in an appearance. Presently newspaper interviews had to be given, preachers and doctors canvassed, hospital arrangements made, banquets set up. Not by anybody, either. Somebody special had to be picked to do these chores. That "somebody" became the group service chairman.

Of course, this was all quite troublesome, for it marred our sometimes fallible serenity. Squabbling began, dark forecasts of our future were made, and everybody yearned to go back into the parlors. But we didn't because we couldn't. We saw we'd have to have service committees or fail to function, perhaps fall apart entirely. We'd actually *have to organize services in order to keep AA simple.*

Hospitals, we early found, disliked drunks. We had been noisy nuisances who ducked paying bills and seldom got well. Yet we quickly saw that many an alcoholic might never get a real chance with AA unless hospitalized. What could we do?

At first, we went in for home "tapering." But instead of "tapering off," our new clients usually "tapered on" — and right back into the bars again. Some groups tried to organize "AA hospitals" with MDs on call. This carried matters too far; it put our groups straight into serious business. All these early attempts were busts. We finally learned that each AA group ought to be primarily a spiritual entity, not a business corporation. Then individual AAs and their friends began to set up rest homes and drunk farms as private enterprises. This worked a lot better, but still it wasn't enough.

At length the medics began to come to our aid. Agreeing with our hard-earned conclusion that doctoring ought to be the affair of doctors, they commenced to help us make hospital connections. Our first attempts to cooperate with hospitals in city areas often led to damaging confusion. Anybody sponsored anybody, and those hospital bills still didn't get paid. Cocksure AAs told doctors how to run wards. This easygoing lack of head or tail in our hospital relations didn't keep AA simple at all. Confusion was general until some hospitals bluntly told metropolitan AA groups that responsible members with whom they could consistently deal would have to be named — or else. Nobody, said the hospitals, could possibly cooperate with an anarchy.

It began to dawn upon AA that group responsibility would have to reach much further than the meeting hall doorstep on Tuesday and Thursday nights only. Otherwise the new man approaching our door might miss his chance, might lose his life.

Slowly, most reluctantly, groups in densely populated areas saw they would have to form associations, open small offices, pay a few full-time secretaries. Terrific outcries went up. To many, this really meant destructive organization, politics, professionalism, big expense, a ruling officialdom, and government. "Believe us," they argued, "a local central office could cost metropolitan AA members fifty cents a month apiece. That could turn into a damned head tax — what about our AA Tradition of no 'fees or dues'?"

Of course these exaggerated fears never materialized. We have lots of good intergroup associations now, voluntarily supported. The new man is getting a better break, the hospitals are pleased. The office of one large association has sponsored and hospitalized 7,000 alcoholics. Prompt interview and phone service is planting the seeds of recovery in other thousands. Local meeting directories are issued, public relations attended to, regional gatherings and dinners set up. We found these last couldn't be carelessly left to anybody who happened to feel like giving interviews or printing up a bundle of tickets and handbills. In short, intergroups do those area chores that no single individual or group could. They unify regions; they make AA tick.

By 1937, some of us realized that AA needed a standard literature. There would have to be a book. Our word-of-mouth program could be garbled, we might be destroyed by dissension over basic principles, and then our public relations would surely go to pot. We'd fall flat on our obligation to the alcoholic who hadn't yet heard unless we put our knowledge on paper.

But not everybody agreed; many were badly scared by this proposal. Money in some quantity would be needed; there would be huge disputes over authorship, royalties, profits, prices, and the contents of the book itself. Some truly believed that this seemingly reckless project would blow our little Society to bits. "Let's avoid trouble, let's keep things simple," they said.

Well, we did quarrel violently over the preparation and distribution of that AA Book. In fact, it took five years for the clamor to die down. Should any AA's dream that the old-timers who put the Book together went about at the time in serene meditation and white robes, then they had best forget it. The inspiration that readers now say they find in the volume must have got there by the grace of God only!

Yet see what has happened. Two hundred thousand AA Books circulated in this year 1951, silently scattering our message worldwide, lighting the path of progress for nearly every incoming member. Without doubt, that Book is the backbone of our unity, it has unbelievably *simplified* our task. Although its preparation was, in part, a very "material" proceeding, indeed, those early labor pains of its creation did help form our Society and cause it to function. The spiritual result, in sobriety, in happiness, and faith, is altogether beyond any reckoning.

This group of Headquarters services enables AA to function as a whole. They guard our Tradition; they issue our principal literature. They watch over our general public relations and so relate us rightly to the world outside. They mediate our difficulties; they guide our policy. Therefore, these indispensable services are AA's principal lifelines to the millions who do not know.

It is this world center of service which constitutes the principal bequest in our recently announced Third Legacy. And it is by the terms of this Legacy of Service that the General Service Conference of Alcoholics Anonymous, a representative body of state and provincial delegates, assumed control and guidance of these principal affairs of AA last April.

That event marked the passing of responsibility for our world services from Dr. Bob, our friends, and myself, to you — the members of Alcoholics Anonymous. Support and guard these assets well; the lives and fortunes of millions, the very survival of AA itself, may depend much upon how well you discharge this, your newfound obligation.

Let us make our services respectable; let us rank them in importance with the Twelve Steps of recovery and the Twelve Principles of AA Tradition. Let us forget our fear of over-organization; let us remember that AA as a whole cannot be organized; but that we must so organize and support our special services that AA can function. Let us forget our early fears of professionalism, of the accumulation of wealth, of government. Experience, now fortified by our Traditions, has already assured us none of these evils are likely to descend upon us.

Above all, let's change our old attitudes about money. Collectively, AA members earn an enormous income because of their sobriety; it's a one-half a billion-dollar bonanza each year. Can we not wisely, gratefully, and humbly reinvest a tiny fraction of this vast sum in those vital services that make AA tick? I think we can, and I think we shall. For in our own lives we have seen sobriety produce money, and in our AA services we have seen a little money produce incalculable spiritual dividends. Let's think this all through again.

By our Twelve Steps we have recovered, by our Twelve Traditions we have unified, and through our Third Legacy — Service — we shall carry the AA message down through all the corridors of time to come. Of this, I am happily confident.

The Vision of Tomorrow

January 1952

Clear vision for tomorrow comes only after a real look at yesterday. That's why we AAs take personal inventory; that's why this issue of the Grapevine directs us to meditate upon the great happenings of 1951. It is our yearly inventory.

Every AA will agree that we have just lived through an awesome, destiny-shaping twelve months.

The greatest event was, I think, AA's assumption of its Third Legacy of Service. Our grown-up Society could for the first time know its own mind, assume the guidance of its principal affairs and the guardianship of its Traditions. The Third Legacy did mark, too, our definite abandonment of the petty squabbles of childhood for a far more mature statesmanship. Upon our cathedral of spirit the spire of service was firmly anchored aloft. High above its great floor symbolizing recovery, high above those protecting walls denoting our unity, AA's spire of service rose to beckon the millions who do not yet know. The last structural job was done. Such, we think, was the inner meaning of the first General Service Conference of Alcoholics Anonymous which met April last at New York.

But great events also bore down upon us from without. Never before did so many theologues, philosophers, sociologists, employers, and political scientists approach AA to see how its principles and structure might fit into their fields of meditation and work. Never before did so many notable clergymen proclaim how the AA Twelve Steps could be used for almost any human problem.

World assault upon the total alcoholic problem intensified; the noted World Health Organization became vigorous. In North America, states and provinces granted large sums to hospitals, clinics, and education. New drugs were offered as palliatives for everything that can ail an alcoholic — from his shakes to his neuroses. In all these ventures, AA invariably received high commendation. A great life insurance company, the Metropolitan, gave us wholesale approval in its advertising. While we could not in the least endorse any of these efforts, we did gladly cooperate with some and were grateful for all.

A climax of public interest was reached in the very special February

1951 issue of the magazine *Fortune*. Right in the middle of this number appeared thousands of good words about AA. This piece was significantly titled "A Uniquely American Phenomenon." Its popularity has continued so great that our Foundation has shipped out tens of thousands of reprints.

The year 1951 finished in still another great blaze. The world of science, as represented by the American Public Health Association, placed upon Alcoholics Anonymous its resounding stamp of complete approval. Last October 30, the stage of San Francisco's historic opera house was filled with leaders in medicine and notables of public life. Then and there AA was presented with the prized Lasker Award which, in the estimate of many, rates with a Nobel Prize. Not only were we recommended for our success with alcoholism, the Lasker citation actually ventured into prophecy. Its closing words declared: "Historians may one day point to Alcoholics Anonymous as a society which did far more than achieve a considerable measure of success with alcoholism and its stigma; they may recognize Alcoholics Anonymous to have been a great venture in social pioneering which forged a new instrument for social action, a new therapy based on the kinship of common suffering, one having vast potential for the myriad other ills of mankind."

So reads the dramatic record for 1951 — one of the finest yesterdays in AA history.

Every AA who ponders these astonishing events will be almost sure humbly to exclaim, "What, indeed, hath God wrought!" Should any be tempted by the dream that AA is becoming great, powerful, or may be destined to save the world, they could well reread the foreword of AA's Tradition where these words are to be seen: "If, as AA members, we can each refuse public prestige and renounce any desire for personal power; if, as a movement, we insist on remaining poor...if we steadfastly decline all political, sectarian or other alliances, we shall avoid internal division and adverse public notoriety; if, as a movement, we remain a spiritual entity concerned *only* with carrying our message to fellow sufferers...then only can we most effectively complete our mission."

Which, in effect, is to pray: "Lead us not into temptation" — let us not be spoiled.

For so long as we shall humbly meditate in this spirit upon our great yesterdays, just so long will God grant us our vision of tomorrow.

Our Final Great Decision

June 1954

Next year, on June 10th, 1955, we shall be celebrating AA's twentieth birthday. But that will not be all. For, in the year of 1955, this Society will take, I trust, the last great decision concerning its final form and substance.

Now exactly what may this grave decision be?

In April, this year, AA's General Service Conference met at New York for the fourth, and the last, of its experimental sessions.

As most of us know, this Conference of ours is the instrument through which we hope that AA, worldwide, will presently be able to assume full guidance and control of its overall services and principal affairs; all those vital activities of service which have long centered around our Foundation, our General Service Office, and in our publication agencies, the AA Publishing and the AA Grapevine.

As a four-year experiment in the guidance of AA by its own group conscience, delegates chosen from all the states and provinces of the United States and Canada have been meeting with our trustees and service staff men and women here at New York to determine whether AA — as a whole — can actually function as such, whether it can now safely gather into its own hands our Third Legacy of Service for all time to come.

We who have anxiously watched our infant Conference take its first steps, and have seen it acquire form, substance, and strength, are today utterly confident. We believe that our Conference, when securely linked to similar conferences in every distant land, can guarantee, *absolutely,* the survival, unity, and functioning of AA throughout the world. We feel the deep assurance that this new beacon light of service can endure every storm and peril that the passage of the years may cast upon us. For the first time, we are certain that AA is safe and secure.

Therefore the great event of 1955 will be our decision to make this newborn General Service Conference a permanent part of AA's life. This irrevocable step will mark the full completion of AA's structure — Recovery, Unity, and now, Service. It will mark that day when, before God and the world, we declare ourselves fully responsible and come of age.

Then the third and last Legacy — the Legacy of Service — will have passed from the hands of the old-timers — people like Dr. Bob and me —

to you, who are the Alcoholics Anonymous of today and of tomorrow.

Such will be the boundless significance of the year of 1955, the day of our 20th Anniversary, and the hour of AA's final decision.

May this be God's will for us all — Amen.

A Letter to the Groups

July 1954

After careful discussion, at the recent General Service Conference, it was voted to remove all discounts to U.S. and Canadian groups on the Big Book and *Twelve Steps and Twelve Traditions.*

Their action was taken by a large majority — sixty-eight to seven — and represented an accurate cross section of AA opinion. It was suggested that I write you, telling why this action was deemed so necessary.

Our experience here at AA Headquarters, in the fifteen years since it was set up, definitely shows, indeed it shouts, that the Foundation must always have on hand *a substantial reserve fund of hard cash* to take care of the frequent deficits that occur and the future possibility of a depression or severe inflation, thereby guaranteeing our world services under all conditions.

This isn't a theory at all. In the first two years of its operation, the entire expense of General Headquarters was paid out of book and pamphlet receipts. Then, in 1941, the groups, by voluntary contributions, commenced to assume the General Headquarters Office expenses. But in only five out of the thirteen years since 1941 have group contributions paid the full bill of the AA General Service Office. And on two occasions reserve book earnings, accumulated in the Foundation, have saved the General Headquarters Office from closing or its service being severely curtailed.

I remember one period when the groups failed to meet office expenses by $2,000 a month. At the same time the Grapevine was losing

$1,000 a month. For almost two years this rate of loss continued. It was only by reason of our reserve of book money in the Foundation that the Grapevine did not go completely out of business. And there would have been severe contraction of the General Service Office at the very time when our fast growing Fellowship needed more services — not less.

Thanks to the General Service Conference, to the activities of its delegates, committee members, and to your better understanding of our service needs down here, we are of course far better off at present. Last year the Grapevine broke a little better than even. And thanks to increased group contributions, the General Service Office bill was just about paid.

Even so, there remained an overall deficit of about $10,000 due to the fact that special contributions of the groups to the expense of the General Service Conference fell that much short.

Again it was book and pamphlet money that made it possible to hold the General Service Conference at all, despite the improvement that has recently taken place.

These are the facts of our history that show the need at all times for a safe reserve fund in the Foundation. This is the money that guarantees the operation of AA's world services, rain or shine.

Due to increased expense and inflation in recent years, our reserve fund *now stands at only nine months' operating expense* for the AA General Service Office.

This — considering the uncertain times in which we are living — was considered by the Conference to be much too low and very unsafe. The Conference realized that a decline of even 15 or 20 percent in group contributions and literature sales could again put us right out on the limb.

Hence the Conference action to suspend all book discounts until the Foundation reserve reaches a figure equal to at least two or three years' operating expense for the General Service Office.

This means that AA Publishing will now charge the Canadian and U.S. groups $3.50 for the Big Book and $2.75 for *Twelve Steps and Twelve Traditions.* It was expressly stipulated that these additional monies were to be placed by the Foundation in its savings bank reserve fund. And, should this fund reach $300,000 during the next few years, it was agreed the book discounts would be restored to the groups. When we think of the immense size and reach of AA, this $300,000 becomes a very small figure — it is a permanent investment of only $2.00 per member so that AA can never, under any conditions, fall apart at its very center.

This action of the Conference gave me immense satisfaction and relief, for it means that your Headquarters will be made depression and calamity-proof.

I trust that all groups will see the great need for this protective accumulation and, at the same time, will fully maintain their voluntary contributions out of which our current General Service Office expenses are met.

A thousand thanks to you all!

The Significance of St. Louis

April 1955

Come next summer, and it will be twenty years since I first set eyes on Dr. Bob — twenty years since the spark that was to be Alcoholics Anonymous was struck and AA's Akron Group Number One took form and substance.

This July, we are having our 1955 Anniversary at St. Louis — all of us who can get there, maybe ten thousand, maybe twenty. And all who can't be there will surely be present in spirit and will be bound to share those meaningful and stirring hours with us as they read the reports.

St. Louis isn't going to be just another anniversary for the very potent reason that there can never be, in all our history to come, another such occasion as this.

As at all anniversaries of the past, we shall thank God for our deliverance out of bondage; we shall pay grateful tribute to those near and dear who sat through the dark night of the soul with us; we shall gratefully recall those friends in the world outside whose ideas, goodwill, and labor without stint have done so much to make AA what it is today. We shall cry out our greetings to each other with a warmth seldom known anywhere. We shall exchange experiences, confess that our Society has its faults, and ask God to show us how to remove them. We shall ponder the meaning of our short but exciting history and, in confident faith, we shall accept whatever destiny Providence has in store for us. All these things we shall do at St. Louis.

But we are also going to do some things that can never be done again: We are going to affirm that the infancy and adolescence of our Society now belongs to its near-miraculous and incredible past; that our Fellowship has now come of age; that we now propose to take full possession and full responsibility for our inheritance coming from the early years of AA — those vital legacies of Recovery, Unity, and Service. No longer will the unity and functioning of our Society depend upon its parents, elders, or founders. That will be the unique significance of St. Louis.

This means that all of us — AA as a whole — are now entirely ready to take over full guardianship of the AA Traditions that guarantee our unity in time to come, and also to take complete charge of those world services which are the means by which we function as an entire Fellowship, and from which radiate our principal lifelines to those millions all over the globe who still need AA.

Maybe this sounds vague, abstract, or visionary. But it really isn't. The basic idea is simple and practical. There comes a time in the life of every family when the parents must say to sons and daughters alike, "You are grown up; here is your inheritance. Do with it as you will. We will watch, we will help, but we must no longer decide for you, act for you, or protect you. You are henceforth responsible for your own lives and well-being. So now take your destiny by the hand. And may God love you." Everybody knows that a good parent must do this. All parents, at some point, simply have to "let go and let God." That's exactly what we old-timers will propose to you at St. Louis. At least that's what I plan to do, as I believe such a decision will be healthy, timely, and right.

On the great stage of the St. Louis Auditorium you will see your elected representatives, the General Service Conference of Alcoholics Anonymous. In the midst of them you will see AA's trustees and your world service staff. When the final hour of our Convention comes, I shall, on behalf of the old-timers. . .

But shucks, here I am, spoiling the show.

Here's hoping that Lois and I will be seeing you at St. Louis!

How AA's World Services Grew
Part I

The following three articles comprise the original version of the historical section of The AA Service Manual. *Portions that contain long-outdated facts, which no longer appear in the* Service Manual, *are retained here as a matter of historical record.*

May 1955

Someday the history of Alcoholics Anonymous will be written. Only then will most of us finally understand what overall national and international services have meant to our Society, how difficult they were to create, and how vital it is to maintain them over future years.

One day in 1937, at Dr. Bob's Akron home, he and I added up the score of nearly three years' work. For the first time we saw that wholesale recovery for alcoholics was possible. We then had two small but solid groups, at Akron and at New York City, plus a sprinkling of members elsewhere. How could these few recovered ones tell millions of alcoholics throughout the world the great news? That was the question.

Forthwith Dr. Bob and I met with eighteen of the Akron Group at the home of T. Henry Williams, a steadfast nonalcoholic friend. Some of the Akron Group still thought we ought to stick to the word-of-mouth process; but the majority felt that we now needed our own hospitals, with paid workers and, above all, a book for other alcoholics that could explain to them our methods and results. This would require considerable money — millions perhaps. We didn't then know that millions would have ruined us even more than no money at all. So the Akron meeting commissioned me to go to New York and raise money. Arrived home, I found the New York Group in full agreement with this idea. Several of us went to work at once.

Through my brother-in-law, Dr. L.V. Strong, Jr., we made a contact with Mr. Willard S. Richardson, a friend and longtime associate of the Rockefeller family. Mr. Richardson promptly took fire and interested a group of his own friends. In the winter of 1937, a meeting was called at the offices of John D. Rockefeller, Jr. Present were Mr. Richardson and his group, Dr. William D. Silkworth, alcoholics from Akron and New York, Dr. Bob, and myself. After a long discussion, we convinced our new friends that we urgently needed money — a lot of it, too.

One of them, a Mr. Frank Amos, soon made a trip to investigate the Akron Group. (Frank has, by the way, remained a friend and trustee of Alcoholics Anonymous to this day.) He returned from the West with a very optimistic report on the Akron situation, a digest of which Mr. Richardson quickly laid before John D. Rockefeller, Jr. This was early in 1938. Though much impressed, Mr. Rockefeller declined to give any large sum for fear of professionalizing AA. He did, however, donate $5,000. This was used to keep Dr. Bob and me going during 1938. We were still a long way from hospitals, missionaries, books, and big money. This looked mighty tough at the time but it was probably one of the best breaks that AA ever had.

In spite of Mr. Rockefeller's views, we renewed our efforts to persuade his friends of our crying need for money. At length, they agreed that we did need more money, certainly enough to prepare a textbook on our methods and experience.

This decision led to the formation of the so-called Alcoholic Foundation in the spring of 1938. The first board of trustees consisted of three of our new friends — Mr. Richardson, Mr. Amos, and Dr. L.V. Strong. The alcoholics were represented by Dr. Bob and a New York member. Supplied with a list of prospects by our new friends, we alcoholics at New York began to solicit funds. Since the Alcoholic Foundation was tax-free, on charitable grounds, we thought the rich would contribute lavishly. But nothing happened. After months of solicitation, we failed to turn up with even a cent. What could we do next?

In the late spring of 1938, I had drafted what are now the first two chapters of the book *Alcoholics Anonymous*. Mimeographed copies of these were used as part of the prospectus for our futile fund-raising operation. At Foundation meetings, then held nearly every month, our nonalcoholic friends commiserated on our lack of success. About half of the $5,000 Mr. Rockefeller advanced had been used to raise the mortgage on Dr. Bob's home. The rest of it, divided between us, would of course soon be exhausted. The outlook was certainly bleak.

Then Frank Amos remembered his old-time friend, Eugene Exman, religious editor at *Harper's*. He sent me to *Harper's* and I showed Mr. Exman two chapters of our proposed book. To my delight, Mr. Exman was impressed. He suggested that *Harper's* might advance me $1,500 in royalties to finish the job. Broke as we then were, that $1,500 looked like a pile of money.

Nevertheless our enthusiasm for this proposal quickly waned. With the book finished, we would be $1,500 in debt to *Harper's*. And if, as we hoped, AA then got a lot of publicity, how could we possibly hire the help to answer the flood of inquiries — maybe thousands!

There was another problem, too, a serious one. If our AA Book became the basic text for Alcoholics Anonymous, its ownership would be in other hands. It was evident that our Society ought to own and publish its own literature. No publisher, however good, ought to own our best asset.

Yet the moment this idea was broached, opposition rose on all sides. We were told that amateurs should never go into the publishing business. They almost never succeeded, it was claimed. But a few of us continued to think otherwise. We had discovered that the printing cost of a book is only a fraction of its retail price. If our Society grew, so would the book sales. With such a big profit margin, real money would surely come in. (Of course we conveniently forgot all the other heavy costs of book production and distribution!) So went the debate. But the opposition lost out because the Foundation had no money and wasn't likely to get any, that we could see. That was the clincher.

So two of us went ahead. A friend and I bought a pad of blank stock certificates and wrote on them, "Works Publishing, par value $25." My friend Hank P. and I then offered shares in the new book company to alcoholics and their friends in New York. They just laughed at us. Who would buy stock, they said, in a book not yet written!

Somehow, these timid buyers had to be persuaded, so we went to the *Reader's Digest* and told the managing editor the story of our budding Society and its proposed book. He liked the notion very much and promised that in the spring of 1939, when we thought that the book would be ready, the *Digest* would print a piece about AA, of course mentioning the new book.

This was the sales argument we needed. With a plug like this, the proposed volume would sell by carloads. How could we miss? The New York alcoholics and their friends promptly changed their minds about Works Publishing stock. They began to buy it, mostly on installments. Our biggest subscriber put in $300. In the end we scraped up forty-nine contributors. They came up with about $4,500 over the next nine months. We also got a loan of $2,500 from Charles B. Towns, proprietor of the hospital where I had often gone. This kept friend Hank, myself, and a secretary named Ruth going until the job was finished.

Ruth typed away as I slowly dictated the chapters of the text for the new book. Fierce argument over these drafts and what ought to go into them featured New York and Akron Group meetings for months on end. I became much more of an umpire than I ever was an author. Meanwhile, the alcoholics at Akron, New York, and a couple at Cleveland, began writing their personal stories — twenty-eight in all. Out west, Dr. Bob was greatly helped in assembling the tales by a newspaperman member, and here in New York, Hank and I kept prodding the amateur writers on.

When the book project neared completion, we visited the managing editor of the *Digest* and asked for the promised article. He gave us a blank look, scarcely remembering who we were. Then the blow fell. He told how months before he had put our proposition to the *Digest* editorial board and how it had been turned down flat. With profuse apologies, he admitted he'd plumb forgot to let us know anything about it. This was a crusher.

Meanwhile, we had optimistically ordered 5,000 copies of the new book, largely on a shoestring. The printer had relied on the *Reader's Digest,* too. Soon there would be 5,000 books in his warehouse and no customers.

The book finally appeared in April, 1939. We got the *New York Times* to do a review and Dr. Harry Emerson Fosdick supplied us with another really good one, but nothing happened. The book simply didn't sell. We were in debt up to our ears. The sheriff appeared at the Newark office where we had been working, and the landlord sold the house where Lois and I lived. She and I were dumped into the street and then onto the charity of AA friends. We thought the printer, the Cornwall Press, might take over the book. But Edward Blackwell, the president, would have none of that. He continued to have faith in us, quite inexplicably. But certain of the alcoholic stock subscribers didn't share his faith. Sometimes they used strong words, not in the least complimentary. Such was the sorry state of our publishing venture.

How we got through the summer of 1939, I'll never quite know. Hank had to get a job. The faithful Ruth accepted shares in the defunct book company as pay. One AA friend supplied us with his summer camp, another with a car. We canvassed magazine publishers in a strenuous effort to get something printed about our Society and its new book.

The first break came in September 1939. *Liberty Magazine,* then headed by our great friend-to-be Fulton Oursler, carried a piece called "Alcoholics and God," written by one Morris Markey. There was an instant response. About 800 letters from alcoholics and their families poured in. Ruth wrote every one of them, enclosing a leaflet about the new book *Alcoholics Anonymous*. Slowly the book began to sell. Then the Cleveland *Plain Dealer* ran a series of pieces about Alcoholics Anonymous. At once, the Cleveland groups mushroomed from a score into many hundreds of members. More books sold. Thus we inched and squeezed our way through that perilous year.

We hadn't heard a thing from Mr. Rockefeller since early 1938. But in February of 1940, he put in a dramatic appearance. His friend, Mr. Richardson, came to a trustees' meeting, smiling broadly. Mr. Rockefeller, he said, wanted to give Alcoholics Anonymous a dinner. The invitation list showed an imposing collection of notables. We figured them to be collectively worth at least a billion dollars. Mr. Richardson told how John D., Jr. had been watching our progress with deep satisfaction and now wanted to lend a hand. Our money troubles were over — so we thought.

The dinner came off the following month at New York's Union League Club. Dr. Harry Emerson Fosdick spoke in praise of us and so did Dr. Foster Kennedy, the eminent neurologist. Then Dr. Bob and I briefed the audience on AA; Akron and New York alcoholics scattered among the notables at the tables responded to questions. The gathering showed a rising warmth and interest. This was it, we thought; our money problems were solved.

To speak for his father, who was ill, Mr. Nelson Rockefeller then rose to his feet. His father was very glad, he said, that those at the dinner had seen the promising beginning of the new Society of Alcoholics Anonymous. Seldom, Nelson continued, had his father shown more interest in anything. But obviously since AA was a work of pure goodwill, one man carrying the good news to the next, little or no money would be required. At this sally, our spirits fell. When Mr. Nelson Rockefeller had finished, the whole billion dollars worth of capitalists got up and walked out, leaving not a dollar behind them.

Next day, Mr. Rockefeller wrote to all those who had attended and even to those who had not. Again he reiterated his complete confidence and high interest. Once more he insisted that little or no money was needed. Then at the very end of his letter, he casually remarked that he was giving Alcoholics Anonymous $1,000!

When the public read the press stories about Mr. Rockefeller's dinner, many rushed to the bookstores to buy the book *Alcoholics Anonymous*. The Foundation trustees solicited the dinner guests for contributions. Knowing the size of Mr. Rockefeller's gift, they acted accordingly. About $3,000 came in, a donation which, as things turned out, we solicited and received each year for just four years more.

Much later we realized what Mr. Rockefeller had really done for us. At risk of personal ridicule, he had stood up before the whole world to put in a plug for a tiny Society of struggling alcoholics. For these unknowns, he'd gone way out on a limb. Wisely sparing of his money, he had given freely of himself. Then and there John D. Rockefeller saved us from the perils of property management and professionalism. He couldn't have done more.

As a result, AA's 1940 membership jumped sharply to about 2,000 at the year's end. Dr. Bob and I each began to receive $30 a week out of the dinner contributions. This eased us greatly. Lois and I went to live in a tiny room at AA's number one clubhouse, 334½ West 24th Street in New York.

Best of all, the increased book sales had made a national Headquarters possible. We moved from 75 William Street, Newark, New Jersey, where the AA book had been written, to 30 Vesey Street, just north of the Wall Street district of New York. We took a modest two-room office right opposite the downtown Church Street Annex Post Office. There the famous Box 658 was ready and waiting to receive the thousands of frantic inquiries that would presently come into it. At this point, Ruth Hock became AA's first national secretary and I turned into a sort of Headquarters handyman.

Through the whole of 1940, book sales were the sole support of the struggling New York office. Every cent of these earnings went to pay for AA work done there. All requests for help were answered with warm personal letters. When alcoholics or their families showed continued interest, we kept on writing. Aided by such letters and the book *Alcoholics Anonymous,* new AA groups began to take form.

More importantly, we had lists of prospects in many cities and towns of the United States and Canada. We turned these lists over to AA traveling businessmen, members of already established groups. With these traveling couriers, we corresponded constantly and they started still more groups. For the further benefit of these travelers, we put out a group directory.

Then came an unexpected activity. Because the newborn groups saw only a little of their traveling sponsors, they turned to the New York office for help with their innumerable troubles. By mail we retailed the experience of the older centers on to them. A little later, as we shall see, this became a major activity.

Meanwhile, some of the stockholders in the book company, Works

Publishing, began to get restive. All the book profits, they complained, were going for AA work in the office. When, if ever, were they going to get their money back? We had to find a way, too, of paying Mr. Towns his $2,500. We also saw that the book *Alcoholics Anonymous* should now become the property of AA as a whole. At the moment, it was owned one-third by the forty-nine subscribers, one-third by my friend Hank, and the remainder by me.

As a first step, we had the book company, Works Publishing, audited and legally incorporated. Hank and I donated our shares in it to the Alcoholic Foundation. This was the stock that we had taken for services rendered. But the forty-nine other subscribers had put in real money. They, and Mr. Towns, would have to be paid cash. But where on earth could we get the money?

The help we needed turned up in the person of Mr. A. LeRoy Chipman. Also a friend and associate of Mr. John D. Rockefeller, he had recently been made a trustee of the Foundation. He persuaded Mr. Rockefeller, two of his sons, and some of the dinner guests to loan the Foundation $8,000. This promptly paid off Mr. Charles B. Towns, settled some incidental debts, and fully reimbursed the forty-nine original subscribers at par. They then turned their shares in to the Foundation. Two years later, the book *Alcoholics Anonymous* had done so well that we were able to pay off this whole loan. Impressed with this considerable show of financial responsibility, Mr. Rockefeller, his sons, and some of the 1940 dinner guests gave half the money they'd lent us back to the Foundation.

These were the transactions that put the book *Alcoholics Anonymous* in trust for our whole Society. Through its Foundation, AA now owned its basic textbook, subject only to royalties payable to Dr. Bob and me. Since the book income was still the sole support of our Headquarters, the trustees quite naturally assumed the management of the AA office at Vesey Street. AA's structure of world service had even then commenced to take on form and substance.

The spring of 1941 brought us a ten strike. The *Saturday Evening Post* decided to do a piece about Alcoholics Anonymous. It assigned its star writer, Jack Alexander, to the job. Having just done an article on the Jersey rackets, Jack approached us somewhat tongue-in-cheek. But he soon became an AA "convert," even though he wasn't an alcoholic. Working early and late, he spent a whole month with us. Dr. Bob and I and elders of the early groups at Akron, New York, Cleveland, Philadelphia, and Chicago spent uncounted hours with him. When he could feel

AA in the very marrow of his bones, he proceeded to write the piece that rocked drunks and their families all over the nation. It was the lead story in the *Post* of March l, 1941.

Came then the deluge. Frantic appeals from alcoholics and their families — six thousand of them — hit the New York office, PO Box 658. At first, we pawed at random through the mass of letters, laughing and crying by turns. How could this heart-breaking mail be answered? It was a cinch that Ruth and I could never do it alone. Form letters wouldn't be enough. Every single one must have an understanding personal reply.

So volunteers with typewriters came to New York's old 24th Street Club. They knew nothing of selling AA by mail, and naturally enough, they weakened in the face of the avalanche. Nothing but full-time paid help could possibly meet this emergency. Yet the AA book income would never pay the bill. Again — what to use for money?

Maybe the AA groups themselves would help. Though we'd never asked anything of them before, this was surely their business, if it was anybody's. An enormous Twelfth Step job had to be done and done quickly. These appeals must never hit the wastebasket. Money we must have.

So we told the groups the story and they responded. The measuring stick for *voluntary contributions* was then set at $1.00 per member per year. The trustees of the Foundation agreed to look after these funds, placing them in a special bank account, earmarking them for AA office work only. While the first returns weren't up to full expectations, they proved to be enough. The AA office took on two full-time workers, and weeks later we caught up.

But this was only a starter. Soon the pins on our office wall map showed AA groups springing up like mushrooms. Most of them had no experienced guidance whatever. Their worries and problems were endless. Moochers mooched, lonely hearts pined, committees quarreled, new clubs had unheard-of headaches, orators held forth, groups split wide open, members turned professional, selling AA by the copy, sometimes whole groups got drunk, local public relations went haywire — such was our truly frightening experience.

Then the amazing story got around that the Foundation, the New York office, and the book *Alcoholics Anonymous* were nothing but another racket for which John D. Rockefeller had foolishly fallen. This was just about the limit.

We had thought we'd proved that AA could sober up alcoholics, but we were certainly a long way from proving that alcoholics could work together or even stay sober under these new and fantastic conditions.

How could AA stay whole, and how could it ever function? Those were the anxious questions of our adolescence. It was to take another ten years of experience to provide the sure answers that we have today.

How AA's World Services Grew
Part II

June 1955

We had started the year 1941 with 2,000 members, but we finished with 8,000. This was the measure of the great impact of the *Saturday Evening Post* piece. But this was only the beginning of uncounted thousands of pleas for help from individuals and from growing groups all over the world that have continued to flow into general service Headquarters to this day.

This phenomenal expansion brought another problem, a very important one. The national spotlight now being on us, we had to begin dealing with the public on a large scale. Public illwill could stunt our growth, even bring it to a standstill. But enthusiastic public confidence could swell our ranks to numbers of which we had only dreamed before. The *Post* piece had proved this. It was not only a big problem, it was a delicate one. Blunders that aroused prejudice could cost lives. A carefully thought out public relations policy had to be formed and put into operation.

Of highest importance would be our relations with medicine and with religion. Under no circumstances must we get into competition with either. If we appeared to be a new religious sect, we'd certainly be done for. And if we moved into the medical field, as such, the result would be the same. So we began to emphasize heavily the fact that AA was *a way of life* that conflicted with no one's religious belief. We told the doctors how much we needed hospitalization, and we urged upon psychiatrists and drying-out places the advantages of cooperating with us. At all times, religion would be the province of clergymen, and the practice of medicine would be for doctors. As laymen, we were only supplying a much-needed missing link.

Maintained over the years since, these attitudes have brought heart-warming results. Today we have the unqualified support of nearly every religious denomination. Most medical practitioners who really understand AA send their alcoholic patients to us. AA members frequently speak before religious gatherings and medical societies. Likewise, the men of medicine and religion are often seen at AA's large open meetings.

Important as they are, medicine and religion proved to be only a fraction of the total public relations field.

How could we best cooperate with press, radio, motion pictures, and more recently, television? How would we deal with employers who wanted special help? What would be the right attitude toward the fields of education, research, and rehabilitation, private and public? What would we say to prisons and hospitals that wanted AA groups within their walls? What were we to say to AAs who went into some of these fields and were tempted to capitalize on the AA name publicly for advertising or fund-raising? What would we say or do if AA were ever publicly exploited, defamed, or attacked by outsiders? Right answers and workable solutions to all these and many more such problems would have to be found or else AA would suffer.

Finding the right answers to all these public relations puzzlers has been a long process. After much trial and error, sometimes punctuated by painful mistakes, the attitudes and practices that would work best for us emerged. The important ones can today be seen in the AA Traditions. One hundred percent anonymity at the public level, no use of the AA name for the benefit of other causes however worthy, no endorsements or alliances, one single purpose for Alcoholics Anonymous, no professionalism, public relations by the principle of attraction rather than promotion — these were some of the hard-learned lessons.

Thus, our board of trustees and the Headquarters office became the focal point around which the AA Traditions were formed. By 1945, order had come out of what had been a chaotic public relations situation. On all sides, the leadership of our Society asked for the experience and guidance of the New York office in these matters. So much success attended these efforts that the average AA member has always taken our excellent public relations record for granted. That was natural since these services were largely invisible to him. Nevertheless, this unseen public relations activity has surely been responsible for much of AA's unbelievable growth.

Thus far in our service story, we have seen the Foundation, the AA Book, the development of pamphlet literature, the answered mass of pleas for help, the satisfied need of groups for counsel on their problems, the beginning of our wonderful relations with the public, all becoming part of a growing service to the whole world of AA. At last, our Society really began to function *as a whole.*

But the 1941-1945 period brought still more developments of significance. The Vesey Street office was moved to 415 Lexington Avenue, just opposite the famed Grand Central Terminal. Our new Post Office Box became 459, Grand Central Annex, New York. We made this move because the need for serving the many AA travelers through New York had become urgent. The moment we located near Grand Central, we were besieged with visitors who, for the first time, began to see Alcoholics Anonymous as a vision for the whole globe. These were only the vanguard of thousands of AAs, their families, their friends, their clergy, their doctors, and their employers who have since visited the New York Headquarters.

Leaving the imprint of her devotion upon our Society for all time, Ruth had left, in 1941, to be married. She was followed at the office by Bobbie B., one whose immense industry was to acquaint her with uncounted thousands of AAs during the next ten years. Hers was to be a signal service in the exciting time of AA's adolescence, when no one could be sure whether we could function or even hang together at all.

The expansion of Alcoholics Anonymous soon became nothing less than staggering. Reaching out into Canada, the U.S. possessions, and numbers of foreign lands, we got under full swing. This foreign development brought us a whole new set of dilemmas to solve. Each new beachhead had to go through its flying blind and its pioneering period just as we had done in the United States. We ran into language barriers, so more and more of our literature was translated into other tongues.

Then too, our foreign friends raised new and special doubts. Maybe AA was just a Yankee gadget that would be no good for Ireland, England, Holland, Scandinavia, Australia, and the Pacific. Since their countries were so different, the alcoholics must be different too. Would AA work in their cultures, they asked.

Again, we resorted to heavy correspondence. Sometimes we were helped by American members who could translate for us. We searched out and briefed AA travelers going abroad. By these means, we gradually made some headway. But it was long indeed before we knew that AA could surely cross all barriers of distance, race, creed, or language. Nevertheless, the AA map shows us today in fifty-two countries and U.S. possessions. This is answer enough. We now know it is only a question of time when every alcoholic in the world will have as good a chance to stay alive and happy as we have had here in America. Serving the foreign groups has therefore become a major activity, though we've scarcely scratched the total problem so far. If AA's Headquarters had never done anything else, this effort alone is worth many times its cost.

Since AA was growing so fast, Headquarters had to grow too. The group contributions and our bulging literature sales soon demanded a full-time bookkeeper. Letter and Kardex files began to appear in rows. The group directory began to look like a suburban telephone book. More alcoholic staff members were engaged. As they divided the work among them, departments began to be created. Today's office has a good many — groups, foreign and public relations, AA Conference and office management, mailing, packing, accounting, stenographic, and special service to prisons and hospitals.

Happily, though, the office did not have to grow as fast as AA did. The bill would never have been paid if it had. AA was getting so big that we couldn't possibly educate all its members on what we were doing. Therefore, many groups failed to help us at all. Less than half of them contributed anything. We had constant deficits which, luckily, could be plugged up with money from the sale of the Big Book, *Alcoholics Anonymous.* That book was not only saving alcoholics, it repeatedly saved the Headquarters too!

The year 1944 unfolded another development of immense value. Down in Greenwich Village, probably in an attic, a few literary, news-minded AAs began to issue a monthly publication. They called it "The Grapevine." It was by no means the first local AA bulletin or magazine. But from the start, it was such a fine job that it caught on nationally. After a time, it became the mirror of AA thought and action, countrywide. It was a magic carpet on which all of us could travel from one distant AA outpost to another. It became a wonderful exchange of our current thought and experience.

But the Grapevine founders, after a while, discovered they had a bear by the tail. It was always fun to get in the material and edit the pieces. But licking all those postage stamps and mailing thousands of copies became impossible for them.

So the Grapeviners came to the Foundation and asked that we take over. The trustees inquired of the groups if they would like to make the Grapevine their national magazine. The answer came back an emphatic "Yes." Forthwith, the journal was incorporated as The AA Grapevine, Inc. Two Foundation trustees were then seated on its five-man board, along with the editors. Funds from the Foundation reserve took up a mounting deficit and, of course, the necessary special workers were hired. But the editors and their successors have continued to serve as volunteers without pay to this day. In ten years, the subscriptions, coming from all over the world, jumped to 30,000. In this fashion, still another Headquarters world service was born and has grown.

As early as 1945, mediating and giving suggestions by mail for the solution of group problems had put a tremendous volume of work on Headquarters. With most of the metropolitan AA centers, correspondence files had grown six inches thick. Seemingly, every contestant in every group argument at every point of the compass wrote us in this period.

It was chiefly from this correspondence, and from our mounting public relations activity, that the basic ideas for the Traditions of Alcoholics Anonymous came. In late 1945, a good AA friend suggested that all this mass of experience might be codified into a set of general principles: principles simply stated which could offer tested solutions to all of AA's problems of living and working together and of relating our Society to the world outside. If we had become sure enough of where we stood on such matters as membership, group autonomy, singleness of purpose, nonendorsement of other enterprises, professionalism, public controversy, and anonymity in its several aspects, then such a code of principles could be written. Such a traditional code could not, of course, ever become rule or law. But it could act as a sure guide for our trustees, Headquarters people and, most especially, for AA groups with bad growing pains. Being at the center of things, we of the Headquarters would have to do the job. Aided by my helpers there, I set to work. The Traditions of Alcoholics Anonymous which resulted were first published in the so-called "long form" in the AA Grapevine of April 1946. Then I wrote some more pieces explaining the Traditions in detail. These came out in later issues of the Grapevine.

Meanwhile, at the Foundation, we had taken another significant action that was forthwith imbedded in these Traditions. In 1945, we had written Mr. Rockefeller and the 1940 dinner guests that we would no longer need their financial help. Book royalties would look after Dr. Bob and me; group contributions would pay the General Office expenses. Since that day when we declared for self-support, the AA Headquarters has steadily refused outside contributions.

The first reception of the Traditions was interesting and amusing. The reaction was mixed, to say the least. Only groups in dire trouble took them seriously. From some quarters there was violent reaction, especially from groups that had long lists of "protective" rules and regulations. There was much apathetic indifference. Several of our "intellectual" members cried loudly that the Traditions reflected nothing more than the sum of my own hopes and fears for Alcoholics Anonymous.

Therefore I began to travel and talk a lot about the new Traditions. People were at first politely attentive, though it must be confessed that some did go to sleep during my early harangues. But after a while, I got letters containing sentiments like this: "Bill, we'd love to have you come and speak. Do tell us where you used to hide your bottles and all about that big, hot-flash spiritual experience of yours. But for Heaven's sake, please don't talk any more about those damned Traditions!"

But time presently changed all that. Only five years later, several thousand AA members, meeting at the 1950 Cleveland Convention, declared that AA's Traditions, by then stated in the now familiar short form, constituted the platform upon which our Fellowship could best function and hold together in unity for all time to come. They saw that the Twelve Traditions were going to be as necessary to the life of our Society as the Twelve Steps were to the life of each member. The AA Traditions were, the Cleveland Convention thought, the key to the unity, the function, and even the survival of us all.

Of course, I realized that I had not been the actual author of the Traditions. I had merely mirrored principles which had already been hammered out on thousands of anvils of AA group experience. It was clear too that AA's general Headquarters, its trustees, and its staff had made the forging of these vital principles possible. Had there been no AA Headquarters to bring our problems into focus, the Twelve Traditions of Alcoholics Anonymous could never have been written.

By this time, AA had found still more favor in the world of medicine. Two of the great medical associations of America did an unprecedented thing. In the year 1944, the Medical Society of the State of New York invited me to read a paper at its annual meeting. Following the reading, three of the many physicians present stood up and gave their highest endorsement. These were Dr. Harry Tiebout, AA's best friend in the psychiatric profession, Dr. Kirby Collier, also a psychiatrist friend and an early advocate of AA, and Dr. Foster Kennedy, the world-renowned neurologist. The Medical Society itself then went still further. They permitted us to print my paper and the recommendations of these three doctors in pamphlet form. Very large numbers of this pamphlet have since been distributed all over the world, carrying the assurance to doctors everywhere that AA is medically sound.

In 1949, the American Psychiatric Association did exactly the same thing. I read a paper at its annual meeting in Montreal. The paper was reprinted in the *American Journal of Psychiatry*, and we were permitted to put it in pamphlet form under the title "The Society of Alcoholics Anonymous." This greatly increased our standing with the psychiatric profession everywhere. These medical papers have served the foreign groups especially well, saving them the years of time that were required here in America to persuade physicians of AA's worth.

While on the topic of medicine, the part Headquarters has played in the field of hospitalization ought to be reviewed.

As all of us know, many hospitals have been reluctant to take us in for the short periods of treatment we usually need to grant our sponsors the necessary visiting privileges, and to cooperate with our area intergroup associations.

During the 1940s, two hospitals did meet all these urgent needs and afforded shining examples of how medicine and AA could cooperate. At St. Thomas Hospital at Akron, Dr. Bob, the wonderful Sister Ignatia, and the hospital's staff presided over an alcoholic ward that had ministered to 5,000 alcoholics by the time Dr. Bob passed away in 1950. At New York, Knickerbocker Hospital provided a ward under the care of our first friend in medicine, Dr. William Duncan Silkworth, where he was assisted by a redheaded AA nurse known as Teddy.

By 1954, 10,000 alcoholics had been referred to Knickerbocker by the New York Intergroup and had passed through this ward, the majority on their road to freedom. It was in these two hospitals and by these pioneering people that the best techniques of combining medicine and AA were worked out.

Since proper hospitalization was, and still is, one of AA's greatest problems, the New York Headquarters has retailed this early hospital experience, along with the many subsequent developments and ramifications, to groups all over the world — still another very vital service.

Meantime, too, the great tide of public approval continued to sweep in. Nothing contributed so much to this as did our friends of the press, radio and, in recent times, television. Long since, the Headquarters office had subscribed to several clipping services. Magazine articles and a never ending deluge of news stories about us continued to feed the Headquarters scrapbooks. Writers asked us to check their manuscripts; members were helped to appear anonymously on radio and TV programs. Hollywood wanted to do motion pictures. Making arrangements for public relations became more than ever a primary effort of the New York Office. How many lives all this saved, how many years of misery were averted for thousands of alcoholics and their families, only God knows.

About this time a serious threat to our longtime welfare made its appearance. Usually meaning well, members began breaking their anonymity all over the place. Sometimes they wanted to use the AA name to advertise and help other causes. Others just wanted their names and pictures in the papers. Being photographed with the governor would really help AA, they thought. (I'd earlier been guilty of this, too.) But at last we saw the appalling risk to AA if all our power-drivers got loose at the public level. Already scores of them were doing it.

So Headquarters got to work. We wrote remonstrances, kind ones of course, to every breaker. Then about every two years, we sent letters to nearly all press and radio outlets, explaining why AAs shouldn't break their anonymity before the public. Nor, we added, did AA solicit money: We paid our own bills.

In a few years the public anonymity breakers were squeezed down to a handful; thus another valuable Headquarters service had gone into action.

To maintain all these ever lengthening service lifelines, the office had to go on expanding. In 1950, we moved to 141 East Forty-Fourth Street, still close to Grand Central. Today, it has the "Do It Now" Henry G., as part-time manager, and the five fine staff members, Helen, Lib, Marian, Eve, and Ann have been seen and heard by thousands on speaking trips, often requested by large regional meetings. On its service staff, twelve nonalcoholics sparked by Grace and Dennis look after the office routines of bookkeeping, filing, and stenography. The enthusiastic receptionist Dolores presides over the outer office. There the visitor sees the walls covered with sectional maps showing the worldwide stretch of our Fellowship. On a table stands a Winged Victory, symbol of the noted Lasker Award given to AA by the American Public Health Association in 1951.

The editorial offices of the Grapevine are on the same floor. Here, volunteer editors headed by Don G. meet with a full-time managing editor, Louise, and her assistant Sarah, to hit the monthly deadline. Further downtown, where rents are cheaper, there is a large floor space where Kitty and her staff look after Grapevine's 30,000 subscribers and their needs — as well as their complaints!

Three blocks away from the main office, we have a good-sized loft space where all our shipping and mailing is done. Six busy young lads do nothing but this. Last year, they shipped about 40,000 books, hundreds of thousands of pamphlets, many of these newly designed and brought out. They mailed about 30,000 letters and bulletins and did huge quantities of mimeographing. Like our three other offices, this place has the best of modern equipment — and needs it!

Down one side of the long packing room, there are shelves reaching to the ceiling. On these can be found, boxed up, tons of the old files of our Headquarters, going clear back to the old days at Vesey Street. The whole world story of AA is hidden in these boxes, waiting only to be dug out. In fact, we have just begun this two-year job. In a partitioned-off corner office near those files, I now have two tireless assistants, Ed and Nell, researching the history of Alcoholics Anonymous. I hope the day will come when I shall be able to write it. In any case it is now sure that the story of AA can never become distorted. Such is our newest vital service.

Moneywise, our present array of services may look like big business to some. But when we think of the size and reach of AA today, that isn't true at all. In 1940, for example, we had one paid worker to every 1,000 AAs; in 1947, one paid worker to every 3,000 AAs. Today, one paid Headquarters worker serves 6,000 AAs. It therefore seems sure that we shall never be burdened with a bureaucratic and expensive service setup.

Here's another illustration of how really small, physically and financially, our Headquarters world operation is. An AA friend of mine owns a garage, filling station, and a small car agency in a suburban town. His building is a hundred feet long and fifty feet wide, about the same total floor space that we have at Headquarters. His showroom holds only two cars for exhibit. His mechanics do repairs out back, and in front stand four gas pumps. This is hardly big business.

Yet my friend tells me that on car sales, repairs, gas and oil, his business takes in and pays out more money yearly than AA's whole world Headquarters, the AA Grapevine, AA Publishing, and the AA General Service Office all put together.

Therefore, our Headquarters is hardly big business either. My friend's garage serves a small community; but AA's Headquarters serves 150,000 members and nearly 6,000 groups. And these services, well maintained, will continue to make the difference between sickness and health, even life or death, to uncounted alcoholics and their families who haven't yet found AA. So let's now have an end to all that talk of big expense and big business at the New York Headquarters!

When we first opened for business at Vesey Street, $1 per member per year was required to do the overall job. But at that time, a dollar was a dollar. Today, a dollar is only fifty cents. If AA's present membership actually sent us a dollar apiece every year, we would still have enough funds to run our Headquarters in spite of the watered dollar. And we could pay all expenses of the General Service Conference besides. But we still have to ask our contributing groups to give *two dollars per member per year* for the distressing reason that only about half of AA's groups give their world Headquarters any support whatever. In fact, group voluntary contributions have fully paid office expenses in only five years out of the last fifteen. That Headquarters reserve of "book money" has had to foot the ten deficits. We have grown so fast that the average member has lost touch and does not understand his world Headquarters and what it does. So I deeply hope that this picture of mine, plus the great work the Conference delegates and committee members are now doing, will be graphic enough to arouse in noncontributors a continuing desire to help. Indeed, I'm certain that it will.

Until 1951 our Headquarters was constantly overhung with even a greater threat to its existence. While this danger still loomed, and if the problem it posed wasn't solved, our whole world service structure might someday wind up in complete collapse.

The danger was this: During our infancy and adolescence, the board of trustees, all friends of Dr. Bob's and mine, had been entirely responsible for the conduct of AA's services — services which had accounted for at least half the size of Alcoholics Anonymous and for much of its unity. As early as 1945, some of us felt that our virtually unknown board of trustees had to be securely linked to AA. None but a trifling fraction of our membership even knew who their trustees were. The main linkage of Headquarters to the movement was through Dr. Bob and me, and we were perishable. The board of trustees had become an isolated island in the middle of a Fellowship sprawled through fifty-two countries. Hence, we began to debate the desirability of some sort of an advisory board of AAs. Or, maybe we needed a Conference of larger numbers elected by AA itself; people who would inspect Headquarters yearly, a body to whom the trustees could become responsible, a guiding conscience of our whole world effort.

But the objections to this were persistent and nothing happened for several years. Such a venture, it was said, would be expensive. And worse still, it might plunge AA into disruptive political activity when Conference delegates were elected. These objections had considerable merit. Therefore, the whole project hung fire until about 1948. But by this time, group contributions nowhere near supported the growing AA office. The Grapevine was losing $1,000 a month, and voluntary contributions for office expenses were in the frightening arrears of $2,000 a month.

Then Dr. Bob fell ill, mortally ill. Finally, in 1950, spurred on by the relentless logic of the situation, the trustees authorized Dr. Bob and me to devise the plan with which this booklet deals. It was a plan for a General Service Conference of AA, a plan by which our Society could assume full and permanent responsibility for the conduct of its most vital affairs.

What Is the Third Legacy?

July 1955

Our Twelfth Step — carrying the message — is the basic service that AA's Fellowship gives; this is our principal aim and the main reason for our existence. Therefore, AA is more than a set of principles; it is a Society of alcoholics *in action*. We must carry the message, else we ourselves can wither and those who haven't been given the truth will die.

Hence, an AA service is *anything whatever* that helps us to reach a fellow sufferer — ranging all the way from the Twelfth Step itself to a ten-cent phone call and a cup of coffee, and to AA's General Service Headquarters for national and international action. The sum total of *all* these services is our Third Legacy.

Services include meeting places, clubs, hospitals, and intergroup offices; they mean pamphlets, books, and good publicity of almost every description. They require committees, delegates, trustees, and Conferences. And, not to be forgotten, they need voluntary money contributions.

These services, whether performed by individuals, groups, areas, or AA as a whole, are utterly vital to our existence and growth. Nor can we make AA simple by abolishing such services. We would only be asking for complication and confusion.

Concerning any given service, we therefore pose but one question: "Is this service really needed?" If it is, then maintain it we must, or fail in our mission to those who seek AA.

The most vital, yet the least understood, group of services that AA has are those which enable us to function as a whole; namely, the AA General Service Office, the AA Publishing, Inc., the AA Grapevine, Inc., and AA's board of trustees, recently renamed as the General Service Board of Alcoholics Anonymous. Our worldwide unity and much of our growth since early times is directly traceable to this cluster of life-giving activities located, since 1938, at New York.

Until 1950, these overall services were the sole function of a few old-time AAs, several nonalcoholic friends, Dr. Bob, and myself. For all the years of AA's infancy, we old-timers had been the self-appointed trustees for Alcoholics Anonymous.

At last we realized that AA had grown up; that our Fellowship was ready and able to take these responsibilities from us. There was also another urgent reason for change. Since we old-timers couldn't live forever, newer trustees would be virtually unknown to the AA groups, now spread over the whole earth. Without direct linkage to AA, future trustees couldn't possibly function alone.

This meant that we had to form a Conference representing our membership which could meet yearly with our trustees at New York and thus assume direct responsibility for the guardianship of AA Tradition and the direction of our principal service affairs. Otherwise, a virtually unknown board of trustees and our too-little-understood service Headquarters operations would someday be bound to face collapse.

Suppose, acting quite on their own, that future trustees were to make a serious blunder. Suppose, with no linkage to AA, that they tried to act for us in time of great trouble or crisis. With no direct guidance from AA as a whole, how could they do this? Collapse of our top services would then be inevitable. And if, under such conditions, our world services did fall apart, how could they ever be reconstructed?

The trustees, Dr. Bob, and I finally saw in 1950 that this appalling risk must no longer be taken. A direct linkage between ourselves and AA had to be built.

These were the conclusions that led to the formation of the General Service Conference of Alcoholics Anonymous, a body of about seventy-five elected delegates from the states and provinces of the United States and Canada. On a trial experimental basis, these delegates commenced in 1951 to sit yearly at New York with our trustees and General Service staff members.

The General Service Conference of Alcoholics Anonymous has proved itself an immense success. Its record of achievement during its four-year trial period has been completely convincing.

Therefore, we who are the old-timers of AA are now entirely ready to deliver the principal affairs of Alcoholics Anonymous into the permanent keeping of this well-tried and tested body of AA members.

Beginning, therefore, with our 20th Anniversary in 1955, the Third Legacy of World Service will henceforth be for all members of Alcoholics Anonymous to have and to hold for so long as God may wish our Society to endure.

THE CONFERENCE IS BORN

It was one thing to say that we ought to have a General Service Conference, but it was quite another to devise a plan which would bring it into successful existence. The cost of holding such a Conference was easily dismissed. Even though the outlay might be $20,000 for each yearly session, this would be only fifteen cents apiece extra for each AA member and mighty well worth it. What member wouldn't give that much to be sure that AA didn't collapse at its center in some future day of great need or crisis?

But how on earth were we going to cut down destructive politics with all its usual struggles for prestige and vainglory? How many delegates would be required and from where should they come? Arrived at New York, how could they be related to the board of trustees? What would be their actual powers and duties? Whatever the plan, it had to be sound enough to work well on the first trial. No blunders big enough to create a fiasco could be allowed.

With these several weighty considerations in mind, and with some misgivings, I commenced work on a draft of a plan, much assisted by Helen B. of the office staff.

Though the Conference might be later enlarged to include the whole world, we felt that the first delegates should come from the United States and Canada only. Each state and province might be allowed one delegate. Those containing heavy AA populations could have additional representatives. To give the Conference continuity, the delegates could be divided into panels. Panel One, elected for two years, would be invited for 1951, the first year. Panel Two, elected for two years, would be seated in 1952. Thereafter, one panel would be elected and one would be retired yearly. This would cause the Conference to rotate. The election of state and provincial committee members and delegates could take place at large centers of population within each state and province. Or, to save expense, such assemblies of group representatives could be held at annual state or provincial conventions.

But how could assemblies of group representatives choose their committee members and delegates without terrific political friction? As veterans of many a group hassle and intergroup brawl, we shivered. Then came a happy thought. We remembered that the usual election troubles were often caused by personal nominations, whether from the floor or from some committee issuing from a back room. Another main cause of trouble was to be seen in close elections, hotly contested. These nearly always left a large and discontented minority.

So we devised the scheme of choosing committee members out of group assemblies by written ballot, with no personal nominations at all. The committee would then be placed in front of the assembly, which could then elect from it the delegate to the Conference in New York. But, sure enough, this was going to be the hottest spot of all! How could we pull the inevitable election pressure down? To accomplish this, it was provided that a delegate must receive a two-thirds vote for election. If a delegate got a majority of this size, nobody could kick much. But if he or she didn't, and the election was close, what then? Well, perhaps the names of the two highest in the running, or the three officers of the committee, or even the whole committee could be put in a hat. One name would be drawn. The winner of this painless lottery would become the delegate. Since the high candidates in the running would all be good ones, we couldn't miss getting fine delegates by this method.

But when these delegates got to New York, what would they do there? We thought they would want to have real authority. So, in the charter drawn for the Conference itself, it was provided that the delegates could issue flat directions to the trustees on a two-thirds vote. And even a simple majority vote would constitute a mighty strong suggestion. It would become traditional too for the trustees, thereafter, to submit the names of all proposed board members to the Conference for confirmation. This would give the Conference an effective voice in the selection of trustees.

Along with a temporary plan for financing the Conference, we put these ideas and their detailed applications into a pamphlet called "The Third Legacy." We shipped about 50,000 of these documents to the groups and asked them to form assemblies for the election of committee members and delegates.

With Dr. Bob's approval, I stumped the country for the Third Legacy plan, talking to large AA audiences and watching assemblies select their delegates in more than two dozen states and provinces.

How well I remember that first tryout in Boston! The Irish turned out in force. To our amazement, the proceedings were as unruffled as a mill pond, even though ballot after ballot failed to get anybody a two-thirds majority for election as a delegate. The assembly finally drew lots among the whole committee, and out of the hat popped a mighty good delegate! Everybody was pleased and happy; the heat was off. If the Irish could do it without a fight, anybody could. Right there we got the first glimmer that AA had begun to move from partisan politics into true statesmanship.

Much the same thing happened at all the other stops. About a third of the delegates chosen were real old-timers. The rest were active AAs, sober four to eight years. The large majority named were chosen by a two-thirds vote, only a few of the elections being decided by lot, as Boston had. And when these few were so chosen, there was never any hard feeling. It was tremendously encouraging.

The first Conference was set for April 1951. In came the delegates. They looked over Headquarters, cellar to garret, got acquainted with the service staff, shook hands with trustees. That evening, we gave them a briefing session, under the name of "What's on your mind?" We answered scores of questions of all kinds. The delegates began to feel at home and reassured. Seeing so much quick understanding and increased confidence, our spirits rose. To a man, we sensed that something very big was happening. One strenuous Conference session followed after another. The delegates overhauled our finances with a microscope. After listening to reports from the board of trustees and from all the services, there was warm but cordial debate on many a question of AA policy. The trustees submitted several of their own serious problems for the opinion of the Conference.

Feeling that everybody was too polite, we set up something called the "Gripe Box." Nothing but excellent questions were dropped into it;

nobody was mad about anything, believe it or not!

So went session after session, morning, afternoon, and evening. The delegates handled several tough puzzlers about which we at Headquarters were in doubt, sometimes giving advice contrary to our own conclusions. In nearly every instance, we saw that they were right. Then and there they proved, as never before, that AA's Tradition Two was correct. The group conscience could safely act as the sole authority and sure guide for Alcoholics Anonymous.

Nobody present will ever forget that final session of the first Conference. We knew that the impossible had happened, that AA could never break down in the middle, that Alcoholics Anonymous was at last safe from any storm the future might bring.

And, as the delegates returned home, they carried this same conviction with them.

Realizing our need for funds and better literature circulation, some did place a little too much emphasis on this necessity; others were a little discouraged, wondering why fellow members did not take fire as they had. They forgot that they themselves had been eyewitnesses to the Conference and that their fellow alcoholics hadn't. But, both here and at home, they made an impression much greater than they knew. The interest of great numbers of AA groups commenced to deepen, something which has continued in all the four Conference years since.

In the midst of this exciting turn of affairs, the Conference agreed that the Alcoholic Foundation ought to be renamed as the General Service Board of Alcoholics Anonymous, and this was done. The word "Foundation" stood for charity, paternalism, and maybe big money. AA would have none of these; from here out we would assume full responsibility and pay our expenses ourselves.

As I watched all this grow, I became entirely sure that Alcoholics Anonymous was at last safe — even from me.

Nearly all of the last dozen years of my life have been invested in the construction of our general Headquarters. My heart is there, and always will be. AA's Headquarters seems that important to me. When, therefore, the hour comes at St. Louis for me to turn over to you this last great asset of the AA inheritance, I shall feel not a little sad that I must no longer be your Headquarters handyman. But I shall rejoice that Alcoholics Anonymous has now grown up and, through its great Conference, can confidently take its destiny by the hand.

So, my dear friends, you now have read my final accounting to you for the world services of Alcoholics Anonymous.

Guardian of AA: Our General Service Conference

April 1958

E very AA wants to make sure of his survival from alcoholism, and his own spiritual well-being afterward. This is just as it should be. He also wants to do what he can for the survival and well-being of his fellow alcoholics. Therefore he is bound to have a vital interest in the permanence and well-being of AA itself.

In his AA group, every good member feels deeply about this. He knows, once the miracle of sobriety has been received, that Providence expects all of us to work and to grow — to do our part in maintaining our blessings in full force. A perpetual miracle — with no effort or responsibility on our part — simply isn't in the cards. We all understand that the price of both personal and group survival is willingness and sacrifice, vigilance and work.

What is so true for each member and for each group must also be true for AA as a whole. Yet many of us have never given this self-evident proposition the thought it deserves. We are apt to take it for granted that AA, as a whole, will go on forever — no special attention or contribution being required of us. Save an occasional glow of pride in AA's size and reach, it is possible that half of AA's members and groups still have little active concern for the total welfare. That isn't negligence on their part at all. They simply haven't seen the need.

There are two good reasons for this. One is that AA as a whole has never run into any trouble. The other is that, until recently, a small group of AA's old-timers — acting as parents — have tended to the perils and problems of our whole Society without consulting the membership very much about such matters.

Never have we had a problem that cut clear across us. The public admires us, our friends love us. Religion and medicine are in our corner. Nobody has seriously exploited us. We have avoided public controversy. The world's political strife hasn't touched us. We haven't had even one full-sized family quarrel. While members and groups have had just about all the woe there is, AA as a whole has never had any. This is the miracle of our twenty-three years of existence.

No wonder so many truly believe that nothing can ever happen to AA itself!

That we have been so long exempt from the pains that all nations and societies must suffer is something for the deepest gratitude. But we certainly cannot presume that this benign phenomenon will last forever. For one, I do not think that it should last. We can never call ourselves "grown-up" until we have successfully met with all those temptations and problems that invariably harass every large grouping of men and women. This will be good for us — very good, I'm sure.

Someday we may have to resist all the pressure that a destruction-bent world can put upon us in this craziest and most perilous century that the human race has ever seen. As a Fellowship, we shall always need to make whatever sacrifices are necessary to insure AA's unity, service, and survival, *under any conditions whatever.* That is why I'm now writing to you about AA's General Service Conference, the guardian of our future.

Until recently, we have behaved like a still-young family. This family, like all families, has had parents. These parents have been the so-called old-timers and originators of AA. I was fortunate enough to have been one of them. Since the earliest days we parents have been more concerned with the future welfare of AA than with anything else. At local levels, we old-timers used to look after things; until very recently, Dr. Bob and I, mightily assisted by dedicated alcoholic and nonalcoholic friends, have been doing the same at national and international levels.

As parents of AA we had to see to it that our growing brood was protected against itself, and against the world outside. Very early, our family had to have principles to live by, and schooling in those principles. The good news of AA had to be spread far and wide so that we could grow in numbers as well as in quality. Such were our responsibilities.

It was in 1937 when Dr. Bob and I first began to see what we must do. We knew there would have to be an AA text of principles and methods. Other old-timers agreed. By 1939, with lots of help, we had published the Big Book, *Alcoholics Anonymous.* This ended all doubt about AA's methods. The 300,000 Big Books today in circulation constitute the platform of recovery upon which our whole Fellowship stands.

We next realized that AA would have to have publicity — lots of it, and of the right kind. We commenced work on this problem. Maybe half of today's members owe their lives and their fortunes to the telling efforts of the press and other means of communication.

From 1940 to 1950, we were beset by group problems of every sort, frightening beyond description. Out of these experiences the Twelve Traditions of AA were forged — Traditions that now protect us against ourselves and the world outside. This effort, requiring immense office correspondence and experience, finally resulted in a whole new literature dealing with AA's unity and services. Under these influences we grew solid.

The news of AA began to spread around the world, finally reaching into seventy lands. This brought a host of new problems and the need to publish AA literature in many tongues. Hospitals and prisons and Loners and men on ships also had to be reached and helped. AA's lifelines had to extend everywhere. AA needed a monthly magazine. Today, the AA Grapevine reaches 40,000 subscribers plus countless thousands of others each month.

These have been the duties and privileges of our parenthood worldwide. We did our best to protect AA so that it could grow undisturbed. Not troubling the growing family about these critical matters, we acted on the principle that "father knows best." In the early days, it was just as simple as that. It was then far too soon to throw the full weight of responsibility onto our whole Fellowship.

From the beginning, Dr. Bob and I found that we needed special help ourselves. Therefore we called upon certain dedicated nonalcoholics to give us a lift. With these men, we formed a trusteeship for Alcoholics Anonymous. It was created 'way back in 1938 and we called it the Alcoholic Foundation (since renamed the General Service Board of AA). In 1940, our trustees acquired the AA Book, assumed full responsibility for AA's general funds, its world service office, its magazine, and its public relations.

To this body of trustees — alcoholic and nonalcoholic — must go most of the credit for making our world Headquarters what it now is. I am very glad that this issue of the Grapevine carries the pictures of two of our distinguished nonalcoholic chairmen of the board, men whose steadfastness saw us through a long season of labor and peril. In the faces of Leonard Harrison and Bernard Smith you can see what these men are. And in our new history book, *AA Comes of Age,* you can read what they and others like them did for us in our pioneering time as the moving drama of AA unfolded.

During the year 1948 we workers at AA's Headquarters got a terrific jolt. Dr. Bob was stricken with a consuming and slowly fatal malady. This created a severe crisis in our affairs because it made us face up to the fact that the old-time parents of our Society weren't going to last forever.

We were filled with foreboding as we realized how insecure were the existing links between our Headquarters and the vast sprawling Fellowship that it served. There was, of course, our small board of trustees. But not one AA in a thousand could name half of them. At the Headquarters office, there were Bobbie, Ann, and Charlotte. There were Dr. Bob and myself. We few were just about the *only links* to worldwide AA!

Meanwhile thousands of our members went serenely about their business. They knew little or nothing about AA's overall problems. They vaguely supposed that God, with maybe a slight assist from Dr. Bob and me, would go right on handling them. Thus they were completely ignorant of the actual state of our affairs and of the awful potential there was for an ultimate collapse.

It was a racking dilemma. Somehow AA as such — *AA as a whole* — would have to take over the full responsibility. Without doubt the groups would have to elect numerous delegates and send them to New York each year, where they could sit with and guide the trustees. Only by so doing could the increasing isolation of the trustees from the movement itself be halted. Only such a body could take binding decisions in any future crisis.

When our scheme for a joint Conference of trustees and delegates was first proposed, a howl went up countrywide. At first it looked as though the AA family didn't want any part of this new and unexpected responsibility. To them, "AA delegates" spelled nothing but politics, controversy, and confusion. "Let's keep it simple," they cried.

But after a couple of years of agitation and education, our Fellowship clearly realized that the ultrasimplicity of the early days could be no more. Direct family responsibility there would have to be, or else AA would fold up at its very center. The erstwhile elders, fathers, and founders would have to be taken off the hook and replaced by delegates. There was no other way. The family would have to "come of age" or suffer dire penalties for the failure to do so.

So we called in some seventy-five delegates from the United States and Canada. Together with the trustees and the Headquarters and Grapevine staff, those delegates formed themselves into the General Service Conference of Alcoholics Anonymous. By then, it was 1951.

At first this was an experiment, pure and simple. If it worked it would mean that AA had truly "come of age" and could really manage its own affairs. Through its representative Conference, it could become the guardian of its own future and the protector of its own lifelines of service.

Well, our Conference did work. Its performance, God be thanked, exceeded all our expectations. At the end of its five-year experimental period, we knew that it could become a permanent part of our Fellowship.

In July of 1955, at AA's 20th Anniversary, I stood before the great St. Louis Convention. Amid a dwindling band of old-timers, and on their behalf, I delivered the destiny of AA into the hands of its chosen representatives, the General Service Conference of Alcoholics Anonymous. I cannot remember any happier day in my life. A gaping chasm had been bridged — AA was secure at last.

Some people still ask these questions: Will the AA family send to the Conference its finest delegates? Will we continue to choose able and wise trustees? Will AAs back their Conference members, their trustees, and their world Headquarters with enough funds, enough interest, and enough understanding?

For me, these are questions no longer. The history of AA shows that whenever a great need arises, that need is always met. In this respect, I'm quite sure that our history will go on repeating itself. Indeed, I can have no doubt whatever.

I think, too, that my own influence at the Headquarters should continue to lessen. Through its Conference, complete authority and responsibility is now fully vested in AA. The parent who overstays his time can only hamper the growth of his offspring. This I must not do. My proper place will soon be along the sidelines, cheering you newer ones as you carry on. Our family is now fully of age, and it should firmly remind me of that fact if I am ever again tempted to take charge.

For these all-compelling reasons, my friends, the future belongs to you. Embrace these new responsibilities eagerly, fear naught, and the grace of God will surely be yours.

Segment

2

Let's Be Friendly with Our Friends

The Psychiatrists

July 1957

It was years ago and we were making our first contacts with mental hospitals. One of them was a New Jersey institution which had paroled two alcoholics who had found AA and had stayed sober for six months. Both of them had been classed as hopeless. Despite AA's unusual methods, the hospital's psychiatrists were not a little impressed.

Forthwith, the eager AA group nearby began to bombard the hospital for visiting privileges. They wanted to bring the good news to every alkie in the place, no delays allowed. The doctors weren't so sure that this was the right idea.

They were still rather cautious, as they had plenty of reason to be.

"Well," said the AA committee, "why don't you doctors come to a meeting?" Two of the psychiatrists allowed this would be fine. They said they would go to New York's AA group the following week.

In that period I think we New Yorkers gathered in a parlor at Steinway Hall. With much delight we had heard about the proposed pilgrimage of the Jersey doctors. Meeting night finally rolled around. But in the interval, my memory had slipped a cog. I forgot all about those psychiatrists. Right after our meeting opened, the beaming AA contingent from Jersey entered the hall and slid into a back row. But even this reminder failed to jog my memory. I certainly had no reason to think that one of my life's worst embarrassments — and one of its best lessons — was just around the corner.

The meeting's first speaker told a fine story; both grim and inspiring. You could have heard a pin drop. It was simply great.

Then up got Jack. He told how he'd been a rising figure in the motion picture industry and had once earned the modest stipend of $50,000 a year. Considering his vaunted abilities, Jack had figured this to be only a starter. Then demon rum began to cut him down. His worried studio produced a psychiatrist. Grudgingly, Jack took some treatments. The results were nil and more psychiatrists were tried. But Jack's ego, his resentments, and his drinking all remained as colossal as before. He worked himself down and finally out of motion pictures — not at all a surprising development. But here he was in AA, sober for months.

However, it soon became apparent that psychiatrists were still among Jack's pet grudges. He actually blamed them for his downfall. Well knowing that two of them were in the room, he saw the chance of a lifetime. Now *he* could dish it out and *they* would have to sit there and take it!

So Jack proceeded to do a job on psychiatry and all its works. As a speaker he packed a huge wallop, and he had great talent for a cynical humor that now suited his purpose exactly. He tore his several psychiatrists apart, one by one. Then he attacked the entire profession, their theories, and their philosophies. He called them "fish worm diggers." All the while he was screamingly funny. Though his talk was nine-tenths fantasy and nonsense, it was nevertheless a real piece of showmanship. The audience was convulsed and I thought I'd never laughed so long or so much. Jack finally sat down amid big applause.

Following the meeting, the Jersey AA contingent pushed toward the platform. They looked both sick and sore, and they definitely were. Mumbling weakly, their spokesman introduced our "honored guests," the two psychiatrists!

I felt an awful sinking sensation in the region of my solar plexus. Just then Jack, obviously much pleased with himself, walked up and genially slapped one of our guests on the back. "Well, doctor," said he, "how did you like 'them apples' I just handed you!" This was the limit. I could have died of mortification.

But the two psychiatrists smilingly rolled with his punch. They insisted that it had been a wonderfully helpful meeting. After all, they declared, their profession ought to be able to stand a little ribbing now and then. To them Jack's talk had been good clean fun and very instructive.

This was an amazing demonstration of friendship and understanding. Under trying conditions these maligned gentlemen had turned the other cheek. They had met Jack's tirade with courtesy, kindness, good humor, and even gratitude. It was a lesson in patience, tolerance, and Christian charity that I hope I shall never forget.

As quickly as possible, I angled the two doctors into a corner and began my apologies. In fact I ate crow. Then one of them looked at me and said, "Think nothing of it, Bill. As you surely see, *some* alcoholics are more maladjusted than others. We understand that perfectly!"

Within a month, this very exceptional doctor opened his hospital to AA visitors and a group began to form within the walls. Ever since that time the psychiatric profession has continued to hold up AA's hands. And I venture to say that it is often their understanding and tolerance, rather than ours, which has brought about this happy state of affairs.

Two more examples: In 1949, the American Psychiatric Association asked me to read a paper on AA before their annual meeting. Going further, the psychiatrists published that paper in their official journal and permitted AA to reprint my material in pamphlet form for public consumption. This one generous act has since brought our Fellowship untold benefit. Only recently a survey was made in Los Angeles to determine how the psychiatrists in that city and county felt about AA. I'm told that they feel fine; 99 percent of them are for us!

Of course this little story has its exaggerations. Great numbers of AAs are today very friendly to psychiatry, and no doubt equally great numbers of psychiatrists who know nothing about us or who have seen only AA failures are still against us. But this is beside the point. The point that I am trying to make is that we AAs should try to be uniformly friendly under all conditions.

Now what became of my old friend Jack? Well, Jack just couldn't make it, though he tried hard. He died three years ago of alcoholism.

Perhaps real friendliness was something which Jack never came to understand.

The Physicians

August 1957

On television recently, I watched as the American Medical Association in convention installed its new president. At first thinking it might be a routine affair, I nearly switched to a "whodunit." I'm now very glad that I did not, for those doctors gave me a most memorable and moving hour.

Up got the new president to make his inauguration address. He said little of the science of medicine. To my surprise he pointed his talk — just as we often do in AA meetings — straight at the newcomers, in this case the young doctors just entering practice. He told them that no doctor, however well trained scientifically, could get far until he was able to make sick people feel that he understood them as human beings; and that every real doctor had to be possessed of the deepest dedication and faith. Such was his theme, and how he did go to town with it. He certainly "carried the message," and I saw as seldom before that we AAs certainly have no monopoly on the practice of Step Twelve.

Several citations for distinguished service were given, one of them to a layman for his outstanding work among the nation's infirm and disabled. He had proven to thousands of sufferers that they need no longer be emotionally or spiritually crippled and that some sort of useful and gainful work could always be theirs. Pointing out that self-pity is a prevalent ailment of the crippled, he quoted the Persian who had no shoes: "I wept because I had no shoes until I saw a man who had no feet!" The beaming man behind the lectern knew whereof he spoke, for he himself had no legs; he had been on artificial limbs for years. Clearly dedication, fortitude, and faith had been his reliances. It was for these things that the AMA had given him such a signal recognition.

This gathering of the doctors, so spiritually centered, set me thinking. I keenly realized that doctoring is mainly a spiritual vocation and that the vast majority of physicians really join the profession to serve their fellow human beings.

We AAs are apt to set a "triple A" rating on ourselves and our Fellowship. But when the names of certain doctors come to mind, doctors who devoted themselves to us in our pioneering time, I wonder how many of us could really match their humility and their dedication.

Take my own doctor, William D. Silkworth. In our forthcoming history book, *AA Comes of Age,* I have drawn a word portrait of him which runs in part as follows:

"As we looked back over those early scenes in New York, we saw often in the midst of them the benign little doctor who loved drunks, William Duncan Silkworth, then physician-in-chief of the Charles B. Towns Hospital in New York, and the man who we now realize was very much a founder of AA. From him we learned the nature of our illness. And he supplied us with the tools with which to puncture the toughest alcoholic ego, those shattering phrases by which he described our illness: *the obsession of the mind* that compels us to drink and *the allergy of the body* that condemns us to go mad or die. Without these indispensable passwords, AA could never have worked. Dr. Silkworth taught us how to till the black soil of hopelessness, out of which every single spiritual awakening in our Fellowship has since flowered. In December 1934 this man of science had sat humbly by my bed following my own sudden and overwhelming spiritual experience, reassuring me: 'No, Bill,' he had said, 'you are not hallucinating. Whatever you have got, you had better hang on to; it is so much better than what you had only an hour ago.' These were great words for the AAs to come! Who else could have said them?

"When I wanted to go to work with alcoholics, he led me to them right there in his hospital, risking his professional reputation.

"After six months of failure on my part to dry up any drunks, Dr. Silkworth again reminded me of Professor William James' observation that truly transforming spiritual experiences are nearly always founded on calamity and collapse. 'Stop preaching at them,' Dr. Silkworth had said, 'and give them the hard medical facts first. This may soften them up at depth so that they will be willing *to do anything* to get well. Then they may accept those moral psychology ideas of yours, and even a Higher Power.'

"Four years later, Dr. Silkworth had helped to convert Mr. Charles B. Towns, the hospital's owner, into a great AA enthusiast and had encouraged him to loan $2,500 to start preparation of the book *Alcoholics Anonymous* — a sum, by the way, which later amounted to over $4,000. Then as our only medical friend at the time, the good doctor boldly wrote the Introduction to our book, where it remains to this day and where we intend to keep it always.

"Perhaps no physician will ever give so much devoted attention to so many alcoholics as did Dr. Silkworth. It is estimated that in his lifetime he saw an amazing 40,000 of them. In the years before his death in 1951, in close cooperation with AA and our redheaded power-house nurse, Teddy, he had ministered to nearly 10,000 alcoholics at New York's Knickerbocker Hospital alone. None of those he treated will ever forget the experience, and the majority of them are sober today."

·So Dr. Silkworth "twelfth-stepped" 40,000 alcoholics. Thousands of these he patiently treated long before AA when the chance for recovery was slim. But he always had faith that one day a way out would be found. He never tired of drunks and their problems. A frail man, he never complained of fatigue. During most of his career he made only a bare living. He never sought distinction; his work was his reward. In his last years he ignored a heart condition and he died on the job — right among us drunks, and with his boots on.

Who of us in AA can match this record of Dr. Silkworth's? Who has his measure of fortitude, faith, and dedication?

So when — twenty-three years after Dr. Silkworth had treated me for the last time — I saw and heard and felt the spirit that was abroad in the great AMA meeting, I thanked God for the doctors, one of the finest groups of friends that AA can ever have.

The Clergy

September 1957

very river has a wellspring at its source. AA is like that, too. In the beginning, there was a spring which poured out of a clergyman, Dr. Samuel Shoemaker. 'Way back in 1934 he began to teach us the principles and attitudes that afterward came to full flower in AA's Twelve Steps for recovery.

If ever there was a living water for drunks, this was it. We took the cup of grace that Sam held out and we drank, not forgetting to pass it on to others. Our gratitude goes up to him whose grace ever fills that cup, and out to Sam who first offered it to us.

But rivers must have tributaries, else they cannot travel far nor grow great. The ever deepening stream of spirit on which we AAs journey to better things now has its myriad tributaries — branches which feed into the main current of the life of our whole Fellowship. The most numerous and most vital of these streams of devotion and service have always come to us from our friends in the clergy.

Let me illustrate: Few know that it was a minister who was the primary figure in forming AA's original Board of Trustees, who were to become the custodians of AA's services, worldwide. I am thinking of Willard S. Richardson, a friend and associate of the Rockefellers. In 1937 we called upon Mr. Richardson to help us find a lot of money for AA work. Instead he helped us to find ourselves. Largely because of his kindness and understanding, his devotion and his hard work, AA's first board of trustees was formed and the writing of the Big Book was begun. His was the kind of giving that had no price tag on it. What our 7,000 groups today owe "Uncle Dick" Richardson, a clergyman, only God could possibly know.

At the Rockefeller dinner meeting of 1940 another man of the cloth appeared. He was no other than Dr. Harry Emerson Fosdick. As the main speaker for the nonalcoholics present, Dr. Fosdick became the first man of religion ever to stand right up before the general public and give us a big pat on the back. I often wonder how much this generous act required of his understanding, love, and sheer nerve. Here was a small bunch of so-called "ex-drunks" — virtually unknown. I still tremble when I think how America would have rocked with mirth if two or three of us AAs had turned up plastered in the spotlight of that famous dinner! Clergyman Fosdick had gone far out on the limb for us. We shall remember this always.

Surely by hundreds, and probably by thousands, our friends in the clergy have since continued to go out on the limb. They install our meetings in their basements and social halls. Never interfering with our affairs, they sit in the back rows — explaining that they have come to AA to learn. When Sunday arrives, they preach sermons about us. They send us prospects and marvel at their progress. When we sometimes ask them to speak to us, they invariably apologize for their own ineffectiveness with alcoholics. This is humility for sure. . . too much of it, perhaps.

When it comes to patience and tolerance they are at their best. Of course they soon learn that, although sober, we AAs can sometimes be grandiose and champion rationalizers. We can also be careless and irresponsible. They listen blandly when we tell (by inference) what a superior Society we have! Once in a while they hear experiences and language at a meeting that would make practically anybody blush. But they never say a word, or bat an eye. They take the nonsense side of AA in stride, sometimes with the patience of Job. They know we are really trying to grow up, and they want to help.

This stirring and round-the-clock demonstration by our friends in religion sets many of us to thinking: "When we consider all that these priests and preachers have done for us, just what have we ever done for them?" This is a good question indeed.

Though the following isn't strictly AA business, I cannot help but report what priests and ministers have done for many of us, personally. Some AAs say, "I don't need religion, because AA *is* my religion." As a matter of fact, I used to take this tack myself.

After enjoying this simple and comfortable view for some years I finally awoke to the probability that there might be sources of spiritual teaching, wisdom, and assurance outside of AA. I recalled that preacher Sam probably had a lot to do with the vital spiritual experience that was my first gift of faith. He had also taught me principles by which I could survive and carry on. AA had provided me with the spiritual home and climate wherein I was welcome and could do useful work. This was very fine, all to the good.

Yet I finally discovered that I needed more than this. Quite rightly, AA didn't try to answer all of my questions, however important they seemed to me. Like any other adolescent, I had begun to ask myself: "Who am I?" "Where did I come from?" "What is my purpose here?" "What is the real meaning of life?" "When the undertaker gets through with me, am I still alive, or not?" "Where, if any place, do I go from here?" Neither science nor philosophy seemed able to supply me convincing answers. Naturally I began to shop about in other directions, and I think I made a little progress.

Though still rather gun-shy about clergymen and their theology I finally went back to them — the place where AA came from. If they had been able to teach me the principles on which I could recover, then perhaps they might now be able to tell me more about growth in understanding, and in belief.

Though my sobriety had come easy, the growing up business hadn't. Both emotional and spiritual growth have always been mighty difficult for me. My quest to understand myself — and better to know God and his design for me — became a matter of great urgency. The clergy, I reflected, must represent the accumulated wisdom of the ages in matters moral and theological. So I began to make friends with them — this time to listen, and not to argue.

I can happily report that one of these clergymen has turned out to be the greatest friend, teacher, and adviser that I ever expect to have. Through the years I have found in Father Ed [Dowling] much of the grace and understanding by which I can now grow, if only a little at a time. He is the finest living example of spirituality that I happen to know. He has often set my feet back on the path when otherwise I might have gone off on an indefinite dry bender. It is characteristic that he has never, in all these years, asked me to join his church.

Therefore it is with the deepest feeling that I here cast up AA's debt to the clergy: without their works for us, AA could never have been born; nearly every principle that we use came from them. Their example, their faith, and their beliefs in some part, we have appropriated and made our own. Almost literally, we AAs owe them our lives, our fortunes, and such salvation as each of us has found.

Surely, this is an infinite debt!

Press, Radio, Television

October 1957

It was the summer of 1939. A few months before, our alcoholic Fellowship, boasting all of one hundred members, had published a book we called *Alcoholics Anonymous*. But nothing else had happened. Our books, five thousand of them, were piled in the warehouse of the printer, Cornwall Press, and nary a one could be sold.

The much-hoped-for piece in the *Reader's Digest* — which might have told the public about us and the new book — had failed to materialize. Panic-stricken, we had rushed from one national magazine to another, pleading for help. But this was in vain. Works Publishing, the little company we had formed to launch the book venture, was flat broke and so was everybody else. There was seemingly no place to turn.

But Providence knew better. Just as we hit this new low, Fulton Oursler, then editor of *Liberty*, had a caller — a free-lance writer named Morris Markey. From Charlie Towns, proprietor of the hospital where I had once been such a good customer, writer Markey had received a terrific build-up on AA, which he now retailed to editor Oursler, one of the most perceptive men I have ever met. Fulton Oursler saw the possibilities in a flash. Said he, "Morris, you've got an assignment. Bring that story in here, and we will print it in September."

Such were the words of AA's first friend of the press. These words were to save the bankrupt book and they also meant that the public was to have its first view of Alcoholics Anonymous.

Just as promised, Morris Markey's article, "Alcoholics and God," was printed in *Liberty* magazine. The results were immediate and electrifying. More than eight hundred urgent pleas for help hit *Liberty*'s office. We carefully answered each one, not forgetting to enclose a book order blank. Orders soon began to come in and, helped by still more letters from our little office on Vesey Street, and by traveling AA members, new groups started up.

Other news-hawkers were not long in following the Oursler example. A month later the public-spirited editor of the Cleveland *Plain Dealer* gave writer Elrick B. Davis an assignment to cover AA and to go the limit. For days on end articles about AA in general and about AA in

Cleveland in particular were a leading feature of the *Plain Dealer.*

Alongside these articles there appeared editorial exhortations which in effect said, "AA is good and it works. Come and get it." Again the deluge. The tiny Cleveland group was swamped. But it happily survived, and in a few months its numbers had shot up into the hundreds. Alcoholics Anonymous had started the year 1939 with less than one hundred members and it finished with more than eight hundred of them.

In February 1940 we got another mighty lift, this time as the result of Mr. Rockefeller's famous dinner at which he introduced us to his own friends and held AA up for the whole world to see. Again the press did a job. This time many newspapers, including the tabloids, said good things about us and the great wire services carried the story worldwide. AA's membership jumped from eight hundred to over two thousand in twelve months.

In the spring of 1941, the same drama was reenacted on a far larger scale. Mr. Curtis Bok, owner of the *Saturday Evening Post*, saw AA at work in Philadelphia and urged his editors to select Jack Alexander to do a feature assignment. When Jack's piece hit the newsstands it brought in a Niagara-like flood of appeals for help. Two years later AA's membership stood at the ten thousand mark.

By telling our story to the American public this small band of early friends had increased AA's ranks by one-hundred-fold in the short space of four years, had made AA a national institution, and had laid the foundation upon which our Society has grown so mightily ever since.

Today the list of AA's friends in press, radio, and television is legion. At our Headquarters we subscribe to an extensive clipping service. Every week the mass of clipsheets tell us the graphic story of what these friends have said and done. It is a never ending and always growing stream of life-giving blood which they pump into our world arteries.

While word of mouth and personal contact have brought in many a newcomer, we can never forget that most of us are able to trace our chance for recovery back to our friends in communications — we read, or maybe we heard, or we saw. That is why AA now has 200,000 active members.

Sometimes we hear members complain about the press as though we were being exploited for stories and profit. They say, "Well, those writers make a good living out of story telling and the publishers make their profits. After all, what is so remarkable about that? They are only acting as they normally would."

However, most of us realize that such statements are far less than half the truth.

Practically every writer and editor of our acquaintance has gone far beyond his call to duty or his natural desire for a stirring story.

Years ago we requested all people in communications to respect the anonymity of our members. This was asking for a great deal because the average reporter couldn't imagine doing business without full names and pictures. But when we explained the "why" of our anonymity — that we dare not allow "big shot-ism" to get going among us — they saw the situation at once; and they have ever since fallen over backward to conform to our needs, despite many a temptation to publicize personally our nationally famous members. On a few occasions, such members have deliberately broken anonymity, but this has seldom been the fault of the press. As a matter of fact, editors have frequently restrained overeager AAs who wanted their membership made public.

In their continuing enthusiasm for AA many of these friends have gone still further. They have personally dedicated themselves to our cause. Jack Alexander, for instance, became a trustee for AA and greatly helped us with our literature problem, and never missed a chance to give us a boost by word and by pen.

Less well known is the relation we had with Fulton Oursler. His was a most brilliant example of personal dedication to Alcoholics Anonymous.

In 1944 it was decided that AA ought to have a monthly magazine. By this time Fulton had seen AA at work close at hand. A person well known to him had made a remarkable recovery. The moment Fulton heard of our magazine project he volunteered at once and, though never an alcoholic, he became a member of the Grapevine's editorial board and one of its founders. He went into his own pocket for organization expenses, gave advice, scanned manuscripts, and wrote a piece for one of the early issues which he called "Alcoholics Are Charming People" [Correct title: "Charming Is the Word for Alcoholics"]. We afterward joshed him about this title. Grinning, he used to say that the title should have been "*Some* Alcoholics Are Charming People"!

In the years afterward I came to know friend Fulton very well. A busier man I have never seen. No matter when he went to bed, nothing short of pneumonia could keep him from being at his desk at five AM, where he wrote until eleven. But his day had then only begun; his countless friends and activities kept him going far into the evening, and I was the one who sometimes kept him up until midnight.

AA was then in the storms of its adolescence. Our Headquarters was just taking on its shape and its responsibility. We needed advice, especially about public relations, and it was to Fulton that I frequently went. It was in this period that Fulton became a senior editor of the *Reader's Digest*, where his helpfulness to us was soon reflected in the wide coverage they began to give us.

Then came the time when we wanted Fulton as a trustee for AA. Knowing his immense burden of work, I was most reluctant to ask him. But I needn't have felt that way, for when I popped the question, his face lit up and he said, "Why, certainly! When do I begin?" Fulton couldn't get to all our meetings, but he was always on tap. I remember once breaking into his busy hours with a request that he help us out in Hollywood where we were in a jam with a motion picture producer. He instantly dropped his work, and got on the long-distance phone. Within an hour he called me back to say that everything was settled, that we need worry no more.

A few months before he died we spent one more evening together. It was then that he told me what AA had meant to him. Most humbly describing his earlier life as a time of prideful agnosticism and sophistication which had led him down a blind alley, he went on to relate how the example of AA had affected him; how he had eventually joined the church of his choice, and how these two influences had inspired him to write about the Bible in "The Greatest Story Ever Told." He had done for AA, he went on to say, only a fraction of what AA had done for him, a nonalcoholic.

These, and a host of other experiences with the men and women of press, radio, and television, plainly tell us of what their dedication has meant. In nearly every city where AA grows today, we see our friends in communications following in the footsteps of Jack Alexander and Fulton Oursler.

For all such couriers of goodwill, let us be everlastingly grateful. And let us always be worthy of their friendship.

On the Alcoholism Front

March 1958

W e are told there are 4,500,000 alcoholics in America. Up to now AA has sobered up perhaps 250,000 of them. That's about one in twenty, or 5 percent of the total. This is a brave beginning, full of significance and hope for those who still suffer. Yet these figures show that we have made only a fair-sized dent on this vast world health problem. Millions are still sick and other millions soon will be.

These facts of alcoholism should give us good reason to think, and to be humble. Surely we can be grateful for every agency or method that tries to solve the problem of alcoholism — whether of medicine, religion, education, or research. We can be open-minded toward all such efforts and we can be sympathetic when the ill-advised ones fail. We can remember that AA itself ran for years on "trial and error." As individual AAs, we can and should work with those that promise success — even a little success.

Nor ought we allow our special convictions or prejudices to overcome our good sense and goodwill. For example, numbers of us think that alcoholism is mainly a spiritual problem. Therefore we have little time for biochemists who would like us to believe that drunks drink mostly because they are bedeviled by bad metabolisms. Likewise, we are apt to get red-hot when psychiatrists wave aside all issues of right or wrong and insist that the real problem of the alcoholic always gathers around the neurotic compulsions which he innocently acquired as a child by reason of being maladjusted by erring parents. Or, when social workers say that the true causes of alcoholism are to be seen in faulty social conditions, we are apt to get restive and say: "Who cares a hang what the causes are, anyway? AA can fix drunks without getting into all that."

In similar fashion some of us AAs decry every attempt at therapy, save our own. We point to certain clinics and committees that have accomplished little; we complain that huge sums are being wasted by state and private sources. We roundly thump every experimental drug that turns out badly. We belittle the attempts of the men and women of religion to deal with us drunks. We believe that sound alcohol education is a good thing. But we are also apt to think that AA — indirectly — is doing the most of it anyhow.

Now this may seem to be a confession of the sins of AA, and in some part it is. It is also a confession that at one time or another, I have myself held many of these often shortsighted views and prejudices. But I do make haste to add that what I've just said applies far more to AA's past than to the present.

Today, the vast majority of us welcome any new light that can be thrown on the alcoholic's mysterious and baffling malady. We don't care too much whether new and valuable knowledge issues from a test tube, a psychiatrist's couch, or from revealing social studies. We are glad of any kind of education that accurately informs the public and changes its age-old attitude toward the drunk. More and more we regard all who labor in the total field of alcoholism as our companions on a march from darkness into light. We see that we can accomplish together what we could never accomplish in separation and in rivalry.

Preoccupied with AA and its affairs, I must admit that I've given too little thought to the total alcohol problem. But I do have a glimpse of it, and that glimpse I would like to share with you.

Take those 4,500,000 drunks in America. What is their condition now? What is being done, and what might be done for them? What about the next generation — yet another 4,000,000 who are still children and adolescents? Excepting for what AA can do, must they be victims, too?

Let's start at the bottom of the heap. Our mental institutions are flooded with the brain damaged and the deeply psychopathic. Here and there a few find their way back, but not many. Most are gone beyond recall; the next world is their best hope. But more research upon their condition may add to our knowledge of prevention for the benefit of others who are approaching the jumping-off place. Great numbers of alcoholics are also to be found in prisons. Either alcohol directly got them into the jams that landed them there, or they had to drink in order to commit the crimes toward which they had compulsive tendencies. Here research — medical, psychiatric, and social — is plainly needed. AA can't do this job, but others have already made a great beginning.

Every large city has its skid row. The so-called derelict alcoholics doubtless number several hundreds of thousands. Some are so "psycho" and so damaged that the mental hospital is their destination. The rest of these countless men and women clog police blotters, courts, jails, and hospitals. To them the cost in suffering is incalculable; the cost to society, even in dollars only, is immense. Huge numbers of these, not yet legally insane, are thus condemned to mill hopelessly about. Can anything be done? In all probability, yes. Perhaps these sufferers can be transferred to farms where in some sort of "quarantine" confinement, they can do enough work to support themselves, be in better health, and save their respective cities great sums and trouble. This and other related experiments are beginning to offer much more hope for the skid-rower. Individual AAs are helping, but most of the work and the money will have to come from elsewhere.

What now of the millions of alcoholics who haven't hit prisons, asylums, or skid rows? These, we are told, constitute the vast majority. At the moment, their best hope of recovery seems to be AA. Well, then, why haven't these millions come to us? Or why haven't they tried to get well by some other method?

Any AA can give you a quick and very accurate answer: "They aren't ready, they don't know how sick they really are. If they did, they would flock to treatment, just as though they had diabetes or cancer." The problem, therefore, is how to expose them to the facts that will convince them they are gravely ill.

More than anything, the answer seems to be in *education* — education in schoolrooms, in medical colleges, among clergy and employers, in families, and in the public at large. From cradle to grave, the drunk and the potential alcoholic will have to be completely surrounded by true and deep understanding and by a continuous barrage of information: the facts about his illness, its symptoms, its grim seriousness. Why should an alcoholic have to wait until he is 55 and be horribly mangled to find out that he is a very sick person, when enough education of the right kind might have convinced him at 30 or 35?

History has shown that whatever their several merits, neither preaching nor moralizing nor other efforts at reform have ever made much impression on alcoholics as a whole. But factual education about the malady has in the last few years shown great promise. Even now we are seeing a great many younger people coming to AA as a direct result of the recently more widespread information about the disease.

We AAs have done a lot of this kind of education, and friends outside AA have done even more. As a result, right now maybe half a million of the U.S.A.'s drunks are trying to get well — or at least thinking seriously about getting well — either on their own, or by actual treatment. Maybe this guess is too high, but it is by no means fanciful. Sound education on alcoholism, and far more of it at all levels, will clearly pay off.

Education will not only pay off in numbers treated; it can pay off even more handsomely in prevention. This means factual education, properly presented to children and adolescents, at home and at school.

Heretofore, much of this education has attacked the immorality of drinking rather than the disease of alcoholism.

We AAs can speak with a lot of conviction about this. Most of our children have been emotionally bunged-up by our drinking behavior, "maladjusted" for sure. Large numbers of them should have turned into problem drinkers by now. But they have done no such thing. Alcoholism, or potential alcoholism, is a rare thing to see among the children of AA parents. Yet we never forbid them to drink, and we don't preach if they do. They simply learn by what they have seen and by what they hear that alcoholism is a ghastly business and that their chances are about one in fifteen of contracting the illness alcoholism if they drink. Most of them don't drink at all. Others drink sparingly. The remainder, after getting into a few ominous jams, are able to quit — and they promptly do. This seems to be preventive education at its best.

Therefore, it is entirely possible that many of these AA attitudes and methods can be widely applied to kids of all kinds.

Now who is going to do all this education? Obviously, it is both a community job and a job for specialists. Individually, we AAs can help, but AA as such cannot, and should not, get directly into this field. Therefore, we must rely on other agencies, on outside friends and their willingness to supply great amounts of money and effort — money and effort which will steer the alcoholic toward treatment as never before, and which will prevent the development of alcoholism in millions of predisposed kids who will otherwise take the road we know so well.

As the following fragment of history will show, great and promising progress, outside of AA, has been made in the field of research, treatment, rehabilitation, and education. It happened that I was a witness to the beginning of modern methods in these areas and this is what I saw:

I well remember Dr. H. W. Haggard of the Yale University faculty. In 1930, four years before I sobered up, this good physician was wondering what ailed drunks. He wanted to begin research — mostly a test tube project at the beginning to see what their chemistry was all about. This so amused some of his colleagues that no funds were forthcoming from Yale treasury. But Dr. Haggard was a man with a mission. He put his hands in his own pockets and begged personal friends to do the same. His project launched, he and an associate, Dr. Henderson, began work.

Later, in 1937, the renowned physiologist Dr. Anton Carlson and a group of interested scientists formed a subsidiary body called the Research Council on Problems of Alcohol. This was to be a more inclusive effort. Some of us early New York AAs went to their meetings — sometimes to cheer, and sometimes, I must confess, to jeer. (AA, you see, then thought it had a monopoly on the drunk-fixing business!)

Presently the Research Council took on a live wire, Dr. E.M. Jellinek. He wasn't an MD, but he was a "doctor" of pretty much everything else. Learning all about drunks was just a matter of catching up on his back reading. Though a prodigy of learning, he was nevertheless mighty popular with us alcoholics. We called him a "dry alcoholic" because he could identify with us so well. Even his nickname was endearing — his Hungarian father had dubbed him "Bunky" which, in that language, means "the little radish." The "little radish" got down to business at once.

At length Bunky and Dr. Haggard joined forces and began in 1940 to publish the *Quarterly Journal of Studies on Alcohol,* which devoted itself to articles covering the total field of alcohol research and inquiry. This brought Dr. Jellinek into partnership and close association with Dr. Haggard.

In 1943, Dr. Haggard and Bunky organized the Yale School for Alcohol Studies. It was seen that a laboratory and technical journal couldn't get far unless a wider audience was found. The idea was advanced that everybody who bumped into drunks or the alcohol problem should be represented at the school.

A strangely assorted crowd turned up at the early sessions. I well remember the venerable Mr. Colvin, he who used to run on the Prohibition ticket for the U.S. presidency. At the other pole of violent opinion there were certain representatives of the liquor industry. Sandwiched in between these were a sprinkling of clergymen, social workers, judges, cops, probation officers, educators, and a certain number of us drunks. Everybody had his own axe to grind and his own cast-iron convictions. The drys and wets were hardly on speaking terms. Every faction wanted us drunks to agree with them. This was very flattering, but we naturally took the independent course and agreed with practically nobody!

It was out of this unpromising miscellany that Drs. Haggard and Jellinek had to bring order. The wets had to be convinced they couldn't brush the alcohol problem under the bed; neither could those drys go on scaring every drinker by brandishing before him a hobnailed liver. We AAs had to see the enormity of the total alcohol problem and to face the fact that we probably weren't going to dry up the world overnight. The school threw in its research findings, everybody else contributed what he had, or thought he had, and Bunky finally showed us that we had to face the actual facts together and be friendly about it besides. His was a stroke of diplomacy; it was perhaps the first beginning of a comprehensive and statesmanlike approach to the problem of alcohol in America.

In the next year, 1944, there were two signal events. The Yale group opened up a clinic where there would be plenty of live drunks to research and to treat experimentally. Here Ray McCarthy, as first administrator, began to sweat out the clinic method with his first batch of alcoholics.

Then along came Marty. As an early AA she knew public attitudes had to be changed, that people had to know that alcoholism was a disease and alcoholics could be helped. She developed a plan for an organization to conduct a vigorous program of public education and to organize citizens' committees all over the country. She brought her plan to me. I was enthusiastic but felt scientific backing was essential, so the plan was sent to Bunky, and he came down to meet with us. He said the plan was sound, the time was ripe, and he agreed with me that Marty was the one to do the job.

Originally financed by the tireless Dr. Haggard and his friends, Marty started her big task. I cannot detail in this space the great accomplishments of Marty and her associates in the present-day National Council on Alcoholism. But I can speak my conviction that no other single agency has done more to educate the public, to open up hospitalization, and to set in motion all manner of constructive projects than this one. Growing pains there have been aplenty, but today the NCA results speak for themselves.

In 1945, Dr. Selden Bacon, the noted sociologist, was appointed chairman of the first program to be supported by state funds, the Connecticut Commission on Alcoholism. This first state effort was the direct result of the work of Dr. Bacon and the Yale group. Our friend Selden has since brought his immense energy and the finest perceptions of his profession to the aid of us alcoholics. He is without doubt one of the best authorities from the social point of view that we now have.

I much wish I could name and tell you of many another dedicated friend of that early pioneering time. They have since been followed by others who are today legion. To all of them I send the timeless gratitude of Alcoholics Anonymous.

Their combined efforts, often sparked by AAs, have since flowered to this general effect: Four universities are now running replicas of the Yale School. Three thousand public and private hospitals have been opened to alcoholics. Industry is revolutionizing its attitude toward its alcoholic employees. Penal institutions, police, and judges alike have taken new heart. Citizens' committees in large numbers are attacking the total problem in their several communities. Over thirty U.S. states and the majority of Canadian provinces have a program of rehabilitation and treatment. Many clergy groups are educating their co-workers. Psychiatric research and treatment is making telling strides. Test tube devotees are working hopefully in their laboratories. The American Medical Association has officially declared alcoholism to be a chronic illness, and has activated its own committee on alcoholism. Medical colleges are beginning to include this subject in their courses. Sparked by Bunky, the World Health Organization is carrying all this good news around the world. School textbooks are being modernized. In the cause of general education, the press, radio, and television are pouring out floods of it daily. This has all happened in the twenty-eight years since Dr. Haggard first decided to find out what makes drunks tick.

Every one of these pioneers in the total field will generously say that had it not been for the living proof of recovery in AA, they could not have gone on. AA was the lodestar of hope and help that kept them at it.

So let us work alongside all these projects of promise to hasten the recovery of those millions who have not yet found their way out. These varied labors do not need our special endorsement; they need only a helping hand when, as individuals, we can possibly give it.

Segment

3

Additional Writings from This Period

Salute to Canada

May 1951

Our congratulations and thanks to Canada; no finer AA exists. This far-flung Society of ours has the odd quality of being everywhere the same, yet everywhere so different. We AAs are totally alike, whether by regions or by nations. This, of course, is just as it should be.

When AA travelers return from Canada they all report how much more they brought away from Canada than they took in.

Nor shall we forget that Canada has brought the AA [now Al-Anon] family groups to their present happy degree of success and to the high favor they found among those of us who heard their testimonies at Cleveland last summer. Nor shall the bright memory ever fade of that day in Montreal when Lois and I heard the Lord's Prayer spoken in French and English — our first meeting in two languages.

We are immeasurably grateful for fast friends from Halifax to Vancouver; they are always the same; devoted workers upon that great fabric which is AA of today — and of tomorrow!

Meet the Nonalcoholic Trustees

November 1951

W hy does AA's Alcoholic Foundation have eight nonalcoholics on its board? What do they do, and how did they get there in the first place? There are some mighty good answers to these oft heard queries.

It all started this way. Back there in 1937 we figured we needed a lot of money. We considered going into the hospital business and thought of putting out some sort of paid AA missionaries. Even more sure, we would have to publish a book. Since we didn't have that kind of cash, we had to look around. These needs, real (and imaginary!), got us on the search for nonalcoholics who had money. Or who could get some for us.

Many have heard me tell the story how, through my brother-in-law, Dr. Leonard V. Strong, we met Mr. Willard S. Richardson, one of the finest friends AA can ever have. In our early extremity we certainly thought he had great promise for, you see, he was a close friend and associate of Mr. John D. Rockefeller, Jr. His interest in us was immediate and lively. Our money problems were solved, we felt sure. Providentially, that was not to be the case. Nevertheless, Mr. Richardson quickly assembled a company of nonalcoholics who were at once infected with his own enthusiasm for what we were doing. Those early friends, Dick Richardson, Leonard Strong, Frank Amos, A. LeRoy Chipman, and Albert Scott, will surely appear in the forefront of any history of Alcoholics Anonymous to be written.

At first, though, they were rather disappointing; these men were not so sure we needed large sums of money — an opinion still more strongly held by Mr. John D. Rockefeller, Jr., when approached later on. Little did we guess that the widsom of these new friends was soon to save Alcoholics Anonymous from professionalism and the perils of great wealth.

By the spring of 1938, however, most of our new sponsors concluded that we could safely use a little money. Our grandiose ideas of hospitals and missionaries had evaporated, but we were still very sure we ought to publish a book of recovery experience. Earlier in the year, Mr. Rockefeller had set aside a sum in assistance to Dr. Bob and me personally. But the end of that was in sight. The book project definitely needed funds.

This was the point at which the Alcoholic Foundation took shape. A trust agreement was drawn in May 1938. Those named above, save Messrs. Scott and Rockefeller, became trustees. We already relied upon their careful judgment and unabating interest. Moreover, AA badly needed friends, people who would stand right up in public and say what they thought about us. Just as Mr. Rockefeller himself did, two years later.

Out of that Foundation creation comes an amusing recollection. None of the alcoholic members of the newly named board were sure they could stay sober. Who, then, would look after the money if all the drunks got drunk? With this potential catastrophe in mind, we inserted into the trust agreement a provision that the number of nonalcoholics on the Board must always exceed the number of alcoholics by one. Just in case!

All during the summer of 1938, with the best of recommendations, we solicited money for our shining new Foundation. There was no result whatever. So in the fall of that year, under the name of Works Publishing, Inc., the New York alcoholics and their friends, forty-nine in all, raised funds for the publication of the AA Book. The Foundation itself had practically no cash until 1940 when Mr. Rockefeller gave his much publicized dinner for Alcoholics Anonymous. That resulted in approximately $3,000 annually for the Foundation over a period of five years. The Rockefeller family later loaned funds to pay off the cash subscribers to the AA book, thereby completing the Foundation's ownership. This was about all the money the Foundation ever had from outside sources.

Right then, the character of the Foundation began to change. After acquiring the book, the trustees came successively into possession of AA's public relations, its contributions for support of the General Office and, in recent years, the AA Grapevine, which had originally been founded by a separate group of journalistic AAs in New York City.

So you can see that what began as a simple committee to help Dr.

Bob and me along has since evolved into an AA service board of custody for our principal affairs. At first concerned only with the problem of money, the board today operates chiefly in the field of overall policy and business management of the AA General Office and the AA Grapevine.

We are apt to forget how remote the Foundation is from the average AA groups, a situation that changed only last April with the advent of the General Service Conference. Even this body will meet but once a year. In this unique and isolated situation the nonalcoholics have, time after time, proved their immense worth to AA. Because of their detached position they have often shown better judgment than we mercurial and prejudiced alcoholics. Not only have they stabilized our Headquarters operation, they have definitely saved the Foundation from disaster on several occasions. What greater tribute than this could we possibly pay them?

So, shake hands with our nonalcoholic trustees. Here they are:

Jack Alexander is the author of the 1941 *Saturday Evening Post* piece that made AA a national institution and brought release to thousands. How well we love that Jack!

Frank Amos is a advertising and newspaper owner, now of Cambridge, Ohio. Frank's tireless interest and patient counsel, in the early days and since, will ever be thankfully remembered.

A. LeRoy Chipman, an associate of Mr. Rockefeller, is a very early board member, a watchful conscientious treasurer, whose great devotion to our cause ought to be better known and appreciated.

Frank Gulden is new to the Foundation. A prominent churchman, member of the board of St. Johns Hospital (which cooperates closely with Brooklyn AA) and owner of the noted food enterprise which bears his name. We deem his keen discernment a real find.

Dr. John Norris is chief physician, Eastman Kodak Company. Recently seated at the Foundation board, Dr. Norris bears a high reputation in the field of industrial medicine. He is notable for his knowledge of alcoholics and is responsible for the wonderful relation that exists between Eastman Kodak and Alcoholics Anonymous.

Fulton Oursler is senior editor of the *Reader's Digest*. Enjoys worldwide renown as an author and public relations expert. Thousands of AAs have read his *Greatest Story Ever Told*. There is no more lovable and ardent AA fan than Fulton.

Bernard Smith is chairman of the Foundation board, well-known corporation lawyer, a friend of exceptional vision and goodwill. His ceaseless advocacy of the General Service Conference idea from the moment it was first proposed entitles him to our everlasting gratitude.

Dr. Leonard V. Strong is the one whose connection with Mr. Willard Richardson led to the creation of the Foundation. He's been secretary virtually ever since. No one has attended more meetings nor worked harder than Leonard to bring the Foundation where it is today. He happens to be my brother-in-law. In the last days of my drinking, his unfailing confidence and medical attention probably saved my life.

Mr. Willard S. Richardson is trustee emeritus. This good friend, retired now, is affectionately remembered by all who served with him as the one who infused wonderful spiritual substance and fine wisdom into our Foundation activity from the beginning. Behind his back, we call him "Uncle Dick." That speaks volumes, doesn't it?

Leonard V. Harrison — no roll call would be complete without him. He served as chairman of the Foundation board during those very uncertain years of AA's adolescence when we shivered for fear the forces which would rend us apart might win out. In this period of severe strain, our friend's steady hand at the Foundation helm kept us off many a shoal. We here record our timeless thanks.

Now you have met our nonalcoholic trustees. Where would AA have been today without them? As for me, I'd rather not guess.

A Fragment of History: Origin of the Twelve Steps

July 1953

A As are always asking: "Where did the Twelve Steps come from?" In the last analysis, perhaps nobody knows. Yet some of the events which led to their formulation are as clear to me as though they took place yesterday.

So far as people were concerned, the main channels of inspiration for our Steps were three in number — the Oxford Groups, Dr. William D. Silkworth of Towns Hospital, and the famed psychologist William James, called by some the father of modern psychology. The story of how these streams of influence were brought together and how they led to the writing of our Twelve Steps is exciting and in spots downright incredible.

Many of us will remember the Oxford Groups as a modern evangelical movement which flourished in the 1920s and early 30s, led by a onetime Lutheran minister, Dr. Frank Buchman. The Oxford Groups of that day threw heavy emphasis on personal work, one member with another. AA's Twelfth Step had its origin in that vital practice. The moral backbone of the "O.G." was absolute honesty, absolute purity, absolute unselfishness, and absolute love. They also practiced a type of confession, which they called "sharing"; the making of amends for harms done they called "restitution." They believed deeply in their "quiet time," a meditation practiced by groups and individuals alike, in which the guidance of God was sought for every detail of living, great or small.

These basic ideas were not new; they could have been found elsewhere. But the saving thing for us first alcoholics who contacted the Oxford Groupers was that they laid great stress on these particular principles. And fortunate for us was the fact that the Groupers took special pains not to interfere with one's personal religious views. Their society, like ours later on, saw the need to be strictly nondenominational.

In the late summer of 1934, my well-loved alcoholic friend and schoolmate, Ebbie, had fallen in with these good folks and had promptly sobered up. Being an alcoholic, and rather on the obstinate side, he hadn't been able to "buy" all the Oxford Group ideas and attitudes. Nevertheless, he was moved by their deep sincerity and felt mighty grateful for the fact that their ministrations had, for the time being, lifted his obsession to drink.

When he arrived in New York in the late fall of 1934, Ebbie thought at once of me. On a bleak November day he rang up. Soon he was looking at me across our kitchen table at 182 Clinton Street, Brooklyn, New York. As I remember that conversation, he constantly used phrases like these: "I found I couldn't run my own life"; "I had to get honest with myself and somebody else"; "I had to make restitution for the damage I had done"; "I had to pray to God for guidance and strength, even though I wasn't sure there was any God"; "And after I'd tried hard to do these things I found that my craving for alcohol left." Then over and over, Ebbie would say something like this: "Bill, it isn't a bit like being on the water-wagon. You don't fight the desire to drink — you get released from it. I never had such a feeling before."

Such was the sum of what Ebbie had extracted from his Oxford Group friends and had transmitted to me that day. While these simple ideas were not new, they certainly hit me like tons of brick. Today we understand just why that was — one alcoholic was talking to another as no one else can.

Two or three weeks later, December 11 to be exact, I staggered into the Charles B. Towns Hospital, that famous drying-out emporium on Central Park West, New York City. I'd been there before, so I knew and already loved the doctor in charge — Dr. Silkworth. It was he who was soon to contribute a very great idea without which AA could never have succeeded. For years he had been proclaiming alcoholism an illness, an obsession of the mind coupled with an allergy of the body. By now I knew this meant me. I also understood what a fatal combination these twin ogres could be. Of course, I'd once hoped to be among the small percentage of victims who now and then escape their vengeance. But this outside hope was now gone. I was about to hit bottom. That verdict of science — the obsession that condemned me to drink and the allergy that condemned me to die — was about to do the trick. That's where medical science, personified by this benign little doctor, began to fit in. Held in the hands of one alcoholic talking to the next, this double-edged truth was a sledgehammer which could shatter the tough alcoholic's ego at depth and lay him wide open to the grace of God.

In my case it was of course Dr. Silkworth who swung the sledge while my friend Ebbie carried to me the spiritual principles and the grace which brought on my sudden spiritual awakening at the hospital three days later. I immediately knew that I was a free man. And with this astonishing experience came a feeling of wonderful certainty that great numbers of alcoholics might one day enjoy the priceless gift which had been bestowed upon me.

At this point a third stream of influence entered my life through the pages of William James's book, *Varieties of Religious Experience*. Somebody had brought it to my hospital room. Following my sudden experience, Dr. Silkworth had taken great pains to convince me that I was not hallucinating. But William James did even more. Not only, he said, could spiritual experiences make people saner, they could transform men and women so that they could do, feel, and believe what had hitherto been impossible to them. It mattered little whether these awakenings were sudden or gradual; their variety could be almost infinite. But the biggest payoff of that noted book was this: In most of the cases described, those who had been transformed were hopeless people. In some controlling area of their lives they had met absolute defeat. Well, that was me all right. In complete defeat, with no hope or faith whatever, I had made an appeal to a Higher Power. I had taken Step One of today's AA program — "Admitted we were powerless over alcohol, that our lives had become unmanageable." I'd also taken Step Three — "Made a decision to turn our will and our lives over to the care of God *as we understood him.*" Thus was I set free. It was just as simple, yet just as mysterious, as that.

These realizations were so exciting that I instantly joined up with the Oxford Groups. But to their consternation I insisted on devoting myself exclusively to drunks. This was disturbing to the O.G.'s on two counts. Firstly, they wanted to help save the whole world. Secondly, their luck with drunks had been poor. Just as I joined they had been working over a batch of alcoholics who had proved disappointing indeed. One of them, it was rumored, had flippantly cast his shoe through a valuable stained glass window of an Episcopal church across the alley from O.G. headquarters. Neither did they take kindly to my repeated declaration that it shouldn't take long to sober up all the drunks in the world. They rightly declared that my conceit was still immense.

After some six months of violent exertion with scores of alcoholics which I found at a nearby mission and Towns Hospital, it began to look like the Groupers were right. I hadn't sobered up anybody. In Brooklyn we always had a houseful of drinkers living with us, sometimes as many as five. My valiant wife, Lois, once arrived home from work to find three of them fairly tight. The remaining two were worse. They were whaling each other with two-by-fours. Though events like these slowed me down somewhat, the persistent conviction that a way to sobriety could be found never seemed to leave me. There was, though, one bright spot. My sponsor, Ebbie, still clung precariously to his newfound sobriety.

What was the reason for all these fiascos? If Ebbie and I could achieve sobriety, why couldn't all the rest find it too? Some of those we'd worked on certainly wanted to get well. We speculated day and night why nothing much had happened to them. Maybe they couldn't stand the spiritual pace of the Oxford Group's four absolutes of honesty, purity, unselfishness, and love. In fact some of the alcoholics declared that this was the trouble. The aggressive pressure upon them to get good overnight would make them fly high as geese for a few weeks and then flop dismally. They complained, too, about another form of coercion —

something the Oxford Groupers called "guidance for others." A "team" composed of nonalcoholic Groupers would sit down with an alcoholic and after a "quiet time" would come up with precise instructions as to how the alcoholic should run his own life. As grateful as we were to our O.G. friends, this was sometimes tough to take. It obviously had something to do with the wholesale skidding that went on.

But this wasn't the entire reason for failure. After months I saw the trouble was mainly in me. I had become very aggressive, very cocksure. I talked a lot about my sudden spiritual experience, as though it was something very special. I had been playing the double role of teacher and preacher. In my exhortations I'd forgotten all about the medical side of our malady, and the need for deflation at depth so emphasized by William James had been neglected. We weren't using that medical sledgehammer that Dr. Silkworth had so providentially given us.

Finally, one day, Dr. Silkworth took me back down to my right size. Said he, "Bill, why don't you quit talking so much about that bright light experience of yours; it sounds too crazy. Though I'm convinced that nothing but better morals will make alcoholics really well, I do think you have the cart before the horse. The point is that alcoholics won't buy all this moral exhortation until they convince themselves that they must. If I were you I'd go after them on the medical basis first. While it has never done any good for me to tell them how fatal their malady is, it might be a very different story if you, a formerly hopeless alcoholic, gave them the bad news. Because of the identification you naturally have with alcoholics, you might be able to penetrate where I can't. Give them the medical business first, and give it to them hard. This might soften them up so they will accept the principles that will really get them well."

Shortly after this history-making conversation, I found myself in Akron, Ohio, on a business venture which promptly collapsed. Alone in the town, I was scared to death of getting drunk. I was no longer a teacher or a preacher, I was an alcoholic who knew that he needed another alcoholic as much as that one could possibly need me. Driven by that urge, I was soon face to face with Dr. Bob. It was at once evident that Dr. Bob knew more of spiritual things than I did. He also had been in touch with the Oxford Groupers at Akron. But somehow he simply couldn't get sober. Following Dr. Silkworth's advice, I used the medical sledgehammer. I told him what alcoholism was and just how fatal it could be. Apparently this did something to Dr. Bob. On June 10, 1935, he sobered up, never to drink again. When, in 1939, Dr. Bob's story first appeared in the book *Alcoholics Anonymous,* he put one paragraph of it in italics. Speaking of me, he said: *"Of far more importance was the fact that he was the first living human with whom I had ever talked, who knew what he was talking about in regard to alcoholism from actual experience."*

Dr. Silkworth had indeed supplied us the missing link without which the chain of principles now forged into our Twelve Steps could never have been complete. Then and there, the spark that was to become Alcoholics Anonymous had been struck.

During the next three years after Dr. Bob's recovery, our growing groups at Akron, New York, and Cleveland evolved the so-called word-of-mouth program of our pioneering time. As we commenced to form a Society separate from the Oxford Group, we began to state our principles something like this:

1. We admitted we were powerless over alcohol.

2. We got honest with ourselves.

3. We got honest with another person, in confidence.

4. We made amends for harms done others.

5. We worked with other alcoholics without demand for prestige or money.

6. We prayed to God to help us to do these things as best we could.

Though these principles were advocated according to the whim or liking of each of us, and though in Akron and Cleveland they still stuck by the O.G. absolutes of honesty, purity, unselfishness, and love, this was the gist of our message to incoming alcoholics up to 1939, when our present Twelve Steps were put to paper.

I well remember the evening on which the Twelve Steps were written. I was lying in bed quite dejected and suffering from one of my imaginary ulcer attacks. Four chapters of the book, *Alcoholics Anonymous,* had been roughed out and read in meetings at Akron and New York. We quickly found that everybody wanted to be an author. The hassles as to what should go into our new book were terrific. For example, some wanted a purely psychological book which would draw in alcoholics without scaring them. We could tell them about the "God business" afterward. A few, led by our wonderful southern friend, Fitz M., wanted a fairly religious book infused with some of the dogma we had picked up from the churches and missions which had tried to help us. The louder these arguments, the more I felt in the middle. It appeared that I wasn't going to be the author at all. I was only going to be an umpire who would decide the contents of the book. This didn't mean, though, that there wasn't terrific enthusiasm for the undertaking. Every one of us was wildly excited at the possibility of getting our message before all those countless alcoholics who still didn't know.

Having arrived at Chapter Five, it seemed high time to state what our program really was. I remember running over in my mind the word-of-mouth phrases then in current use. Jotting these down, they added up to the six named above. Then came the idea that our program ought to be more accurately and clearly stated. Distant readers would have to have a precise set of principles. Knowing the alcoholic's ability to rationalize, something airtight would have to be written. We couldn't let the reader wiggle out anywhere. Besides, a more complete statement would help in the chapters to come where we would need to show exactly how the recovery program ought to be worked.

At length I began to write on a cheap yellow tablet. I split the word-of-mouth program up into smaller pieces, meanwhile enlarging its scope considerably. Uninspired as I felt, I was surprised that in a short time, perhaps half an hour, I had set down certain principles which, on being counted, turned out to be twelve in number. And for some unaccountable reason, I had moved the idea of God into the Second Step, right up front. Besides, I had named God very liberally throughout the other Steps. In one of the Steps I had even suggested that the newcomer get down on his knees.

When this document was shown to our New York meeting, the protests were many and loud. Our agnostic friends didn't go at all for the idea of kneeling. Others said we were talking altogether too much about God. And anyhow, why should there be Twelve Steps when we had done five or six? Let's keep it simple, they said.

This sort of heated discussion went on for days and nights. But out of it all there came a ten-strike for Alcoholics Anonymous. Our agnostic contingent, speared by Hank P. and Jim B., finally convinced us that we must make it easier for people like themselves by using such terms as "a Higher Power" or "God as we understand him." Those expressions, as we so well know today, have proved lifesavers for many an alcoholic. They have enabled thousands of us to make a beginning where none could have been made had we left the Steps just as I originally wrote them. Happily for us there were no other changes in the original draft and the number of Steps still stood at twelve. Little did we then guess that our Twelve Steps would soon be widely approved by clergy of all denominations and even by our latter-day friends, the psychiatrists.

This little fragment of history ought to convince the most skeptical that nobody invented Alcoholics Anonymous.

It just grew — by the grace of God.

Another Fragment of History: Sister Ignatia and Dr. Bob

·

February 1954

It was December 13, 1953. The occasion was the first anniversary of the opening of Rosary Hall, the newly remodeled alcoholic ward at Cleveland's famed St. Vincent's Charity Hospital. It had been a great AA meeting. The small auditorium was crammed with alcoholics and their friends. So was the balcony. One thousand people now rose to their feet, clapping wildly.

The slight figure of a nun in a gray habit reluctantly approached the lectern's microphone. The uproar redoubled, then suddenly subsided as the little nun commenced to give her thanks. She was embarrassed, too. For had not the program she'd helped write for the occasion definitely stated that "The Sisters of Charity and the members of Alcoholics Anonymous who have assisted, decline all individual credit." Sister Ignatia's attempted anonymity was busted wide open, for no one there wanted to let her get away with it this time. And anyway, she was just about as anonymous in that part of our AA world as baseball's Cleveland Indians. This was a tribute to her which had been years in the making.

As I sat watching this scene, I vividly remembered Dr. Bob's struggles to start Akron's AA Group Number One and what this dear nun and her Sisters of Charity of St. Augustine had done to make that possible. I tried to envision all the vast consequences which have since flowed from their early effort. Seeking hospitalization for his newfound prospects, Dr. Bob, I recalled, had begged one Akron institution after another to take them in. Two hospitals had tried for a time but finally gave up in favor of folks with broken legs, ailing gall bladders, etc. — really sick people!

Then in desperation, the good doctor bethought himself of Sister Ignatia, that shy but beaming nun who handled admissions at St. Thomas Hospital in Akron where he had occasionally operated. In an atmosphere of some secrecy he approached her with his proposal. In nothing flat, he got results. This rare pair immediately bootlegged a shaking alkie into a tiny two-bed ward. Because the new customer kicked like a steer at this glaring lack of privacy for his delicate condition, Sister Ignatia moved him to the hospital's flower room. Here AA's co-founder Bob and Sister Ignatia ministered to this newcomer, who presently left his bed for the world outside, there to mend his ways and his broken life.

Through Sister Ignatia and Bob, God had wrought a divine conspiracy of medicine, religion, and Alcoholics Anonymous which was to bring sobriety within reach of more than 5,000 alcoholics who were to pass through the alcoholic ward of St. Thomas up to the time of Dr. Bob's death in 1950. But when that first customer was shaking it out in the flower room way back there in 1939, the trustees of the hospital little guessed that St. Thomas had become the first religious institution ever to open its doors to AA.

Not long before Dr. Bob passed out of our sight and hearing, I was asked to inscribe a plaque which could always be seen on the wall of the alcoholic ward and which would commemorate the great events which there took place.

Two years after Dr. Bob's death, Sister Ignatia was transferred by the order to which she belongs to Charity Hospital at Cleveland.

But no account of the activity of church hospitals in this area would be complete without a recital of what happened at Charity Hospital over the years *before* her arrival there.

Old-time AAs will recall the wonderful publicity which the Cleveland *Plain Dealer* gave us in the fall of 1939. When these stories broke there was scarcely a score of AAs in the whole town. Because the pieces appearing on the Cleveland *Plain Dealer's* editorial page were accompanied by strong editorials and ran consecutively for about ten days, the ensuing excitement in the town was immense. The little band of alcoholics, some of them dry only months, were flooded by hundreds of telephone calls and frantic pleas for help. The *Plain Dealer* had said to the good people of Cleveland "Come and get it!" And they certainly did.

This startling development ushered in an entirely new phase of AA.

Pioneering had gone on since 1935 and the AA Book was already off the press. But growth in Akron and New York had been discouragingly slow. A handful of Clevelanders had dried up by contact with Akron but held no meeting of their own until early 1939. It was then commonly supposed that nobody but "greybeards" could look after new people. The supply of seasoned AAs in Cleveland was of course painfully small. What could these few do with the hundreds of alcoholics who now descended on them like a landslide? Was mass production of sobriety possible?

Well, those early Clevelanders proved that it was. Cases were dumped into hospitals willy-nilly all over town. Whether their hospital bills would be paid, no one knew. An AA would appear at a new man's bedside, snatch him out and take him to a meeting. The new man would thereupon rush to another bedside with the glad tidings. Then and there it was discovered that very new people could drive the opening wedge into a fresh case almost as well as anybody. Out of this confused scramble there soon evolved the great idea of organized personal sponsorship for each and every new man and woman.

Meanwhile Cleveland's membership soared to hundreds in a matter of months. There at Cleveland in the winter of 1939, they proved that mass production of sobriety was a glad fact. This is Cleveland's great and rightful claim to distinction as a pioneer group.

But this prodigious effort had to have help from the town's hospitals. Such amazing results could have been obtained in no other way. As in Akron, after the excitement died down, some of the hospitals got weary of drunks. But Cleveland's Charity Hospital never did. Since 1940 it has admitted alcoholics and has provided a ward for them. Though Cleveland was lacking a "Dr. Bob," the Charity ward did nevertheless prosper nobly under the guidance and devoted interest of Sister Victorine and Father Nagle, the hospital's chaplain. Though work with the alcoholics could take up only a fraction of their time, and though Father Nagle suffered constantly from ill health, they continued to press on with such a result that their work will always stand as a shining mark in our annals. St. John's Hospital in Cleveland, too, did provide a two-bed ward for a time under the devoted Sister Merced, who was finally transferred to Akron where she became associated with Sister Ignatia and Dr. Bob.

With the arrival of Sister Ignatia at Cleveland's Charity Hospital in 1952, plenty more began to happen. Suddenly thousands of AAs from near and far who had sobered up in these wonderful institutions began to realize their long-standing debt of gratitude. Permission was obtained to modernize completely the battered old ward at Charity. Sister Ignatia, helped by the hospital authorities and the sisters of her order, and further buttressed by an enthusiastic committee of AAs, went to work. Money, and much more, flowed in. With special dispensations from their respective unions, AA carpenters, plumbers, and electricians worked long nights. When they were done, the ward gleamed; it was possessed of every modern device. Neither were two indispensable adjuncts forgotten — the chapel and the coffee bar! A plumbing inspector summed it all up when, after looking at this astonishing result, he remarked: "This was no professional job. The folks who worked on this thing had their hearts in it." More than $60,000 in funds and night work was thus expended on this urgent labor of love.

In the one short year since Sister Ignatia came to Charity, one thousand alcoholics have there seen the light of their new day. Sister Ignatia, who has kept in touch with many of them, believes that about seven hundred are sober at this moment.

Is it any wonder, then, that the anniversary meeting of the opening of Rosary Hall was turned into a declaration of our personal love for Sister Ignatia and all her works? If the plumbing inspector had been present at this great meeting, he would have again exclaimed, "This is no professional job. It comes from the heart."

The Bill W. – Yale Correspondence

February 1978

Early in 1954, Bill W. declined an honorary degree of Doctor of Laws offered by Yale University. Following is the correspondence between Bill and Reuben A. Holden, then secretary of the university.

The exchange of letters followed a personal visit to Bill from Mr. Holden and Professor Selden Bacon in January of 1954.

January 21, 1954

Dear Mr. W —:

I enclose a suggested draft of a citation which might be used in conferring upon you the proposed honorary degree on June 7th.

If your trustees approve this formula, I should then like to submit it to the Yale Corporation for their consideration.

The wording can be considerably improved. We shall work on that during the next few months, but in every instance we shall be sure it has your unqualified blessing.

Thanks for your hospitality on Tuesday and for your thoughtful consideration of our invitation.

Very sincerely yours,
Reuben A. Holden

W.W.:

Co-founder of Alcoholics Anonymous. For twenty years, this Fellowship has rendered a distinguished service to mankind. Victory has been gained through surrender, fame achieved through anonymity, and for many tens of thousands, the emotional, the physical, and the spiritual self has been rediscovered and reborn. This nonprofessional movement, rising from the depths of intense suffering and universal stigma, has not only shown the way to the conquest of a morbid condition of body, mind, and soul, but has invigorated the individual, social, and religious life of our times.

Yale takes pride in honoring this great anonymous assembly of men and women by conferring upon you, a worthy representative of its high purpose, this degree of Doctor of Laws, admitting you to all its rights and privileges.

February 2, 1954

Dear Mr. Holden,

This is to express my deepest thanks to the members of the Yale Corporation for considering me as one suitable for the degree of Doctor of Laws.

It is only after most careful consultation with friends, and with my conscience, that I now feel obligated to decline such a mark of distinction.

Were I to accept, the near term benefit to Alcoholics Anonymous and to legions who still suffer our malady would, no doubt, be world-wide and considerable. I am sure that such a potent endorsement would greatly hasten public approval of AA everywhere. Therefore, none but the most compelling of reasons could prompt my decision to deny Alcoholics Anonymous an opportunity of this dimension.

Now this is the reason: The Tradition of Alcoholics Anonymous — our only means of self-government — entreats each member to avoid all that particular kind of personal publicity or distinction which might link his name with our Society in the general public mind. AA's Tradition Twelve reads as follows: "Anonymity is the spiritual foundation of all our Traditions, ever reminding us to place principles before personalities."

Because we have already had much practical experience with this vital principle, it is today the view of every thoughtful AA member that if, over the years ahead, we practice this anonymity *absolutely,* it will guarantee our effectiveness and unity by heavily restraining those to whom public honors and distinctions are but the natural stepping-stones to dominance and personal power.

Like other men and women, we AAs look with deep apprehension upon the vast power struggle about us, a struggle in myriad forms that invades every level, tearing society apart. I think we AAs are fortunate to be acutely aware that such forces must never be ruling among us, lest we perish altogether.

The Tradition of personal anonymity and no honors at the public level is our protective shield. We dare not meet the power temptation naked.

Of course, we quite understand the high value of honors outside our Fellowship. We always find inspiration when these are deservedly bestowed and humbly received as the hallmarks of distinguished attainment or service. We say only that in our special circumstances it would be imprudent for us to accept them for AA achievement.

For example: My own life story gathered for years around an implacable pursuit of money, fame, and power, anticlimaxed by my near sinking in a sea of alcohol. Though I survived that grim misadventure, I well understand that the dread neurotic germ of the power contagion has survived in me also. It is only dormant, and it can again multiply and rend me — and AA, too. Tens of thousands of my fellow AAs are temperamentally just like me. Fortunately, they know it, and I know it. Hence our Tradition of anonymity, and hence my clear obligation to decline this signal honor with all the immediate satisfaction and benefit it could have yielded.

True, the splendid citation you propose, which describes me as

"W.W.," does protect my anonymity for the time being. Nevertheless, it would surely appear on the later historical record that I had taken an LL.D. The public would then know the fact. So, while I might accept the degree within the letter of AA's Tradition as of today, I would surely be setting the stage for a violation of its spirit tomorrow. This would be, I am certain, a perilous precedent to set.

Though it might be a novel departure, I'm wondering if the Yale Corporation could consider giving AA itself the entire citation, omitting the degree to me. In such an event, I will gladly appear at any time to receive it on behalf of our Society. Should a discussion of this possibility seem desirable to you, I'll come to New Haven at once.

Gratefully yours,
William G. W—

February 8, 1954

Dear Mr. W—:

I have waited to respond to your letter of February 2 until we had a meeting of the Committee on Honorary Degrees, which has now taken place, and I want to report to you on behalf of the committee that after hearing your magnificent letter, they all wish more than ever they could award you the degree — though it probably in our opinion isn't half good enough for you.

The entire committee begged me to tell you in as genuine a way as I can how very deeply they appreciated your considering this invitation as thoroughly and thoughtfully and unselfishly as you have. We understand completely your feelings in the matter, and we only wish there were some way we could show our deep sense of respect for you and AA. Some day, the opportunity will surely come.

Meanwhile, I should say that it was also the feeling of the committee that honorary degrees are, like knighthoods, bestowed on individuals, and that being the tradition, it would seem logical that we look in other ways than an honorary-degree award for the type of recognition that we should like to give the organization in accordance with the suggestion you made in your last paragraph. I hope this may be possible.

I send you the warmest greetings of the president of Yale University and of the entire corporation and assure you of our sincere admiration and good wishes for the continued contribution you are making to the welfare of this country.

Cordially yours,
Reuben A. Holden

March 1, 1954

Dear Mr. Holden,

Your letter of February 8th, in which you record the feelings of the Yale Corporation respecting my declination of the degree of Doctor of Laws, has been read with great relief and gratitude. I shall treasure it always.

Your quick and moving insight into AA's vital need to curb its future aspirants to power, the good thought you hold of me, and your hope that the Yale Corporation might presently find the means of giving Alcoholics Anonymous a suitable public recognition, are something for the greatest satisfaction.

Please carry to the president of Yale and to every member of the board my lasting appreciation.

Devotedly yours,
Bill W—

Why Alcoholics Anonymous Is Anonymous

January 1955

As never before the struggle for power, importance, and wealth is tearing civilization apart. Man against man, family against family, group against group, nation against nation.

Nearly all those engaged in this fierce competition declare that their aim is peace and justice for themselves, their neighbors, and their nations: Give us power and we shall have justice; give us fame and we shall set a great example; give us money and we shall be comfortable and happy. People throughout the world deeply believe that, and act accordingly. On this appalling dry bender, society seems to be staggering down a dead-end road. The stop sign is clearly marked. It says "Disaster."

What has this got to do with anonymity and Alcoholics Anonymous?

We of AA ought to know. Nearly every one of us has traversed this identical dead-end path. Powered by alcohol and self-justification, many of us have pursued the phantoms of self-importance and money right up to the disaster stop sign. Then came AA. We faced about and found ourselves on a new high road where the direction signs said never a word about power, fame, or wealth. The new signs read, "This way to sanity and serenity — the price is self-sacrifice."

Our new book, *Twelve Steps and Twelve Traditions,* states that "anonymity is the greatest protection our Society can ever have." It says also that "the spiritual substance of anonymity is sacrifice."

Let's turn to AA's twenty years of experience and see how we arrived at that belief, now expressed in our Traditions Eleven and Twelve.

At the beginning we sacrificed alcohol. We had to, or it would have killed us. But we couldn't get rid of alcohol unless we made other sacrifices. Big-shotism and phony thinking had to go. We had to toss self-justification, self-pity, and anger right out the window. We had to quit the crazy contest for personal prestige and big bank balances. We had to take personal responsibility for our sorry state and quit blaming others for it.

Were these sacrifices? Yes, they were. To gain enough humility and self-respect to stay alive at all we had to give up what had really been our dearest possession — our ambitions and our illegitimate pride.

But even this was not enough. Sacrifice had to go much further. Other people had to benefit too. So we took on some Twelfth Step work; we began to carry the AA message. We sacrificed time, energy, and our own money to do this. We couldn't keep what we had unless we gave it away.

Did we demand that our new prospects give us anything? Were we asking them for power over their lives, for fame for our good work, or for a cent of their money? No, we were not. We found that if we demanded any of these things our Twelfth Step work went flat. So these natural desires had to be sacrificed; otherwise, our prospects received little or no sobriety. Nor, indeed, did we.

Thus we learned that sacrifice had to bring a double benefit, or else little at all. We began to know about the kind of giving of ourselves that had no price tag on it.

When the first AA group took form, we soon learned a lot more of this. We found that each of us had to make willing sacrifices for the group itself, sacrifices for the common welfare. The group, in turn, found that it had to give up many of its own rights for the protection and welfare of each member, and for AA as a whole. These sacrifices had to be made or AA couldn't continue to exist.

Out of these experiences and realizations, the Twelve Traditions of Alcoholics Anonymous began to take shape and substance.

Gradually we saw that the unity, the effectiveness — yes, even the survival — of AA would always depend upon our continued willingness to sacrifice our personal ambitions and desires for the common safety and welfare. Just as sacrifice meant survival for the individual, so did sacrifice mean unity and survival for the group and for AA's entire Fellowship.

Viewed in this light, AA's Twelve Traditions are little else than a list of sacrifices which the experience of twenty years has taught us that we must make, individually and collectively, if AA itself is to stay alive and healthy.

In our Twelve Traditions we have set our faces against nearly every trend in the outside world.

We have denied ourselves personal government, professionalism, and the right to say who our members shall be. We have abandoned do-goodism, reform, and paternalism. We refuse charitable money and prefer to pay our own way. We will cooperate with practically everybody, yet we decline to marry our Society to anyone. We abstain from public controversy and will not quarrel among ourselves about those things that so rip society asunder — religion, politics, and reform. We have but one purpose: to carry the AA message to the sick alcoholic who wants it.

We take these attitudes not at all because we claim special virtue or wisdom; we do these things because hard experience has told us that we must — if AA is to survive in the distraught world of today. We also give up rights and make sacrifices because we ought to — and, better yet, because we want to. AA is a power greater than any of us; it must go on living or else uncounted thousands of our kind will surely die. This we know.

Now where does anonymity fit into this picture? What is anonymity anyhow? Why do we think it is the greatest single protection that AA can ever have? Why is it our greatest symbol of personal sacrifice, the spiritual key to all our Traditions and to our whole way of life?

The following fragment of AA history will reveal, I deeply hope, the answer we all seek.

Years ago a noted ball player sobered up through AA. Because his comeback was so spectacular, he got a tremendous personal ovation in the press and Alcoholics Anonymous got much of the credit. His full name and picture, as a member of AA, were seen by millions of fans. It did us plenty of good; alcoholics flocked in. We loved this. I was specially excited because it gave me ideas.

Soon I was on the road, happily handing out personal interviews and pictures. To my delight, I found I could hit the front pages, just as he could. Besides, he couldn't hold his publicity pace, but I could hold mine. I only needed to keep traveling and talking. The local AA groups and newspapers did the rest. I was astonished when recently I looked at those old newspaper stories. For two or three years I guess I was AA's number one anonymity breaker.

So I can't really blame any AA who has grabbed the spotlight since. I set the main example myself, years ago.

At the time, this looked like the thing to do. Thus justified, I ate it up. What a bang it gave me when I read those two-column spreads about "Bill the Broker," full name and picture, the guy who was saving drunks by the thousands!

Then this fair sky began to be a little overcast. Murmurs were heard from AA skeptics who said, "This guy Bill is hogging the big time. Dr. Bob isn't getting his share." Or, again, "Suppose all this publicity goes to Bill's head and he gets drunk on us?"

This stung. How could they persecute me when I was doing so much good? I told my critics that this was America and didn't they know I had the right of free speech? And wasn't this country and every other run by big-name leaders? Anonymity was maybe okay for the average AA. But co-founders ought to be exceptions. The public certainly had a right to know who *we* were.

Real AA power-drivers (prestige-hungry people, folks just like me) weren't long in catching on. They were going to be exceptions, too. They said that anonymity before the general public was just for timid people; all the braver and bolder souls, like themselves, should stand right up before the flash bulbs and be counted. This kind of courage would soon do away with the stigma on alcoholics. The public would right away see what fine citizens recovered drunks could make. So more and more members broke their anonymity, all for the good of AA. What if a drunk *was* photographed with the governor? Both he and the governor deserved the honor, didn't they? Thus we zoomed along, down the dead-end road!

The next anonymity-breaking development looked even rosier. A close AA friend of mine wanted to go in for alcohol education. A department of a great university interested in alcoholism wanted her to go out and tell the general public that alcoholics were sick people, and that plenty could be done about it. My friend was a crack public speaker and writer. Could she tell the general public that she was an AA member? Well, why not? By using the name Alcoholics Anonymous she'd get fine publicity for a good brand of alcohol education and for AA, too. I thought it an excellent idea and therefore gave my blessing.

AA was already getting to be a famous and valuable name. Backed by our name and her own great ability, the results were immediate. In nothing flat her own full name and picture, plus excellent accounts of her educational project, and of AA, landed in nearly every large paper in North America. The public understanding of alcoholism increased, the stigma on drunks lessened, and AA got new members. Surely there could be nothing wrong with that.

But there was. For the sake of this short-term benefit, we were taking on a future liability of huge and menacing proportions.

Presently an AA member began to publish a crusading magazine devoted to the cause of Prohibition. He thought Alcoholics Anonymous ought to help make the world bone dry. He disclosed himself as an AA member and freely used the AA name to attack the evils of whiskey and those who made it and drank it. He pointed out that he too was an "educator," and that his brand of education was the "right kind." As for putting AA into public controversy, he thought that was exactly where we should be. So he busily used AA's name to do just that. Of course, he broke his anonymity to help his cherished cause along.

This was followed by a proposal from a liquor trade association that an AA member take on a job of "education." People were to be told that too much alcohol was bad for anyone and that certain people — the alcoholics — shouldn't drink at all. What could be the matter with this?

The catch was that our AA friend had to break his anonymity; every piece of publicity and literature was to carry his full name as a member of Alcoholics Anonymous. This of course would be bound to create the definite public impression that AA favored "education," liquor-trade style.

Though these two developments never happened to get far, their implications were nevertheless terrific. They spelled it right out for us. By hiring out to another cause, and then declaring his AA membership to the whole public, it was in the power of an AA to marry Alcoholics Anonymous to practically any enterprise or controversy at all, good or bad. The more valuable the AA name became, the greater the temptation would be.

Further proof of this was not long in showing up. Another member started to put us into the advertising business. He had been commissioned by a life insurance company to deliver a series of twelve "lectures" on Alcoholics Anonymous over a national radio hookup. This would of course advertise life insurance and Alcoholics Anonymous — and naturally our friend himself — all in one good-looking package.

At AA Headquarters, we read the proposed lectures. They were about 50 percent AA and 50 percent our friend's personal religious convictions. This could create a false public view of us. Religious prejudice against AA would be aroused. So we objected.

Our friend shot back a hot letter saying that he felt "inspired" to give these lectures, and that we had no business to interfere with his right of free speech. Even though he was going to get a fee for his work, he had nothing in mind except the welfare of AA. And if we didn't know what was good for us, that was too bad! We and AA's board of trustees could go plumb to the devil. The lectures were going on the air.

This was a poser. Just by breaking anonymity and so using the AA name for his own purposes, our friend could take over our public relations, get us into religious trouble, put us into the advertising business and, for all these good works, the insurance company would pay him a handsome fee.

Did this mean that any misguided member could thus endanger our Society any time or any place simply by breaking anonymity and telling himself how much good he was going to do for us? We envisioned every AA advertising man looking up a commercial sponsor, using the AA name to sell everything from pretzels to prune juice.

Something had to be done. We wrote our friend that AA had a right of free speech too. We wouldn't oppose him publicly, but we could and would guarantee that his sponsor would receive several thousand letters of objection from AA members if the program went on the radio. Our friend abandoned the project.

But our anonymity dike continued to leak. AA members began to take us into politics. They began to tell state legislative committees — publicly, of course — just what AA wanted in the way of rehabilitation, money, and enlightened legislation.

Thus, by full name and often by pictures, some of us became lobbyists. Other members sat on benches with police court judges, advising which drunks in the lineup should go to AA and which to jail.

Then came money complications involving broken anonymity. By this time, most members felt we ought to stop soliciting funds publicly for AA purposes. But the educational enterprise of my university-sponsored friend had meanwhile mushroomed. She had a perfectly proper and legitimate need for money and plenty of it. Therefore, she asked the public for it, putting on drives to this end. Since she was an AA member and continued to say so, many contributors were confused. They thought AA was in the educational field or else they thought AA itself was raising money when indeed it was not and didn't want to.

So AA's name was used to solicit funds at the very moment we were trying to tell people that AA wanted no outside money.

Seeing what happened, my friend, wonderful member that she is, tried to resume her anonymity. Because she had been so thoroughly publicized, this has been a hard job. It has taken her years. But she has made the sacrifice, and I here want to record my deep thanks on behalf of us all.

This precedent set in motion all sorts of public solicitations by AAs for money — money for drying-out farms, Twelfth Step enterprises, AA boarding houses, clubs, and the like — powered largely by anonymity breaking.

We were next startled to learn that we had been drawn into partisan politics, this time for the benefit of a single individual. Running for public office, a member splashed his political advertising with the fact that he was an AA and, by inference, sober as a judge! AA being popular in his state, he thought it would help him win on election day.

Probably the best story in this class tells how the AA name was used to back up a libel lawsuit. A member, whose name and professional attainments are known on three continents, got hold of a letter which she thought damaged her professional reputation. She felt something should be done about this and so did her lawyer, also an AA. They assumed that both the public and AA would be rightfully angry if the facts were known. Forthwith, several newspapers headlined how Alcoholics Anonymous was rooting for one of its lady members — named in full, of course — to win her suit for libel. Shortly after this, a noted radio commentator told a listening audience, estimated at twelve million people, the same thing. This again proved that the AA name could be used for purely personal purposes — this time on a nationwide scale.

The old files at AA Headquarters reveal many scores of such experiences with broken anonymity. Most of them point up the same lessons.

They tell us that we alcoholics are the biggest rationalizers in the world; that fortified with the excuse we are doing great things for AA we can, through broken anonymity, resume our old and disastrous pursuit of personal power and prestige, public honors, and money — the same implacable urges that when frustrated once caused us to drink; the same forces that are today ripping the globe apart at its seams. Moreover, they make clear that enough spectacular anonymity breakers could someday carry our whole Society down into that ruinous dead end with them.

So we are certain that if such forces ever rule our Fellowship, we will perish too, just as other societies have perished throughout human history. Let us not suppose for a moment that we recovered alcoholics are so much better or stronger than other folks; or that because in twenty years nothing has ever happened to AA, nothing ever can.

Our really great hope lies in the fact that our total experience, as alcoholics and as AA members, has at last taught us the immense power of these forces for self-destruction. These hard-won lessons have made us entirely willing to undertake every personal sacrifice necessary for the preservation of our treasured Fellowship.

This is why we see anonymity *at the general public level* as our chief protection against ourselves, the guardian of all our Traditions, and the greatest symbol of self-sacrifice that we know.

Of course, no AA need be anonymous to family, friends, or neighbors. Disclosure there is usually right and good. Nor is there any special danger when we speak at group or semi-public AA meetings, provided press reports reveal first names only.

But before the general public — press, radio, films, television, and the like — the revelation of full names and pictures is the point of peril. This is the main escape hatch for the fearful destructive forces that still lie latent in us all. Here the lid can and must stay down.

We now fully realize that 100 percent personal anonymity before the public is just as vital to the life of AA as 100 percent sobriety is to the life of each and every member. This is not the counsel of fear; it is the prudent voice of long experience. I am sure that we are going to listen; that we shall make every needed sacrifice. Indeed, we have been listening. Today only a handful of anonymity breakers remain.

I say all this with what earnestness I can; I say this because I know what the temptation of fame and money really is. I can say this because I was once a breaker of anonymity myself. I thank God that years ago the voice of experience and the urging of wise friends took me out of that perilous path into which I might have led our entire Society. Thus I learned that the temporary or seeming good can often be the deadly enemy of the permanent best. When it comes to survival for AA, nothing short of our very best will be good enough.

We want to maintain 100 percent anonymity for still another potent reason, one often overlooked. Instead of securing us more publicity, repeated self-serving anonymity breaks could severely damage the wonderful relation we now enjoy with press and public alike. We could wind up with a poor press and little public confidence at all.

For many years, news channels all over the world have showered AA with enthusiastic publicity, a never ending stream of it, far out of proportion to the news values involved. Editors tell us why this is. They give us extra space and time because their confidence in AA is complete. The very foundation of that high confidence is, they say, our continual insistence on personal anonymity at the press level.

Never before had news outlets and public relations experts heard of a society that absolutely refused personally to advertise its leaders or members. To them, this strange and refreshing novelty has always been proof positive that AA is on the square, that nobody has an angle.

This, they tell us, is the prime reason for their great goodwill. This is why, in season and out, they continue to carry the AA message of recovery to the whole world.

If, through enough anonymity lapses, we finally caused the press, the public, and our alcoholic prospects themselves to wonder about our motives, we'd surely lose this priceless asset; and, along with it, countless prospective members. Alcoholics Anonymous would not then be getting more good publicity; it would be getting less and worse. Therefore the handwriting on the wall is clear. Because most of us can already see it, and because the rest of us soon will, I'm fully confident that no such dark day will ever fall upon our Society.

For a long time now, both Dr. Bob and I have done everything possible to maintain the Tradition of anonymity. Just before he died, some of Dr. Bob's friends suggested that there should be a suitable monument or mausoleum erected in honor of him and his wife, Anne, something befitting a founder. Dr. Bob declined, with thanks. Telling me about this a little later, he grinned and said, "For Heaven's sake, Bill, why don't you and I get buried like other folks?"

Last summer I visited the Akron cemetery where Bob and Anne lie. Their simple stone says never a word about Alcoholics Anonymous. This made me so glad I cried. Did this wonderful couple carry personal anonymity too far when they so firmly refused to use the words "Alcoholics Anonymous," even on their own burial stone?

For one, I don't think so. I think that this great and final example of self-effacement will prove of more permanent worth to AA than could any spectacular public notoriety or fine mausoleum.

We don't have to go to Akron, Ohio, to see Dr. Bob's memorial. Dr. Bob's real monument is visible throughout the length and breadth of AA. Let us look again at its true inscription — one word only, which we AAs have written. That word is sacrifice.

Respecting Money

November 1957

Here in the States it is Thanksgiving time. The whole of AA takes its cue from this occasion and we rejoice worldwide in gratitude for the blessings that our Fellowship has bestowed upon us. It is traditional, too, that this is the season for taking stock of our progress as a Fellowship. We look at our Society and ask, "How are we doing?"

AA's Twelve Traditions are the measuring rods that we use. "How well are we sticking to the Twelve Traditions?" is the prime question of each Thanksgiving week. Every year we see more clearly that adherence to our hard-won traditional principles is the basis for our unity and the effective carrying of our message; that indifference, lack of understanding, or rebellion against these principles could result in widespread dissension and maybe ruin. We keenly realize that the practice of the Twelve Traditions is quite as vital to the life of AA as a whole as is the practice of the Twelve Steps to the life and sobriety of each member.

The Grapevine has asked me to write about the Traditions in this issue. Accordingly I've selected those which deal with the often misunderstood and sometimes unpopular topic of money — its use and its misuse. About this, our Traditions make two short and simple declarations. In Tradition Seven we read: "Every AA group ought to be fully self-supporting, declining outside contributions." Tradition Eight states: "Alcoholics Anonymous should remain forever nonprofessional, but our service centers may employ special workers."

These few words pack immense meaning. They are the outcome of the huge controversies and struggles of our pioneering time when we knew that AA would have to come up with a sound and workable money policy or else face endless ineffectiveness and possible collapse. If ever a matter was taken seriously, it was the question of money.

The money debates of that time veered crazily between two extreme poles of opinion. The conservatives said that AA as such should use no money at all. Meetings would be confined to homes; we could spread our message by word of mouth. There would be no publicity, no literature, no treasurers, no committees, no intergroups, and no trustees. There would be no paid workers; hence no army of bureaucrats and therefore no possibility of any government. By refusing to collect money, we'd stay completely out of business. Everything would be done spontaneously, each member following his own conscience. Cried the conservatives, "Lead us not into temptation. Let's keep it just that simple."

At the other extreme we had the radicals, the promoters. They said we had to have vast sums. We must employ press agents; we'd need a great literature. We would have to own chains of hospitals; there would need to be regiments of paid workers of every description, even paid missionaries to carry the message to distant cities and far lands. As we got going there would have to be vast public rallies. Squads of members, riding sound trucks, would criss-cross the country. As world-famous men and women joined up with us, they would gladly stand on the rooftops to shout the good word. Thus the AA message, pure and ungarbled, would whiz around the world quite as fast as did Jules Verne's hero — in just about eighty days! No fantasy was too impossible, no idea too grandiose for the promoters. And where would they get the money? From the public, of course; the rich would send in millions.

Today we can see that the conservatives would have rotted us by doing nothing. On the other hand, the promoters would have surely ruined us by trying to do everything.

The process of separating the sense from the nonsense was long and painful. We were vastly confused because nobody had any monopoly on good sense. In their prudence the conservatives seemed right when they said that great sums would endanger us. But when fear got the upper hand and they insisted on no money or services whatever, they seemed to be talking arrant foolishness. Their program could lead only to great confusion and a snail's pace growth. It was much the same with the promoters. In their enthusiasms they sometimes urged dangerous schemes. Yet wisdom was often theirs nonetheless.

Slowly, as the hammers of the promoters beat on the stubborn anvils of the conservatives, our two "money" Traditions were fashioned.

At first we made certain concessions to the radicals. We conceded that, though unorganized as a whole, we would nevertheless have to create committees or service boards so that AA could function and carry our message and, at regional and international levels, we would sometimes have to hire a few full-time workers. This was going to cost money, but never a lot of it, never enough to pose any great problem or future temptation.

This obvious necessity did, however, pose the question of professionalism. There was a widespread and justified fear in the early days that AA might be saddled with a class of paid Twelfth Step workers — people who would want salaries or fees for carrying the AA message person-to-person and face-to-face. It did not take us long to see that such a development would certainly kill the spirit of our whole undertaking. The Twelfth Step simply couldn't be sold for money.

This great fear of professionalism sideswiped us even when we hired an AA janitor or cook. And it doubly bedeviled us when we finally had to hire a few AA members to work full-time as area or international secretaries. For a while, they carried the awful stigma of professionalism. They were, we said, making money out of AA. Believe it or not, they were personally avoided by many a fearful and righteous member. Even the committees and boards for whom they worked often regarded them as a sort of necessary but heretical evil. In them we were "mixing the material with the spiritual." To keep these borderline "professionals" in a proper "spiritual condition" we mixed in the smallest amount of money we could; meaning that we paid them the least salaries for which they could possibly consent to work.

However, the radicals had partially made their point. AA did have to have some paid workers, if only a few. We finally saw that these people were primarily paid for making good and effective Twelfth Step work possible. Today they are not regarded as professionals at all and we try to pay them well. They are among the most dedicated AAs that we know. Hence, Tradition Eight declares, "Alcoholics Anonymous should remain forever nonprofessional, but our service centers may employ special workers."

But the conservatives also had their victory when we finally took the decision to build a dike against the inrush of contributions from the world outside. We began to decline all such gifts, large and small. Our service centers would never wax rich from the contributions of AA members. But our well-meaning friends, by gift and bequest, could endow us with huge funds.

Once we began to accept donations of this kind, there would be no end. Though easily able to pay our own small service bills, we would nevertheless begin to accept huge amounts of charity. Worse still, rich AA service boards would embark on all sorts of needless and compromising adventures. A large paid bureaucracy would certainly take shape and the worst fears of the conservatives would be realized. Respecting gifts and grants, their wisdom had been supremely right. Thus we developed Tradition Seven: "Every AA group ought to be fully self-supporting, declining outside contributions."

Not long after this Tradition was written, AA's trustees turned down a bequest of $10,000 at a moment when money was badly needed. It was a time when, by a considerable margin, the AA groups were failing to support their own world Headquarters.

Nevertheless our Trustees promptly plugged that first threatened leak in our newly constructed dike against the temptation to take money from outside AA. Thereafter AA would pay for its services or do without them. That decision still stirs me. It was one of the great turning points in our history.

To conclude: Our spiritual way of life is safe for future generations if, as a Society, we resist the temptation to receive money from the outside world. But this leaves us with a responsibility — one that every member ought to understand. We cannot skimp when the treasurer of our group passes the hat. Our groups, our areas, and AA as a whole will not function unless our services are sufficent and their bills are paid.

When we meet and defeat the temptation to take large gifts, we are only being prudent. But when we are generous with the hat we give a token that we are grateful for our blessings and evidence that we are eager to share what we have found with all those who still suffer.

Problems Other Than Alcohol

February 1958

Perhaps there is no suffering more horrible than drug addiction, especially that kind which is produced by morphine, heroin, and other narcotics. Such drugs twist the mind and the awful process of withdrawal racks the sufferer's body. Compared with the addict and his woes, we alcoholics are pikers. Barbiturates, carried to extremes, can be almost as bad. In AA we have members who have made great recoveries from both the bottle and the needle. We also have a great many others who were — or still are — victimized by "goof balls" and even by the new tranquilizers.

Consequently, this problem of drug addiction in its several forms lies close to us all. It stirs our deepest interest and sympathy. In the world around us we see legions of men and women who are trying to cure or to escape their problems by this means. Many AAs, especially those who have suffered these particular addictions, are now asking, "What can we do about drugs — within our Fellowship, and without?"

Because several projects to help pill and drug takers are already afloat — projects which use AA's Twelve Steps and in which AA members are active — there has arisen a whole series of questions as to how these efforts, already meeting with not a little success, can be rightly related to the AA groups and to AA as a whole.

Specifically, here is a list of questions: 1) Can a nonalcoholic pill or drug addict become an AA member? 2) Can such a person be brought, as a visitor, to an "open" AA meeting for help and inspiration? 3) Can a pill or drug taker, who also has a genuine alcoholic history, become a member of AA? 4) Can AAs who have suffered both alcoholism and addiction form themselves into special purpose groups to help other AAs who are having drug trouble? 5) Could such a special purpose group call itself an AA group? 6) Could such a group also include nonalcoholic drug users? 7) If so, should these nonalcoholic pill or drug users be led to believe that they have become AA members? 8) Is there any objection if AAs who have had the dual problem join outside groups, such as Addicts Anonymous or Narcotics Anonymous?

While some of these questions almost answer themselves, others do not. But all of them, I think, can readily be resolved to the satisfaction of everyone if we have a good look at the AA Traditions which apply, and another look at our long experience with the special purpose groups in which AAs are active today — both within and without our Society.

Now there are certain things that AA cannot do for anybody, regardless of what our several desires or sympathies may be.

Our first duty, as a Society, is to insure our own survival. Therefore we have to avoid distractions and multipurpose activity. An AA group, as such, cannot take on *all* the personal problems of its members, let alone the problems of the whole world.

Sobriety — freedom from alcohol — through the teaching and practice of the Twelve Steps, is the sole purpose of an AA group. Groups have repeatedly tried other activities and they have always failed. It has also been learned that there is no possible way to make nonalcoholics into AA members. We have to confine our membership to alcoholics and we have to confine our AA groups to a single purpose. If we don't stick to these principles, we shall almost surely collapse. And if we collapse, we cannot help anyone.

To illustrate, let's review some typical experiences. Years ago, we hoped to give AA membership to our families and to certain nonalcoholic friends who had been greatly helpful. They had their problems, too, and we wanted them in our fold. Regretfully, we found that this was impossible. They couldn't make straight AA talks; nor, save a few exceptions, could they identify with new AA members. Hence, they couldn't do continuous Twelfth Step work. Close to us as these good folks were, we had to deny them membership. We could only welcome them at our open meetings.

Therefore I see no way of making nonalcoholic addicts into AA members. Experience says loudly that we can admit no exceptions, even though drug users and alcoholics happen to be first cousins of a sort. If we persist in trying this, I'm afraid it will be hard on the drug user himself, as well as on AA. We must accept the fact that no nonalcoholic, whatever his affliction, can be converted into an alcoholic AA member.

Suppose, though, that we are approached by a drug addict who nevertheless has had a genuine alcoholic history. There was a time when such a person would have been rejected. Many early AAs had the almost comical notion that they were "pure alcoholics" — guzzlers only, no other serious problems at all. When alcoholic ex-cons and drug users first turned up there was much pious indignation. "What will people think?" chanted the pure alcoholics. Happily, this foolishness has long since evaporated.

One of the best AAs I know is a man who had been seven years on the needle before he joined up with us. But prior to that, he had been a

terrific alcoholic and his history proved it. Therefore he could qualify
for AA and this he certainly did. Since then, he has helped many AAs
and some non-AAs with their pill and drug troubles. Of course, that is
strictly his affair and is no way the business of the AA group to which he
belongs. In his group he is a member because, in actual fact, he is an
alcoholic.

Such is the sum of what AA *cannot* do — for narcotics addicts or
for anybody else.

Now, then, what *can* be done? Very effective answers to problems
other than freedom from alcohol have always been found through special purpose groups, some of them operating within AA and some on
the outside.

Our first special purpose group was created 'way back in 1938.
AA needed a world service office and some literature. It had a service
problem that could not be met by an AA group, as such. Therefore, we
formed a board of trustees (the Alcoholic Foundation) to look after
these matters. Some of the trustees were alcoholics, and some were
nonalcoholics. Obviously, this was not an AA group. Instead, it was a
group of AAs and non-AAs who devoted themselves to a special task.

Another example: In 1940, the New York AAs got lonesome and installed themselves in a club. The club had directors and dues-paying AA
members. For a long time, the club members and directors thought that
they were an AA group. But after a while, it was found that lots of AAs
who attended meetings at "Old 24th" didn't care one hoot for the club,
as such. Hence, the management of the club (for its social purpose) had
to be completely separated from the management of the AA group that
came there to hold its meetings. It took years of hassling to prove that
you couldn't put an AA group into the club business and make it stick.
Everywhere today, club managements and their dues-paying members
are seen as special purpose groups, not as AA groups.

The same thing has happened with drying-out places and "Twelfth
Step houses" managed by AAs. We never think of these activities as AA
groups. They are clearly seen as the functions of interested individuals
who are doing helpful and often very valuable jobs.

Some years ago, numbers of AAs formed themselves in "retreat
groups" having a religious purpose. At first, they wanted to call themselves AA groups of various descriptions. But they soon realized this
could not be done because their groups had a dual purpose: both AA and
religion.

At another time a number of us AAs wanted to enter the field of alcohol education. I was one of them. We associated ourselves with some nonalcoholics, likewise interested. The nonalcoholics wanted AAs because they needed our experience, philosophy, and general slant. Things were fine until some of us AAs publicly disclosed our membership in the educational group. Right away, the public got the idea that this particular brand of alcoholic education and Alcoholics Anonymous were one and the same thing. It took years to change this impression. But now that this correction has been made, plenty of AA members work with this fine group and we are glad that they do.

It was thus proven that, as individuals, we can carry the AA experience and ideas into *any outside field whatever,* provided that we guard anonymity and refuse to use the AA name for money-raising or publicity purposes.

I'm very sure that these experiences of yesterday can be the basis of resolving today's confusions about the narcotic problem. This problem is new, but the AA experience and Tradition which can solve it is already old and time-tested. I think we might sum it up like this:

We cannot give AA membership to nonalcoholic narcotics addicts. But like anyone else, they should be able to attend certain open AA meetings, provided, of course, that the groups themselves are willing.

AA members who are so inclined should be encouraged to band together in groups to deal with sedative and drug problems. But they ought to refrain from calling themselves AA groups.

There seems to be no reason why several AAs cannot join, if they wish, with a group of straight addicts to solve the alcohol and the drug problem together. But, obviously, such a dual purpose group should not insist that it be called an AA group nor should it use the AA name in its title. Neither should its straight addict contingent be led to believe that they have become AA members by reason of such an association.

Certainly there is every good reason for interested AAs to join with outside groups, working on the narcotic problem, provided the Traditions of anonymity and of "no endorsements" are respected.

In conclusion, I want to say that throughout AA's history, most of our special purpose groups have accomplished very wonderful things. There is great reason to hope that those AAs who are now working in the grim regions of narcotic addiction will achieve equal success.

In AA, the group has strict limitations, but the individual has scarcely any. Remembering to observe the Traditions of anonymity and nonendorsement, the AA member can carry AA's message into every troubled area of this very troubled world.

Let's Make Practical and Spiritual Sense

The 1958 General Service Conference unanimously voted down a proposal for a paperback edition of the Big Book. Believing that all AAs should fully understand why this was done, Bill asked the Grapevine to reprint portions of a letter he had written to an old friend on this long-debated topic.

August 1958

Dear ———,

It was fine to hear from you again. We old-timers are getting more and more separated. My nostalgia for the old days is often with me and letters like yours bring it back.

You raised a time-tested question, "What about a cheap edition of the AA book — maybe a fifty-cent paperback?" This question raises a considerable number of other questions, having both a practical and spiritual bearing.

First, let's take a look at the early history of the cheap book question. The issue of a low-priced book versus a higher-priced one was seriously and heatedly debated for several years after the Big Book came out in 1939 at $3.50. In this era, the majority of AAs were doubtless in favor of a one-dollar job. When we announced the $3.50 price, the reaction was very strong (and to some extent unreasonable): "Bill had let AA down," "The price is too high for the poor drunk," "Since everything in AA is free, why not a giveaway book?" "Because AA is nonprofit, why should the groups and the New York Headquarters make a profit?" As for royalties to Dr. Bob and me — well, some said that made us profiteers, if not racketeers.

From the point of view of many of the membership, these were powerful arguments. A giveaway book was the purest kind of spiritual enterprise. But a volume decently bound and priced within the normal trade range, a volume which would help carry the expenses of AA's Headquarters, was looked upon as a pretty fearsome evil. Consequently, I fell under the severest criticism of my whole AA life.

Yet our history proves that the sometimes idealistic majority of that day was seriously mistaken. Had there been no book earnings for the Headquarters and no royalties for Dr. Bob and me, AA would have taken a very different and probably disastrous course. Dr. Bob and Sister Ignatia could not have looked after those 5,000 drunks in their hospital pioneering at Akron. I would have had to quit full-time work fifteen years ago. Our book would have been in the hands of an outside publisher. There could have been no Twelve Traditions and no General Service Conference. Financially crippled, the Headquarters could not have spread AA around the world. Indeed, it might have folded up completely.

All of this would have come to pass had not earnings of the Big Book plugged up the often large deficits in group contributions to Headquarters. In the 1945-1950 period, for example, I saw our reserve fund of $100,000 drop to $40,000 in three hectic years. In these years the AA General Service Office and the AA Grapevine once reached a combined deficit of $3,000 a month. It was the book money that kept us afloat and enabled us to reorganize the service office and put today's General Service Conference into operation. A cheap AA book would have been a practical and spiritual mistake of major proportions. The AA message would have been carried to the few instead of to the many. There is not the slightest doubt about it. Everybody who now wants a fifty-cent paperback should bear this part of our history seriously in mind.

AA's trusteeship, our General Service Board, has a reserve fund which has been slowly accumulated out of book earnings over the years. This fund is equal to one year's running expense of the Headquarters. We think it is our chief protection against hard times and the possibility of a large drop in group contributions. Even in good times, group contributions have often failed to pay Headquarters' expenses by a considerable margin. If we could actually collect from every recovered AA member, the annual cost to each would be only one dollar a year. In practice, we ask for $2.00 a member and average considerably less. The AA office ran $15,000 in the red in 1957 and the Grapevine had an operating deficit of $10,000. Since this is a frequent situation in good times, what would actually happen to us in hard times?

In hard times, AA members and their groups will surely look after themselves. But in such circumstances, how well would they take care of general Headquarters? Having never been through such a time, nobody can say. We can't even make an informed guess. We simply know that our Headquarters still runs deficits. We also know that one-third of the AA groups, representing 50,000 members, send Headquarters nothing, even in boom times. We therefore have no reason to believe in Santa Claus. That is why we have insisted on building up our reserve fund. It is our primary protection against the impairment or collapse of AA's general services; those services which have spread the good word throughout the world and which we ought to maintain in full strength under all conditions.

There are those who feel that a fifty-cent book would not seriously cut into the sales of our $4.50 edition. But would it not? At Headquarters we are finding many able volunteer service workers. One of these is the vice president of a large book publishing house. He understands book markets, inside AA and out. He emphatically points out that ultracheap AA books, especially paperbacks, would severely damage our present sales and income. Wouldn't it therefore be wise to ask ourselves, "Can we afford those cheap books now?"

There has been some hope that the volume of fifty-cent book sales would be so huge on the public market that we would not lose much money anyhow. But this is one of those situations on which no reliable estimate can be made. As AA cannot go into newsstand or drugstore distribution, we would have to let an outside publisher do the job for us. Such a publisher would be the sole source of supply. Even if such a paperback house sold a million copies a year, the return to AA Publishing, Inc., in royalties and profits, would not exceed $10,000. This estimate may, of course, be far too optimistic. A preliminary investigation among publishers indicates that such a sale is to be questioned. Horse sense suggests this, too.

The main market for cheap paperbacks is dominated by former best-sellers, murder mysteries, sex novels, science fiction, and the like. Large and sustained volume is possible because of the huge public interest. Now the AA book has been on sale for almost twenty years, in bookstores. Alcoholics Anonymous and its Big Book have received vast advertising in all public media and this still continues. Nevertheless, our sale to the public has never been more than a dribble; it hasn't averaged 1,500 copies a year. So how can we have any assurance if we put a fifty-cent AA book on newsstands and in drugstores that sales are suddenly going to jump from 1,500 books to one million, or one hundred thousand, or even ten thousand? Nobody seems to be able to predict with confidence what a specialized textbook like ours would do if put on cheap sale with whodunits and science fiction in these city outlets. If we did fail to sell a large volume, we would have mostly failed our spiritual purpose of carrying the AA message. Compared to the vast publicity that AA already gets, the effect of a cheap book could not be very great in any case.

Next let us inquire if there is any real shortage of AA books and reading material inside AA. Let's also ponder whether our poorest members are really deprived of their chance at the AA book because we still lack a fifty-cent edition. Also, whether our excellent pamphlet literature cannot pretty well fill the need of such newcomers when necessary. We know that 350,000 AA books have already been distributed and that a half-million good pamphlets hit AA members every year. Who knows anyone in AA that hasn't been given a book, who can't borrow a book, or who can't buy one from his group on partial payment, or find the Big Book in a local library? Hardly anyone need be deprived of reading the present volume if he will make even a little effort to lay hold of a copy. Of course there are some exceptions, but these are being met; we already send gift copies of the Big Book to prisons and the institutional groups.

There might be certain spiritual advantages in a cheap book literature, but there would also be definite spiritual disadvantages.

There is the question of who is best able to pay for a given service — in this case, a giveaway book program. Is it the individual AAs, the AA groups, or is it AA as a whole? Obviously, the combined wealth and income of individual AA members is the real reservoir and source of money. The combined income of all alcoholics who have recovered in AA is easily one billion dollars a year. Compared with this, the money coming into our 7,000 AA group treasuries is a trickle. Compared to the funds that flow into local treasuries, the contributions to AA Headquarters are drops in a bucket. Our international treasury and reserve fund doesn't contain even one dollar for each alcoholic who has recovered in AA. Neither do these alcoholics supply these reserve funds; the book buyers do it. Probably half of the alcoholics who have recovered in AA over the years have never, directly or indirectly, sent a cent to Headquarters. Maybe our Headquarters financial statements look like big money to some. But these monies represent only the tiniest fraction of the total wealth and earning power of the members of Alcoholics Anonymous. AA Headquarters — AA as a whole, if you like — is relatively as poor as a church mouse. Should the Headquarters, the poorest part of AA, now undertake to finance the richest part — the individual AAs — with a fifty-cent book?

Does this make sense — practically or spiritually?

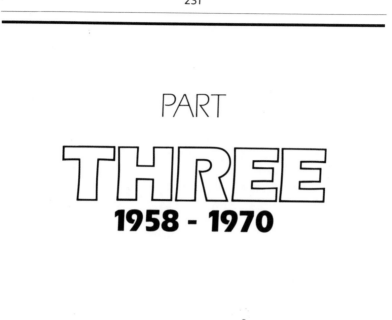

PART

THREE

1958 - 1970

By 1961, when Bill announced his final retirement from leadership in AA, he believed that he had completed all the major tasks he needed to do for the Fellowship. In his talk to the 1961 General Service Conference (see "Again at the Crossroads," page 324), Bill emphasized the importance of the principle of rotation, and of the need for him to step down as a leader and let AA's group conscience operate. While declaring his intention to move to the sidelines in AA, he also expressed his desire to continue writing for the Grapevine:

"...one primary channel of communication still stands wide open — my writing for the Grapevine. This I would certainly like to continue. Just now, for example, I'm doing a series of articles entitled 'Practicing These Principles in All Our Affairs.' Maybe these pieces can later be expanded into a full-sized book which would try to deal with the whole problem of living, as seen by us AAs. If it turns out that I can write it, such a volume might be of permanent value.

"There is another factor that bears upon my decision. Like every AA member I have a definite responsibility to become a citizen of the world around me...Therefore, I'm already exploring certain areas of outside activity in which I may be able to make a helpful, and possibly a meaningful, contribution.''

Among those areas of outside activity were a return, in a limited fashion, to work on Wall Street, and pursuit of an interest in niacin therapy. The full-sized book Bill hoped to write was never completed, partially because of his increasing outside involvement and also because his emphysema was growing worse as the 1960s progressed. Three articles (pages 251, 254, and 259) were introduced in the Grapevine as parts of the series on ''Practicing These Principles in All Our Affairs.'' No other articles were earmarked for the book, though much of the material reprinted here deals explicitly with its theme.

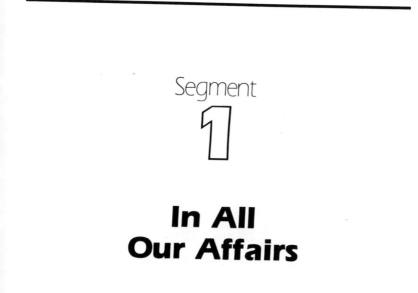

Segment 1

In All
Our Affairs

The Greatest Gift of All

December 1957

The greatest gift that can come to anybody is a spiritual awakening. Without doubt this would be the certain verdict of every well-recovered alcoholic in AA's entire Fellowship.

So, then, what is this "spiritual awakening," this "transforming experience"? How can we receive it and what does it do?

To begin with, a spiritual awakening is our means of finding sobriety. And to us of AA sobriety means life itself. We know that a spiritual experience is the key to survival from alcoholism and that for most of us it is the only key. We must awake or we die.

So we do awake, and we are sober. Then what? Is sobriety all that we are to expect of a spiritual awakening? Again, the voice of AA speaks up. No, sobriety is only a bare beginning, it is only the first gift of the first awakening. If more gifts are to be received, our awakening has to go on. And if it does go on, we find that bit by bit we can discard the old life — the one that did not work — for a new life that can and does work under any conditions whatever. Regardless of worldly success or failure, regardless of pain or joy, regardless of sickness or health or even of death itself, a new life of endless possibilities can be lived if we are willing to continue our awakening.

Soon after he entered AA, a certain newcomer approached me and he said: "I'm sober and it's mighty near a miracle. I admitted that I was licked, came to a few meetings, began to get honest with myself and my sponsor. Then that awful urge for a drink suddenly left me. There's been no more booze-fighting; the desire for alcohol has simply evaporated and I can't yet understand just why or just how. Here in AA the folks are wonderful. They care and they understand. It's a brand-new world to me.

"But," continued Mr. Newcomer, "I'm still plumb puzzled. I don't see just how this God business fits into practical living. And when they talk about a 'new life for an old one,' I can't take it all in. Sure enough I'm sober, and that's new. But now that I've gone ex-grog, what's the matter with trying to live my old life? That was okay, until the liquor got me. I was going places, on the way to making my pile. Things weren't too bad at home, either, until my wife yelled she'd had enough of me, and left. All I need is sobriety, and AA can keep on giving me that. Now I can go about my business. I'm sure I can make a better job of it this time."

Four years later, I ran across that same "newcomer." "Well, Joe," said I, "have you made your pile yet, and did your wife come back?"

With a half-smile, Joe looked at me steadily and replied: "No, Bill, nothing of the kind happened. For a whole year I had the devil of a time. How I stayed sober was more of a miracle than getting sober in the first place. I had to make that pile and get her back or else I was going to be miserable. And miserable I certainly was. But little by little, I woke up to the possibility that God hadn't put me on earth for the purpose of getting all the money, prestige, and romance that I could lay my hands on. I finally had to face the fact that I would have to settle for less, a lot less. And if I couldn't accept this, I'd probably get drunk again.

"So I quit giving lip service to AA's Serenity Prayer and really began to use it. Over and over I kept saying, 'God grant me the serenity to accept the things I cannot change, courage to change the things I can, and wisdom to know the difference.'

"As I slowly learned acceptance, my pain subsided. I began to wake up and look around. I began to see that my modest job was a means of living, and of serving society. The bigger and the better job could no longer be my chief aim. Then I looked at AA. What had I done for the Fellowship that had saved my life? Mighty little, I had to confess. So I began to go to meetings with a very different attitude. I quit my envy of financially well-heeled AAs and listened closely to what they said. I learned that their money was no longer a symbol of prestige; it was a trust for the best use to which it could be put. They also showed me that the temptations of riches could sometimes be worse than the pains of poverty. I also found that there was *no such thing* as an 'unfortunate' AA — that is, if he were a real member. If sick, he was, by fine example, an inspiration to those both sick and well. If poor in pocket, he could often be rich in spirit, an eager worker and servant of our Society.

"I now see that awakening and growing is something that never need stop and that growing pains are never to be feared, provided I am willing to learn the truth about myself from them.

"The other day an old-time AA gave me an example which I'll never forget. Jack is a real old-timer. In fact, he started AA in my town. I used to envy him because he was a millionaire.

"They told me he was in our local hospital, deathly sick, and about to die. In a way, I hated to go there, it would be so sad. When I walked into the room it was filled with AAs all in a happy mood. They were happy because Jack was happy. He was telling funny drinking stories, now and then wiping away the blood that ran down his chin from a cancerous mouth. He sat upright, his legs and bare feet hanging from the edge of the bed. A nurse came in, remonstrating, begging him to lie down. Waving her away, he said, 'If I lie down flat on this bed, I might die now. And that would be too bad, because I want to go to our AA state convention next week.'

"We saw that this was no bravado; he really meant it.

"A little later Jack again spoke of death. He said that he'd had a wonderful life. Whiskey had brought him great pain but, as a result, AA had given him great joy. With his 'awakening' in AA had come the utter conviction, indeed the sure knowledge, that 'in my Father's house there are many mansions.' Everybody there could see that to Jack, death was but a fresh awakening. He never did get to the AA convention.

"But Jack knew, and we know, that this didn't really matter, for Jack was in full possession of 'the greatest gift of all.' "

The Next Frontier: Emotional Sobriety

This article is the substance of a letter Bill wrote to a close friend who also had troublesome depressions.

January 1958

I think that many oldsters who have put our AA "booze cure" to severe but successful tests still find they often lack emotional sobriety. Perhaps they will be the spearhead for the next major development in AA — the development of much more real maturity and balance (which is to say, humility) in our relations with ourselves, with our fellows, and with God.

Those adolescent urges that so many of us have for top approval, perfect security, and perfect romance — urges quite appropriate to age seventeen — prove to be an impossible way of life when we are at age forty-seven or fifty-seven.

Since AA began, I've taken immense wallops in all these areas because of my failure to grow up, emotionally and spiritually. My God, how painful it is to keep demanding the impossible, and how very painful to discover, finally, that all along we have had the cart before the horse! Then comes the final agony of seeing how awfully wrong we have been, but still finding ourselves unable to get off the emotional merry-go-round.

How to translate a right mental conviction into a right emotional result, and so into easy, happy, and good living — well, that's not only the neurotic's problem, it's the problem of life itself for all of us who have got to the point of real willingness to hew to right principles in all our affairs.

Even then, as we hew away, peace and joy may still elude us. That's the place so many of us AA oldsters have come to. And it's a hell of a spot, literally. How shall our unconscious — from which so many of our fears, compulsions, and phony aspirations still stream — be brought into line with what we actually believe, know, and want! How to convince our dumb, raging, and hidden "Mr. Hyde" becomes our main task.

I've recently come to believe that this can be achieved. I believe so because I begin to see many benighted ones — folks like you and me — commencing to get results. Last autumn, depression, having no really rational cause at all, almost took me to the cleaners. I began to be scared that I was in for another long chronic spell. Considering the grief I've had with depressions, it wasn't a bright prospect.

I kept asking myself, "Why can't the Twelve Steps work to release depression?" By the hour, I stared at the St. Francis Prayer... "It's better to comfort than to be comforted." Here was the formula, all right. But why didn't it work?

Suddenly I realized what the matter was. My basic flaw had always been dependence — almost absolute dependence — on people or circumstances to supply me with prestige, security, and the like. Failing to get these things according to my perfectionist dreams and specifications, I had fought for them. And when defeat came, so did my depression.

There wasn't a chance of making the outgoing love of St. Francis a workable and joyous way of life until these fatal and almost absolute dependencies were cut away.

Because I had over the years undergone a little spiritual development, the *absolute* quality of these frightful dependencies had never before been so starkly revealed. Reinforced by what grace I could secure in prayer, I found I had to exert every ounce of will and action to cut off these faulty emotional dependencies upon people, upon AA, indeed, upon any set of circumstances whatsoever. Then only could I be free to love as Francis had. Emotional and instinctual satisfactions, I saw, were really the extra dividends of having love, offering love, and expressing a love appropriate to each relation of life.

Plainly, I could not avail myself of God's love until I was able to offer it back to him by loving others as he would have me. And I couldn't possibly do that so long as I was victimized by false dependencies.

For my dependency meant demand — a demand for the possession and control of the people and the conditions surrounding me.

While those words "absolute dependency" may look like a gimmick, they were the ones that helped to trigger my release into my present degree of stability and quietness of mind, qualities which I am now trying to consolidate by offering love to others regardless of the return to me.

This seems to be the primary healing circuit: an outgoing love of God's creation and his people, by means of which we avail ourselves of his love for us. It is most clear that the real current can't flow until our paralyzing dependencies are broken, and broken at depth. Only then can we possibly have a glimmer of what adult love really is.

Spiritual calculus, you say? Not a bit of it. Watch any AA of six months working with a new Twelfth Step case. If the case says "To the devil with you," the twelfth-stepper only smiles and turns to another case. He doesn't feel frustrated or rejected. If his next case responds, and in turn starts to give love and attention to other alcoholics yet gives none back to him, the sponsor is happy about it anyway. He still doesn't feel rejected; instead he rejoices that his one-time prospect is sober and happy. And if his next following case turns out in later time to be his best friend (or romance), then the sponsor is most joyful. But he well knows that his happiness is a by-product — the extra dividend of giving without any demand for a return.

The really stabilizing thing for him was having and offering love to that strange drunk on his doorstep. That was Francis at work, powerful and practical, minus dependency and minus demand.

In the first six months of my own sobriety, I worked hard with many alcoholics. Not a one responded. Yet this work kept me sober. It wasn't a question of those alcoholics giving me anything. My stability came out of trying to give, not out of demanding that I receive.

Thus I think it can work out with emotional sobriety. If we examine every disturbance we have, great or small, we will find at the root of it some unhealthy dependency and its consequent unhealthy demand. Let us, with God's help, continually surrender these hobbling demands. Then we can be set free to live and love; we may then be able to Twelfth Step ourselves and others into emotional sobriety.

Of course I haven't offered you a really new idea — only a gimmick that has started to unhook several of my own "hexes" at depth. Nowadays my brain no longer races compulsively in either elation, grandiosity, or depression. I have been given a quiet place in bright sunshine.

Take Step Eleven

June 1958

When it comes to the practice of AA's Step Eleven — "Sought through prayer and meditation to improve our conscious contact with God as we understood him, praying only for knowledge of his will for us and the power to carry that out" — I'm sure I am still very much in the beginner's class; I'm almost a case of arrested development.

Around me I see many people who make a far better job of relating themselves to God than I do. Certainly it mustn't be said I haven't made any progress at all over the years; I simply confess that I haven't made the progress that I might have made, my opportunities being what they have been, and still are.

My twenty-fourth AA anniversary is just ahead; I haven't had a drink in all this time. In fact, I've scarcely been tempted at all. This is some evidence that I must have taken and ever since maintained Step One: "We admitted we were powerless over alcohol — that our lives had become unmanageable." Step One was easy for me.

Then, at the very beginning, I was fortunate enough to receive a tremendous spiritual awakening and was instantly "made conscious of the presence of God" and "restored to sanity" — at least so far as alcohol is concerned. Therefore I've had no difficulty with AA's Step Two because, in my case, its content was an outright gift. Step Four and Step Five, dealing with self-survey and confession of one's defects, have not been overly difficult, either.

Of course, my self-analysis has frequently been faulty. Sometimes I've failed to share my defects with the right people; at other times, I've confessed *their* defects, rather than my own; and at still other times, my confession of defects has been more in the nature of loud complaints about my circumstances and my problems.

Nevertheless, I think I've usually been able to make a fairly thorough and searching job of finding and admitting my personal defects. So far as I know, there isn't at this moment a single defect or current problem of mine which hasn't been discussed with my close advisers. Yet this pretty well-ventilated condition is nothing for self-congratulation. Long ago I was lucky enough to see that I'd have to keep up my self-analysis or else blow my top completely. Though driven by stark necessity, this continuous self-revelation — to myself and to others — was rough medicine to take. But years of repetition has made this job far easier. Step Nine, making restitution for harms done, has fallen into much the same bracket.

In Step Twelve — carrying the AA message to others — I've found little else than great joy. We alkies are folks of action and I'm no exception. When action pays off as it does in AA, it's small wonder that Step Twelve is the most popular and, for most of us, the easiest one of all.

This little sketch of my own "pilgrim's progress" is offered to illustrate where I, and maybe lots of other AAs, have still been missing something of top importance. Through lack of disciplined attention and sometimes through lack of the right kind of faith, many of us keep ourselves year after year in the rather easy spiritual kindergarten I've just described. But almost inevitably we become dissatisfied; we have to admit we have hit an uncomfortable and maybe a very painful sticking point.

Twelfth-stepping, talking at meetings, recitals of drinking histories, confessions of our defects and what progress we have made with them no longer provide us with the released and the abundant life. Our lack of growth is often revealed by an unexpected calamity or a big emotional upset. Perhaps we hit the financial jackpot and are surprised that this solves almost nothing; that we are still bored and miserable, notwithstanding.

As we usually don't get drunk on these occasions, our bright-eyed friends tell us how well we are doing.

But inside, we know better. We know we aren't doing well enough. We still can't handle life, as life is. There must be a serious flaw somewhere in our spiritual practice and development.

What, then, is it?

The chances are better than even that we shall locate our trouble in our misunderstanding or neglect of AA's Step Eleven — prayer, meditation, and the guidance of God. The other Steps can keep most of us sober and somehow functioning. But Step Eleven can keep us growing, if we try hard and work at it continually. If we expend even five percent of the time on Step Eleven that we habitually (and rightly) lavish on Step Twelve, the results can be wonderfully far-reaching. That is an almost uniform experience of those who constantly practice Step Eleven.

In this article, I'd like to develop Step Eleven further — for the benefit of the complete doubter, the unlucky one who can't believe it has any real merit at all.

In lots of instances I think that people find their first great obstacle in the phrase "God as we understand him." The doubter is apt to say: "On the face of it, nobody can understand God. I half believe that there is a First Cause, a something, and maybe a Somebody. But I can't get any further than this. I think people are kidding themselves when they say they can. Even if there were a Somebody, why should he bother with little me, when, in making the cosmos run, he already has plenty to do? As for those folks who claim that God tells them where to drill for oil, or when to brush their teeth — well, they just make me tired."

Our friend is clearly one who believes in some kind of God — "God as he understands him." But he doesn't believe any bigger concept or better feeling about God to be possible. So he looks upon meditation, prayer, and guidance as the means of a self-delusion. Now what can our hard-pressed friend do about this?

Well, he can strenuously try meditation, prayer, and guidance, just as an experiment. He can address himself to whatever God he thinks there is. Or, if he thinks there is none, he can admit — just for experimental purposes — that he might be wrong. This is all-important. As soon as he is able to take this attitude, it means that he has stopped playing God himself; his mind has opened. Like any good scientist in his laboratory, our friend can assume a theory and pray to a "higher power" that *may* exist and *may* be willing to help and guide him. He keeps on experimenting — in this case, praying — for a long time. Again he tries to behave like the scientist, an experimenter who is never supposed to give up so long as there is a vestige of any chance of success.

As he goes along with his process of prayer, he begins to add up the results. If he persists, he will almost surely find more serenity, more tolerance, less fear, and less anger. He will acquire a quiet courage, the kind that doesn't strain him. He can look at so-called failure and success for what they really are. Problems and calamity will begin to mean instruction, instead of destruction. He will feel freer and saner. The idea that he may have been hypnotizing himself by autosuggestion will become laughable. His sense of purpose and of direction will increase. His tensions and anxieties will commence to fade. His physical health is likely to improve. Wonderful and unaccountable things will start to happen. Twisted relations in his family and on the outside will unaccountably improve.

Even if few of these things happen, he will still find himself in possession of great gifts. When he has to deal with hard circumstances he can face them and accept them. He can now accept himself and the world around him. He can do this because he now accepts a God who is

All — and who loves all. When he now says, "Our Father who art in Heaven, hallowed be thy name," our friend deeply and humbly means it. When in good meditation and thus freed from the clamors of the world, he knows that he is in God's hand; that his own destiny is really secure, here and hereafter.

A great theologian once declared: "The chief critics of prayer are those who have never really tried it enough." That's good advice, good advice I'm trying to take ever more seriously for myself. Many AAs have long been striving for a better conscious contact with God and I trust that many more of us will presently join with that wise company.

I've just finished rereading the chapter on Step Eleven in our book *Twelve Steps and Twelve Traditions.* This was written almost five years ago. I was astonished when I realized how little time I had actually been giving to my own elementary advice on meditation, prayer, and guidance — practices that I had so earnestly recommended to everybody else!

In this lack of attention I probably have plenty of company. But I do know that this is a neglect that can cause us to miss the finest experiences of life, a neglect that can seriously slacken the growth that God hopes we may achieve right here on earth; here in this great day at school, this very first of our Father's many mansions.

The Language of the Heart

July 1960*

My workshop stands on a hill back of our home. Looking over the valley, I see the village community house where our local group meets. Beyond the circle of my horizon lies the one world of AA: eight thousand groups, a quarter of a million of us. How in twenty-five years did AA get the way it is? And where are we going from here?

*From the Grapevine book AA Today, *published on the occasion of AA's twenty-fifth anniversary.*

Often, I sense the deep meaning of the phenomenon of Alcoholics Anonymous, but I cannot begin to fathom it. Why, for instance, at this particular point in history has God chosen to communicate his healing grace to so many of us? Who can say what this communication actually is — so mysterious and yet so practical? We can only partly realize what we have received and what it has meant to each of us.

It occurs to me that every aspect of this global unfoldment can be related to a single crucial word. The word is *communication*. There has been a lifesaving communication among ourselves, with the world around us, and with God.

From the beginning, communication in AA has been no ordinary transmission of helpful ideas and attitudes. It has been unusual and sometimes unique. Because of our kinship in suffering, and because our common means of deliverance are effective for ourselves only when constantly carried to others, our channels of contact have always been charged with *the language of the heart*. And what is that? Let's see if I can communicate to you something of what it means to me.

At once, I think of my own doctor, William Duncan Silkworth, and how he ministered to me with the language of the heart during the last shattering years of my alcoholism. Love was his magic, and with it he accomplished this wonder: He conveyed to the foggy mind of the drunk that here was a human being who understood, and who cared without limit. He was one who would gladly walk the extra mile with us, and if necessary (as it often was), even the last mile of all. At that time he had already tried to help over twenty thousand drunks, and he had failed with nearly all. Only here and there had this dismal experience of futility been brightened by a genuine recovery. People wondered how he could go on, how he could still believe in the possibility of help for chronic alcoholics. Yet he did believe with a faith that never faltered. He kept saying, "Someday we'll find the answer."

He had developed some ideas of his own about what ailed drunks: They had an *obsession* to drink, a veritable and a destructive lunacy. Observing that their bodies could no longer tolerate alcohol, he spoke of this as an *allergy*. Their obsession made them drink, and their allergy was the guarantee that they would go mad or die if they kept it up. Here, in contemporary terms, was the age-old dilemma of the alcoholic. Total abstinence, he knew, was the only solution. But how to attain that? If only he could understand them more and identify with them better, then his educational message could perhaps reach into those strange caverns of the mind where the blind compulsion to drink was entrenched.

So the little doctor who loved drunks worked on, always in hope that the very next case might somehow reveal more of the answer. When I came to him, his more recent concepts and tactics had begun to produce slightly improved results. So he was encouraged, and he went after my situation with something of the enthusiasm and hope of a young doctor on his first critical case. He told me what an infernal malady alcoholism is, and why. He made no promises, and he did not try to conceal the poor recovery rate. For the first time, I saw and felt the full gravity of my problem. I learned, also for the first time, that I was a sick man emotionally and physically. As every AA today knows, this knowledge can be an enormous relief. I no longer needed to consider myself essentially a fool or a weakling.

This new insight, plus the little doctor's account of a few of his good recoveries, brought me a surge of hope. But above all, my confidence rested on the understanding, the interest, and the affection he so freely gave me. I was not alone anymore with my problem. He and I could work it through. Despite several discouraging slips, I truly believed this for quite a while. And so did he.

But the hour finally arrived when he knew that I was not going to be one of his exceptions. He would have to begin to walk that last mile with my wife Lois and me. Characteristically, he found the courage gently but frankly to tell us the whole truth: Neither mine nor his nor any other resources he knew could stop my drinking; I would have to be locked up or suffer brain damage or death within perhaps a year.

It was a verdict I would not have accepted from any other person. He had spoken to me in the language of the heart, and so I was able to receive the truth he offered me. But it was a terrible and hopeless truth. He spoke in the name of science, which I deeply respected, and by science I seemed condemned. Who else could have driven home this indispensable principle on which every recovery depends? I seriously doubt that any other man alive could have done it.

Today, every AA member implants in his new prospect just what Dr. Silkworth so powerfully lodged in me. We know that the newcomer has to hit bottom; otherwise, not much can happen. Because we are "drunks who understand," we can use that nutcracker of the-obsession-plus-the-allergy as a tool of such power that it can shatter the newcomer's ego at depth. Only thus can he be convinced that on his own unaided resources he has little or no chance.

I was in precisely this state of inner collapse when, in November of

1934, I was visited by Ebby. He was an old friend, an alcoholic, and my sponsor-to-be. Why was it that he could communicate with me in areas that not even Dr. Silkworth could touch?

Well, first of all, I already knew that he himself was a hopeless case — just like me. Earlier that year, I had heard that he, too, was a candidate for the lockup. Yet here he was, sober and free. And his powers of communication now were such that he could convince me in minutes that he really felt he had been released from his drinking compulsion. He represented something very different from a mere jittery ride on the water-wagon. And so he brought me a kind of communication and evidence that even Dr. Silkworth could not give. Here was *one drunk talking to another.* Here was hope indeed.

Ebby told me his story, carefully detailing his drinking experiences of recent years. Thus he drew me still closer to him. I knew beyond doubt that he had lived in that strange and hopeless world where I still was. This fact established his *identification* with me. At length, our channel of communication was wide open, and I was ready for his message.

And what was his message? All AAs know what it was: honesty with oneself, leading to a fearless moral inventory of character defects; a revelation of these defects to another human being, the first humble and faltering steps away from isolation and guilt; willingness to face up to those we had harmed, making all possible restitution. A thorough housecleaning inside and out was indicated, and then we were ready to devote ourselves in service to others, using the understanding and language of the heart, and seeking no gain or reward. Then there was that vital attitude of dependence on God, or a higher power.

None of Ebby's ideas were really new. I'd heard them all before. But coming over his powerful transmission line, they were not at all what in other circumstances I would have regarded as conventional cliches for good church behavior. They appeared to me as living truths *which might liberate me as they had liberated him.* He could reach me at depth.

But in one respect I still backed away. I could not go for God, because I could not believe there *was* any God. Ebby sold me his other ideas at once, but not this one. I could not share his faith, as much as I had to admit its very evident result.

I had struck an impasse with which thousands of incoming AAs have since collided.

Mine was exactly the kind of deep-seated block we so often see today in new people who say they are atheistic or agnostic. Their will to disbelieve is so powerful that apparently they prefer a date with the undertaker to an open-minded and experimental quest for God. Happily for me, and for most of my kind who have since come along in AA, the constructive forces brought to bear in our Fellowship have nearly always overcome this colossal obstinacy. Beaten into complete defeat by alcohol, confronted by the living proof of release, and surrounded by those who can speak to us from the heart, we have finally surrendered. And then, paradoxically, we have found ourselves in a new dimension, the real world of spirit and of faith. Enough willingness, enough open-mindedness — and there it is!

When my own time for open-mindedness and surrender finally came, that new world of spirit burst upon me in a flash of overwhelming conviction and power. And as a result, freedom from obsession, faith in God, and a consciousness of his presence have remained with me ever since, regardless of subsequent ups and downs. The gift of faith instantaneously became built into me. My pride had paid a very high price. In despair, I had cried out, "Now I am willing to do anything. If there is a God, will he show himself!" And he did. This was my first conscious contact, my first awakening. I asked from the heart, and I received.

With this illumination came the vision of a possible chain reaction, one alcoholic working with the next. I was convinced that I could give to fellow sufferers that which Ebby had given to me, and for months afterward I tried to carry the message. But nobody sobered up, and a wonderful lesson came out of the experience: I was painfully learning *how not to communicate*. No matter how truthful the words of my message, there could be no deep communication if what I said and did was colored by pride, arrogance, intolerance, resentment, imprudence, or desire for personal acclaim — even though I was largely unconscious of these attitudes.

Without realizing it, I had fallen pretty heavily into these errors. My spiritual experience had been so sudden, brilliant, and powerful that I had begun to be sure I was destined to fix just about all the drunks in the world. Here was pride. I kept harping on my mystical awakening, and the customers were uniformly repelled. Here was imprudence. I began to insist that every drunk should have a "bright-light uplift" just about like mine. I ignored the fact that God comes to man in many ways. I had begun in effect to say to my clients, "You must be as I am, believe as I believe, do as I do." Here was the sort of unconscious arrogance that no drunk can stand! I loudly began to point out the sins of my prospects (mostly, of course, the sins I supposed I didn't have), and the prospects got sore and so did I. When they got drunk, I got mad. And here was hurt pride again.

My new Oxford Group friends (the religious group in which Ebby had made his first, but not final, recovery) objected to the idea of alcoholism as an illness, so I had quit talking about the-allergy-plus-the-obsession. I wanted the approval of these new friends, and in trying to be humble and helpful, I was neither. Slowly I learned, as most of us do, that when the ego gets in the way it blocks communication.

I needed another big dose of deflation, and I got it. The realization dawned on me that for six months I had failed completely. Then Dr. Silkworth gave me this crisp advice: "Quit preaching, quit harping on your odd spiritual experience. Tell your own story. Then pour it into those drunks how medically hopeless alcoholism is. Soften them up enough first. *Then* maybe they will buy what you really have to say. You've got the cart before the horse."

My meeting with Dr. Bob in Akron was my first successful rapport with another alcoholic. I followed Dr. Silkworth's advice to the letter. Dr. Bob did not need spiritual instruction. He already had more of that than I did. What he did need was the deflation at depth and the understanding that only one drunk can give another. What I needed was the humility of self-forgetfulness and the kinship with another human being of my own kind. I thank God for providing it.

One of the first insights Dr. Bob and I shared was that all true communication must be founded on mutual need. Never could we talk down to anyone, certainly not to a fellow alcoholic. We saw that each sponsor would have to humbly admit his own needs as clearly as those of his prospect. Here was the foundation for AA's Twelfth Step to recovery, the Step in which we carry the message.

Our next great adventure in communication was the book *Alcoholics Anonymous*. After four strenuous years, we had produced three small groups and less than a hundred recoveries. We knew we could communicate face-to-face. But it was very slow going. As we prepared the book, we all wondered, "Could the written word carry the message?" Could the book speak the language of the heart to the drunk who read it? We didn't know; we simply hoped. But now we do know.

Alcoholics Anonymous appeared in 1939. At that time, there were one hundred drunks who had recovered in AA. And there were five million alcoholics and their families in America alone who had never heard of Alcoholics Anonymous. There were perhaps another twenty million sufferers in other parts of the world. How were we going to get the good news to even a fraction of all these? There was now a book about AA, but almost nobody outside the Fellowship knew about it.

It became apparent that we would have to have the help of press and radio, that we would need communication resources of every kind. Would these agencies really be interested? Would they be friendly? Would they be able to place a true image of AA before the alcoholic and his family and friends?

The answer turned out to be yes. In the fall of 1939, Elrick Davis, a fine reporter, wrote a series of pieces about us in the Cleveland *Plain Dealer*. These pieces embodied truly wonderful insight into what AA really is and what it can do, and within a few days *several hundred* alkies and their families literally swamped the small AA group in Cleveland with pleas for help. In the next year, Jack Alexander wrote his famous *Saturday Evening Post* feature article on Alcoholics Anonymous, published in 1941. And for the first time we saw what communication in the language of the heart could mean nationwide.

The impact of his article upon the alcoholics of America, upon their families, and upon the general public was tremendous. There was an immediate deluge of calls for information and for help — not hundreds, but thousands. We were flabbergasted. It was evident that our recovery message could be transmitted all over the country — if we did our part.

As our Fellowship now entered its period of rapid growth, the Traditions of AA gradually took form. The Twelve Traditions communicate our principles of unity as the Twelve Steps communicate our principles of recovery. The Traditions show how an AA member can best relate himself to his group, the group to other groups, and AA as a whole to the world around us. They show what AA membership is; they reveal AA's experience in matters of authority and money; they guard against compromising alliances, professionalism, and our very natural desires for personal public acclaim. The Twelve Traditions were slowly evolved during an era when large-scale publicity was causing new groups to spring up like popcorn on a hot griddle. Many a power-driven ego ran hog-wild among us in those days, and it was the Traditions that finally brought order, coherence, and effective functioning out of the noisy anarchy which for a time threatened us with collapse.

The Traditions are neither rules, regulations, nor laws. No sanctions or punishments can be invoked for their infraction. Perhaps in no other area of society would these principles succeed. Yet in this Fellowship of alcoholics, the unenforceable Traditions carry a power greater than that of law. For years now, we have seldom seen a serious departure from them. The example of the very few who have persistently ignored them has not caused others to follow suit. We obey our Traditions willingly because of the need for AA survival. We obey them because we ought to and because we want to. Perhaps the secret of their power lies in the fact that these life-giving communications spring out of living experience and are rooted in sacrificial love.

Even in the very earliest days of AA, we began to find that the kinship of having suffered severe alcoholism was in itself not enough. We saw that, in order to cross certain barriers, our channels of communication had to be broadened and deepened. For example, practically all of AA's first members were what we today call last-gasp or low-bottom cases. When the mildly afflicted or high-bottom cases began to turn up, they often said, "But we were never jailed. We were never in mental hospitals. We never did those frightful things you fellows talk about. Maybe AA is not for people like us."

For years, we old-timers simply could not communicate with such folks. Then, out of much experience, a new approach was developed. To each new high-bottom, we emphasized the medical view that alcoholism is a fatal and *progressive* malady. We concentrated on the earlier periods in our drinking careers. We recalled how sure we were that "next time we could control ourselves" when we took a few drinks. Or how our drinking was the fault of unfortunate circumstances or the behavior of other people.

Then we took the prospect through the parts of our histories which proved how insidious and irresistible the progress of the illness is. We showed him how, years before we realized it, we had actually gone much beyond the point of no return so far as our own resources of strength and will were concerned. We kept pointing out how right the doctors are in their assessment of this malady.

Slowly but surely, this strategy began to pay off. The low-bottoms began to communicate at depth with the high-bottoms. And the high-bottoms began talking to each other. As soon as any AA locality took in even a small number of high-bottom drunks, progress with this class of sufferer became very much faster and easier. It is probable that about half of today's AA membership has been spared that last five, ten, or even fifteen years of unmitigated hell that we low-bottoms know all too well.

In the beginning, it was four whole years before AA brought permanent sobriety to even one alcoholic woman. Like the high-bottoms, the women also said they were different. But as communication was improved, mostly by the women themselves, the picture changed. Today, our sister AAs are many thousands strong.

The skid row man said he was different. Even more loudly, the socialite (or Park Avenue stumblebum) said the same. So did the practitioners of the arts and the professions. So did the rich, the poor, the religious, the agnostics, the Indians, the Eskimos, the veterans, and the prisoners. But that was years ago. Nowadays, they all talk about how very much alike we alcoholics are when the chips are down.

By 1950, this one big question remained unanswered: Could we communicate overseas? Could AA transcend the barriers of race, language, religion, culture, and wars? What about the Norwegians, the Swedes, the Danes, and the Finns? What about the Dutch, the Germans, the French, the English, the Scots, and the Israelis? How about the Africans, the Boers, the Aussies, the Latins, the Japanese, the Hindus, and the Mohammedans?

So Lois and I wondered a lot as we headed for Europe and Britain to see for ourselves that year. The moment we alighted in Norway, *we knew that AA could and would go everywhere.* We understood not one word of Norwegian. Scenes and customs alike were new and strange to us. Yet there was a marvelous communication from the first moment. There was an incredible sensation of oneness, of being completely at home. The Norwegians were our people. Norway was our country, too. They felt the same way about us. It shone in their faces.

As we journeyed from land to land, we had the same magnificent adventure in kinship over and over again. In Britain, we met with the most wonderful love and understanding. In Ireland, we were at one with the Irish. Everywhere, everywhere, it was the same. This was something much greater than people cordially meeting people. This was no merely interesting comparison of mutual experiences and aspirations. This was far more; this was the communication of heart to heart in wonder, in joy, and in everlasting gratitude. Lois and I then knew that AA could circle the globe — and it has.

God As We Understand Him: The Dilemma of No Faith

April 1961

The phrase "God as we understand him" is perhaps the most important expression to be found in our whole AA vocabulary. Within the compass of these five significant words there can be included every kind and degree of faith, together with the positive assurance that each of us may choose his own. Scarcely less valuable to us are those supplemental expressions — "a higher power" and "a power greater than ourselves." For all who deny or seriously doubt a deity, these frame an open door over whose threshold the unbeliever can take his first easy step into a reality hitherto unknown to him — the realm of faith.

In AA such breakthroughs are everyday events. They are all the more remarkable when we reflect that a working faith had once seemed an impossibility of the first magnitude to perhaps half of our present membership of three hundred thousand. To all these doubters has come the great discovery that as soon as they could cast their main dependence upon a "higher power" — even upon their own AA groups — they had turned that blind corner which had always kept the open highway from their view. From this time on — assuming they tried hard to practice the rest of the AA program with a relaxed and open mind — an ever deepening and broadening faith, a veritable gift, had invariably put in its sometimes unexpected and often mysterious appearance.

We much regret that these facts of AA life are not understood by the legion of alcoholics in the world around us. Any number of them are bedeviled by the dire conviction that if ever they go near AA they will be pressured to conform to some particular brand of faith or theology. They just don't realize that faith is never a necessity for AA membership; that sobriety can be achieved with an easily acceptable minimum of it; and that our concepts of a higher power and God as we understand him afford everyone a nearly unlimited choice of spiritual belief and action.

How to transmit this good news is one of our most challenging problems in communication, for which there may be no fast or sweeping answer. Perhaps our public information services could begin to emphasize this all-important aspect of AA more heavily. And within our own ranks we might well develop a more sympathetic awareness of the acute plight of these really isolated and desperate sufferers. In their aid we can settle for no less than the best possible attitude and the most ingenious action that we can muster.

We can also take a fresh look at the problem of "no faith" as it exists right on our own doorstep. Though three hundred thousand did recover in the last twenty-five years, maybe half a million more have walked into our midst, and then out again. No doubt some were too sick to make even a start. Others couldn't or wouldn't admit their alcoholism. Still others couldn't face up to their underlying personality defects. Numbers departed for still other reasons.

Yet we can't well content ourselves with the view that all these recovery failures were entirely the fault of the newcomers themselves. Perhaps a great many didn't receive the kind and amount of sponsorship they so sorely needed. We didn't communicate when we might have done so. So we AAs failed them. Perhaps more often than we think, we still make no contact at depth with those suffering the dilemma of no faith.

Certainly none are more sensitive to spiritual cocksureness, pride, and aggression than they are. I'm sure this is something we too often forget. In AA's first years I all but ruined the whole undertaking with this sort of unconscious arrogance. God as *I* understood him *had* to be for everybody. Sometimes my aggression was subtle and sometimes it was crude. But either way it was damaging — perhaps fatally so — to numbers of nonbelievers. Of course this sort of thing isn't confined to Twelfth Step work. It is very apt to leak out into our relations with everybody. Even now, I catch myself chanting that same old barrier-building refrain, "Do as *I* do, believe as *I* do — or else!"

Here's a recent example of the high cost of spiritual pride. A very tough-minded prospect was taken to his first AA meeting. The first speaker majored on his own drinking pattern. The prospect seemed impressed. The next two speakers (or maybe lecturers) each themed their talks on "God as *I* understand him." This could have been good, too, but it certainly wasn't. The trouble was their attitude, the way they presented their experience. They did ooze arrogance. In fact, the final speaker got far overboard on some of his personal theological convictions. With perfect fidelity, both were repeating my performance of years before. Quite unspoken, yet implicit in everything they said, was the same idea — "Folks, *listen to us. We* have the only true brand of AA — and you'd better get it!"

The new prospect said he'd had it — and he had. His sponsor protested that this wasn't real AA. But it was too late; nobody could touch him after that. He also had a first class alibi for yet another bender. When last heard from, an early appointment with the undertaker seemed probable.

Fortunately, such rank aggression in the name of spirituality isn't often seen nowadays. Yet this sorry and unusual episode can be turned to good account. We can ask ourselves whether, in less obvious but nevertheless destructive forms, we are not more subject to fits of spiritual pride than we had supposed. If constantly worked at, I'm sure that no kind of self-survey could be more beneficial. Nothing could more surely increase our communication with each other and with God.

Many years ago a so-called unbeliever brought me to see this very clearly. He was an MD and a fine one. I met him and his wife Mary at the home of a friend in a midwestern city. It was purely a social evening. Our Fellowship of alcoholics was my sole topic and I pretty much monopolized the conversation. Nevertheless, the doctor and his lady seemed truly interested and he asked many questions. But one of them made me suspect that he was an agnostic, or maybe an atheist.

This promptly triggered me, and I set out to convert him, then and there. Deadly serious, I actually bragged about my spectacular spiritual experience of the year before. The doctor mildly wondered if that experience might not be something other than I thought it was. This hit me hard, and I was downright rude. There had been no real provocation; the doctor was uniformly courteous, good-humored, and even respectful. Not a little wistfully, he said he often wished he had a firm faith, too. But plainly enough, I had convinced him of nothing.

Three years later I revisited my midwestern friend. Mary, the doctor's wife, came by for a call and I learned that he had died the week before. Much affected, she began to speak of him.

His was a noted Boston family, and he'd been Harvard educated. A brilliant student, he might have gone on to fame in his profession. He could have enjoyed a wealthy practice and a social life among old friends. Instead, he had insisted on being a company doctor in what was a strife-torn industrial town. When Mary had sometimes asked why they didn't go back to Boston, he would take her hand and say, "Maybe you are right, but I can't bring myself to leave. I think the people at the company really need me."

Mary then recalled that she had never known her husband to complain seriously about anything, or to criticize anyone bitterly. Though he appeared to be perfectly well, the doctor had slowed down in his last five years. When Mary prodded him to go out evenings, or tried to get him to the office on time, he always came up with a plausible and good-natured excuse. Not until his sudden last illness did she know that all this while he had carried about a heart condition that could have done him in at any moment. Except for a single doctor on his own staff, no one had an inkling. When she reproached him about this, he simply said, "Well, I could see no good in causing people to worry about me — especially you, my dear."

This was the story of a man of great spiritual worth. The hallmarks were plain to be seen: humor and patience, gentleness and courage, humility and dedication, unselfishness and love — a demonstration I might never come near to making myself. This was the man I had chided and patronized. This was the "unbeliever" I had presumed to instruct!

Mary told us this story more than twenty years ago. Then, for the first time, it burst in upon me how very dead faith can be — when minus responsibility. The doctor had an unwavering belief in his ideals. But he also practiced humility, wisdom, and responsibility. Hence his superb demonstration.

My own spiritual awakening had given me a built-in faith in God — a gift indeed. But I had been neither humble nor wise. Boasting of my faith, I had forgotten my ideals. Pride and irresponsibility had taken their place. By so cutting off my own light, I had little to offer my fellow alcoholics. Therefore my faith was dead to them. At last I saw why many had gone away — some of them forever.

Therefore, faith is more than our greatest gift; its sharing with others is our greatest responsibility. So may we of AA continually seek the wisdom and the willingness by which we may well fulfill that immense trust which the giver of all perfect gifts has placed in our hands.

Humility for Today

June 1961

There can be no absolute humility for us humans. At best, we can only glimpse the meaning and splendor of such a perfect ideal. As the book *Alcoholics Anonymous* says: "We are not saints...we claim spiritual progress rather than spiritual perfection." Only God himself can manifest in the absolute; we human beings must needs live and grow in the domain of the relative. We seek humility for today.

Therefore our practical question is this: "Just what do we mean by 'humility for today' and how do we know when we have found it?"

We scarcely need be reminded that excessive guilt or rebellion leads to spiritual poverty. But it was a very long time before we knew we could go even more broke on spiritual pride. When we early AAs got our first glimmer of how spiritually prideful we could be, we coined this expression: "Don't try to get too damned good by Thursday!" That old-time admonition may look like another of those handy alibis that can excuse us from trying for our best. Yet a closer view reveals just the contrary. This is our AA way of warning against pride-blindness, and the imaginary perfections that we do not possess.

Now that we no longer patronize bars and bordellos; now that we bring home the paychecks; now that we are so very active in AA; and now that people congratulate us on these signs of progress — well, we naturally proceed to congratulate ourselves. Yet we may not be within hailing distance of humility. Meaning well, yet doing badly, how often have I said or thought, "I am right and you are wrong," "My plan is correct and yours is faulty," "Thank God your sins are not my sins," "You are hurting AA and I'm going to stop you cold," "I have God's guidance, so he is on my side." And so on, indefinitely.

The alarming thing about such pride-blindness is the ease with which it is justified. But we need not look far to see that this deceptive brand of self-justification is a universal destroyer of harmony and of love. It sets person against person, nation against nation. By it, every form of folly and violence can be made to look right, and even respectable. Of course it is not for us to condemn. We need only investigate ourselves.

How, then, can we do more and more about reducing our guilt, rebellion, and pride?

When I inventory such defects, I like to draw a picture and tell myself a story. My picture is that of a Highway to Humility, and my story is an allegory. On one side of my Highway, I see a great bog. The Highway's edge borders a shallow marsh which finally shelves down into that muddy morass of guilt and rebellion in which I have so often floundered. Self-destruction lies in wait out there, and I know this. But the country on the other side of the road looks fine. I see inviting glades, and beyond them great mountains. The countless trails leading into this pleasant land look safe. It will be easy, I think, to find one's way back.

Together with numbers of friends, I decide to take a brief detour. We pick our path and happily plunge along it. Elatedly, somebody soon says, "Maybe we'll find gold on top of that mountain." Then to our amazement we do strike gold — not nuggets in the streams, but fully minted coins. The heads of these coins each declare, "This is pure gold — twenty-four carats." Surely, we think, this is the reward for our patient plodding back there in the everlasting brightness of the Highway.

Soon, though, we begin to notice the words on the tails of our coins, and we have strange forebodings: Some pieces carry rather attractive inscriptions. "I am Power," "I am Acclaim," "I am Wealth," "I am Righteousness," they say. But others seem very strange. For example: "I am the Master Race," "I am the Benefactor," "I am Good Causes," "I am God." This is very puzzling. Nevertheless we pocket them. But next come real shockers. They read: "I'm Pride," "I'm Revenge," "I'm Disunity," "I'm Chaos." Then we turn up a single coin — just one — which declares: "I am the Devil himself." Some of us are horrified and we cry, "This is fool's gold, and this is a fool's paradise — let's clear out of here!"

But many would not return with us. They said, "Let's stay here and sort over those damned coins. We'll pick only the ones that carry the lucky inscriptions. For instance, those that say, 'Power' and 'Glory' and 'Righteousness.' You fellows are going to be sorry you didn't stick around." Not strangely, it was years before this part of our original company returned to the Highway.

They told us the story of those who had sworn never to return. They had said, "This money is real gold, and don't tell us any different. We're going to pile up all we can. Sure, we don't like those fool mottoes. But there's plenty of firewood here. We'll just melt all this stuff down into good solid gold bricks." Then our late arrivals added: "This is how the gold of Pride claimed our brothers. They were already quarreling over their bricks when we left. Some were hurt and a few were dying. They had begun to destroy each other."

This symbolic picture graphically tells me that I may attain "humility for today" only to the extent that I am able to avoid the bog of guilt and rebellion, and that fair but deceiving land which is strewn with the coin of Pride. This is how I can find and stay on the Road to Humility which lies in between. Therefore, a constant inventory which can reveal when I am off the road is always in order.

Of course, our first attempts at such inventories are apt to prove very unrealistic. I used to be a champ at *unrealistic* self-appraisal. I wanted to look only at the part of my life which seemed good. Then I would greatly exaggerate whatever virtues I supposed I had attained. Next I would congratulate myself on the grand job I was doing. So my unconscious self-deception never failed to turn my few good assets into serious liabilities. This astonishing process was always a pleasant one. Naturally this generated a terrible hankering for still more "accomplishments," and still more approval. I was falling straight back into the pattern of my drinking days. Here were the same old goals — power, fame, and applause. Besides, I had the best alibi known — the spiritual alibi. The fact that I really did have a spiritual objective always made this utter nonsense seem perfectly right. I couldn't tell a good coin from a bad one; it was spiritual gold-bricking at its worst. I shall forever regret the damage I did to people around me. Indeed, I still tremble when I realize what I might have done to AA and to its future.

In those days I wasn't much bothered about the areas of life in which I was standing still. There was always the alibi. "After all," I said to myself, "I'm far too busy with much more important matters." That was my near perfect prescription for comfort and complacency.

But sometimes I would simply have to look at certain situations where, on the face of them, I was doing very badly. Right away, a rousing rebellion would set in. Then the search for excuses would become frantic. "These," I would exclaim, "are really a good man's faults." When that pet gadget finally broke apart, I would think, "Well, if those people would only treat me right, I wouldn't have to behave the way I do." Next in order was this: "God well knows that I do have *awful compulsions.* I just can't get over this one. So *he* will have to release me." At last came the time when I would shout, *"This,* I positively *will not do; I won't even try."* Of course my conflicts went right on mounting because I was simply loaded with excuses and refusals.

When these troubles had finally exhausted me enough, there was yet another escape. I would commence to wallow in the bog of guilt. Here pride and rebellion would give way to depression. Though the variations were many, my main theme always was, "How god-awful I am." Just as I had exaggerated my modest attainments by pride, so now I would exaggerate my defects through guilt. I would race about, confessing all (and a great deal more!) to whoever would listen. Believe it or not, I took that to be great humility on my part, and I counted this as my sole remaining asset and consolation!

During those bouts with guilt, there was never a decent regret for the harms I had done, nor was there any serious thought of making such restitution as I could. The idea of asking God's forgiveness, let alone any forgiveness of myself, never occurred to me. Of course my really big

liability — spiritual pride and arrogance — was not examined at all. I
had shut out the light by which I might have seen it.

Today I think I can trace a clear linkage between my guilt and my
pride. Both of them were certainly attention-getters. In pride I could say,
"Look at me, I am wonderful." In guilt I would moan, "I'm awful."
Therefore guilt is really the reverse side of the coin of pride. Guilt aims at
self-destruction, and pride aims at the destruction of others.

*This is why I see humility for today as that safe and secure stance
midway between these violent emotional extremes. It is a quiet place where
I can keep enough perspective, and enough balance, to take my next small
step up the clearly marked road that points toward eternal values.*

Many of us have experienced far greater emotional gyrations than I.
Others have experienced less. But all of us still have them at times. Yet I
think we need not regret these conflicts. They seem to be a necessary part
of growing up, emotionally and spiritually. They are the raw material
out of which much of our progress has to be made.

Does anyone ask if AA is but a retching pit of pain and conflict?
The answer is "Certainly not." In great measure, we AAs have really
found peace. However haltingly, we have managed to attain an increasing humility whose dividends have been serenity and legitimate joy. We
do not detour as much or as far as we once did.

At the outset of this meditation, it was thought that absolute ideals
are far beyond our attainment, or even our comprehension; that we
would be sadly lacking in humility if we really felt that we could achieve
anything like absolute perfection in this brief span of earthly existence.
Such a presumption would certainly be the acme of spiritual pride.

Reasoning thus, many people will have no truck at all with absolute
spiritual values. Perfectionists, they say, are either full of conceit because they fancy they have reached some impossible goal, or else they are
swamped in self-condemnation because they have not done so.

Yet I think that we should not hold this view. It is not the fault of
great ideals that they are sometimes misused and so become shallow
excuses for guilt, rebellion, and pride. On the contrary, we cannot grow
very much unless we constantly try to envision what the eternal spiritual
values are. As Step Eleven of AA's recovery program says, we "Sought
through prayer and meditation to improve our conscious contact with
God as we understood him, praying only for knowledge of his will for us
and the power to carry that out." This surely means that we ought to
look toward God's perfection as our guide rather than as a goal to be
reached in any foreseeable time.

I'm sure, for instance, that I ought to seek out the finest definition of humility that is possible for me to envision. This definition doesn't have to be absolutely perfect — I am only asked to try. Suppose I choose one like this: "Perfect humility would be a state of complete freedom from myself, freedom from all the claims that my defects of character now lay so heavily upon me. Perfect humility would be a full willingness, in all times and places, to find and do the will of God."

When I meditate upon such a vision, I need not be dismayed because I shall never attain it, nor need I swell with presumption that one of these days its virtues shall all be mine.

I only need to dwell on the vision itself, letting it grow and ever more fill my heart. This done, I can compare it with my last-taken personal inventory. Then I get a sane and healthy idea of where I actually stand on the Highway to Humility. I see that my journey toward God has scarce begun. As I thus get down to my right size and stature, my self-concern and importance become amusing. Then faith grows that I do have a place on this Highway; that I can advance upon it with deepening peace and confidence. Once more I know that God is good; that I need fear no evil. This is a great gift, this knowledge that I do have a destiny.

As I continue to contemplate God's perfection, I discover still another joy. As a child, hearing my first symphony, I was lifted up into its indescribable harmony, though I knew little of how or whence it came. So today, when I listen for God's music of the spheres, I can now and again hear those divine chords by which I am told that the great composer loves me — and that I love him.

This Matter of Honesty

August 1961

The problem of honesty touches nearly every aspect of our lives. There are, for example, the widespread and amazing phenomena of self-deception. There are those rather dreadful brands of reckless truth-telling, which are so often lacking in prudence and love. Then there are

those countless life situations in which nothing less than utter honesty
will do, no matter how sorely we may be tempted by the fear and pride
that would reduce us to half-truths or inexcusable denials.

Let's first see what self-deception can do to one's integrity.

Well remembered is the comfort I used to take from an exaggerated
belief in my own honesty. My New England kinsfolk had thoroughly
taught me the sanctity of all business commitments and contracts. They
insisted that "a man's word is his bond." I delighted in the Lincoln story
which tells how Honest Abe once walked six miles to return the six pennies
he had overcharged a poor woman at his grocery. After this rigorous con-
ditioning, business honesty always came easy, and it stayed with me. Even
in Wall Street, where I landed years later, I never flimflammed anyone.

However, this small fragment of easy-won virtue did produce some
interesting liabilities. I was so absurdly proud of my business standards
that I never failed to whip up a fine contempt for those of my fellow Wall
Streeters who were prone to shortchange their customers. This was
arrogant enough, but the ensuing self-deception proved even worse. My
prized business honesty was presently converted into a comfortable
cloak under which I could hide the many serious flaws that beset other
departments of my life. Being certain of this one virtue, it was easy to
conclude that I had them all. For years on end, this prevented me from
taking a good look at myself. This is a very ordinary example of the
fabulous capacity for self-deception that nearly all of us can display at
times. Moreover, the deception of others is nearly always rooted in the
deception of ourselves.

As further illustrations, two extreme cases come to mind. One
shows self-delusion in a very obvious form — obvious, that is, to all but
the victim himself. The other depicts the more subtle brand of self-delusion, from which no human being can be entirely exempt.

One of my good friends used to be a safecracker. He told me this revealing tale. Said he: "You know, Bill, I used to think I was a kind of
one-man revolution against society. All over the world I could see the
'have-nots' taking it away from the 'haves.' This seemed very reasonable. After all, those damn 'haves' just wouldn't share their wealth. The
revolutions that took it away from them were apt to get a lot of applause.
But guys like me, who could also make those 'haves' share their wealth,
got no such glad hand. After a while I figured this out: the plain fact was
that nobody liked burglars. Revolutions, yes — but burglars, no. Anyway, I couldn't see anything wrong about blowing safes, excepting
getting caught. Even after years in jail, I still couldn't see it. When AA

showed up, I slowly began to get it through my head that there were good revolutions and bad ones. Bit by bit it dawned on me how I'd completely fooled myself. I could see that I had been pretty crazy. How I could have been *that* dumb, I'll never be able to explain in any other way.''

Now I have another AA friend, a good and gentle soul. He recently joined one of the great religious orders, one in which the friars spend many hours a day in contemplation. So my friend has plenty of time to take his inventory. The more he looks, the more unconscious self-deception he finds. And the more astonished he becomes at the elaborate and devious excuse-making machinery by which he had been justifying himself. He has already come to the conclusion that the prideful righteousness of "good people" may often be just as destructive as the glaring sins of those who are supposedly not so good. So he daily looks inward upon himself and then upward toward God, the better to discover just where he stands in this matter of honesty. Out of each of his meditations there always emerges one dead certainty, and this is the fact that he still has a long way to go.

Just how and when we tell the truth — or keep silent — can often reveal the difference between genuine integrity and none at all. Step Nine of AA's program emphatically cautions us against misusing the truth when it states: "Made direct amends to such people wherever possible, except when to do so would injure them or others." Because it points up the fact that the truth can be used to injure as well as to heal, this valuable principle certainly has a wide-ranging application to the problem of developing integrity.

In AA, for instance, we talk a great deal about each other. Provided our motives are thoroughly good, this is not in the least wrong. But damaging gossip is quite something else. Of course, this kind of scuttlebutt can be well grounded in fact. But no such abuse of the facts could ever be twisted into anything resembling integrity. It can't be maintained that this sort of superficial honesty is good for anyone. So the need to examine ourselves is very much with us. Following a gossip binge we can well ask ourselves these questions: "Why did we say what we did? Were we only trying to be helpful and informative? Or were we not trying to feel superior by confessing the other fellow's sins? Or, because of fear and dislike, were we not really aiming to damage him?" This would be an honest attempt to examine ourselves, rather than the other fellow. Here we see the difference between the use of the truth and its misuse. Right here we begin to regain the integrity we had lost.

Sometimes, though, our true motives are not so easily determined.

There are times when we think we must reveal highly damaging facts so that we may stop the depredations of certain evildoers. "All for the good of AA" — or what have you — now becomes our cry. Armed with this often false justification, we righteously press our attack. True enough, there may be a genuine need to remedy a damaging condition. True enough, we may have to make use of some unpleasant facts. But the real test is how we handle ourselves. We must be ever so certain that we are not pots who call the kettles black. Therefore it is wise if we pose ourselves these questions: "Do we really understand the people who are involved in this situation? Are we certain that we have *all* of the facts? Is any action or criticism on our part really necessary? Are we positive that we are neither fearful nor angry?" Only following such a scrutiny can we be sure to act with the careful discrimination and in the loving spirit that will always be needed to maintain our own integrity.

Now here is another aspect of the honesty problem. It is very possible for us to use the alleged dishonesty of other people as a most plausible excuse for not meeting our own obligations. I once had a spell of this myself. Some rather prejudiced friends had exhorted me never to go back to Wall Street. They were sure that the rampant materialism and double-dealing down there would be sure to stunt my spiritual growth. Because this sounded so high-minded, I continued to stay away from the only business that I knew.

When finally my household went quite broke, I woke up to the fact that I hadn't been able to face the prospect of going back to work. So I returned to Wall Street after all. And I have ever since been glad that I did. I needed to rediscover that there are many fine people in New York's financial district. Then, too, I needed the experience of staying sober in the very surroundings where alcohol had cut me down. I did receive all these benefits and a great deal more. Indeed, there was one colossal dividend that resulted directly from my grudging decision to reenter the market place. It was a Wall Street business trip to Akron, Ohio, in 1935, that first brought me face to face with Dr. Bob — AA's co-founder-to-be. So the birth of AA itself actually hinged on the fact that I had been trying to meet my bread-and-butter responsibilities.

We must now leave the absorbing topic of self-delusion and look at some of those trying life situations which we have to meet foursquare and head-on. Suppose we are handed an employment application that asks, "Have you ever suffered from alcoholism, and were you ever hospitalized?" Here, we AAs can assuredly make a good report of ourselves. Almost to a man we believe that nothing short of the absolute truth will do in situations of this type. Most employers respect our Fellowship and they like this rugged brand of honesty, especially when we reveal our AA membership and its results. Of course many another life problem calls for this identical brand of forthrightness. For the most part, situations requiring utter honesty are clear-cut, and readily recognizable. We simply have to face up to them, our fear and pride regardless. Failing to do this, we shall be sure to suffer those ever mounting conflicts which can only be resolved by plain honesty.

There are, nevertheless, certain occasions where reckless truth-telling may create widespread havoc and permanent damage to others. Whenever this seems possible, we are likely to find ourselves in a bad jam indeed. We shall be torn between two temptations. When conscience agonizes us enough, we may well cast all prudence and love to the winds. We may try to buy our freedom by telling the brutal truth, no matter who gets hurt or how much. But this is not the usual temptation. It is far more probable that we shall veer to the other extreme. We will paint for ourselves a most unrealistic picture of the awful damage we are about to inflict on others. By claiming great compassion and love for our supposed victims, we are getting set to tell the Big Lie — and be thoroughly comfortable about it, too.

When life presents us with a racking conflict like this, we cannot be altogether blamed if we are confused. In fact, our very first responsibility is to admit that we *are* confused. We may have to confess that, for the time being, we have lost all ability to tell right from wrong. Most difficult, too, will be the admission that we cannot be certain of receiving God's guidance because our prayers are so cluttered with wishful thinking. Surely this is the point at which we must seek the counsel of our finest friends. There is nowhere else to go.

Had I not been blessed with wise and loving advisers, I might have cracked up long ago. A doctor once saved me from death by alcoholism because he obliged me to face up to the deadliness of that malady. Another doctor, a psychiatrist, later on helped me save my sanity because he led me to ferret out some of my deep-lying defects. From a clergyman I acquired the truthful principles by which we AAs now try to live. But these precious friends did far more than supply me with their professional skills. I learned that I could go to them with any problem whatever. Their wisdom and their integrity were mine for the asking. Many of my dearest AA friends have stood with me in exactly this same relation. Oftentimes they could help where others could not, simply because they *were* AAs.

Of course we cannot wholly rely on friends to solve all our difficulties. A good adviser will never do all our thinking for us. He knows that each final choice must be ours. He will therefore help to eliminate fear, expediency, and self-deception, so enabling us to make choices which are loving, wise, and honest.

The choice of such a friend is an all-important matter. We should look for a person of deep understanding, and then carefully listen to what he has to say. In addition, we must be positive that our prospective adviser will hold our communications in the strictest of confidence. Should he be a clergyman or doctor or lawyer, this can be taken for granted. But when we consult an AA friend, we should not be reluctant to remind him of our need for full privacy. Intimate communication is normally so free and easy among us that an AA adviser may sometimes forget when we expect him to remain silent. The protective sanctity of this most healing of human relations ought never be violated.

Such privileged communications have priceless advantages. We find in them the perfect opportunity to be as honest as we know how to be. We do not have to think of the possibility of damage to other people, nor need we fear ridicule or condemnation. Here, too, we have the best possible chance of spotting self-deception.

If we are fooling ourselves, a competent adviser can see this quickly. And, as he guides us out of our fantasies, we are surprised to find that we have few of the usual urges to defend ourselves against unpleasant truths. In no other way can fear, pride, and ignorance be so readily melted. After a time, we realize that we are standing firm on a brand-new foundation for integrity.

Let us therefore continue our several searches for self-deception, great or small. Let us painstakingly temper honesty with prudence and love. And let us never flinch from entire forthrightness whenever this is the requirement.

How truth makes us free is something that we AAs can well understand. It cut the shackles that once bound us to alcohol. It continues to release us from conflicts and miseries beyond reckoning; it banishes fear and isolation. The unity of our Fellowship, the love we cherish for each other, the esteem in which the world holds us — all of these are products of such integrity as, under God, we have been privileged to achieve. May we therefore quicken our search for still more genuine honesty, and deepen its practice in all our affairs.

This Matter of Fear

January 1962

A s the AA Book says, "Fear is an evil, corroding thread; the fabric of our lives is shot through with it." Fear is surely a bar to reason, and to love, and of course it invariably powers anger, vainglory, and aggression. It underlies maudlin guilt and paralyzing depression. President Roosevelt once made the significant remark that "We have nothing to fear but fear itself."

This is a severe indictment, and it is possibly too sweeping. For all its usual destructiveness, we have found that fear can be the starting point for better things. Fear can be a stepping-stone to prudence and to a decent respect for others. It can point the path to justice, as well as to hate. And the more we have of respect and justice, the more we shall begin to find the love which can suffer much, and yet be freely given. So fear need not always be destructive, because the lessons of its consequences can lead us to positive values.

The achievement of freedom from fear is a lifetime undertaking, one that can never be wholly completed. When under heavy attack, acute illness, or in other conditions of serious insecurity, we shall all react, well or badly, as the case may be. Only the vainglorious claim perfect freedom from fear, though their very grandiosity is really rooted in the fears they have temporarily forgotten.

Therefore the problem of resolving fear has two aspects. We shall have to try for all the freedom from fear that is possible for us to attain. Then we shall need to find both the courage and the grace to deal constructively with whatever fears remain. Trying to understand our fears, and the fears of others, is but a first step. The larger question is how, and where, we go from there.

Since AA's beginning, I have watched as thousands of my fellows became more and more able to understand and to transcend their fears. These examples have been of unfailing help and inspiration. Perhaps, then, some of my own experiences with fear and the shedding of it to an encouraging degree may be appropriate.

As a child I had some pretty heavy emotional shocks. There was deep family disturbance; I was physically awkward and the like. Of course other kids have such emotional handicaps and emerge unscathed.

But I didn't. Evidently I was oversensitive, and therefore overscared. Anyhow, I developed a positive phobia that I wasn't like other youngsters, and never could be. At first this threw me into depression and thence into the isolation of retreat.

But these child miseries, all of them generated by fear, became so unbearable that I turned highly aggressive. Thinking I never could belong, and vowing I'd never settle for any second-rate status, I felt I simply had to dominate in everything I chose to do, work or play. As this attractive formula for the good life began to succeed, according to my then specifications of success, I became deliriously happy. But when an undertaking occasionally did fail, I was filled with a resentment and depression that could be cured only by the next triumph. Very early, therefore, I came to value everything in terms of victory or defeat — all or nothing. The only satisfaction I knew was to win.

This was my false antidote for fear and this was the pattern, ever more deeply etched, that dogged me through school days, World War I, the hectic drinking career in Wall Street, and down into the final hour of my complete collapse. By that time adversity was no longer a stimulant, and I knew not whether my greater fear was to live or to die.

While my basic fear pattern is a very common one, there are of course many others. Indeed, fear manifestations and the problems that trail in their wake are so numerous and complex that in this brief article it is not possible to detail even a few of them. We can only review those spiritual resources and principles by which we may be able to face and deal with fear in any of its aspects.

In my own case, the foundation stone of freedom from fear is that of faith: a faith that, despite all worldly appearances to the contrary, causes me to believe that I live in a universe that makes sense. To me, this means a belief in a Creator who is all power, justice, and love; a God who intends for me a purpose, a meaning, and a destiny to grow, however little and haltingly, toward his own likeness and image. Before the coming of faith I had lived as an alien in a cosmos that too often seemed both hostile and cruel. In it there could be no inner security for me.

Dr. Carl Jung, one of the three founders of modern depth psychology, had a profound conviction upon this great dilemma of the world today. In paraphrase, this is what he had to say about it: "Any person who has reached forty years of age, and who still has no means of comprehending who he is, where he is, or where he is next going, cannot avoid becoming a neurotic — to some degree or other. This is true whether his youthful drives for sex, material security, and a place in society have been satisfied, or not satisfied." When the benign doctor said "becoming neurotic" he might just as well have said "becoming fear-ridden."

This is exactly why we of AA place such emphasis on the need for faith in a higher power, define that as we may. We have to find a life in the world of grace and spirit, and this is certainly a new dimension for most of us. Surprisingly, our quest for this realm of being is not too difficult. Our conscious entry into it usually begins as soon as we have deeply confessed our personal powerlessness to go on alone, and have made our appeal to whatever God we think there is — or may be. The gift of faith and the consciousness of a higher power is the outcome. As faith grows, so does inner security. The vast underlying fear of nothingness commences to subside. Therefore we of AA find that our basic antidote for fear is a spiritual awakening.

It so happens that my own spiritual perception was electrically sudden and absolutely convincing. At once I became a part — if only a tiny part — of a cosmos that was ruled by justice and love in the person of God. No matter what had been the consequences of my own willfulness and ignorance, or those of my fellow travelers on earth, this was still the truth. Such was the new and positive assurance, and this has never left me. I was given to know, at least for the time being, what the absence of fear could be like. Of course my own gift of faith is not essentially different from those spiritual awakenings since received by countless AAs — it was only more sudden. But even this new frame of reference — critically important though it was — only marked my entrance into that long path which leads away from fear, and toward love. The old and deeply carved etchings of anxiety were not instantly and permanently rubbed out. Of course they reappeared, and sometimes alarmingly.

Being the recipient of such a spectacular spiritual experience, it was not surprising that the first phase of my AA life was characterized by a great deal of pride and power-driving. The craving for influence and approval, the desire to be *the* leader, was still very much with me. Better still, this behavior could be now justified — all in the name of good works!

It fortunately turned out that this rather blatant phase of my grandiosity, which lasted some years, was followed by a string of adversities. My demands for approval, which were obviously based on the fear that I might not get enough of it, began to collide with these identical traits in my fellow AAs. Hence their saving of the Fellowship from me, and I saving it from them, became an all-absorbing occupation. This of course resulted in anger, suspicion, and all sorts of frightening episodes. In this remarkable and now rather amusing era of our affairs, any number of us commenced playing God all over again. For some years AA power-drivers ran hog-wild. But out of this fearsome situation, the Twelve Steps and the Twelve Traditions of AA were formulated. Mainly these were principles designed for ego reduction, and therefore for the reduction of our fears. These were the principles which we hoped would hold us in unity and increasing love for each other and for God.

Gradually we began to be able to accept the other fellow's sins as well as his virtues. It was in this period that we coined the potent and meaningful expression, "Let us always love the best in others — and never fear their worst." After some ten years of trying to work this brand of love and the ego-reducing properties of the AA Steps and Traditions into the life of our Society, the awful fears for the survival of AA simply vanished.

The practice of AA's Twelve Steps and Twelve Traditions in our personal lives also brought incredible releases from fear of every description, despite the wide prevalence of formidable personal problems. When fear did persist, we knew it for what it was, and under God's grace we became able to handle it. We began to see each adversity as a God-given opportunity to develop the kind of courage which is born of humility, rather than of bravado. Thus we were enabled to accept ourselves, our circumstances, and our fellows. Under God's grace we even found that we could die with decency, dignity, and faith, knowing that "the Father doeth the works."

We of AA now find ourselves living in a world characterized by destructive fears as never before in history. But in it we nevertheless see great areas of faith and tremendous aspirations toward justice and brotherhood. Yet no prophet can presume to say whether the world outcome will be blazing destruction or the beginning, under God's intention, of the brightest era yet known to mankind. I am sure we AAs well comprehend this scene. In microcosm, we have experienced this identical state of terrifying uncertainty, each in his own life. In no sense pridefully, we AAs can say that we do not fear the world outcome, whichever course it may take. This is because we have been enabled to deeply feel and say, "We shall fear no evil — thy will, not ours, be done."

Often told, the following story can nevertheless bear repeating. On the day that the staggering calamity of Pearl Harbor fell upon our country, a friend of AA, and one of the greatest spiritual figures that we may ever know, was walking along a street in St. Louis. This was, of course, our well-loved Father Edward Dowling of the Jesuit Order. Though not an alcoholic, he had been one of the founders and a prime inspiration of the struggling AA group in his city. Because large numbers of his usually sober friends had already taken to their bottles that they might blot out the implications of the Pearl Harbor disaster, Father Ed was understandably anguished by the probability that his cherished AA group would scarcely settle for less. To Father Ed's mind, this would be a first-class calamity, all of itself.

Then an AA member, sober less than a year, stepped alongside and engaged Father Ed in a spirited conversation — mostly about AA. As Father Ed saw, with relief, his companion was perfectly sober. And not a word did he volunteer about the Pearl Harbor business.

Wondering happily about this, the good father queried, "How is it that you have nothing to say about Pearl Harbor? How can you roll with a punch like that?"

"Well," replied the AA, "I'm really surprised that you don't know. Each and every one of us in AA has already had his own private Pearl Harbor. So, I ask you, why should we alcoholics crack up over this one?"

What Is Acceptance?

March 1962

One way to get at the meaning of the principle of acceptance is to meditate upon it in the context of AA's much used prayer, "God grant me the serenity to accept the things I cannot change, courage to change the things I can, and the wisdom to know the difference."

Essentially this is to ask for the resources of grace by which we may make spiritual progress under all conditions. Greatly emphasized in this wonderful prayer is a need for the kind of wisdom that discriminates between the possible and the impossible. We shall also see that life's formidable array of pains and problems will require many different degrees of acceptance as we try to apply this valued principle.

Sometimes we have to find the right kind of acceptance for each day. Sometimes we need to develop acceptance for what may come to pass tomorrow, and yet again we shall have to accept a condition that may never change. Then, too, there frequently has to be a right and realistic acceptance of grievous flaws within ourselves and serious faults within those about us — defects that may not be fully remedied for years, if ever.

All of us will encounter failures, some retrievable and some not. We shall often meet with defeat — sometimes by accident, sometimes self-inflicted, and at still other times dealt to us by the injustice and violence of other people. Most of us will meet up with some degree of worldly success, and here the problem of the right kind of acceptance will be really difficult. Then there will be illness and death. How indeed shall we be able to accept all these?

It is always worthwhile to consider how grossly that good word *acceptance* can be misused. It can be warped to justify nearly every brand of weakness, nonsense, and folly. For instance, we can "accept" failure as a chronic condition, forever without profit or remedy. We can "accept" worldly success pridefully, as something wholly of our own making. We can also "accept" illness and death as certain evidence of a hostile and godless universe. With these twistings of *acceptance,* we AAs have had vast experience. Hence we constantly try to remind ourselves that these perversions of acceptance are just gimmicks for excuse-making: a losing game at which we are, or at least have been, the world's champions.

This is why we treasure our Serenity Prayer so much. It brings a new light to us that can dissipate our old-time and nearly fatal habit of fooling ourselves. In the radiance of this prayer we see that defeat, rightly accepted, need be no disaster. We now know that we do not have to run away, nor ought we again try to overcome adversity by still another bull-dozing power drive that can only push up obstacles before us faster than they can be taken down.

On entering AA, we become the beneficiaries of a very different experience. Our new way of staying sober is literally founded upon the proposition that "Of ourselves, we are nothing, the Father doeth the works." In Steps One and Two of our recovery program, these ideas are specifically spelled out: "We admitted we were powerless over alcohol — that our lives had become unmanageable" — "Came to believe that a Power greater than ourselves could restore us to sanity." We couldn't lick alcohol with our own remaining resources and so we accepted the further fact that dependence upon a higher power (if only our AA group) could do this hitherto impossible job. The moment we were able to fully accept these facts, our release from the alcohol compulsion had begun. For most of us this pair of acceptances had required a lot of exertion to achieve. Our whole treasured philosophy of self-sufficiency had to be cast aside. This had not been done with old-fashioned willpower; it was instead a matter of developing the willingness to *accept* these new facts of living. We neither ran nor fought. But *accept* we did. And then we were free. There had been no irretrievable disaster.

This kind of acceptance and faith is capable of producing 100 percent sobriety. In fact it usually does; and it must, else we could have no life at all. But the moment we carry these attitudes into our emotional problems, we find that only relative results are possible. Nobody can, for example, become completely free from fear, anger, and pride. Hence in this life we shall attain nothing like perfect humility and love. So we shall have to settle, respecting most of our problems, for a very gradual progress, punctuated sometimes by heavy setbacks. Our old-time attitudes of "all or nothing" will have to be abandoned.

Therefore our very first problem is to accept our present circumstances as they are, ourselves as we are, and the people about us as they are. This is to adopt a realistic humility without which no genuine advance can even begin. Again and again, we shall need to return to that unflattering point of departure. This is an exercise in acceptance that we can profitably practice every day of our lives. Provided we strenuously avoid turning these realistic surveys of the facts of life into unrealistic alibis for apathy or defeatism, they can be the sure foundation upon which increased emotional health and therefore spiritual progress can be built. At least this seems to be my own experience.

Another exercise that I practice is to try for a full inventory of my blessings and then for a right acceptance of the many gifts that are mine — both temporal and spiritual. Here I try to achieve a state of joyful gratitude. When such a brand of gratitude is repeatedly affirmed and pondered, it can finally displace the natural tendency to congratulate myself on whatever progress I may have been enabled to make in some areas of living. I try hard to hold fast to the truth that a full and thankful heart cannot entertain great conceits. When brimming with gratitude, one's heartbeat must surely result in outgoing love, the finest emotion that we can ever know.

In times of very rough going, the grateful acceptance of my blessings, oft repeated, can also bring me some of the serenity of which our prayer speaks. Whenever I fall under acute pressures I lengthen my daily walks and slowly repeat our Serenity Prayer in rhythm to my steps and breathing. If I feel that my pain has in part been occasioned by others, I try to repeat, "God grant me the serenity to love their best, and never fear their worst." This benign healing process of repetition, sometimes necessary to persist with for days, has seldom failed to restore me to at least a workable emotional balance and perspective.

Another helpful step is to steadfastly affirm the understanding that pain can bring. Indeed pain is one of our greatest teachers. Though I still find it difficult to accept today's pain and anxiety with any great degree of serenity — as those more advanced in the spiritual life seem able to do — I can, if I try hard, give thanks for present pain nevertheless. I find the willingness to do this by contemplating the lessons learned from past suffering — lessons which have led to the blessings I now enjoy. I can remember, if I insist, how the agonies of alcoholism, the pain of rebellion and thwarted pride, have often led me to God's grace, and so to a new freedom. So, as I walk along, I repeat still other phrases such as these, "Pain is the touchstone of progress" . . . "Fear no evil" . . . "This, too, will pass" . . . "This experience can be turned to benefit."

These fragments of prayer bring far more than mere comfort. They keep me on the track of right acceptance; they break up my compulsive themes of guilt, depression, rebellion, and pride; and sometimes they endow me with the courage to change the things I can, and the wisdom to know the difference.

To those who never have given these potent exercises in acceptance a real workout, I recommend them highly the next time the heat is on. Or, for that matter, at any time!

Where Willpower Comes In

May 1962

There has always been a lot of confusion about this matter of exerting the will. When the Twelve Steps say "We admitted we were powerless over alcohol. . ." we assert what has always been a fact about that malady — namely, that a frontal attack by the will on the desire to drink almost never works.

This hard fact is the premise upon which we must start — the recognition that actual lunacy cannot be subdued by straight willpower. God knows drunks have tried hard enough to do just this and have generally failed. Nobody would expect much result were every kleptomaniac to take the pledge not to steal. Respecting stealing, the kleptomaniac is as compulsively nutty as he can be. Though this compulsive condition is not so generally recognized in the alcoholic, because drinking is socially acceptable, it is nevertheless true that he is just about as crazy. Therefore our First Step is realistic when it declares that we are powerless to deal with the alcohol hex on our own resources or will.

But even AA's First Step asks for willingness — the willingness to admit that our willpower is not going to work head-on. But that's only a starter. All of the rest of AA's Twelve Steps require both willingness and willpower. They certainly deal in religious and moral values.

For example, we must acquire the willingness to take a moral inventory. This much accomplished, we then must needs muster the gumption to actually do that. We can become willing to believe in the efficacy of AA's Twelfth Step — carrying the message to others. But if we are aroused from sleep at 12 o'clock at night to make a Twelfth Step call — well, the actual making of that visit may call for a considerable amount of willpower.

Another example: It is especially required of the atheist and agnostic that he become open-minded on the subject of God. This seems to require a considerable exertion indeed. If then we suggest that he address himself to whatever God there may be, in meditation and prayer, he usually finds this takes a lot of discipline to do, even as an experiment.

The net result of willingness and will, as applied to the life problem in general, does eventuate in a release from the desire to drink, thereby getting around any heavy exertion of willpower on the alcohol problem itself. Precisely why this release comes to most of us is totally unexplained. We *are* restored to sanity, provided we condition ourselves for the gift of restoration — or, to put it in religious terms, to the inflow of God's grace which results in the expulsion of the obsession.

Nor does it seem to matter how we define God's grace. We can still claim if we like that we have tapped a hidden or unused inner resource. We don't need to actually define just where that came from. Or we can believe, as most of us finally do, that we have tapped the resources of God as he exists in us and in the cosmos generally. None of us can presume to know exactly how this is.

Of course I do not mean to say that no willpower respecting the alcohol problem is ever to be used. During my first couple of years, I had two or three severe temptations to drink. But having practiced the AA program pretty faithfully, I was fully able to see the consequences of so doing at the time I was tempted. The usual blinding rationalizations were not present. I had been restored to sanity, respecting alcohol. I nevertheless had to make a choice. But under these conditions it was not hard. And the choice did require a certain modicum of willpower. Or of willingness to choose rightly.

I think this exercise of the will is appropriate and necessary during the interval in which one is developing a general release from the problem. But a general and complete release is quite possible, after considerable practice of AA's program. I know because I have been under enormous emotional strain since AA started. I had a neurotic depression that lasted from 1943 until 1955, one from which I never fully surfaced. About three years of this was suicidal. But the release from alcohol had been so thorough that I was never tempted during this long siege to resort to drink.

So this is the substance of the AA party line as I happen to see it. But please be assured you don't necessarily have to see it the same way. Plenty of people differ with me, and yet remain sober. Nevertheless the experience of most of us seems to back up what I have just said. Those who try to work the program in other ways, and who succeed by so doing, are in my belief staying dry the hard way. AA's orthodoxy, if it can be called that, is merely what the majority experience suggests. You can still take your pick!

Spiritual Experiences

July 1962

It is the intention of the Grapevine to carry occasional accounts of spiritual experiences. To this interesting project I would like to say a few introductory words. There is a very natural tendency to set apart those experiences or awakenings which happen to be sudden, spectacular, or vision-producing. Therefore any recital of such cases always produces mixed reactions. Some will say, "I wish I could have an experience like that!" Others, feeling that this whole business is too far out on the mystic limb for them, or maybe hallucinatory after all, will say, "I just can't buy this business. I can't understand what these people are talking about."

As most AAs have heard, I was the recipient in 1934 of a tremendous mystic experience or "illumination." It was accompanied by a sense of intense white light, by a sudden gift of faith in the goodness of God, and by a profound conviction of his presence. At first it was very natural for me to feel that this experience staked me out for somebody very special.

But as I now look back upon this tremendous event, I can only feel very specially grateful. It now seems clear that the only special feature of my experience was its electric suddenness and the overwhelming and immediate conviction that it carried to me.

In all other respects, however, I am sure that my own experience was not in the least different from that received by every AA member who has strenuously practiced our recovery program.

How often do we sit in AA meetings and hear the speaker declare, "But I haven't yet got the spiritual angle." Prior to this statement, he had described a miracle of transformation which had occurred in him — not only his release from alcohol, but a complete change in his whole attitude toward life and the living of it. It is apparent to nearly everyone else present that he has received a great gift; and that this gift was all out of proportion to anything that might be expected from simple AA activity, such as the admission of alcoholism and the practice of Step Twelve. So we in the audience smile and say to ourselves, "Well, that guy is just reeking with the spiritual angle — except that he doesn't seem to know it yet!" We well know that this questioning individual will tell us six months or a year hence that he has found faith in God.

Moreover, he may by then be displaying "spiritual qualities" and a performance that I myself have never been able to duplicate — my sudden spiritual experience notwithstanding.

So nowadays when AAs come to me, hoping to find out how one comes by those sudden experiences, I simply tell them that in all probability they have had one just as good — and that theirs is identical excepting it has been strung out over a longer period of time.

Then I go on to say that if their transformation in AA extending over six months had been condensed into six minutes — well, they then might have seen the stars, too!

In consequence of these observations I fail to see any great difference between the sudden experiences and the more gradual ones — they are certainly all of the same piece. And there is one sure test of them all: "By their fruits, ye shall know them."

This is why I think we should question no one's transformation — whether it be sudden or gradual. Nor should we demand anyone's special type for ourselves, because our own experience suggests that we are apt to receive whatever may be the most useful for our needs.

The Bill W. – Carl Jung Letters

After his retirement from AA leadership in 1961, Bill embarked on a task he had long desired to undertake — acknowledging AA's debt to those who had contributed to its creation. One of those people was Dr. Carl Jung, to whom Bill wrote on January 23, 1961.

January 1963

My dear Dr. Jung:
This letter of great appreciation has been very long overdue.

May I first introduce myself as Bill W., a co-founder of the Society of Alcoholics Anonymous. Though you have surely heard of us, I doubt if you are aware that a certain conversation you once had with one of your patients, a Mr. Rowland H., back in the early 1930s, did play a critical role in the founding of our Fellowship.

Though Rowland H. has long since passed away, the recollections of his remarkable experience while under treatment by you has definitely become part of AA history. Our remembrance of Rowland H.'s statements about his experience with you is as follows:

Having exhausted other means of recovery from his alcoholism, it was about 1931 that he became your patient. I believe he remained under your care for perhaps a year. His admiration for you was boundless, and he left you with a feeling of much confidence.

To his great consternation, he soon relapsed into intoxication. Certain that you were his "court of last resort," he again returned to your care. Then followed the conversation between you that was to become the first link in the chain of events that led to the founding of Alcoholics Anonymous.

My recollection of his account of that conversation is this: First of all, you frankly told him of his hopelessness, so far as any further medical or psychiatric treatment might be concerned. This candid and humble statement of yours was beyond doubt the first foundation stone upon which our Society has since been built.

Coming from you, one he so trusted and admired, the impact upon him was immense.

When he then asked you if there was any other hope, you told him that there might be, provided he could become the subject of a spiritual or religious experience — in short, a genuine conversion. You pointed out how such an experience, if brought about, might remotivate him when nothing else could. But you did caution, though, that while such experiences had sometimes brought recovery to alcoholics, they were, nevertheless, comparatively rare. You recommended that he place himself in a religious atmosphere and hope for the best. This I believe was the substance of your advice.

Shortly thereafter, Mr. H. joined the Oxford Groups, an evangelical movement then at the height of its success in Europe, and one with which you are doubtless familiar. You will remember their large emphasis upon the principles of self-survey, confession, restitution, and the giving of oneself in service to others. They strongly stressed meditation and prayer. In these surroundings, Rowland H. did find a conversion experience that released him for the time being from his compulsion to drink.

Returning to New York, he became very active with the "O.G." here, then led by an Episcopal clergyman, Dr. Samuel Shoemaker. Dr. Shoemaker had been one of the founders of that movement, and his was a powerful personality that carried immense sincerity and conviction.

At this time (1932-34) the Oxford Groups had already sobered a number of alcoholics, and Rowland, feeling that he could especially identify with these sufferers, addressed himself to the help of still others. One of these chanced to be an old schoolmate of mine, named Edwin T. ["Ebby"]. He had been threatened with commitment to an institution, but Mr. H. and another ex-alcoholic "O.G." member procured his parole and helped to bring about his sobriety.

Meanwhile, I had run the course of alcoholism and was threatened with commitment myself. Fortunately I had fallen under the care of a physician — a Dr. William D. Silkworth — who was wonderfully capable of understanding alcoholics. But just as you had given up on Rowland, so had he given me up. It was his theory that alcoholism had two components — an obsession that compelled the sufferer to drink against his will and interest, and some sort of metabolism difficulty which he then called an allergy. The alcoholic's compulsion guaranteed that the alcoholic's drinking would go on, and the allergy made sure that the sufferer would finally deteriorate, go insane, or die. Though I had been one of the few he had thought it possible to help, he was finally obliged to tell me of my hopelessness; I, too, would have to be locked up. To me, this was a shattering blow. Just as Rowland had been made ready for his conversion experience by you, so had my wonderful friend, Dr. Silkworth, prepared me.

Hearing of my plight, my friend Edwin T. came to see me at my home where I was drinking. By then, it was November 1934. I had long marked my friend Edwin for a hopeless case. Yet here he was in a very evident state of "release" which could by no means be accounted for by his mere association for a very short time with the Oxford Groups. Yet this obvious state of release, as distinguished from the usual depression, was tremendously convincing. Because he was a kindred sufferer, he could unquestionably communicate with me at great depth. I knew at once I must find an experience like his, or die.

Again I returned to Dr. Silkworth's care where I could be once more sobered and so gain a clearer view of my friend's experience of release, and of Rowland H.'s approach to him.

Clear once more of alcohol, I found myself terribly depressed. This seemed to be caused by my inability to gain the slightest faith. Edwin T. again visited me and repeated the simple Oxford Groups' formulas. Soon after he left me I became even more depressed. In utter despair I cried out, "If there be a God, will he show himself." There immediately came to me an illumination of enormous impact and dimension, something which I have since tried to describe in the book *Alcoholics Anonymous* and also in *AA Comes of Age,* basic texts which I am sending to you.

My release from the alcohol obsession was immediate. At once I knew I was a free man.

Shortly following my experience, my friend Edwin came to the hospital, bringing me a copy of William James' *Varieties of Religious Experience.* This book gave me the realization that most conversion experiences, whatever their variety, do have a common denominator of ego collapse at depth. The individual faces an impossible dilemma. In my case the dilemma had been created by my compulsive drinking and the deep feeling of hopelessness had been vastly deepened by my doctor. It was deepened still more by my alcoholic friend when he acquainted me with your verdict of hopelessness respecting Rowland H.

In the wake of my spiritual experience there came a vision of a society of alcoholics, each identifying with and transmitting his experience to the next — chain style. If each sufferer were to carry the news of the scientific hopelessness of alcoholism to each new prospect, he might be able to lay every newcomer wide open to a transforming spiritual experience. This concept proved to be the foundation of such success as Alcoholics Anonymous has since achieved. This has made conversion experiences — nearly every variety reported by James — available on an almost wholesale basis. Our sustained recoveries over the last quarter century number about 300,000. In America and through the world there are today 8,000 AA groups.

So to you, to Dr. Shoemaker of the Oxford Groups, to William James, and to my own physician, Dr. Silkworth, we of AA owe this tremendous benefaction. As you will now clearly see, this astonishing chain of events actually started long ago in your consulting room, and it was directly founded upon your own humility and deep perception.

Very many thoughtful AAs are students of your writings. Because of your conviction that man is something more than intellect, emotion, and two dollars worth of chemicals, you have especially endeared yourself to us.

How our Society grew, developed its Traditions for unity, and structured its functioning will be seen in the texts and pamphlet material that I am sending you.

You will also be interested to learn that in addition to the "spiritual experience," many AAs report a great variety of psychic phenomena, the cumulative weight of which is very considerable. Other members have — following their recovery in AA — been much helped by your practitioners. A few have been intrigued by the "I Ching" and your remarkable introduction to that work.

Please be certain that your place in the affection, and in the history of our Fellowship, is like no other.

Gratefully yours,
William G. W.
Co-founder
Alcoholics Anonymous

January 30, 1961

Dear Mr. W.

Your letter has been very welcome indeed.

I had no news from Rowland H. anymore and often wondered what has been his fate. Our conversation which he has adequately reported to you had an aspect of which he did not know. The reason that I could not tell him everything was that those days I had to be exceedingly careful of what I said. I had found out that I was misunderstood in every possible way. Thus I was very careful when I talked to Rowland H. but what I really thought about, was the result of many experiences with men of his kind.

His craving for alcohol was the equivalent, on a low level, of the spiritual thirst of our being for wholeness, expressed in medieval language: the union with God.

How could one formulate such an insight in a language that is not misunderstood in our days?

The only right and legitimate way to such an experience is, that it happens to you in reality and it can only happen to you when you walk on a path which leads you to higher understanding. You might be led to that goal by an act of grace or through a personal and honest contact with friends, or through a higher education of the mind beyond the confines of mere rationalism. I see from your letter that Rowland H. has chosen the second way, which was, under the circumstances, obviously the best one.

I am strongly convinced that the evil principle prevailing in this world leads the unrecognized spiritual need into perdition, if it is not counteracted either by real religious insight or by the protective wall of human community. An ordinary man, not protected by an action from above and isolated in society, cannot resist the power of evil, which is called very aptly the Devil. But the use of such words arouses so many mistakes that one can only keep aloof from them as much as possible.

These are the reasons why I could not give a full and sufficient explanation to Rowland H. But I am risking it with you because I conclude from your very decent and honest letter that you have acquired a point of view above the misleading platitudes one usually hears about alcoholism.

You see, alcohol in Latin is "spiritus" and you use the same word for the highest religious experience as well as the most depraving poison. The helpful formula therefore is: *spiritus contra spiritum.*

Thanking you again for your kind letter.

I remain

yours sincerely

C. G. Jung

Dr. Jung, Dr. Silkworth, and AA

The article that follows comprises excerpts from Bill's talk at his 33rd AA anniversary sponsored by New York City Intergroup. He was the third and final speaker, preceded by Jim from Long Island and Kirsten from Scarsdale.

January 1968

As Kirsten said so poignantly just now, "The years laid waste by the locusts are over. . . ." And as Jim so simply remarked, "There is a God and there is a grace. . . ."

Tonight I think I would like to tell you my own story in terms, first, of the "years laid waste" and the reasons I now see why this was so — what in my early life contributed to my alcoholism — and then, in terms of my belief that "there is a God and there is a grace" and what the outcome has been for me and for so many because of that belief.

Our chairman tonight remarked on the wonderful friends that AA has had from the start. He might have said the wonderful friends we have had since before AA was even a gleam in the eye of any of us!

Long before I was sober, long before there was any idea that there would be this AA way for alcoholics to help themselves, certain men and women were gaining skills and insights that were to make all the difference to us in later years. The thing that characterized all of these early friends of ours who were to donate their skill and wisdom to us in AA was this: In each case where telling contributions were made, the man or woman was *spiritually centered, spiritually animated.*

Tonight I would like to sketch just one of the historical situations out of which our Fellowship sprang. Many of you have heard parts of the story before, the story of how Rowland H., an American business-man, was getting progressively worse in alcoholism — undergoing one treatment, one so-called cure after another, with no result. Finally, as a refuge of last resort, he went to Europe and literally cast himself upon the care of a psychiatrist, Dr. Carl Jung, who was to prove, in the event, a great and good friend of AA.

You will recall Dr. Jung as one of the three first pioneers in the art of psychiatry. The thing that distinguished him from his colleagues, Freud and Adler, was the fact that he was spiritually animated — something that was to make all the difference to each and every one of us now here, and will make the difference for all yet to come....

I never realized what a very great man in spiritual dimensions Carl Jung was until, in 1961, I wrote him a very belated letter of gratitude for the part he had played in originating our Society of Alcoholics Anonymous.

This was the last year of Dr. Jung's life. He was old. Nevertheless, he sat down and wrote me a letter. It looks like he tapped it out on a typewriter with one finger. It is one of my most cherished possessions. Lois framed it and it will always be with us.

We ought to note very carefully what Dr. Jung said in that letter, so obviously written in profound love and understanding — in the language of the heart. His insight into what was needed for recovery from alco-holism, an insight that came to me through Rowland and Ebby at a crucial point in my own deterioration, meant everything for AA when it was still in embryo. His humble willingness to speak the truth, even when it meant disclosing the limitations of his own art, gives the measure of the man.

There was another spiritually animated man, Dr. William D. Silk-worth, whose contribution to AA paralleled Dr. Jung's. Unlike Jung,

Dr. Silkworth was a man in obscure position, but he was spiritually centered — he had to be! He declared to all comers, after twenty years of almost absolute defeat in trying to help alcoholics, that he did love alcoholics and wanted to go on working with and for them. Every alcoholic who came his way felt that love. A very few recovered. He thought I might recover. Then the day came when it was clear that I would not, that I could not.

By this time Dr. Silkworth had defined alcoholism as a sickness of the emotions, coupled with a sickness of the body which he loosely described as an allergy. These words of his are to be seen in the foreword of the Big Book, *Alcoholics Anonymous,* entitled, "The Doctor's Opinion," and over the intervening years they have been incorporated into the consensus that is AA.

As Jung had told Rowland that his case was hopeless and that medicine and psychiatry could do nothing more for him, so Silkworth told Lois on a fateful day in the summer of 1934: "I am afraid that Bill will have to be committed. There is nothing that I can do for him, or anything else that I know." These were words of great humility from a professional.

They scared me into sobriety for two months, although I soon resumed my drinking. But the message that Ebby had brought me from Dr. Jung and from the Oxford Groups, and the sentence that Dr. Silkworth pronounced over me, continued to occupy my mind in every waking hour thereafter. I began to be very resentful. Here was Dr. Silkworth, who had defined alcoholism — the obsession that condemns you to drink against your will and true interests, even unto destruction, and the bodily sensitivity that guarantees madness and death if you drink at all. And here came Dr. Jung via Rowland and Ebby confirming that there was no way out known to the doctors. My god, science, the only god I had then, had declared me hopeless.

But Ebby had also brought hope. Not much later, I was back in the hospital, in Dr. Silkworth's care after what proved to be my last drunk. Ebby came to visit me again. I asked him to repeat once more what he had said over my kitchen table in Brooklyn that first time he told me how he had gotten sober.

"Well," he said, "you know, you get honest with yourself; you make a self-survey; you talk it out with the other guy; you quit living alone and begin to get straight with the world around by making restitution; you try the kind of giving that demands no reward either in approval, prestige, or money; and you ask whatever higher power there is, even if it is just as an experiment, to help you find the grace to be released from alcoholism.''

As Ebby put it, it was quite simple, quite matter-of-fact, and said with a smile. But this was it.

So Ebby finally took his leave. Now the jaws of the dilemma really crushed. I hit an all-time block. I can only suppose that any particle of belief that there was a single thing I could do for myself alone was for the moment rubbed out. And I found myself as a child, utterly alone in complete darkness. And I cried out as a child, expecting little — indeed, expecting nothing. I simply said, ''If there is a God, will he show himself?'' Then I was granted one of those instantaneous illuminations. The sort of thing that really defies description. I was seized with great joy and ecstasy beyond all possible expression. In the mind's eye, it seemed to me I stood on a high mountain. I was taken there, I had not climbed it. And then the great thought burst upon me: ''Bill, you are a free man! This is the God of the Scriptures.'' And then I was filled with a consciousness of a presence. A great peace fell over me, and I was with this I don't know how long.

But then the dark side put in an appearance, and it said to me, ''Perhaps, Bill, you are hallucinating. You better call in the doctor.''

So the doctor came, and haltingly I told him of the experience. Then came great words for Alcoholics Anonymous. The little man had listened, looking at me so benignly with those blue eyes of his, and at length he said to me, ''Bill, you are not crazy. I have read about this sort of thing in the books but I have never seen it firsthand. I don't know what it is you have, Bill, but it must be some great psychic event, and you had better hang on to it — it is so much better than what you had only an hour ago.''

So I hung on, and then I knew there was a God and I knew there was a grace. And through it all, I have continued to feel, if I may presume to say it, that I do *know* these things.

Then, of course, being trained as an analyst of sorts, I began to ask myself why this had happened to me. And why had it so seldom happened to drunks before? Why shouldn't this be the heritage of any drunk? And while I was wondering, Ebby came again the next day and he had in his hands a message from another great man, William James, and the message came to me in a book called *Varieties of Religious Experience.* I read the book cover to cover, and naturally I found experiences corresponding with my own. I found other experiences, however, that were very gradual. I found experiences that occurred outside of any religious association.

But nearly all of these experiences that were capable of transforming motivations had common denominators over and above any explanation by associations, or common discipline, or faith, or what have you. These gifts of grace, whether they came in a rush or very gradually, were all founded on a basis of hopelessness. The recipients were people who in some controlling area of life found themselves in a situation that could not be gotten over, around, or under. Their defeat had been absolute, and so was mine.

Then I wondered about that defeat, and I realized what part my god of science, as personified by Dr. Carl Jung and Dr. Silkworth, had played in it. They had transmitted to me the very bad news that the chance of recovery on my own unaided resources or merely by medication was just about nil. This was deflation at depth — this made me ready for the gift when it came.

Now, actually, although this is the great experience of my life, I do not think it in any way superior or in its essentials very different at all than the experience which all AAs have had — the transforming experience — the spiritual awakening. They are all from the same source: the divine peace.

So, with my own experience had come the possibility of a chain reaction. I realized nothing had happened to me until certain messages had been transmitted, striking into me at great depth, by another alcoholic. Therefore, the thought came of one alcoholic talking to another just as Oxford Group people were talking to each other — in the language of the heart. Maybe this could be the transmission belt. So I started working among alcoholics.

I went to a few Oxford Group meetings and to the missions. Dr. Silkworth let me work with a few people in the hospital at the risk of his reputation. And lo and behold! Nothing happened. Because — some of my old grandeur had come back, I had thought my experience was something very special. The old ego began to boom again. I was destined to fix all the drunks in the world — quite a large order.

Naturally nothing happened until — again — the deflation came. It came on that day when, in the Mayflower Hotel in Akron, I was tempted to take a drink for the first time since my hospital experience. That was when I first realized that I would need other alcoholics to preserve myself and maintain that original gift of sobriety. It was not just a case of trying to *help* alcoholics. If my own sobriety were to be maintained, I *had* to find another alcoholic to work with. So when Dr. Bob and I sat down for the first time face-to-face, it was a very different act. I said, ''Bob, I am speaking because I need you as much as you could possibly need me. I am in danger of slipping back down the drain.''

So there is the story. There is the nature of the illness as explained by Dr. Jung and Dr. Silkworth — and there is one drunk talking to another, telling his story of recovery through reliance on the grace of God.

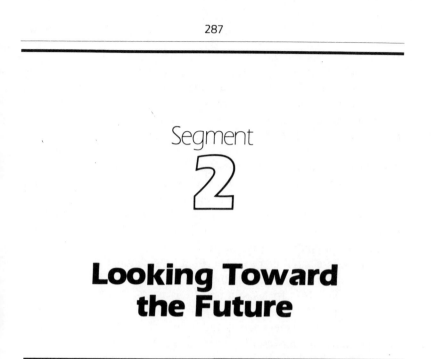

Segment
2

Looking Toward the Future

Leadership in AA: Ever a Vital Need

April 1959

No society can function well without able leadership in all its levels, and AA can be no exception. It must be said, though, that we AAs sometimes cherish the thought that we can do without any leadership at all. We are apt to warp the traditional idea of "principles before personalities" around to such a point that there would be no "personality" in leadership whatever. This would imply rather faceless automatons trying to please everybody, regardless.

At other times we are quite as apt to demand that AA's leaders must necessarily be people of the most sterling judgment, morals, and inspiration — big doers, prime examples to all, and practically infallible.

Real leadership, of course, has to function in between these entirely imaginary poles of hoped-for excellence. In AA, certainly, no leader is faceless and neither is any leader perfect. Fortunately our Society is blessed with any amount of *real* leadership — the active people of today and the potential leaders for tomorrow as each new generation of able members swarms in. We have an abundance of men and women whose dedication, stability, vision, and special skills make them capable of dealing with every possible service assignment. We have only to seek these folks out and trust them to serve us.

Somewhere in our literature there is a statement to this effect: "Our leaders do not drive by mandate, they lead by example." In effect we are saying to them, "Act for us, but don't boss us."

A leader in AA service is therefore a man (or a woman) who can personally put principles, plans, and policies into such dedicated and effective action that the rest of us want to back him up and help him with his job. When a leader power-drives us badly, we rebel; but when he too meekly becomes an order-taker and he exercises no judgment of his own — well, he really isn't a leader at all.

Good leadership originates plans, policies, and ideas for the improvement of our Fellowship and its services. But in new and important matters, it will nevertheless consult widely before taking decisions and actions. Good leadership will also remember that a fine plan or idea can come from anybody, anywhere. Consequently, good leadership will often discard its own cherished plans for others that are better, and it will give credit to the source.

Good leadership never passes the buck. Once assured that it has, or can obtain, sufficient general backing, it freely takes decisions and puts them into action forthwith, provided of course that such actions be within the framework of its defined authority and responsibility.

A "politico" is an individual who is forever trying to "get the people what they want." A statesman is an individual who can carefully discriminate when, and *when not* to do this. He recognizes that even large majorities, when badly disturbed or uninformed, can, once in a while, be dead wrong. When such an occasional situation arises, and something very vital is at stake, it is always the duty of leadership, even when in a small minority, to take a stand against the storm — using its every ability of authority and persuasion to effect a change.

Nothing, however, can be more fatal to leadership than opposition for opposition's sake. It never can be, "Let's have it our way or no way at all." This sort of opposition is often powered by a visionless pride or a gripe that makes us want to block something or somebody. Then there is the opposition that casts its vote saying, "No, we don't like it." No real reasons are ever given. This won't do. When called upon, leadership must always give its reasons, and good ones.

Then too a leader must realize that even very prideful or angry people can sometimes be dead right, when the calm and the more humble are quite mistaken.

These points are practical illustrations of the kinds of careful discrimination and soul-searching that true leadership must always try to exercise.

Another qualification for leadership is "give and take" — the ability to compromise cheerfully whenever a proper compromise can cause a situation to progress in what appears to be the right direction. Compromise comes hard to us "all-or-nothing drunks." Nevertheless, we must never lose sight of the fact that progress is nearly always characterized by *a series of improving compromises*. We cannot, however, compromise always. Now and then it is truly necessary to stick flat-footed to one's conviction about an issue until it is settled. These are situations for keen timing and a most careful discrimination as to which course to take.

Leadership is often called upon to face heavy and sometimes long-continued criticism. This is an acid test. There are always the constructive critics, our friends indeed. We ought never fail to give them a careful hearing. We should be willing to let them modify our opinions or change them completely. Often, too, we shall have to disagree and then stand fast without losing their friendship. Then we have those who we like to call our "destructive" critics. They power-drive, they are "politickers," they make accusations. Maybe they are violent, malicious. They pitch gobs of rumors, gossip, and general scuttlebutt to gain their ends — all for the good of AA, of course! Well, in AA at least, we have at last learned that these folks, who may be a trifle sicker than the rest of us, need not be really destructive at all, depending entirely on how we relate ourselves to them.

To begin with, we ought to listen very carefully to what they say. Sometimes they are telling the whole truth; at other times, a little truth. More often, though, they are just rationalizing themselves into nonsense. If we are within range, the whole truth, the half truth, or even no truth at all can equally hurt us. That is why we have to listen so carefully. If they've got the whole truth, or even a little truth, then we'd better thank them and get on with our respective inventories, admitting we were wrong, regardless. If it's nonsense, we can ignore them. Or we can lay all the cards on the table and try to persuade them. Failing this, we can be sorry they are too sick to listen and we can try to forget the whole business. We can think of few better means of self-survey, of developing genuine patience, than these usually well-meaning but erratic brother members can afford us. This is always a large order and we shall sometimes fail to make good on it ourselves. But we must needs keep trying.

Now comes that all-important attribute of vision. Vision is, I think, the ability to make good estimates, both for the immediate and for the more distant future. Some might feel this sort of striving to be a sort of heresy because we AAs are constantly telling ourselves, "One day at a time." But that valued maxim really refers to our emotional lives and means only that we are not to repine over the past nor wishfully fantasy or daydream about our future.

As individuals and as a Fellowship, we shall surely suffer if we cast the whole job of planning for tomorrow onto a kind Providence. God has endowed us human beings with considerable capability for foresight and he evidently expects us to use it. Therefore we must needs distinguish between wishful dreaming for a happy tomorrow and today's use of our powers of thoughtful estimate — estimate of the kind which we trust will bring future progress rather than unforeseen woe.

Vision is therefore the very essence of prudence — a sound virtue if ever there was one. Of course we shall often miscalculate the future in whole or in part. But even so, this will be far better than to refuse to think at all.

The making of estimates has several aspects. We look at past and present experience to see what we think it means. From this, we derive a tentative idea or policy. Looking first at the nearby future, we ask how our idea or policy might work. Following this estimate we ask how our policies and ideas might work under the several differing conditions that could arise in the longer future. If an idea looks like a good bet, we try it on — always experimentally, when that is possible. Somewhat later, we revalue the situation and ask whether our estimate is, or may soon be, working out.

At about this stage, we may have to take a critical decision. Maybe we have a policy or plan that still looks fine and is apparently doing well.

Nevertheless we ought to ponder very carefully what its longtime effect will be. Will today's nearby advantages boomerang into large liabilities for tomorrow? The temptation will almost always be to seize the nearby benefits and quite forget about the harmful precedents or consequences that we may be setting in motion.

These are no fancy theories. We have found that we must use these principles of estimate constantly, especially at world service levels where the stakes are high. In public relations, for example, we must estimate the reaction both of AA groups and the general public, both short-term and long-term. The same thing goes for our literature. Our finances have to be estimated and budgeted. We must think about our service needs as they relate to general economic conditions, group capability, and willingness to contribute. On many such problems we must very often try to think many months and even years ahead.

As a matter of fact, all of AA's Twelve Traditions were at first questions of estimate and vision for the future. Years ago we slowly evolved an idea about AA being self-supporting. There had been trouble here and there about outside gifts. Then still more trouble developed. Consequently we began to devise a policy of no outside gifts. We began to suspect that large sums would tend to make us irresponsible and could divert us from our primary aim. Finally we saw that for the long pull, outside money could ruin us utterly. At this point, what had been just an idea or general policy hardened firmly down into an AA Tradition. We saw that we must sacrifice the quick, nearby advantage for long-term safety.

We went through this same process on anonymity. A few public breaks had looked good. But finally the vision came that many such breaks could raise havoc among us. So it went — first a gleam in the eye, then an experimental policy, then a firm policy, and finally a deep conviction — a vision for tomorrow. Such is our process of estimating the future. Our responsible world leadership must be especially and constantly proficient in this vital activity. This is an ability much to be desired, especially among our trustees, and I think most of them should be chosen on the basis that they have already proved their aptness for foresight in business or professional careers.

We shall continually need many of these same attributes, insofar as they can be had, among our leaders of AA services at all levels. The principles of leadership will be just about the same, no matter what the size of the operation.

This discussion on leadership may look, at first glance, like an attempt to stake out a specially privileged and superior type of AA member. But this is not really so. We are simply recognizing that our talents vary greatly. The conductor of an orchestra is not necessarily good at finance or foresight. And it is even less likely that a fine banker could be much of a musical success. When, therefore, we talk about AA leadership, we only declare that we ought select that leadership on the basis of obtaining the best talent we can find, making sure that we land that talent, whatever it is, in the spot where it will do us the most good.

While this article was first thought of in connection with our world service leadership, it is quite possible that many of its suggestions can be useful to everyone who takes an active part in our Society.

Nowhere could this be more true than in the area of Twelfth Step work itself — something at which nearly all of us most eagerly work. Every sponsor is necessarily a leader. The stakes are huge. A human life, and usually the happiness of a whole family, hangs in the balance. What the sponsor does and says, how well he estimates the reactions of his prospects, how well he times and makes his presentation, how well he handles criticisms, and how well he leads his prospect on by personal spiritual example — well, these attributes of leadership can make all the difference, often the difference between life and death.

Thank God that Alcoholics Anonymous is blessed with so much leadership in each and all of its great affairs!

AA Communication Can Cross All Barriers

October 1959

E veryone must agree that we AAs are unbelievably fortunate people; fortunate that we have suffered so much; fortunate that we can know, understand, and love each other so supremely well — these attributes and virtues are scarcely of the earned variety. Indeed, most of us are well aware that these are rare gifts which have their true origin in our kinship born of a common suffering and a common deliverance by the grace of God. Thereby we are privileged to communicate with each other to a degree and in a manner not very often surpassed among our nonalcoholic friends in the world around us.

From AA's very beginning our success with each new prospect has always rested squarely on our ability to identify with him or her in experience, in language, and especially in feeling — that profound feeling for each other that goes deeper than words. This is what we really mean when we say "one alcoholic talking to another."

Years ago, however, we found that the kinship of having suffered severe alcoholism was often not enough in itself. To cross all barriers, our channels of communication had to be broadened and deepened.

Practically all of AA's first members were, for example, what we today call "last gasp" (or low-bottom) cases. We oldsters, for the most part, were at the jumping-off place. When the still mildly afflicted (or high-bottom) cases began to turn up, they usually said, "But we were never jailed. We were never clapped into mental hospitals. We never did those horrendous things you fellows talk about. Surely AA can't be for people like us."

For years we old-timers simply couldn't communicate with folks like these. Somehow our transmission lines to them had to be increased in numbers and in power. Otherwise we'd never get through. Out of much experience a means and a method was developed.

To each new high-bottom we hammered home the verdict of noted doctors that "alcoholism is a fatal and *progressive* malady." Then we would go back to those earlier periods in our drinking careers when we too were mild, or seemingly not too serious, cases ourselves. We would recall how very sure we were that "next time" we could control ourselves when we took a few drinks, or maybe how we rather admired the notion that, on occasions, unrestrained grog consumption was after all no more than a good "he-man's" fault. Or, in the next phase, how our dram consumption was the fault of unfortunate circumstances or the distressing behavior of other people.

This much identification achieved, we'd proceed to regale the prospect with many a tale showing just how insidious and irresistible the progress of our illness had been; how, years before we realized it, we had actually gone much beyond the "point of no return" so far as our own resources of strength and will were concerned. We kept pointing out how right the doctors were.

Slowly but surely this strategy commenced to pay off. With the aid of the authority of medical science and by a better presentation, the low-bottoms had begun to communicate at depth with the high-bottoms. But this tedious process and its sparse results didn't have to go on forever. We joyfully discovered that the moment any AA locality was possessed of even a small group of high-bottom drunks, then progress into this class of toper became progressively faster and easier. Today we know why — one high-bottom can talk to another high-bottom as nobody else ever could. So this segment of our Fellowship grew and grew. It is probable that one-half of today's AA membership has been spared that last five, ten, or even fifteen years of unmitigated hell that we low-bottoms know all too well.

Since these first elemental problems of communication were solved, AA has taken on and has successfully communicated with every single area of life and living where alcoholics dwell.

In the beginning, for instance, it was four whole years before AA brought permanent sobriety to even one alcoholic woman. Like the high-bottoms the women said they were different; AA couldn't be for them. But as the communication was perfected, mostly by the women themselves, the picture changed. Spread all over the globe, our sister AAs must be thirty thousand strong by now.

In like manner, this process of identification and transmission has gone on and on. The skid rower said he was different. Even more loudly the socialite (or Park Avenue stumble bum) said the same — so did the arts and the professions, the rich, the poor, the religious, the agnostics, the Indians and the Eskimos, the veterans, and the prisoners.

But nowadays all of these, and legions more, soberly talk about how very much alike all of us alcoholics are when we all admit that the chips are finally down; when we see that it is really a question of do or die in our wide world Fellowship of "the common suffering and the common deliverance."

Now this is our yearly international issue of the AA Grapevine. Here we feature the news and views of our far-flung and treasured groups beyond the seas who today return to us in double measure the inspiration that years ago we tried to send to them. In those days there was a problem of communications indeed. Could we possibly identify ourselves by mail, by our literature and its then scarce translations, and through random AA travelers abroad?

By 1950, we weren't any too sure. So Lois and I wondered a lot as we headed for Europe and Britain to see for ourselves in that wonderful year. Could AA really and fully transcend all of those formidable barriers of race, language, religion, and culture; all of those scars of wars, recent and ancient; all of those kinds of pride and prejudice of which we knew we had our share in America? What about the Norwegians, the Swedes, the Danes, and the Finns? What about the Dutch, the Germans, the French, the English, the Scots, and the Israelis? How about the Africans, the Boers, the Aussies, the Latins, the Japanese, the Hindus, the Mohammedans, and, of course, the Eskimos! Could AA finally cross all of the very barriers that had, as never before, divided and shattered the world of our time?

The moment we alighted in Norway, we knew that AA could and would go everywhere. We understood not one word of Norwegian, and translators were sometimes scarce. Scenes and customs alike were new and strange to us. Yet there was a marvelous communication from the first moment. There was an incredible sensation of oneness, of being completely at home — Norwegians were our people, Norway was our country, too. They felt the same way about us; it shone in their faces; they reached our hearts.

As we journeyed from land to land, it was the same everywhere. In Britain we were accepted as Britons; in Ireland we were at one with the Irish. Everywhere, everywhere it was the same. It was so much more than minds cordially meeting minds; it was no simple and merely interesting comparison of mutual experiences and aspirations. This was much, much more; this was the forming of heart to heart in wonder, in joy, and in everlasting gratitude. Lois and I then knew that AA could circle the globe — and it has!

For us no more proof will ever be needed. Should any AA still doubt, he ought to have heard the sweet and stirring story told me only last week.

Here it is: It's about a small English-speaking AA group in Japan. More properly, it's about two of its members — two Japanese who can't understand a word of English. It should also be known that the rest of the group — the English-speaking — don't know a word of Japanese. The language barrier is complete. The two Japanese have probably read a translation of the Twelve Steps, that's about all.

For months now the two Japanese have not missed a meeting. They are bone-dry, too. So there they sit in the meeting place, their faces wreathed in beautiful smiles. Their concentration on every speaker is intense; they act as though they savor and understand every word that is said. Those English words — as words — are still without meaning. Yet these speakers, and that meeting, are nevertheless full of meaning for them. We all know why. The speakers are talking far more than English;

they are speaking the universal language of deep and abiding brother-hood — the language of the heart.

The once lonely and solitary Japanese are no longer alone; they see, they feel, they understand. And, thank God, so do all the rest of us.

After Twenty-Five Years

March 1960

It is very wonderful to know that most of our worldwide anniversary gatherings will be so widely shared by our families and by our dedicated friends — the ones who have seen us through, the ones who have watched and who have so much helped our passage from the darkness of alcoholism into the bright sunlight of AA.

For Lois and me, and for AA people everywhere, this 25th Anniversary time is one of warm and happy recollection; of gratitude for the sobriety and the new life that the last quarter century has brought to so many of us once hopeless people; of gratitude for the ever-widening opportunity to serve man and God which is today ours, an opportunity that will require of us an ever-deepening dedication to our cherished AA principles of recovery, unity, and service — those themes of our 25th Anniversary now on every tongue.

We are thinking deeply, too, of all those sick ones still to come to AA — thousands, surely, and perchance millions. As they try to make their return to faith and to life, we want them to find everything in AA that we have found, and yet more, if that be possible. On our part, therefore, no care, no vigilance, no effort to preserve AA's constant effectiveness and spiritual strength will ever be too great to hold us in full readiness for the day of their homecoming.

When I think of our small and quiet unnoticed beginnings of only twenty-five years ago; when I recollect the early struggles, uncertainties, and perils of our pioneering time, I now find it both incredible and infinitely moving to realize that all this will be climaxed July next when Lois and I will be seeing so many thousands of you face to face at our International Convention in Long Beach, California. From now until then, we shall surely be exclaiming to each other, "Indeed, what hath God wrought?" This meaningful exclamation will be our constant reminder that AA is truly God's creation. No single one of us, nor any single group of us alcoholics got together to invent Alcoholics Anonymous. Contemplating the totality of all that has happened in these twenty-five years we see that he has worked through the willing hearts and minds and hands of thousands. For this reason Dr. Bob and I have often deplored being called co-founders because such titles may create the impression that we pretty much invented, structured, and spread AA all by ourselves.

Nothing could, in fact, be further from the truth.

To illustrate, we might review for a moment the basic ideas on which our recovery program is founded and then ask whence these ideas came to us — and just who brought them.

Our recovery Step One reads thus: "We admitted we were powerless over alcohol — that our lives had become unmanageable." This simply means that all of us have to hit bottom and hit it hard and lastingly. But we can seldom make this sweeping admission of personal hopelessness until we fully realize that alcoholism is a grievous and often fatal malady of the mind and body — an obsession that condemns us to drink joined to a physical allergy that condemns us to madness or death.

So, then, how did we first learn that alcoholism is such a fearful sickness as this? Who gave us this priceless piece of information on which the effectiveness of Step One of our program so much depends? Well, it came from my own doctor, "the little doctor who loved drunks," William Duncan Silkworth. More than twenty-five years ago at Towns Hospital, New York, he told Lois and me what the disease of alcoholism actually is.

Of course, we have since found that these awful conditions of mind and body invariably bring on the third phase of our malady. This is the sickness of the spirit; a sickness for which there must necessarily be a spiritual remedy. We AAs recognize this in the first five words of Step Twelve of the recovery program. Those words are: "Having had a spiritual awakening. . ." Here we name the remedy for our threefold sickness of body, mind, and soul. Here we declare the necessity for that all-important spiritual awakening.

Who, then, first told us about the utter necessity for such an awakening, for an experience that not only expels the alcohol obsession, but which also makes effective and truly real the practice of spiritual principles "in all our affairs"?

Well, this life-giving idea came to us of AA through William James, the father of modern psychology. It came through his famous book, *Varieties of Religious Experience,* when my friend Ebby handed me that volume at Towns Hospital immediately following my own remarkable spiritual experience of December 1934.

William James also heavily emphasized the need for hitting bottom. Thus did he reinforce AA's Step One and so did he supply us with the spiritual essence of today's Step Twelve.

Having now accounted for AA's Steps One and Twelve, it is natural that we should next ask, "Where did the early AAs find the material for the remaining ten Steps? Where did we learn about moral inventory, amends for harm done, turning wills and lives over to God? Where did we learn about meditation and prayer and all the rest of it?"

The spiritual substance of our remaining ten Steps came straight from Dr. Bob's and my own earlier association with the Oxford Groups, as they were then led in America by that Episcopal rector, Dr. Samuel Shoemaker.

At this point in our very early experience there remained, however, one missing link — an absolutely vital one. We still lacked a full comprehension of the terrific impact at great depth which one alcoholic talking to another could make. I had partly realized this when my alcoholic friend and sponsor, Ebby, told me about his own drinking, his release from it and of the Oxford Group principles which had made this possible. Still more realization came during my own spiritual experience which had included the vision of a chain reaction among alcoholics, one alcoholic talking to the next. But it was not until I met Dr. Bob that I knew I needed him as much as he could ever need me. This was perfect mutuality, this was full brotherhood. This was the crucial and the final answer. The missing link was then fully forged and somehow we knew this at once.

To those wonderful friends who thus brought Dr. Bob and me within reach of recovery, our debt is quite beyond calculation or repayment. But even these great gifts could not have amounted to anything had they not been passed from hand to hand in these last twenty-five years. You, the members of AA, have continued to forge countless fresh links in the chain of recovery that now encircles the world. It is your example, your influence, and, under God, your work which has already brought hope and health and happiness to millions — alcoholics and nonalcoholics alike.

A great many of you can well recall the perils of AA's time of frantic mushroom growth. You remember how we feared that an all-too-human scramble for money, fame, and power might ruin us. You remember how we feared any public exploitation of the AA name, whether by our own members or by others. Then there were the bogies of political and religious strife — bogies that might break loose and smash us. There was the fear, too, that if we ever created a world service organization, our servants working there might presently become our masters and so saddle us with an expensive and disastrous government. There was apprehension about wide publicity, lest it turn into promotional ballyhoo that could garble our message and could bring ridicule upon us and so keep alcoholics and their families at a distance. We also feared that we might be tempted to take great gifts of money, thus making us dependent upon the charity of others and tempting us to foolishly scatter our energies into outside projects that could be better handled by others. You can remember our fierce hostility toward any and all AA members who had the temerity to enter these other ventures in the field of alcoholism. You can recall how we lambasted any AA who, for any purpose, received a cent of our money; how we so feared professionalism that we scarcely dared hire any full-time AAs to answer the phones in our local offices. Above all, you remember how we shuddered at that first rash of public anonymity breaks by both well-meaning and self-seeking members.

Such were our fears — some of them ridiculous and some of them abundantly justified. What, then, could we do?

For a long and anxious time we simply did not know whether we could live and work with each other or with the world about us. Could we hold in unity at all levels, could we effectively function to carry AA's message? We simply did not know.

Then, little by little, we moved away from the fear of our growing pains. We began to learn from these experiences. Genuine prudence replaced destructive fear. And out of our collective experience in working and living together there finally emerged the Twelve Traditions of Alcoholics Anonymous — the present-day basis for the truly splendid unity that is nearly everywhere ours; the basis for an excellent service structure now so highly effective that not many more years can pass before alcoholics everywhere will have the marvelous opportunity for sanity and for sobriety that we who are gathered here know so well. Certainly it is not only to the few that we owe these remarkable developments in our unity and in our ability to carry AA's message everywhere. It is to the many; indeed it is to the labors of all of us that we owe these prime blessings.

This is the brand of dedication and unity that, little by little, has enabled us to cross nearly every barrier of race and creed, of nationality and of language. In fact, we have been gradually learning to deal with all conditions and with all obstacles. With joy we have watched the good news catch up with the young and not too badly damaged alcoholics, as we have learned to raise the bottom and hit them with it, so saving them years of misery. With equal satisfaction we have witnessed the salvage of the very rich and the very poor. Today we see them learning what true wealth of spirit can be.

We note with high interest how so many of us are trying to practice AA's principles in all of our affairs, how the quest for emotional and spiritual growth is quickening and is being reflected at home, at work, and in the world at large. Our families, too, have adopted AA's Twelve Steps as their own. Their Al-Anon groups, now numbering more than a thousand, are growing prodigiously. Again this reflects the progress of the many, of all of us.

Such is a mere glimpse of the vast panorama of AA today, and it surely must be a good token of still finer things to come. Of course this recital of past accomplishment and the vision we have of our hoped-for future cannot possibly create any mood of complacency or self-congratulation. We well know that our defects, as people and as a Society, have been and still are very great. And we hope that we shall never cease to rededicate ourselves to their correction.

May we so continue to deepen our humility and our devotion to man and to God that we may meet and transcend all future problems and perils. Let us pray that both we of today and the new generations of our tomorrow will become increasingly worthy of the happy and useful destiny that our Creator is most surely holding in store for us all.

What Is Freedom in AA?

May 1960

The Traditions and customs of Alcoholics Anonymous reveal a charter for individual and group freedom, the like of which history has never before produced. We have no humanly administered government whatever.

Once upon a time there was an AA member who got the notion that his own group was a little too stuffy, respectable, and intolerant. Hence it was, he thought, overfearful of the lapses and deviations of its members. Tongue in cheek, he pondered a remedy. Finally he hung a placard in the clubroom. It read as follows: "Folks, just about anything goes in here. But if you happen to be drunk at this meeting, don't be too noisy about it. And please don't smoke your opium in the club elevators!"

True, our friend had gone overboard to make out his case. An AA drunk at an AA meeting is seldom seen, and it's probable that nobody has yet smoked opium in a clubhouse. Nevertheless any of us can read between the lines of that placard, and to good effect.

Our prankster was really saying to each of the respectable and the fearful, "But for the grace of God, there go I." To disturbers of the group peace he was saying, "Nobody can compel you to behave, or punish you if you do not. AA has Twelve Steps for recovery and for spiritual growth. It has Twelve Traditions for the unity of every AA group and our whole Fellowship. These Traditions show how we can all stay in one piece, if we will. Now this meeting place costs some money. We hope you will put some cash in the hat but don't want to make you do it. You can attack us, but you'll probably find that most of us won't fight back. You can bust your anonymity in public and misuse the AA name for your own prestige and pocketbook. If you insist on such foolishness, we can't stop you. The same is true if you drag the AA name into public controversy. We hope you won't do any of these things to us, or to yourself. We simply say that you will have to practice AA's principles because you want them for yourself — not because we insist. The choices are yours; this is your charter of freedom in AA."

For any other society such unlimited freedom for the individual would be disastrous. Sheer anarchy would take it over in jig-time. How is it, then, that we AAs can stand this amount of liberty, a liberty which sometimes looks like a license to do exactly as we please, individually and collectively? Then, too, is this unheard-of charter of liberty made possible by our virtues? Or is it actually powered by our necessities?

Well, our necessities are certainly immense and compelling. Each of us must conform reasonably well to AA's Steps and Traditions, or else we shall go mad or die of alcoholism. Therefore the compulsion among most of us to survive and to grow soon becomes far stronger than the temptation to drink or to misbehave. Literally, we must "do or die." So we make the choice to live. This, in turn, means the choice of AA principles, practices, and attitudes that can salvage us from total disaster by insuring our sobriety. This is our first great and critical choice. Admittedly this is made under the fearful and immediate lash of John Barleycorn, the killer. Plainly enough, this first choice is far more a necessity than it is an act of virtue.

But once over this hump, we commence to make another kind of choice. We begin to see that AA principles are good ones. Though we are still beset with much rebellion, we increase the practice of these principles out of a sense of responsibility to ourselves, our families, and our groups. We begin to obey because we feel we *ought* to obey. Though painful, we see that this is the right thing to do. As we try for results we see that we are growing. This is an earned satisfaction. Life still isn't easy, but it's a whole lot better. Besides, we have a lot of company. All around us there are plenty of fellow travelers, individuals or groups. We can do together what we can't do in separation.

Finally, we see that there is still another dimension of choice which may now and then be attained. This is the point where we can take an attitude, engage in a practice or obey a sound principle, because, without reservation or rebellion, that is what we really want. When our willingness and acceptance become this complete, we find that all rebellion disappears. Now we conform because we fully want to conform. Or to put it another way: We want nothing else but God's will for us, and his grace for our fellows.

Looking back we see that our freedom to choose badly was not, after all, a very real freedom. When we chose because we "must," this was not a free choice either. But it got us started in the right direction. When we chose because we "ought to" we were really doing better. This time we were earning some freedom, making ourselves ready for more. But when, now and then, we could gladly make right choices without rebellion, holdout, or conflict, then we had our first view of what perfect freedom under God's will could be like. Few indeed can long remain on that lofty plateau; for most of us its permanent attainment has to be a lifetime and, more probably, an eternal job. But we know that this highest plateau is really there — a goal someday to be reached.

Such are the several freedoms in AA, and this is how they seem to work among us. To gain these insights took a long time. It was not until 1945, ten years after I met Dr. Bob, that we even dared put the Traditions of Alcoholics Anonymous on paper. There had been a period in which we continually feared what erratic members within and the world without might do to us. It was difficult to believe that our group conscience could be a reliable guide. Hence we questioned the wisdom of giving every AA group its local autonomy.

Still more, we questioned whether we shouldn't throw out undesirables and even unbelievers. To give every alcoholic in the world an exclusive right to say whether or not he would be an AA member was a breathtaking decision. Such were the fears of those days, and such were the restrictions that we were tempted to place upon each other. After all, these were the restrictions that even the more benign of societies and governments had had to place on their members and citizens. Why should we be the exception?

Happily, however, we adopted no governmental measures. Instead, we cast up the Twelve Traditions of AA. These were truly the utterance of our entire group conscience. The amazing degree of today's voluntary conformity to them is something for the greatest wonder and thanksgiving. We now know that we shall always practice these principles: first because we must, then because we ought to, and finally because the majority of us will deeply want to do just that. There cannot be the slightest question of this.

We trust that we already know what our several freedoms truly are; that no future generation of AAs will ever feel compelled to limit them. Our AA freedoms create the soil in which genuine love can grow — the love of each for the other, and all for God himself.

Let's Keep It Simple — But How?

July 1960

This Grapevine will be read as we celebrate AA's 25th Anniversary in July at Long Beach, California. We shall be stepping over a new threshold into our future. We shall rejoice as we think of the gifts and the wonders of yesterday. And, as we rededicate ourselves to fulfilling the immense promise of AA's tomorrow, we shall certainly survey how we stand today. Have we really "kept AA simple"? Or, unwittingly, have we blundered?

Thinking on this, I began to wonder about our fundamental structure: those principles, relationships, and attitudes which are the substance of our Three Legacies of Recovery, Unity, and Service. In our Twelve Steps and Twelve Traditions we find twenty-four definitely stated principles. Our Third Legacy includes a charter for world service that provides thousands of general service representatives, hundreds of local committee members, eighty General Service Conference delegates, fifteen General Service Board trustees, together with our Headquarters legal, financial, public relations, editorial experts, and their staffs. Our group and area services add still more to this seeming complexity.

Twenty-two years ago last spring, we were just setting about the formation of a trusteeship for AA as a whole. Up to that moment, we had neither stated principles nor special services. Our Twelve Steps weren't even a gleam in the eye. As for the Twelve Traditions — well, we had only forty members and but three years' experience. So there wasn't anything to be "traditional" about. AA was two small groups: one at Akron and another in New York. We were a most intimate family. Dr. Bob and I were its "papas." And what we said in those days went. Home parlors were meeting places. Social life ranged around coffeepots on kitchen tables. Alcoholism was of course described as a deadly malady. Honesty, confession, restitution, working with others, and prayer was the sole formula for our survival and growth. These were the uncomplicated years of halcyon simplicity. There was no need for the maxim, "Let's keep it simple." We couldn't have been less complicated.

The contrast between then and now is rather breathtaking. To some of us it is frightening. Therefore we ask, "Has AA really kept faith with Dr. Bob's warning, 'Let's keep it simple'? How can we possibly square today's Twelve Steps, Twelve Traditions, General Service Conferences and International Conventions with our original coffee-and-cake AA?"

For myself I do not find this difficult to do. Genuine simplicity for today is to be found, I think, in whatever principles, practices, and services can permanently insure our widespread harmony and effectiveness. Therefore it has been better to state our principles than to leave them vague; better to clarify their applications than to leave these unclear; better to organize our services than to leave them to hit-or-miss methods, or to none at all.

Most certainly indeed, a return to the kitchen table era would bring no hoped-for simplicity. It could only mean wholesale irresponsibility, disharmony, and ineffectiveness. Let's picture this: There would be no definite guiding principles, no literature, no meeting halls, no group funds, no planned sponsorship, no stable leadership, no clear relations with hospitals, no sound public relations, no local services, no world services. Returning to that early-time brand of simplicity would be as absurd as selling the steering wheel, the gas tank, and the tires off our family car. The car would be simplified all right — no more gas and repair bills, either! But our car wouldn't go anyplace. The family life would hardly be simplified; it would instantly become confused and complicated.

A formless AA anarchy, animated only by the "Let's get together" spirit, just isn't enough for AAs here and now. What worked fine for two score members in 1938 won't work at all for more than 200,000 of them in 1960. Our added size and therefore greater responsibility simply spells the difference between AA's childhood and its coming of age. We have seen the folly of attempting to recapture the childhood variety of simplicity in order to sidestep the kind of responsibility that must always be faced to "keep it simple" for today. We cannot possibly turn back the clock and shouldn't try.

The history of our changing ideas about "simplicity for today" is fascinating. For example, the time came when we actually had to codify — or organize, if you please — the basic principles that had emerged out of our experience. There was a lot of resistance to this. It was stoutly claimed by many that our then simple (but rather garbled) word-of-mouth recovery program was being made too complicated by the publication of AA's Twelve Steps. We were "throwing 'simplicity' out the window," it was said. But that was not so. One has only to ask, "Where would AA be today without its Twelve Steps?" That these principles were carefully defined and published in 1939 has done only the Lord knows how much good. Codification has vastly simplified our task. Who could contest that now?

In 1945, a similar outcry arose when sound principles of living and working together were clearly outlined in AA's Twelve Traditions. It was then anything but simple to get agreement about them. Yet who can now say that our AA lives have been complicated by the Traditions? On the contrary, these sharply defined principles have immensely *simplified* the task of maintaining unity. And unity for us AAs is a matter of life or death.

The identical thing has everywhere happened in our active services, particularly in world services. When our first trusteeship for AA was created there were grave misgivings. The alarm was great because this operation involved a certain amount of legality, authority, and money, and the transaction of some business. We had been running happily about saying that AA had "completely separated the spiritual from the material." It was therefore a shocker when Dr. Bob and I proposed world services; when we urged that these had to head up in some kind of a permanent board; and further stated that the time had come — at least in this realm — when we would have to learn how to make "material things" serve spiritual ends. Somebody with experience had to be at the steering wheel and there had to be gas in the AA tank.

As our trustees and their co-workers began to carry our message worldwide, our fears slowly evaporated. AA had not been confused — it had been simplified. You could ask any of the tens of thousands of alcoholics and their families who were coming into AA because of our world services. Certainly their lives had been simplified. And, in reality, so had ours.

When our first General Service Conference met in 1951, we again drew a long breath. For some, this event spelled sheer disaster. Wholesale brawling and politicking would now be the rule. Our worst traits would get out in front. The serenity of the trustees and everybody else would be disturbed (as indeed it sometimes was!). Our beautiful spirituality and the AA therapy would be interfered with. People would get drunk over this (and indeed a few did!). As never before, the shout went up, "For God's sake, let's keep this thing simple!" Cried some members, "Why can't Dr. Bob and Bill and the trustees go right on running those services for us? That's the only way to keep it simple."

But few knew that Dr. Bob was mortally sick. Nobody stopped to think that there would soon be less than a handful of old-timers left; that soon they would be gone, too. The trustees would be quite isolated and unconnected with the Fellowship they served. The first big gale could well bowl them over. AA would suffer heart failure at its vital center. Irretrievable collapse would be the almost certain result.

Therefore we AAs had to make a choice: what would really be the simpler? Would we get that General Service Conference together, despite its special expense and perils? Or, would we sit on our hands at home, awaiting the fateful consequences of our fear and folly? What, in the long run, we wondered, would really be the better — and therefore the simpler? As our history shows, we took action. The General Service Conference of Alcoholics Anonymous has just held its tenth annual meeting. Beyond doubt we know that this indispensable instrument has cemented our unity and has insured the recovery of the increasing hosts of sufferers still to come.

Therefore I think that we *have* kept the faith. As I see it, this is how we have made AA truly simple!

Some may still ask, "Are we nevertheless moving away from our early Tradition that 'AA, as such, ought never be organized'?" Not a bit of it. We shall never be "organized" until we create a government; until we say who shall be members and who shall not; until we authorize our boards and service committees to mete out penalties for nonconformity, for nonpayment of money, and for misbehavior. I know that every AA heart shares in the conviction that none of these things can ever happen. We merely organize our principles so that they can be better understood, and we continue so to organize our services that AA's lifeblood can be transfused into those who must otherwise die. That is the all-in-all of AA's "organization." There can never be any more than this.

A concluding query: "Has the era of coffee-and-cake and fast friendships vanished from the AA scene because we are going modern?" Well, scarcely. In my home town I know an AA who has been sober several years. He goes to a small meeting. The talks he hears are just like those Dr. Bob and I used to hear — and also make — in our respective front parlors. As neighbors, my friend has a dozen AA cronies. He sees them constantly over kitchen tables and coffee cups. He takes a frequent whack at Twelfth Step cases. For him, nothing has changed; it's just like AA always was.

At meetings, my friend may see some books, pamphlets, and Grapevines on a table. He hears the lady secretary make her timid announcement that these are for sale. He thinks the New York Intergroup is a good thing because some of his fellow members were sponsored through it. On world services, he is not so clear. He hears some pros and cons about them. But he concludes they are probably needed. He knows his group sends in some money for these undertakings, and this is okay. Besides, his group's hall rent has to be paid. So when the hat comes by, he cheerfully drops a buck into it.

As far as my friend is concerned, these "modernizations" of AA are not a big shattering to his serenity or to his pocketbook. They merely represent his responsibility to his group, his area, and to AA as a whole. It has never occurred to him that these are any but the most obvious obligations.

If you tried to tell my friend that AA is being spoiled by money, politics, and overorganization, he would just laugh. He'd probably say, "Why don't you come over to my house after the meeting and we'll have another cup of coffee."

AA Tomorrow

July 1960*

T his book has given us some wonderful glimpses of the panorama of AA at work in the twenty-fifth year of its founding. We marvel and rejoice that the near impossible has really happened. All this has indeed depended on our many channels of communication and our singular ability to use them.

Now comes the question: Where do we go from here and what is our responsibility for today and for tomorrow?

Clearly our first duty to AA's future is to maintain in full strength what we now have. Only the most vigilant caretaking can assure this. Never should we be lulled into complacent self-satisfaction by the wide acclaim and success that is everywhere ours. This is the subtle temptation which could stagnate us today, perchance disintegrate us tomorrow. We have always rallied to meet and transcend failure and crisis. Problems have been our stimulants. How well, though, shall we be able to meet the problems of success?

Will we continue to search out the ever present flaws and gaps in our communications? With enough imagination, courage, and dedication, will we resolutely address ourselves to those many tasks of repair and improvement which even now the future is calling upon us to undertake? Still clearer vision and an ever mounting sense of responsibility can be the only answers to these questions.

What, then, is the real size and reach of our foreseeable responsibilities? During the last twenty-five years it is quite certain that 25 million men and women throughout the world have suffered alcoholism. Nearly all of these are now sick, mad, or dead. AA has brought recovery to something like 250,000. The rest are still out of reach or else gone beyond recall. An even larger generation of drunks is right now in the making. Facing the enormity of this situation, shall any of us sit comfortably and say, "Well, people, here we are. We hope you hear about us and come around. Then maybe we can give you a hand."

Of course we shall do nothing of the sort. We know that we are going to open, wider and wider, every conceivable means and channel

*From the Grapevine book AA Today, published on the occasion of AA's twenty-fifth anniversary.

through which these kinsfolk of ours may be reached. We shall remember Dr. Bob and his marvelous co-worker, Sister Ignatia — how they worked in Akron. We shall remember the many years of Silky's unstinted labor for us. Ten thousand AAs still around will remember how they literally owe their lives to these three people. Each of us will remember his own sponsor, the one who cared enough. As the inheritors of such a tradition of service, how many could ever say, "Let George do that Twelfth Step job; he likes to work with drunks anyhow. Besides, I'm busy." Surely there could not be many! Complacency would be impossible.

Our next great area of future responsibility may be this one: I'm thinking about the total problem of alcohol and about all of those who still must suffer the appalling *consequences* of alcoholism. Their number is astronomical; it runs into hundreds of millions. Here's just a sampling of that problem:

Because of our drinking, most of us banged up our kids. Their emotional scars should have made them "naturals" for alcoholism. Yet it is startlingly true that teenage children of good AA members show almost no sign of becoming drunks. They drink moderately or not at all. If a few of the vulnerable do hit the bottle, and the telltale symptoms and episodes show up, most can stop — and they do. Now why is this?

The answer is "alcohol education" — AA style. Of course we have never told our kids not to drink. But for years, around the house and at meetings, they have heard what the score really is, what alcoholism can do to people. They have seen the old man in action, first as an alcoholic, then as an AA member. This is the kind of education that has no doubt already saved a hundred thousand of our children.

But what about other people's kids — have we no concern for them? Of course we do have concern. While we appreciate that AA itself cannot very well get into alcohol education or into any of the related activities that touch the total problem, we do know that, as peculiarly well-informed citizens, there is plenty we can, and should, do in these fields.

Enterprises of this sort — governmental, state, and private — have been springing up everywhere in recognition of the fact that alcoholism is a top priority problem of health. Nearly every one of these agencies tells us it has been inspired to work on by the example we AAs have set them. They now take their turn as pioneers. Naturally, they are bound to make some mistakes. Certainly, we can understand this. In fact, we like to say that we ourselves have progressed mostly by trial and error. A good number of these undertakings are now going places and their promise is very large.

Nevertheless, I gather the impression that many of us are so intent on their few errors, especially the errors of those AAs associated with them, that we often fail to give these dedicated people the encouragement they much need. Now that we AAs have so amazingly unified around our single purpose and the Twelve Traditions, the risk that we could be much hurt by anything done in these outside ventures is virtually nonexistent.

Let's instead keep focused on the fact that there are some 24,750,000 drunks left in the world. Could not still more friendly and widespread cooperation with outside agencies finally lead us to countless alcoholics who will otherwise be lost? Maybe we are beginning to stand in our own light. Perhaps we are blocking a communication that has a tremendous potential. Shouldn't we therefore have a fresh look at this?

Inside AA — well, how do we stand?

It is a fact, and a perfectly explicable one, that the number of Al-Anon Family Groups has jumped from a handful to 1,300 of them in the last ten years. They are tackling one of the toughest problems that an alcoholic and his family can have, inside AA or out. This is the terrific distortion that we alcoholics force upon our wives (and husbands) through destructive drinking — drinking that has led us into a highly abnormal dependency upon them. Active drunks frequently turn themselves into rebellious and wayward children, thereby compelling their marriage partners to become their protective custodians — their "mamas" and "papas." This has often resulted in a built-in pattern, one most difficult to erase. The coming of sobriety in AA is seldom a remedy. Indeed sobriety sometimes aggravates this often intolerable condition.

The Al-Anon Family Groups, comprised of wives and husbands of alcoholics, now see this picture clearly — far more clearly, in fact, than do most of us AAs. In their own groups they are now working to repair that damage — along with their other defects — by the practice of AA's Twelve Steps. More than some of us, these life partners of ours are trying hard to "practice AA principles in all their affairs." The Family Groups have already made a big dent in this mighty tough problem and there is evidence of far more to come. Can't we therefore give this remarkable project our greatest possible understanding and encouragement? And let each of us do his full share of that repair job at home!

Then there is among us AAs the ever present need for further spiritual growth. Here most of us show a heavy deficit and I'm a notable example. The simplest self-questioning can reveal such deficiencies. For instance: "Am I trying to 'practice these principles' in all my own affairs? Or am I simply complacent and quite content with just enough spiritual nourishment to keep me sober? Do I really possess the spiritual resources to see me through some rough going? Or do I think pretty well of my spiritual demonstration because: a) things are pretty good at home, b) I got a big raise, and c) they made me vice-president of my lodge? Or if things go badly and I begin to be jittery, depressed, anxious, or resentful, do I then justify my resulting self-pity and guilt by blaming my 'bad breaks' or, more usually, the behavior of other people? Or do I fall back on the old refrain that I'm a 'sick alcoholic' and therefore not responsible?"

Nearly all of us, when we think about it, agree that we are a long, long way from being anywhere near grown-up, from almost any point of view. We can clearly see that our job as individuals and as a Fellowship is to keep right on growing by the constant use of our Twelve Steps.

Of course, we may be certain that this will be a slow business. But we also know we can never take our plodding progress as the slightest alibi for setting ourselves second-rate goals. Our high aim can be emotional sobriety, full emotional maturity — and that's good. However, I think most of us may prefer a still larger definition, one with a still broader and higher reach. Perhaps there can be no "relative" in the universe unless somewhere there is an "absolute." To most of us this "absolute" is "God as we understand him." We feel that we were born to this life to grow — if only a little — toward that likeness and image. However small and prudent our next immediate step on the path of progress may be, we of AA can never set any hampering limitation upon the ultimate destiny of ourselves and our Fellowship, nor any whatever upon God's love for us all. Individually and collectively, structurally and spiritually, we shall ever need to build for the future. We are still laying down the foundation on which all coming generations of AAs will have to stand, perhaps for centuries.

Our Fellowship has been permitted to achieve — though still in miniature — the "one world" dream of philosophers. Ours is a world in which we can hotly differ, yet never think of schism or conflict as a solution. As a Fellowship we ask nothing of wealth or power. As we better use the "language of the heart," our communications grow apace: already we find ourselves in safe passage through all those barriers of distance and language, of social distinctions, nationality and creed, that so divide the world of our time.

For so long as we remain sure that our "one world of AA" is God's gift rather than any virtue earned or created by ourselves; and for so long as our "one world" continues to be ever more inclusive of those in need; and for so long as we speak and try to perfect the language of love — for just so long may we count upon making whatever rendezvous with destiny that God would have us.

Our Pioneers Overseas

October 1960

I 've just finished reading the printer's galleys for this international number of our Grapevine. There are deeply stirring communications from South Africa, Northern Rhodesia, and the Congo; from Japan, Indonesia, New Guinea, Tasmania, Australia; from Cuba, Trinidad, and Jamaica; from Saudi Arabia and from West Germany, Denmark, Holland, Finland, Ireland, Scotland, and England.

Yet this eye-arresting array of AA's overseas beachheads and bases reveals scarcely more than a quarter of our total activity in distant places and countries. Out on those far reaches there are hundreds of groups and thousands of fellow members. Our language of the heart is already spoken in perhaps a dozen tongues. This is the pioneering front of AA today.

We often speak of our Loners, of our solitary groups, and of our several large centers abroad, as beachheads, bases, and fronts. But in a very real sense these descriptions are misnomers. Though our AA Loners and groups do live and do carry our message in many areas of danger and revolution, there is no evidence that they fear their surroundings; there is little sign that their presence in these hot spots is unwanted. Their entire nonaggressiveness, their single purpose of bringing a new light to all who suffer alcoholism, is perfectly clear. Theirs are beachheads for health and for faith, and this is for all to see.

Witness the AA who, on an errand of peace, recently drove alone across the whole African continent and emerged unscathed; then think of those Loners stationed in other areas of strife — how they continue to maintain their sobriety and struggle to start new groups; please remember the intense concern of the AA who felt he had failed a fellow member who had committed suicide; ponder the good humor of the Middle East AA meeting as its members gather in a secret rendezvous lest the military authorities or some of our Mohammedan friends (who never drink!) might be offended. Consider, in these articles, the problems of those fast-growing overseas centers just now emerging from their pioneering time — how they have slowly gained the confidence of medicine, religion, and the press; how they have finally grown into unity through an ever better application of our Twelve Traditions; how they have tried to make good their desperate lack of language translations; and how they have well begun to cross all barriers of race, creed, or social condition. This, and more, can be read in and between these special lines which they have penned for this GV international issue.

Beyond doubt, this exciting pioneering front of AA today brings great promise of a vast worldwide unfoldment for tomorrow. Our friends abroad well understand that this is no time for complacent relaxation; their letters eloquently portray their intense industry and dedication.

So then, what can we do — we here in North America?

Well, we can greatly increase the tempo of what we have been doing. Let's scan just a small sampling of our overseas projects:

Americans and Canadians alike are much traveled in these days. Therefore let each traveler remember that many a group abroad has been started by a voyaging AA like himself or herself. We have a world directory. Let all such messengers be supplied with this valuable means of communication. This can mean untold inspiration to the Loner or the group to be found at many a destination.

Here, for instance, is a crying current need. As this Grapevine goes to press, pandemonium has broken loose in Paris. One paper there is carrying a series of sensational pieces about AA in America. To say the least, that characteristic desire of the French to be dramatic has been going pretty far.

One of these articles describes my first meeting in 1934 with my own sponsor, Ebby. It displays a screaming headline about two inches high. Allegedly, I say over the phone: *"Come quickly, Ebby, I have gin!"* Despite this astounding and most comical distortion of our Twelfth Step approach, the French alkies are nevertheless flocking to the AA colors.

Our tiny group at Paris is nearly swamped. Scarcely a one of them can speak French. So, AA travelers, there in Paris is your chance — especially if you can "parlez vous"!

Then we have the men on ships, those Internationalists of ours. May their numbers and their dedication continue to grow. They have already planted and nurtured AA all over the world. To them we all exclaim, "May your plantings increase and may your harvests bulge the AA granaries!"

Now look into our efforts at GSO — AA's world Headquarters. We can surely enlarge those overseas services. To eliminate the distressing garble that has plagued many distant AA groups for years, we shall need to furnish far more and better translations of our basic literature. Sheer lack of an understanding of AA's Twelve Traditions has routinely created chaotic conditions in many a land. Even our book *Alcoholics Anonymous* has seen but two complete translations. In mimeograph form the bare text of the book can be read in only two more tongues. Of course this challenge has to be met, and very soon, we believe.

Our whole foreign department at New York Headquarters must be enlarged. There is an urgent need for more staff work — which would mean far better communication with those abroad. Until recently, no overseas group had ever been visited by anyone from our world Headquarters — excepting Lois and me. That visit was ten years ago. Of course we deeply hope that we can still make a few similar journeys. But even these, if made, could scarcely add up to the consistent personal contact that will one of these days be needed.

So, AAs in America, let us back our overseas pioneers to the limit. Without delay, let's back them with a still more lively understanding, with still more dedicated travelers, and with every bit of aid and information and inspiration that we can send to them across the waters. In this respect no single agency can do more than our world Headquarters. Here all of us can participate. Here a few more contribution dollars can make an enormous difference — something that we shall be bound to remember every time the hat is specially passed for this great and unique service purpose.

I am sure that we shall soon press these and many more projects into a far higher gear. Then our pioneers beyond the seas will feel that they have something more than our interested approval and occasional help. They will know that our constant and unstinted love has become theirs — and theirs for keeps!

Freedom Under God:
The Choice Is Ours

November 1960

In its deeper sense AA is a quest for freedom — freedom under God. Of course the immediate object of our quest is sobriety — freedom from alcohol and from all its baleful consequences. Without this freedom, we have nothing at all.

Paradoxically, though, we can achieve no liberation from the alcohol obsession until we become willing to deal with those character defects which have landed us in that helpless condition. Even to gain sobriety only, we must attain some freedom from fear, anger, and pride; from rebellion and self-righteousness; from laziness and irresponsibility; from foolish rationalization and outright dishonesty; from wrong dependencies and destructive power-driving.

In this freedom quest, we are always given three choices. A rebellious refusal to work upon our glaring defects can be a ticket to destruction. Or, for a time, we can stay sober with a minimum of self-improvement and settle ourselves into a comfortable but often dangerous mediocrity. Or we can continuously try hard for those sterling qualities which can add up to greatness of spirit and action — true and lasting freedom under God, the freedom to find and do his will.

For most of us this last choice is really ours; we must never be blinded by the futile philosophy that we are just the hapless victims of our inheritance, our life experience, and our surroundings — that these are the sole forces that make our decisions for us. This is not the road to freedom. We have to believe that we can really choose.

Similarly, our whole Society, and every group in it, will constantly face these identical decisions. Shall we settle for destruction? Shall we try only for the temporary comforts of a complacent mediocrity? Or shall we consistently face the disciplines, make the sacrifices, and endure the discomforts that will qualify us to walk the path that invariably leads toward true greatness of spirit and action?

These reflections are meant to be background for the theme of this article — the Twelve Traditions of Alcoholics Anonymous.

AA's Traditions are the yardstick by which our Fellowship can accurately measure its progress — or the lack of it. In our Traditions we see such wisdom as we have been able to muster in a quarter of a century of living and working together. That these principles stake out the path we ought to follow there can be little doubt.

As we contemplate the Traditions we see that they have two main characteristics, and that each of these aspects reinforces the other.

The first aspect of the Twelve Traditions is *protection;* the second aspect is *progress.* We are first reminded what our Fellowship's temptations really are and by what means we may best deal with them. This is our basis for a continuous moral inventory of our collective behavior — the first step to actively casting aside our road blocks. In the affirmative or positive aspect of the Traditions we learn, both directly and impliedly, how we may best apply the high ideals of sacrifice and willing responsibility, trust and love, in our relations with each other and with the world around us. Out of these practices flows the spiritual energy that moves us along the road to full liberation.

As we ponder *protection,* we see that our Traditions warn against the perils of public fame and power, against the perils of great wealth, against the making of compromising alliances, against professionalism. We are reminded that we may deny no alcoholic his membership, that we must never create an authoritative government of men. We are cautioned that we should never force AA's message upon the world by aggressive promotional schemes, and that we should shun public controversy as the Devil himself.

Such are typical examples of the protective prudence which our Twelve Traditions directly express, or clearly imply. Some claim that these warnings are nothing but the sum of our collective fears. Once upon a time this was very true. In our first years, every violation of these precepts seemed to threaten our actual existence. We then doubted if our rebellious membership could ever resist its great temptations. But we *have* resisted, and so we have survived. Therefore the stark fears of yesterday have since given way to a vigilant prudence — something quite different from unreasoning panic.

Of course, we know that we shall always have to deal with the fearful forces which are released when the human ego runs amok — the same forces that are shattering the world of our time. *Deliver us from temptation* must therefore continue to be a prime ingredient of our every attitude, practice, and prayer. When things go well, we must never fall into the error of believing that no great ill can possibly befall us. Nor should we accuse ourselves of "negative thinking" when we insist on facing the destructive forces in and around us, both realistically and effectively. Vigilance will always be the price of survival.

This is the protective aspect of our Traditions. But AA's Twelve Traditions should provide us with far more than protection against mediocrity and dissolution — and they do.

Let's now think about the positive, the progressive side of AA's Traditions; the disciplined sacrifices and responsibilities that we shall need to undertake; the degree of mutual trust and love that we shall need to achieve if we are to find the greater freedom we seek. The length of this article will not admit a full examination of all Twelve Traditions in this respect, but a few examples can serve to illustrate just what we mean.

Take Tradition One. It says that AA's common welfare comes first. This really means that our personal ambitions will have to be set aside every time they conflict with the safety or the effectiveness of our Fellowship. It means that we must sometimes love our Society more than ourselves.

Tradition Two states: "For our group purpose there is but one ultimate authority — a loving God as he may express himself in our group conscience. Our leaders are but trusted servants; they do not govern." This is a study in mutual trust in God, in ourselves, and in our service leadership. This has been one of our finest experiments and it has succeeded far beyond our expectations.

Tradition Three defines the personal liberty of the AA member. It says, in effect, that any alcoholic can be an AA member the moment he says so. Neither can any of us deprive him of that membership, no matter what his behavior. Perhaps no other society has ever staked out such a broad expanse of liberty for the individual as this. Every AA newcomer feels at once that he is wanted and trusted and loved. How well we understand his needs; certainly we have had them ourselves. Seldom has any alcoholic taken unfair advantage of that unlimited charter for freedom. We took this decision for individual freedom years ago. We are glad that we did; there has never been any cause for regret.

Tradition Four is yet another confident declaration of mutual trust and love as it flows from each AA group to the other. We give each group full autonomy, the undisturbed right to manage its own affairs. To make this condition doubly permanent and secure, we have guaranteed to all AA groups that they will never be subjected to any centralized government or authority. In turn each group agrees that it will never take any action that could injure us all. Rarely indeed has any AA group ever forgotten that precious trust.

Tradition Seven proclaims AA's principle of self-support. In it, we undertake to pay every cent of our own service expenses, meanwhile declining outside contributions.

The fact that we don't take money from the outside world builds confidence in every alcoholic who thinks of approaching us. This we know. Public goodwill has also been increased because people like the idea that the once irresponsible alcoholics have now become responsible. There is no doubt, either, that this salutary practice takes us in the direction of increased freedom for ourselves. By resolutely declining outside funds, whether offered by individual donors or by governments, we are making dead sure that we shall always preserve our own liberty of action. Hence the old adage, "Who pays the piper calls the tune" will never be descriptive of us.

There is little question that large sums could be raised today for AA — that is, if we ever gave the word. Perhaps no greater calamity could befall our Fellowship than such a development. We would be at once absolved from the beneficial responsibility of raising our own funds. With lots of other people's money available, our idea-a-minute members would doubtless conceive countless schemes for doing good. In those few past instances where we have taken outside money, distraction and contention within has been the almost uniform result. Therefore we are well aware that the responsibility for full self-support brings us great spiritual and practical blessings. This is sacrificial prudence at its best — chief bulwark to our cherished freedoms.

Another example: Tradition Ten is an emphatic warning against public controversy. This was perhaps the first AA Tradition ever to take shape. Of course we did reserve that sometimes enjoyable right of quarreling among ourselves about lesser matters! But when it came to the awful issues that rock society about us, such as politics, religion, reform, and the like — well, the early AAs knew these terrible conflicts were surely not for them.

Later on, a new aspect of this same peril came into view. All sorts of people and organizations begged us to "take stands," "deliver opinions," and "fight evils," all up and down the line. Again we instantly saw that if we ever embarked upon such a course, it would certainly be our finish. Drunks by the thousands would be kept away from AA through sheer prejudice. The same old peril would again menace us. This time it would crash in from the outside.

This was when we AAs knew for sure that we had to be at peace —

internally, and with the world around us. No doubt mankind has wrung many a freedom out of violent controversy and bitter war. Yet we AAs have had to learn that the kinds of freedom that we must possess cannot possibly be obtained by violence. As a Fellowship, we cannot fight anybody, anywhere or at any time. This has been proved. When we had directly attacked John Barleycorn, we had lost. Booze fighting had never worked. When we quarrel too much with each other, we get drunk.

Hence genuine peace will always be a chief ingredient of AA's freedom. But let none suppose that we shrink from major conflict only because we are afraid. Nowadays we believe we keep the peace because we love each other.

Let's now examine that vital Tradition Eleven. It deals with our public relations. Here is our greatest channel of communication to the alcoholic who still suffers. Tradition Eleven reads: "Our public relations policy is based on attraction rather than promotion; we need always maintain personal anonymity at the level of press, radio, and films." Since this great Tradition describes the most important application of AA's principle of anonymity, and because it sets the pitch and tone of our entire public relations policy, nothing can be more critically important. If personal ambitions ever invade our public relations we shall be badly crippled, perhaps lost altogether.

The danger, of course, is the possibility that we may one day recklessly abandon the principle of personal anonymity at the top public level. This possibility arises from the fact that many of us AAs have been, and sometimes still are, possessed by enormous power drives. These are frequently fueled by an almost irresistible craving for money, approval, and public acclaim. My own past history is outstanding in this respect. I can well understand the constant temptation to turn oneself into a public figure. Therefore I have urged, in season and out, that we AAs maintain our personal anonymity at the top level, no matter what the personal sacrifices may be.

Our chief hope for the future is that these appalling urges of ours will be held in restraint by self-discipline, by love of AA, and by firm group and public opinion. These powerful constructive forces, all working together, have thus far been enough. We pray that they may always prevail.

Let's look once more at how immense this temptation really is. A vast communications net now covers the earth, even to its remotest reaches. Granting all its huge public benefits, this limitless world forum is nevertheless a hunting ground for all those who would seek money, acclaim, and power at the expense of society in general. Here the forces of good and evil are locked in struggle. All that is shoddy and destructive contests all that is best.

Therefore nothing can matter more to the future welfare of AA than the manner in which we use this colossus of communication. Used unselfishly and well, the results can surpass our present imagination. Should we handle this great instrument badly, we shall be shattered by the ego demands of our own people — often with the best of intention on their part. Against all this, the sacrificial spirit of AA's anonymity at the top public level is literally our shield and our buckler. Here again we must be confident that love of AA, and of God, will always carry the day.

Last, in Tradition Twelve, we see "anonymity is the spiritual foundation of all our Traditions, ever reminding us to place principles before personalities."

This principle, and its enormous implications, touches every aspect of our lives. Anonymity is humility at work. To maintain the humility of our Society we shall constantly take stock of our temptations and of our defects. The spirit of anonymity calls upon each of us for personal sacrifice in every level of our Fellowship's undertakings. Only through such willing sacrifices can we AAs meet our responsibilities to ourselves, to the victims of alcoholism everywhere, and to society as a whole. Here we clearly see that only sacrifice can fulfill responsibility; that only high responsibility can lead to mutual trust; and that only mutual trust can be the foundation for great love — each of us for the other, and all of us for God.

In just this spirit, all of those present at AA's 25th Anniversary in Long Beach rededicated themselves to the service of AA. They knew that the choice was theirs, and they made it. These were their telling words:

"By God's grace we are here assembled in grateful remembrance of the Twenty-fifth Anniversary of the founding of our Fellowship.

"At this meaningful quarter century mark we are deeply aware that we stand upon the threshold of a great door which opens wide into our future. Ours can be a destiny of ever-increasing promise and fulfillment. Our faith in this vision has never faltered.

"But the future would still lack its full use and meaning did it not bring us fresh problems and even acute perils — problems and perils through which we can grow into true greatness of action and spirit.

"To these ends we have pledged our lives and fortunes. We here re-dedicate ourselves to an ever deepening love of each other — love for the wondrous creation in which we live and serve, and love for its supreme author, God himself.

"We now entrust you of AA's distant reaches — you who so well symbolize the unique and loving communication that is ours in this universal Fellowship — to carry this message to fellow members everywhere; and most especially to all those others who still know not, and who, God willing, may soon issue out of their darkness into light."

The Shape of Things to Come

February 1961

AA's first quarter century is now history. Our next twenty-five years lie in prospect before us. How, then, can we make the most of this new grant of time?

Perhaps our very first realization should be that we can't stand still. Now that our basic principles seem established, now that our functioning is fairly effective and widespread, it would be temptingly easy to settle down as merely one more useful agency on the world scene. We could conclude that "AA is fine, just the way it is."

Yet how many of us, for example, would presume to declare, "Well, I'm sober and I'm happy. What more can I want, or do? I'm fine the way I am." We know that the price of such self-satisfaction is an inevitable backslide, punctuated at some point by a very rude awakening. We have to grow or else deteriorate. For us, the "status quo" can only be for today, never for tomorrow. Change we must; we cannot stand still.

Just how, then, can AA go on changing for the better? Does this mean that we are to tinker with our basic principles? Should we try to amend our Twelve Steps and Twelve Traditions? Here the answer would seem to be "no." Those twenty-four principles have first liberated us, have then held us in unity, and have enabled us to function and to grow as AA members and as a whole. Of course, perfect truth is surely something better understood by God than by any of us. Nevertheless we have come to believe that AA's recovery Steps and Traditions do represent the approximate truths which we need for our particular purpose. The more we practice them, the more we like them. So there is little doubt that AA principles continue to be advocated in the form they stand now.

So then, if our basics are so firmly fixed as all this, what is there left to change or to improve? The answer will immediately occur to us. While we need not alter our truths, we can surely improve their application to ourselves, to AA as a whole, and to our relation with the world around us. We can constantly step up "the practice of these principles in all our affairs."

As we now enter upon the next great phase of AA's life, let us therefore rededicate ourselves to an ever greater responsibility for our general welfare. Let us continue to take our inventory as a Fellowship, searching out our flaws and confessing them freely. Let us devote ourselves to the repair of all faulty relations that may exist, whether within or without.

And above all, let us remember that great legion who still suffer from alcoholism and who are still without hope. Let us, at any cost or sacrifice, so improve our communication with all these that they may find what we have found — a new life of freedom under God.

The Far Reaches

October 1961

Stirring in its implications and exciting in its drama, this is the Grapevine's international issue. In and between its lines, we are given a wonderful glimpse of AA today, out on the farthest reaches of our Fellowship. Unfailingly, everyone who reads this issue will get a magnificent preview of what AA worldwide will be like tomorrow.

One of our South Africa contributors, himself an old-timer down there, ends his article with these strange words: *"Hamba gahle, hlala gahle.* " These are Zulu greetings and mean "travel in peace" and "abide in peace." These poignant expressions, of course, deeply reveal the aspirations and the longings of the whole Zulu community.

Surely we of AA can identify with these words quite as well as the Zulus themselves. For is this not exactly what we ourselves have been seeking — first as active alcoholics, and then as AA members? We have always wanted to go out from the place where we were, to a place where there would be peace. The story of AA is the story of our own travels together, in the quest for better things.

As our contributor recounts, it is small wonder that his Zulu, Bantu, and Hindu alcoholic friends are now finding their cherished hopes realized as they flock to AA in the Transvaal, and from the regions about. They are traveling with us, and they are finding quiet.

The spread of AA abroad is most certainly the story of AAs who have thus traveled, both in the flesh and in the spirit. In these GV pages we find the moving experience of the wife of a diplomat. For descriptive purposes, we call her "a Loner." Yet she tells us how she was not in the least alone as she flitted first to Norway and then to Indonesia. At this moment she is living even more joyfully in Haiti.

Then there is the English lady — also one of our alcoholic sisters — who tells how she fell apart in Singapore, as a necessary prelude to finding herself now well and happy at Malta, where she and another woman form an AA group of two!

And by all means read about our British friend, an army officer and founding father of AA over there, as he describes how, as a so-called Loner, he was able to stay perfectly sober in Malaya during a trying season of guerrilla warfare; and then share with him what he found in AA on his return to England.

Don't miss, either, that picture of AA in Australia as drawn by an old-timer from Down Under. I choked up as I read this one, because I could remember when AA had started on that continent with a single letter and a Big Book sent from New York twenty years ago.

Neither should you fail to take in that strange and incredible Twelfth Step job recently done in South Africa. Our GV contributor worked day and night to sponsor a young Hungarian who, along with his mother, had been living in absolute isolation and misery. The language barrier at first seemed impossible to cross. But the sponsor and his client could each read a little from a Latin Bible, and that helped. But the barrier was more than language. The erring prospect turned out to be a deaf mute. Yet he did sober up, and the story of how that was brought off is amazing.

In fact, you ought to read every scrap of this GV international issue. You will surely discover some fresh ideas on how to get from where you are now, to where there is still more quiet. I know that I did.

"Hamba gahle, hlala gahle"!

Again at the Crossroads

November 1961

We AAs are everywhere developing a keener sense of our history and the meaning of its turning points. Moreover, I believe that we are getting a right sense of our history; something of the utmost importance indeed. The world's past reveals that many societies and nations have fallen victims to fear and pride or to their aggressive designs. Thus they lost their sense of meaning, purpose, and right destiny, and so they disintegrated and vanished. Neither power nor glory nor wealth could in the least guarantee their longtime survival.

There is little on the record of AA's first quarter century to suggest such a fate for us. In our personal lives, and therefore in our Fellowship itself, we have steadily striven to lay aside all those vainglorious clamors for prestige, power, and possessions which had ruined so many of us in the drinking days. With those fearful experiences vividly before us, it is not strange that AA's Twelve Steps continually remind us of the stark need for ego reduction; that our Twelve Traditions warn heavily against the perils of concentrated wealth, the vain pursuit of fame, and the ever present temptation to controversy and attack.

We did not come to such wisdom by reason of our virtues; our better understanding is rooted in our former follies. In the nick of time, and by God's grace, each of us has been enabled to develop a growing sense of the meaning and purpose of his own life. Because this has been the essence of our individual experience, it is also the essence of our experience as a Fellowship. We have suffered enough to learn something of the love of God and of each other. Thus we have been taught to choose those principles and practices by which we can surely survive and grow. This is the spiritual climate in which we AAs are today privileged to live.

Even our sometimes erratic behavior since sobriety has never changed this all-pervading climate of humility and love. This, we think, is the spiritual condition which has invited into our midst so much wise and providential guidance. We say this in no conceit; it is an obvious fact of our experience. We only need to ponder the long series of apparently correct choices that we have been enabled to make over the past twenty-six years; choices respecting our principles and right methods of communicating them. Not a single one of these major decisions has yet shown the slightest sign of being a mistake. Up to now AA seems to have taken the right turning at each new crossroad. This could scarcely have been our doing alone. Our Fellowship has afforded a convincing proof of that wise old adage which declares that "man's extremity is God's opportunity." This being our record, we can surely face the next hour of decision in confident faith.

The fact is that AA does now stand at a new turning point in its affairs. This has to do with the future world service leadership of AA as a whole. Therefore, we shall have to take a new look at the shape of things to come. At this particular crossroad a crucial decision is required of me. And here it is:

It is my conviction that I should now retire from all active management of AA world service affairs, and that my leadership in these matters should be fully transferred to the trustees of AA's General Service Board.

This is not at all a new concept; it is simply the last step in a play which has been in development for more than ten years. It was in mind when, in 1948, Dr. Bob and I jointly wrote an article for the Grapevine which was called, "Why Can't We Join AA, Too?" It was even more in mind when our first General Service Conference was experimentally assembled in 1951. And when, at St. Louis in 1955, the full authority and responsibility for the maintenance of world services was transferred to our Conference, my retirement from active service leadership was definitely foreshadowed.

Yet a vestige of my old-time status remains, and this should be explained. Following the St. Louis transference there were a few tasks that still required my full attention. But these are now virtually completed. During the last six years I have, respecting these particular matters, exercised a joint leadership with our trustees. This sustained activity has no doubt tended to confirm me, in the minds of many AAs, as a continuing fact and symbol of AA leadership worldwide. This is the last remainder of my service leadership.

For this action there are excellent and even compelling reasons. The basic one is the present need to strictly apply AA's Tradition Two to every area of our world service operation. This means that I should no longer act in service leadership for the group conscience of AA. This must now become fully the function of our trustees, as guided by the Conference delegates. Consider, too, AA's very healthy tradition of rotating leadership. Everywhere today this is a strictly applied principle — excepting to me. This is a leftover inconsistency that ought to be eliminated by my own retirement to the sidelines, where practically all of AA's old-timers now are.

But this is not all. My continued activity at AA's Headquarters may be covering up unforeseen flaws in our organizational structure. These should be given an opportunity to reveal themselves, if they exist. Moreover, the excellent leadership that we now have among the trustees and in the Headquarters should be allowed to operate without further collaboration with me. We know that, in the long run, double-headed management is highly unsound. My retirement from active service would cure this defect.

There are also psychological reasons of the deepest import. AA is very much a family, of which we elders have surely been the spiritual parents. Now the parent who quits before his family has arrived at the age of responsibility, has unquestionably forsaken his trust. But the parent who far overstays his time can be extremely damaging, too. If he insists on continuing his parental authority and the protective custody of his wards well after they have reached the age of responsibility, he is simply robbing them of the priceless privilege of facing life on their own. What was perfectly right for their infancy and adolescence becomes strictly no good for their maturity. So the wise parent always changes his status accordingly. Of course he is still one who, if asked, will lend a hand in serious emergencies. But he knows that he simply must let his heirs make and repair most of their own mistakes, live their own lives, and grow up. Tradition Two of the AA program deeply recognizes this universal truth when it declares: "There is but one ultimate authority — a loving God as he may express himself in our group conscience."

Of course I am not suggesting a complete withdrawal; I propose only to change my relationship with AA. For example, I expect to be available at trustee and Conference meetings. Should marked defects appear in our present service structure, I shall, if asked, be very happy to aid in the work of repair. In short, I expect to be "on tap" but never again "on top," this being precisely the stance that AA hopes all its old-timers will take.

My coming shift to the sidelines will necessarily involve other changes. Save for the possibility of a future visit or two overseas, and my attendance at whatever International Conventions there may be, I think that my days of traveling and speaking are over. Practically speaking, it is no longer possible for me to respond to the hundreds of invitations that now come in. It is very clear, too, that continued appearances would increase my prominence in AA at the very time when this should greatly diminish. There is much the same situation respecting my very large correspondence which has grown so far out of hand that I can no longer do it justice.

Nevertheless, one primary channel of communication still stands wide open — my writing for the Grapevine. This I would certainly like to continue. Just now, for example, I'm doing a series of articles entitled "Practicing These Principles in All Our Affairs." Maybe these pieces can later be expanded into a full-sized book which would try to deal with the whole problem of living, as seen by us AAs. If it turns out that I can write it, such a volume might be of permanent value.

There is another factor that bears upon my decision. Like every AA member I have a definite responsibility to become a citizen of the world around me; to channel into it the experience of living and working which has been mine in our Fellowship. Therefore, I'm already exploring certain areas of outside activity in which I may be able to make a helpful, and possibly a meaningful, contribution. For the first time, I now feel at liberty to follow the constructive example already set by uncounted numbers of my fellow members. But, of course, my principal reason for taking this new direction is the deep and confident belief that this will prove to be in the best longtime interest of Alcoholics Anonymous.

It scarce needs be said that I approach this new crossroad for AA and for me with a lump in my throat, and with a heart very full of gratitude for all those unexampled privileges and gifts with which I have so long been blessed.

Responsibility Is Our Theme

July 1965

Marking AA's thirtieth year we shall, in this month of July 1965, hold our International Convention at Toronto. It is most fitting that the chosen keynote for this gala occasion will be "AA's Responsibility." There we shall review the three decades of AA life that are now history. Stirred by gratitude beyond expression, we shall give thanks to God whose grace has made it possible for us to achieve the quality of responsibility, individual and collective, that has brought our Fellowship into its present state of well-being and worldwide reach.

Looking back through the years, we shall be unable to conceive more than a mere fraction of what God has wrought among us. None will be able to imagine the sum of the suffering that was once ours, or the misery borne by those near and dear. Who will really understand the inner nature of our transforming spiritual experiences, those gifts of God, that opened to us a new world of being and doing and living? Indeed our blessings have been quite beyond any human comprehension.

At our international gathering, we shall look into new faces. Many from afar will be heard to speak in other tongues. We shall see that the sun never sets upon AA's Fellowship, that 350,000 of us have now recovered from our malady; that we have everywhere begun to transcend those formidable barriers of race, creed, and nationality. This assurance that so many of us have been able to meet our responsibilities for sobriety and for growth and effectiveness in the troubled world where we live, will surely fill us with the deepest joy and satisfaction. But as a people who have nearly always learned the hard way, we shall certainly not congratulate ourselves. We shall perceive these assets to be God's gifts, which have been in part matched by an increasing willingness on our part to find and do his will for us.

Then we shall remember, too, how the pains of our illness literally drove us to what for most of us was the first responsible act of years — that of joining AA. Alcoholism had literally lashed us to such a point of collapse that we became willing to do whatever was necessary to get well; it was a matter of life or death.

Thus propelled we finally did join the AA Fellowship and there had our first glimpse of its quite new world of understanding and loving concern. Soon we took a look at AA's Twelve Steps for recovery but many of us promptly forgot ten of them, as perhaps not needed. We bought only the concept that we were alcoholics; that attendance at meetings and a helping hand to the newcomers would be sufficient to solve the booze problem, and probably all problems. We looked with approval on that dear old cliche which says that "drinking is but a good man's fault." Once off the grog, life should be as pleasant as eating cherries. By happily warming our hands at the AA fire, all seemed well.

But by degrees certain dissatisfactions set in, even with our own group; it was not as wonderful as we had first supposed. There was, perhaps, some rock-throwing at a scandal, or a distressing row over who would become the group's next chair. There were people we simply did not like, and the ones we did admire failed to give us the attention we thought we deserved. At home we were also shocked. After the pink cloud had departed from the household, things seemed as bad as ever. The old wounds weren't healing at all. Though impressed with our sobriety, the bank nevertheless asked when were we going to pay up. Our boss likewise demanded in firm tones that we "get with it."

So each of us looked up his sponsor and regaled him with these woes. Our resentments, anxieties, and depressions were definitely caused, we claimed, by our unfortunate circumstances and by the inconsiderate behavior of other people. To our consternation, our sponsors didn't seem impressed either. They had just grinned and said, "Why don't we sit down and take a hard look at all of AA's Twelve Steps? Maybe you have been missing a lot — in fact, nearly everything."

Then we began to take our own inventories, rather than the other fellow's. Getting into the swing of self-examination, we finally began to discover our real responsibilities toward ourselves and toward those around us. Though a tough assignment, it did by degrees get easier. We began to make restitution to those we had harmed, grudgingly at first, and then more willingly. Little by little, we found that all progress, material or spiritual, consisted of finding out what our responsibilities actually were and then proceeding to do something about them. These activities began to pay off. We found that we didn't always have to be *driven* by our own discomforts as, more willingly, we picked up the burdens of living and growing.

Then, most surprisingly, we discovered that full acceptance and action upon any clear-cut responsibility almost invariably made for true happiness and peace of mind. Moreover, these durable satisfactions were redoubled when we realized that our now-better quality of willingness made it possible in meditation to find God's will. At last we discovered that we joyfully wanted to live responsibly.

Such has been the course of spiritual unfoldment in AA; our pilgrim's progress, if you like.

As it has been with each AA member, so it has been with each group, and with AA as a whole. I have often seen our Society timid and fearful, angry and prideful, apathetic and indifferent. But I have also seen these negatives fade as the lessons of experience were learned and gladly applied.

Let us recall a few instances:

In the early days, we were so timid that we were sure AA should be a secret society. We shunned publicity because we still labored under the stigma of alcoholism — also because we might be overwhelmed by an influx of so-called undesirable people. We have often been angered at criticism from within and from the outside world. We have generally been far better at dishing out criticism than taking it. Sometimes we have boasted of AA as the know-all and do-all of alcoholism, so alienating our friends. Quite understanding the perils of accumulated wealth, we have converted this fear into an alibi for failing to meet our trivial group, intergroup, and world service expenses — those vital arms of service so indispensable to carrying AA's message into the world about us. By poor sponsorship we have sometimes failed the needs of newly arrived sufferers.

Then at certain great turning points of our history, we have, in anger or sheer indifference, backed away from what should have been clearly visible responsibilities. Disastrous results were on a few occasions barely averted. Old-timers can recall that the book *Alcoholics Anonymous* might never have been printed because some avowed that we did not need it, while others shrank from the risks of preparing that invaluable text. There was a great outcry against formation of the General Service Conference of Alcoholics Anonymous, that indispensable body of delegates which today links our Society with the AA trustees of our world services. There was almost no belief that such a linkage could be effectively forged; even an attempt at such a project would ruin us, many thought. In consequence, this utterly vital undertaking nearly fell by the wayside from the sheer burden of indifference, heavy attack, and little faith.

Yet, in God's time, our spiritual assets have invariably come to exceed even such large liabilities. AA recovery goes forward on a large scale. Practice of AA's Twelve Traditions has amazingly cemented our unity. Our intergroup associations and our General Service Conference have made possible a wide spreading of our message, at home and abroad. Our pains and our necessities first called us reluctantly to responsibility. But in the latter years, a joyous willingness and a confident faith have more and more permeated all the affairs of our Fellowship.

Despite this happy transcendence of the difficulties of yesterday and of today, we nevertheless deeply realize that our negative traits are still with us, and always will be. Therefore our constant responsibility should be that of taking a fearless inventory of our defects as we go along, the better to undertake their mending.

At Toronto, we shall therefore be asking ourselves, "What sort of heritage are we leaving, for the use of all those future generations that will people our Society? Is this heritage as good as we can make it? While there is yet time, what can we still do that may multiply our assets and decrease our liabilities?"

In so surveying our Society of today, I hope that I shall not be regarded as the wise and righteous elder who would admonish and exhort his fellows. If I inventory AA's shortcomings, be also assured that I am also taking stock of my own. I know that my errors of yesterday still have their effect; that my shortcomings of today may likewise affect our future. So it is, with each and all of us.

Therefore, let us together take a look at the more important areas in the life of our Fellowship where the call for improvement will always be insistent.

Our first concern should be with those sufferers that we are still unable to reach. Let's first humbly realize that throughout the world of today there are 20,000,000 alcoholics, 5,000,000 of these being in the United States alone. Of course, these vast numbers are in all stages of sickness. Some cannot be reached because they are not hurt enough, others because they are hurt too much. Many sufferers have mental and emotional complications that seem to foreclose their chances. Yet it would be conservative to estimate that at any particular time there are 4,000,000 alcoholics in the world who are able, ready, and willing to get well — if only they knew how! Clearly, all these sufferers need to know what alcoholism is and to recognize that they are so afflicted. Being thus readied, they need to be brought within our reach by every resource of public information and word of mouth that will tell them exactly what steps they can take in finding the road to recovery. When we remember that in the thirty years of AA's existence, we have reached less than 10 percent of those who might have been willing to approach us, we begin to get an idea of the immensity of our task and of the responsibilities with which we will always be confronted.

These facts point straight to our next responsibility: that of intelligently and lovingly sponsoring each man and woman who comes among us asking help. The care and concern with which we individually and collectively do this can make all the difference. Besides, this is the greatest expression of gratitude that we can give for what we ourselves have received. Without much doubt, a million alcoholics have approached AA during the last thirty years. We can soberly ask ourselves what became of the 600,000 who did not stay. How much and how often did we fail all these?

In no circumstances should we feel that Alcoholics Anonymous is the know-all and do-all of alcoholism. We have in the United States and Canada alone perhaps one hundred agencies engaged in research, alcohol education, and rehabilitation. Research has already come up with significant and helpful findings, and can still do far more. Those engaged in education are carrying the message that alcoholism is a definite illness and that something can be done about it. All these workers can make our efforts more effective. It is a statistical fact that rehabilitation agencies in the United States and Canada treat something like 50,000 alcoholics annually. True, their approach is often different from our own. But what does that matter, when the greater part of them are, or could become, entirely willing to cooperate with AA? Too often, I think, we have deprecated and even derided these projects of our friends just because we do not always see eye to eye with them. We should very seriously ask ourselves how many alcoholics have gone on drinking simply because we have failed to cooperate in good spirit with these many agencies — whether they be good, bad, or indifferent. No alcoholic should go mad or die merely because he did not come straight to AA at the beginning.

Now let's look at the matter of criticism — criticism of AA that is made in the world about us. For years AA has been amazingly exempt from those barbs which society pitches at all endeavors of any consequence, whether they be social, medical, religious, or political. So we register surprise, shock, and anger when people find fault with AA. We are apt to be disturbed to such an extent that we cannot benefit by constructive criticism. Nor are we able to be good-natured about criticism which isn't so good. While these attitudes are not general among us, it is nevertheless a fact that many AAs do so react when they are hit where they live. Surely this sort of resentment makes no friends and achieves no constructive purpose. Certainly this is an area in which we can improve.

Alcoholics Anonymous is not a religion, nor is it a medical treatment, nor does it profess expertise in respect of unconscious motivations for behavior. These are facts all too often overlooked. Here and there we hear our members proclaiming AA as the great new religion. Except for strictly sobering-up operations, we are also apt to underrate medical contributions to our welfare. The fact that psychiatry does not yet sober up many alcoholics sometimes inclines us to think in unflattering terms of that profession. Again we are forgetting that to religion and to the medical arts we owe our very existence. In its cardinal principles and attitudes, AA has made great use of all of these resources. It is chiefly our friends who first gave us the principles and attitudes that enable us to live and to move today. Therefore, the credit of all these vital contributors should stand aces-high among us. Certainly we drunks did put AA together, but all of its basic components were supplied by others. Here, especially, our maxim should be, "Let's be friendly with our friends."

It is an historical fact that practically all groupings of men and women tend to become more dogmatic; their beliefs and practices harden and sometimes freeze. This is a natural and almost inevitable process. All people must, of course, rally to the call of their convictions, and we of AA are no exception. Moreover, all people should have the right to voice their convictions. This is good principle and good dogma. But dogma also has its liabilities. Simply because we have convictions that work well for us, it becomes very easy to assume that we have all the truth. Whenever this brand of arrogance develops, we are certain to become aggressive; we *demand* agreement with us; we play God. This isn't good dogma; it's very bad dogma. It could be especially destructive for us of AA to indulge in this sort of thing.

Newcomers are approaching AA at the rate of tens of thousands yearly. They represent almost every belief and attitude imaginable. We have atheists and agnostics. We have people of nearly every race, culture, and religion. In AA we are supposed to be bound together in the kinship of a common suffering. Consequently, the full individual liberty to practice any creed or principle or therapy whatever should be a first consideration for us all. Let us not, therefore, pressure anyone with our individual or even our collective views. Let us instead accord each other the respect and love that is due to every human being as he tries to make his way toward the light. Let us always try to be inclusive rather than exclusive; let us remember that each alcoholic among us is a member of AA, so long as he or she so declares.

Some of our more obvious perils will always attach to money, to controversies within AA, and to the ever-present temptation to scramble within AA and outside it for distinction, prestige, and even power. The world around us is today shattered by these untoward forces. As drinkers we have been more subject to these forms of destruction than most other people. Here, thank God, we do have, and I trust we shall continue to have, a tremendous amount of awareness of our responsibilities for improvement.

However, the fear of these forces should not deceive us into absurd rationalizations. In the fear of accumulated wealth and bureaucracy, we should not discover an alibi for failure to pay AA's legitimate service expenses. For fear of controversy, our leadership should not go timid when lively debate and forthright action is a necessity. And for fear of accumulating prestige and power, we should never fail to endow our trusted leaders with proper authority to act for us.

Let us never fear needed change. Certainly we have to discriminate between changes for worse and changes for better. But once a need becomes clearly apparent in an individual, a group, or in AA as a whole, it has long since been found out that we cannot stand still and look the other way. The essence of all growth is a willingness to change for the better and then an unremitting willingness to shoulder whatever the responsibility.

In conclusion, it is only fair to say that we of AA have been able in most areas of our lives together to make substantial gains in both our willingness and our capability for the acceptance and discharge of responsibility, something that our great gathering in Toronto will symbolize and demonstrate.

As we look into the future, we clearly see that an ever greater willingness will certainly be the key to that progress which God intends for us as we move toward his appointed destiny.

The Guidance of AA's World Affairs

January 1966

Speaking on behalf of AA's board of trustees, our devoted friend and chairman, Dr. Jack Norris, has called upon us to face a far-reaching responsibility. Future AA historians will no doubt record this occasion as a major turning point in the unfoldment of our well-loved Fellowship. This is because we are now to reconsider, and perhaps to recast, the whole nature and composition of AA's future world leadership. As we meditate upon this long unresolved problem, it would be well to recall that in the affairs of new societies and of nations, the determination of their ultimate leadership has ever been a matter of crucial importance. This is the teaching of all human history.

Dr. Jack has specifically requested us of Alcoholics Anonymous — at the level of our board of trustees — to assume the primary role in the conduct of AA's world affairs. He has presented a detailed program for achieving this, a plan almost unanimously recommended by his fellow trustees. Should we adopt this new concept in 1966, the chief responsibility for the guidance of our world affairs would then be shifted from the nonalcoholics of our present board to the alcoholic trustees of the new board.

Our recast board would then be composed of fourteen AA trustees and seven nonalcoholic trustees. Seven of the AA members would be chosen from suitable areas of the United States and Canada on the basis of their AA leadership qualifications. The remaining seven AAs would be selected on the basis of their several high standards of business, professional, and administrative skills. This would add up to a balanced board of twenty-one members, in which the AAs would function in a majority of two to one. That would compare with our present board of ten nonalcoholics and nine AAs. The chief posts of the new board would be open to its AA members at any time such a change might be desirable. For practical reasons alone, the improved balance between the three classes of trustees should commend itself to us all.

However, the trustees' plan, as outlined by Dr. Jack, has far greater implications than mere practicality: It carries deep spiritual values; it is a call to the highest of AA's responsibilities. In effect, it is also a declaration that AA has now evolved to such a point of stability and competence that it should no longer need to function under what has been, since 1938, the symbol of protective custody by nonalcoholic friends. As you know, the present structure was created long ago — in a time when AA had but three groups and only forty members.

It is worth pausing here to recall why our General Service Board was originally so constituted. For us of AA, the year 1938 was one of anguished uncertainty. There was no proof that alcoholics could stay sober indefinitely. Nor was there convincing evidence that we had the emotional stability to look after ourselves, even though sober. Besides, we had no public standing; people did not even know that we existed. Then, too, how many distant AA groups would think of sending their money contributions to a board of trustees composed wholly of New York alcoholics? This was the climate of fear and indecision that darkly overcast us in that early time.

Nevertheless, it had already become clear that our infant Society would have to head up somewhere. At the top of our growing pyramid of membership, there would need to be erected a beacon light whose illumination might carry AA's message to those who still suffered from alcoholism. Lest one day its radiance be snuffed out by drinking relapses and irresponsibility, we felt sure that we dare not tend this lighthouse all by ourselves.

Some kind of certain protection we must have — but what protection? The answer that we proposed in 1938 is now history. We requested carefully chosen nonalcoholic friends to become a majority of our projected trusteeship, and we agreed to make this status legal. We further stipulated that, traditionally, there should always be a nonalcoholic chairman and likewise a nonalcoholic treasurer. Frankly admitting that AA would absolutely have to have such a protectorate, we somberly estimated that, should all the AA trustees get drunk, our board could nevertheless continue to function by reason of its nonalcoholic guardianship!

Happily, we can now smile at all these excessive fears and elaborate precautions. During the past twenty-seven years, only two AA trustees have been waylaid by alcohol. Meanwhile, our message has been carried worldwide, and most effectively indeed. It is probably no exaggeration to estimate that one-half of our present membership and much of our remarkable unity has been due, in large measure, to the efforts of AA world servants, both on the board of trustees and in the General Service Office.

Of course, we have sometimes witnessed emotional storms, but none more serious than those which afflict most other societies. In every single instance these disturbances have been successfully overcome by the immense spirit of dedication that has always characterized every level of our worldwide effort. The record speaks for itself. Today we know that we need not fear alcoholism, nor excessive emotional instability.

Next, let us inquire into what has been the value of our nonalcoholic trustees over all these years. Without hesitation, I can tell you that their value has been quite beyond reckoning. Only God could add their score. Therefore I deeply hope that a sizable contingent of these friends will continue to remain with us, just as our new plan provides.

In the days when AA was unknown, it was the nonalcoholic trustees who held up our hands before the general public. They supplied us with ideas that are now a part of the working structures of our Headquarters. They voluntarily spent hours on end, working side by side with us and among the grubbiest of details. They gave freely of their professional and financial wisdom. Now and then they helpfully mediated our difficulties.

In the early years especially, their very presence on our board was quite able to command full confidence and the respect of many faraway groups. Meanwhile, they assured the world around us of AA's worth. These are the unusual services which indeed they still render. Then, too, these are the men who stood fast during that exciting but perilous time between 1940 and 1950 when AA's unity and its collective responsibility were put to the acid test — a time our Twelve Traditions were being forged out of the lessons of that experience.

Having myself been a constant resident of AA's house of world service for over a quarter of a century, no one could better understand what these devoted friends have meant to us. To gratefully set my testimony of their magnificent contributions on the record in this article is something for the deepest and most enduring of satisfactions. Nor could any expression of our gratitude be complete unless I were to tell you of the indispensable contribution that was once made to AA's welfare by a nonalcoholic friend and trustee. I write of a man that many of you know — our onetime chairman, Mr. Bernard Smith. During the most serious crisis that this Fellowship has ever experienced, it was Bern who persuaded us to meet and to shoulder our clear and rightful obligations.

As individuals, it must be confessed that we AAs have never been over-anxious to meet heavy responsibilities. All of us were at first driven to AA under the lash of alcohol. Arriving in the midst of the newfound life, we were soon confronted with the Twelve Steps and Twelve Traditions. More often than not, we proceeded to adopt these principles in a rather piecemeal fashion. However, as inevitably time went by, the quality of our conformity began to improve. We commenced to practice AA principles because we knew them to be right for us, even though many were still difficult. Nonetheless, it was a very long time before many of us could come to the point where we would accept our heavier obligations with that full and joyful willingness which finally grants to us a consistent spiritual effectiveness.

It is also observable that, like other people, we AAs are apt to resist any proposal for great change, especially when all seems to go well. Often enough, these reluctances have been based upon our fears. But sometimes they have represented a genuine prudence. This latter quality of conservatism has occasionally prevented ill-considered or hasty decisions upon important matters.

What has been true of us as individuals has necessarily been true of AA as a whole. I can vividly remember the heavy opposition to the creation of our world trusteeship in 1938, to the publication of our textbook *Alcoholics Anonymous* in 1939, and I still tremble when I recall the truly fierce resistance that arose when, in 1946, the General Service Conference of Alcoholics Anonymous was first projected. In those times it was seriously believed by a majority of AAs that the temptations and risks of such complex ventures as these would be far too much for us. However, we can now thank God that we finally did face and accept those vital and clear-cut responsibilities.

Nevertheless we found on each of these occasions that we had to be strongly persuaded of the absolute need for change. There had to be manifest a solid core of constructive and convincing personal leadership.

This is exactly what our remarkable friend, Bern Smith, gave to us when, in 1950, after years of great heat but little light, we had failed to arrive at a decision to form AA's General Service Conference. It was his personal leadership that saved the day.

Let me now background this statement. By 1946, certain facts of AA life were becoming visible. Our trusteeship — then called the Alcoholic Foundation — was becoming more and more isolated as our groups fanned out over the globe. Indeed, the only linkage between our board and all these thousands of members consisted of a few tireless AAs at the General Service Office, Dr. Bob, and myself. The trustees themselves were virtually unknown. Dr. Bob had fallen ill, perhaps fatally. Our linkage was perishable and far too thin. Hence some of us felt it imperative that our board of trustees should be directly related without delay to AA as a whole.

There was still another reason: A majority of our groups had already declared that they would no longer live under the protection and management of their local founders and old-timers — no matter how well-loved these were. For better or worse, our groups were taking the decision to look after themselves.

This was the AA revolution which led to the writing of Tradition Two, whose principles of AA function provide that the group conscience shall be the final authority for all active services and that trusted servants named by the groups shall act in their behalf.

Certainly our long isolated board members *were* trusted servants. But it was nonetheless true that these trustees had no direct connection to the group conscience of our Society, nor were they directly accountable to it. It was therefore becoming evident that we here at New York were still operating as a protectorate, something that had by then become obsolete and quite inconsistent with the provisions and spirit of AA's Second Tradition.

Consequently, it was proposed to assemble a General Service Conference of delegates who could squarely meet these deficiencies. As news of this project got into circulation, resistance began to mount. The more the Conference was urged, the more the opposition dug in. Many AAs were deeply frightened. They imagined themselves engulfed in a wave of prestige-seeking, shabby politics, financial troubles, and all the rest of it. Under such conditions, many good members were quite unable to see the urgent need for radical change. Observing their protests, our board naturally concluded that AAs most emphatically did not want a General Service Conference. I'm afraid, too, that the growing impasse was made still worse by my incessant bulldozing of the Conference issue.

Then Bern Smith came upon the scene. With matchless diplomacy and tact he began to point out that the actual risk of the Conference venture was, in his belief, far less than the risk of doing nothing at all — a policy which he thought would, in the future, result in a collapse or certainly a grievous impairment of AA at its very heart of service. He deeply felt that we must not risk such a debacle at our Headquarters, a calamity from which we might never recover.

He also continued to remind us that *self-direction was the very first responsibility* of every democratic society, such as ours had said it was in Tradition Two. As we know, these views of Bern's were finally accepted, and I shall never forget that wonderful day in his office when the trustees' committee on structure recommended immediate creation of the General Service Conference of AA. To our friend Bern we therefore owe it that we have our annual Conference.

Certainly his story has a deep and clear relevance to this all-important matter of AA's future leadership; the question that is again before us and one which has been ten years under debate.

It is ever so evident that Dr. Jack has been performing for us a similar service of unique importance. To him and to his fellow trustees, we therefore owe a similar tribute. It is greatly due to Dr. Jack's wise and patient leadership in this time of change that we have the trustees' plan before us at this time — a plan which, if adopted, would mark the last basic step in the evolution of AA's world service structure.

Most assuredly, I hardly need say that I *do* endorse the trustees' plan; its unfoldment in the 1965 Conference was one of the most inspiring and heartwarming events of my entire AA life.

Finally, let us reflect together upon the high spiritual content of this all-important plan.

As we know, all AA progress can be reckoned in terms of just two words: humility and responsibility. Our whole spiritual development can be accurately measured by our degree of adherence to these magnificent standards. Ever deepening humility, accompanied by an ever greater willingness to accept and to act upon clear-cut obligations — these are truly our touchstones for all growth in the life of the spirit. They hold up to us the very essence of right being and right doing. It is by them that we are enabled to find and to do God's will.

Let us therefore consider the spiritual gifts which our friends have today offered for AA's future welfare. They have offered to reduce their numbers by three. Being still a board majority, and still holding its chief posts, our nonalcoholics have all these years been cast in the role of guardianship, a responsibility that they have never been called upon to meet. Therefore this old-time symbol of protection has long since become meaningless. Recognizing this, the new trustees' plan provides that our friends would, in the future, act in a minority, thus becoming our associates. In making this humble offer, they have called upon us to assume the highest of responsibilities — the guidance, under God, of our own life as a Fellowship.

If this, then, is their demonstration of humility, what is going to be our demonstration of responsibility? As to a family just coming of age, they have in substance told us, "The world of the future stretches before you, and you are well prepared. Go out into it, fearing nothing. Our faith in you is confident and strong. As you move onward toward your destiny, may you always remember that God in his wisdom has granted you three precious graces: freedom from a deadly affliction; a life experience that enables you to carry that priceless freedom to others; and a vision, ever widening, of God's reality and of his love."

May we of Alcoholics Anonymous remain ever worthy of these three gifts of grace and of the supreme responsibilities that are now ours, for so long as a bountiful God may wish AA to endure.

First World Service Meeting

October 1969

$\mathbb{S}$ urely the time will come when our overseas AA population may well exceed that of the United States and Canada. In *The Third Legacy Manual* [now *The AA Service Manual*] and in other writings, the principle has already been enunciated that the General Service Office in New York should one day become the "senior service center" among a number of national and zonal offices around the globe.

This attitude has already been of immense value in forwarding our effort overseas. It has banished all possible suspicion that GSO in New York is going to run the whole world of AA.

It is obvious that we cannot actually manage and conduct public information and relations with medicine and religion in South Africa, Australia, the British Isles, or anywhere else, for that matter. In the area of literature, distribution centers are needed that take into account both language and shipping problems. We are too remote to do these jobs, and for psychological reasons we should never make the attempt.

But we can help by sharing with other countries the thirty-year history and experience of GSO. AA is taking a giant step toward world-wide AA unity in New York, October 9 to 11, 1969.

The first World Service Meeting will be held for these three days, bringing twenty-six delegates from twelve countries overseas, the zone of Central America, and the North American Conference. These delegates will sit in sharing conferences in New York with trustees on the General Service Board and the staffs of GSO and the Grapevine.

This meeting is, of course, undertaken with the approval of our General Service Board, the North American Conference, and the boards or committees of all participating countries.

The objectives of the World Service Meeting are: 1) to consider the future development of world services; 2) to strengthen general service work already existing abroad; 3) to increase the number of service centers; 4) to provide for them an orderly plan of evolution; 5) to assist in strengthening their self-support.

We welcome our delegate friends from around the world as we join together to assure that help will always be available for sick alcoholics wherever they are or whatever language they speak.

Segment 3

Additional Writings from This Period

The Antidote for Fear: Prudence, Trust, and Faith

November 1959

This Conference opened on the keynotes of prudence, trust, and faith, and its proceedings have been characterized by these attitudes and practices throughout. Confidence has therefore abounded among us and in this year's session we have gone nearly scot-free of any worry or fear. Indeed, we have gone along so quietly that we have rather missed the usual excitements of hot debate and "viewing with alarm for the good of the movement."

But there has been an excitement nevertheless; a healthier excitement of quite another quality and kind. For instance, I found a most satisfying excitement as I watched the real eagerness, discipline, and dedication with which this assembly has waded for days through a great pile of humdrum but very necessary routine work. It made me most happy when I heard you delegates pay repeated and grateful tributes to the folks back home — to those hundreds of committee members and thousands of general service representatives whose combined labor had been, and always must be, the final foundation on which our whole world service structure and effort can securely rest. AA service leadership, you said, was not for delegates and trustees alone; it had to be out there in the grass roots — and it already was there.

Then, too, we have all been gladdened by reports from nearly every quarter of our Fellowship to the effect that confidence and real trust in our world services and servants has been much on the increase; that the fears of other days have almost evaporated. These are some of the newer and healthier excitements that we have felt in this notable Conference of 1959.

Fresh in memory is that great big laugh we had when one of you delegates, addressing me, rose and said, "Bill, we all heard you give that convincing pitch on trust and faith the night we got here. Now what would you say if I told you that out in our country we have a member who was supposed to be acting as our treasurer for a pretty large and important meeting; that the minute the tickets were sold and the money was banked, he developed a terrific thirst, drew out all that dough, and took off on a traveling winging that blazed a cross-country trail a thousand miles long?" We all remember how our fellow delegates grinned as he spoke and how we roared with mirth as he finished.

Now there was a time, years back, when such a thirsty and absconding treasurer could have shattered our confidence wholesale. How well I remember the first one! I can remember, too, my own shock and chagrin when one of my best friends attacked me unmercifully because he didn't like the way I was acting. I remember those first breaks of anonymity at the top public level and all of the fear and violent controversy that followed in their wake. Such were the alarms of AA's early time. We feared we couldn't stay sober, we feared our group couldn't survive, we really feared that AA might collapse completely.

But how times have changed! What was once a big fear is today a big laugh — take that one about the erring treasurer. In it I think we can find some wonderful things. Let it be recalled that in that laugh there

wasn't a trace of contempt or anger. There wasn't the slightest thought
of punishment and I'll wager that not one soul here would have thought
to call him a thief. Underneath that laugh there was sympathetic understanding, there was the realization that any one of us was still capable of
an equal folly. Because we understood so well, we could forgive lightly
and easily. Of course, we were laughing at the startled and penniless convention as it heard the bad news. But I think our laugh had a far deeper
meaning than this.

In reality I'm sure we were laughing at ourselves, at our old and far-
fetched fears. We were rejoicing because they had gone. Gone was the
awful fear of what an individual's failure or behavior might do to us all,
gone was the longtime fear that the pressures and conflicts of the world
around us might one day infiltrate and crush AA. We laughed, I think,
because we had no bondage to fear and felt free. We had ceased to doubt
our collective safety and security.

This brings me to another thought, another reason for reassurance.
Of most nations and societies it seems true that their collective behavior
has often been far worse than the individual behavior of their mem-
berships. For example, few individuals in the world of today are hankering for war. Yet many nations crave conquest and armed conflict.
Nations notable for the individual honesty of their citizens will keep
phony books, inflate their currencies, load their people with debts that
can't be paid, and engage in all sorts of fraudulent propaganda and practices. Even the great religions, as organizations, have, quite contrary to
their own teachings, sometimes gone in for a degree of violence and
bigotry which the majority of their adherents would never have dreamed
of imitating in their own personal lives. Mobs do all sorts of things that
most of the individuals composing them would seldom do separately and
on their own.

While it's not for us to take a moral inventory of the world in any
sense of pride or superiority, I do think it fair and timely to point out we
AAs have thus far demonstrated a collective behavior probably much
superior to our individual conduct. The whole, in our case, seems to be
rather better than the sum of its individual parts. We are pretty much a
bunch of power-drivers. Yet AA, as a whole, has never quarreled with
anybody. We like money for ourselves but we keep our Fellowship treasuries poor. We like prestige, yet we somehow remain anonymous. As
individuals we are apt to be aggressive, yet our Society as a whole is quite
nonaggressive, minding its own business.

In short, we are in a strange contrast to the world about us, and we devoutly hope we shall stay that way. In these perilous times this will be the sort of collective prudence that we shall constantly need. It will guarantee our effectiveness, safety, and survival as nothing else can.

Our collective prudence respecting money, fame, and controversy — derived of course from our Twelve Traditions — has continued to make AA new hosts of friends, and, just as importantly, no enemies. May this benign process never stop, within and without our Fellowship.

As this wonderful Conference has so well shown, the absence of fear has made way for wisdom and prudence; prudence has led us to confidence and trust and faith — faith in our fellow man, faith in ourselves, and faith in God's love.

Our Critics Can Be Our Benefactors

When a magazine criticizing aspects of AA raised questions about AA's relationships to medicine, religion, and the world at large, the Grapevine editors consulted Bill. He suggested a rereading of the following relevant portions of AA Comes of Age *and* Twelve Concepts for World Service.

April 1963

As a Society we must never become so vain as to suppose that we have been the authors and inventors of a new religion. We will humbly reflect that each of AA's principles, *every one of them,* has been borrowed from ancient sources. We shall remember that we are laymen, holding ourselves in readiness to cooperate with all men of goodwill, whatever creed or nationality.

Speaking for Dr. Bob and myself I would like to say that there has never been the slightest intent, on his part or mine, of trying to found a new religious denomination. Dr. Bob held certain religious convictions, and so do I. This is, of course, the personal privilege of every AA member.

Nothing, however, could be so unfortunate for AA's future as an attempt to incorporate any of our personal theological views into AA teaching, practice, or tradition. Were Dr. Bob still with us, I am positive he would agree that we could never be too emphatic about this matter.

Then, too, it would be a product of false pride to believe that Alcoholics Anonymous is a cure-all, even for alcoholism. Here we must remember our debt to the men of medicine. Here we must be friendly and, above all, open-minded toward every new development in the medical or psychiatric art that promises to be helpful to sick people. We should always be friendly to those in the fields of alcoholic research, rehabilitation, and education. We should endorse none especially but hold ourselves in readiness to cooperate so far as we can with them all. Let us constantly remind ourselves that the experts in religion are the clergymen; that the practice of medicine is for physicians; and that we, the recovered alcoholics, are their assistants.

There are those who predict that Alcoholics Anonymous may well become a new spearhead for a spiritual awakening throughout the world. When our friends say these things they are both generous and sincere. But we of AA must reflect that such a tribute and such a prophecy could well prove to be a heady drink for most of us — that is, if we really came to believe this to be the real purpose of AA, and if we commenced to behave accordingly. Our Society, therefore, will prudently cleave to its single purpose; the carrying of the message to the alcoholic who still suffers. Let us resist the proud assumption that since God has enabled us to do well in one area we are destined to be a channel of saving grace for everybody.

On the other hand, let us never be a closed corporation; let us never deny our experience for whatever it may be worth to the world around us. Let our individual members heed the call to every field of human endeavor. Let them carry the experience and spirit of AA into all these affairs, for whatever good they may accomplish. For not only has God saved us from alcoholism; the world has received us back into its citizenship. Yet believing in paradoxes as we do, we must still realize that the more the Society of Alcoholics Anonymous as such tends to its own affairs and minds its own business, the greater will be our general influence, the less will be any opposition to us, and the wider will be the circle in which our Fellowship will be likely to enjoy the confidence and respect of men.

— Alcoholics Anonymous Comes of Age

Now let us suppose that AA does fall under sharp public attack or heavy ridicule; and let us take the particular case where such pronouncements happen to have little or no justification in fact.

Almost without exception it can be confidently estimated that our best defense in these situations would be no defense whatever — namely, complete silence at the public level. Unreasonable people are stimulated all the more by opposition. If in good humor we leave them strictly alone, they are apt to subside the more quickly. If their attacks persist and it is plain that they are misinformed, it may be wise to communicate with them in a temperate and informative way; also in such a manner that they cannot use our communication as a springboard for fresh assault. Such communications need seldom be made by the Conference officially. Very often we can use the good offices of friends. Such messages from us should never question the motives of the attackers; they should be purely informative. These communications should also be private. If made public, they will often be seized upon as a fresh excuse for controversy.

If, however, a given criticism of AA is partly or wholly justified, it may be well to acknowledge this privately to the critics, together with our thanks....

— Twelve Concepts for World Service

In the years ahead we shall, of course, make mistakes. Experience has taught us that we need have no fear of doing this, providing that we always remain willing to confess our faults and to correct them promptly. Our growth as individuals has depended upon this healthy process of trial and error. So will our growth as a Fellowship. Let us always remember that any society of men and women that cannot freely correct its own faults must surely fall into decay if not into collapse. Such is the universal penalty for the failure to go on growing. Just as each AA must continue to take his moral inventory and act upon it, so must our whole Society do if we are to survive and if we are to serve usefully and well.

— Alcoholics Anonymous Comes of Age

A Message from Bill

May 1964

I 'm glad indeed that we so often say to each other, "Faith without works is dead — action is the magic word!" As we strive to devise better ways of carrying the AA message to those who still suffer, I hope that we will also try to create a wider understanding of the operation and needs of AA's world services — that all-important cluster of activities which enables our Fellowship to function as a whole. Because these far-flung services reach into every quarter of the world, their direct influence for good is too often unseen, and therefore unknown.

Without that global effort, we would now be in a most sorry and chaotic state. Let me illustrate this by two examples:

Suppose, for instance, that, during the last twenty-five years, AA had never published any standard literature — no books, no pamphlets. We need little imagination to see that by now our message would be hopelessly garbled. Our relations with medicine and religion would have become a shambles. To alcoholics generally we would today be a joke and the public would have thought us a riddle. Without its literature, AA would certainly have bogged down in a welter of controversy and disunity.

Nevertheless, effective literature was prepared, and in 1939 the publication of the Big Book became our very first world service. From that time on, it became perfectly clear what AA is, what it believes, and how it works. Millions of our pamphlets and hundreds of thousands of our books are today in circulation. AA's message can never be garbled; anyone at all can find out about us with ease. What the dividends of this single project in world communication have been, only God himself knows.

One more illustration. Our Fellowship enjoys a vast goodwill everywhere. In large measure this is directly due to another AA world service — the service of public information. For many years wonderful accounts of AA have poured from the press and from other media of communication. This astounding success has required of your general service people great labor, top skills, and unstinted dedication. There is no question that this continued torrent of favorable publicity has brought to AA one-half its present membership.

But just suppose that these great channels of communication had been left wide open to the winds of chance; or, worse still, had never been developed by us at all. Had there been such a failure, we may well shudder at the dire consequences. Tens of thousands of today's AA membership would still be drinking. Many indeed would now be mad or dead.

I'm sure you have already seen that AA world service is utterly necessary to our future unity and growth — even to our survival as a Fellowship.

To maintain these life-giving arteries of world communication in full flow, and in good repair, will always be a top priority task for each new generation of our Society. This will require of us a greatly increased understanding of the immense need to be met, and a sustained devotion of the highest order.

The world of today harbors the appalling total of twenty million alcoholic men and women. Without doubt a large fraction of these fellow sufferers could begin to find their sobriety and a new way of life if only they could see and hear just one AA meeting. Experience has already proved that our world services constitute the largest and the most powerful single agency that we shall ever possess to bring those legions of sufferers within reach of what we — AAs around the world — have so providentially discovered for ourselves.

Knowing this Fellowship, I feel entirely confident that we will eagerly shoulder and discharge well this most high responsibility to our Third Legacy.

As we continue in the language of the heart to carry AA's message across all distances and all barriers, may God bless us.

AA's Tradition of Self-Support

October 1967

A A 's far-flung Twelfth Step activities, carrying the message to the next sufferer, are the very lifeblood of our AA adventure. Without this vital activity, we would soon become anemic; we would literally wither and die.

Now where do AA's services — worldwide, area, local — fit into our scheme of things? Why should we provide these functions with money? The answer is simple enough. Every single AA service is designed to make more and better Twelfth Step work possible, whether it be a group meeting place, a central or intergroup office to arrange hospitalization and sponsorship, or the world service Headquarters to maintain unity and effectiveness all over the globe.

Though not costly, these service agencies are absolutely essential to our continued expansion — to our survival as a Fellowship. Their costs are a collective obligation that rests squarely upon all of us. Our support of services actually amounts to a recognition on our part that AA must everywhere function in full strength — and that, under our Tradition of self-support, *we are all going to foot the bill.*

We have long known that Alcoholics Anonymous has no need for charitable contributions from any source. Our Fellowship is self-supporting. Neither do AA groups try to meet the rehabilitation expenses of thousands of newcomers. Long ago we learned that this was impractical.

Instead, AA offers to the new person a spiritual way of life that can eliminate the alcohol problem. With this accomplished, the new person, in the company of his fellow sufferers, can then begin the solution of his personal problems — including the financial one.

So AA groups themselves accept no charitable funds — and give none away. At first glance, this attitude may seem to be hard-nosed, even callous. An immense experience tells us otherwise. Money gifts — as a prerequisite of getting sober — are usually worthless when made a function of an AA group.

Of course, we see AA's primary charity in the Twelfth Step activities of tens of thousands of us as we daily carry the AA message to newcomers. We travel millions of miles; we absent ourselves from business and home. In the aggregate, we lay out large sums. As individuals, we do not hesitate to give temporary financial aid to the newcomer, if and when he seems to want sobriety first. Here, then, is money charity aplenty, always given on a very personal, face-to-face basis. And perhaps even this cannot be called wholly charitable, since every Twelfth Step effort means more certain sobriety and added spiritual growth for the sponsor.

Both these principles we understand: that AA wants no charity; that we support our own services. We understand — but we sometimes forget.

A Christmas Message

December 1970

Gratitude is just about the finest attribute we can have, and how deeply we of AA realize this at Christmastime. Together, we count and ponder our blessings of life, of service, of love.

In these distraught times, we have been enabled to find an always increasing measure of peace within ourselves. Together with all here at AA's General Service Office, Lois joins me in warmest greetings to each and all of you, and we share our confident faith that the year to come will be counted among the best that our Fellowship has ever known.

Memorial Articles

Anne S.

July 1949

A nne S. has taken her leave of us. She died on Wednesday, June 1. To the hundreds who really knew her, this was a meaningful and moving event. With those who knew her not, I wish to share the inspiration which she gave to Lois and me. Anne was the wife of Dr. Bob, co-founder of Alcoholics Anonymous. She was, quite literally, the mother of our first group, Akron Number One.

Her wise and beautiful counsel to all, her insistence that the spiritual come before anything else, her unwavering support of Dr. Bob in all his works; all these were virtues which watered the uncertain seed that was to become AA. Who but God could assess such a contribution? We can only say that it was priceless and magnificent. In the full sense of the word, she was one of the founders of Alcoholics Anonymous.

Not a soul who knew Anne will say that she is really gone. Each knows that her abiding love and influence will live forever. And none knows better than Dr. Bob, Lois and I, who saw these things from the beginning. Nor do we think we shall never see her again. For, like nearly all our fellow AA members, we believe there is no death. She is only out of our sight and hearing for a little while.

Dr. Bob: A Tribute

January 1951

$\mathbb{S}$erenely remarking to his attendant, "I think this is it," Dr. Bob passed out of our sight and hearing November 16, 1950 at noonday. So ended the consuming malady wherein he had so well shown us how high faith can rise over grievous distress. As he had lived, so he had died, supremely aware that in his Father's house are many mansions.

In all those he knew, memory was at floodtide. But who could really say what was thought and felt by the 5,000 sick ones to whom he personally ministered and freely gave a physician's care; who could possibly record the reflections of his townsmen who had seen him sink almost within the grasp of oblivion, then rise to anonymous world renown; who could express the gratitude of those tens of thousands of AA families who had so well heard of him but had never seen him face to face? What, too, were the emotions of those nearest him as they thankfully pondered the mystery of his regeneration fifteen years ago and all its vast consequence since? Not the smallest fraction of this great benefaction could be comprehended. He could only declare, "What indeed hath God wrought?"

Never would Dr. Bob have us think him saint or superman. Nor would he have us praise him or grieve his passing. He can almost be heard, saying, "Seems to me you folks are making heavy going. I'm not to be taken so seriously as all that. I was only a first link in that chain of providential circumstance which is called AA. By grace and great fortune my link did not break; though my faults and failures might often have brought on that unhappy result. I was just another alcoholic trying to get along — under the grace of God. Forget me, but go you and do likewise. Securely add your own link to our chain. With God's help, forge that chain well and truly." In this manner would Dr. Bob estimate himself and counsel us.

It was a Saturday in May 1935. An ill-starred business venture had brought me to Akron where it immediately collapsed, leaving me in a precarious state of sobriety. That afternoon I paced the lobby of Akron's Mayflower Hotel. As I peered at the gathering crowd in the bar, I became desperately frightened of a slip. It was the first severe temptation since my New York friend had laid before me what were to become the basic principles of AA, in November 1934. For the next six months I had felt utterly secure in my sobriety. But now there was no security; I felt alone, helpless. In the months before I had worked hard with other alcoholics. Or, rather, I had preached at them in a somewhat cocksure fashion. In my false assurance I felt I couldn't fall. But this time it was different. Something had to be done at once.

Glancing at a church directory at the far end of the lobby, I selected the name of a clergyman at random. Over the phone I told him of my need to work with another alcoholic. Though I'd had no previous success with any of them I suddenly realized how such work had kept me free from desire. The clergyman gave me a list of ten names. Some of these people, he was sure, would refer me a case in need of help. Almost running to my room, I seized the phone. But my enthusiasm soon ebbed. Not a person in the first nine called could, or would, suggest anything to meet my urgency.

One uncalled name still stood at the end of my list — Henrietta Seiberling. Somehow I couldn't muster courage to lift the phone. But after one more look into the bar downstairs something said to me, "You'd better." To my astonishment a warm Southern voice floated in over the wire. Declaring herself no alcoholic, Henrietta nonetheless insisted that she understood. Would I come to her home at once?

Because she had been enabled to face and transcend other calamities, she certainly did understand mine. She was to become a vital link to those fantastic events which were presently to gather around the birth and development of our AA Society. Of all names the obliging rector had given me, she was the only one who cared enough. I would here like to record our timeless gratitude.

Straightaway, she pictured the plight of Dr. Bob and Anne. Suiting action to her word, she called their house. As Anne answered, Henrietta described me as a sobered alcoholic from New York who, she felt sure, could help Bob. The good doctor had seemingly exhausted all medical and spiritual remedies for his condition. Then Anne replied, "What you say, Henrietta, is terribly interesting. But I am afraid we can't do anything now. Being Mother's Day, my dear boy has just brought in a fine potted plant. The pot is on the table but, alas, Bob is on the floor. Could we try to make it tomorrow?" Henrietta instantly issued a dinner invitation for the following day.

At five o'clock next afternoon, Anne and Dr. Bob stood at Henrietta's door. She discreetly whisked Bob and me off to the library. His words were, "Mighty glad to meet you, Bill. But it happens I can't stay long; five or ten minutes at the outside." I laughed and observed, "Guess you're pretty thirsty, aren't you?" His rejoinder was, "Well, maybe you *do* understand this drinking business after all." So began a talk which lasted hours.

How different my attitude was this time. My fright of getting drunk had evoked a much more becoming humility. After telling Dr. Bob my story, I explained how truly I needed him. Would he allow me to help him, I might remain sober myself. The seed that was to flower as AA began to grow toward the light. But as dear Anne well guessed, that first tendril was a fragile thing. Practical steps had better be taken. She bade me come and live at their menage for a while. There I might keep an eye on Dr. Bob. And he might on me. This was the very thing. Perhaps we could do together what we couldn't do separately. Besides I might revive my sagging business venture.

For the next three months I lived with these two wonderful people. I shall always believe they gave me more than I ever brought them. Each morning there was devotion. After the long silence Anne would read out of the good book. James was our favorite. Reading him from her chair in the corner, she would softly conclude "Faith without works is dead."

But Bob's travail with alcohol was not quite over. That Atlantic City Medical Convention had to be attended. He hadn't missed one in twenty years. Anxiously waiting, Anne and I heard nothing for five days. Finally his office nurse and her husband found him early one morning at the Akron railroad station in some confusion and disarray — which puts it mildly. A horrible dilemma developed. Dr. Bob had to perform a critical surgical operation just three days hence. Nor could an associate substitute for him. He simply had to do it. But how? Could we ever get him ready in time?

He and I were placed in twin beds. A typical tapering down process was inaugurated. Not much sleep for anybody, but he cooperated. At four o'clock on the morning of the operation he turned, looked at me, and said, "I am going through with this." I inquired, "You mean you are going through with the operation?" He replied, "I have placed both the operation and myself in God's hands. I'm going to do what it takes to get sober and stay that way." Not another word did he say. At nine o'clock he shook miserably as we helped him into his clothes. We were panic stricken. Could he ever do it? Were he too tight or too shaky, it would make little difference, his misguided scalpel might take the life of his patient. We gambled. I gave him one bottle of beer. That was the last drink he ever took. It was June 10, 1935. The patient lived.

Our first prospect appeared; a neighboring parson sent him over. Because the newcomer faced eviction, Anne took in his whole family, wife and two children. The new one was a puzzler. When drinking, he'd go clean out of his mind. One afternoon Anne sat at her kitchen table, calmly regarding him as he fingered a carving knife. Under her steady gaze, his hand dropped. But he did not get sober then. His wife despairingly betook herself to her own parents and he disappeared. But he did reappear fifteen years later for Dr. Bob's last rites. There we saw him, soundly and happily sober in AA. Back in 1935 we weren't so accustomed to miracles as we are today; we had given him up.

Then came a lull on the Twelfth Step front. In this time Anne and Henrietta infused much needed spirituality into Bob and me. Lois came to Akron on vacation from her grind at a New York department store, so raised our morale immensely. We began to attend Oxford Group meetings at the Akron home of T. Henry Williams. The devotion of this good man and his wife is a bright page in memory. Their names will be inscribed on page one of AA's book of first and best friends.

One day Dr. Bob said to me, "Don't you think we'd better scare up some drunks to work on?" He phoned the nurse in charge of admissions at Akron City Hospital and told her how he and another drunk from New York had a cure for alcoholism. I saw the old boy blush and look disconcerted. The nurse had commented, "Well, Doctor, you'd better give that cure a good workout on yourself."

Nevertheless the admitting nurse produced a customer. A dandy, she said he was. A prominent Akron lawyer, he had lost about everything. He'd been in City Hospital six times in four months. He'd arrived at that very moment; had just knocked down a nurse he'd thought was a pink elephant. "Will that one do you?" she inquired. Said Dr. Bob, "Put him in a private room. We'll be down when he's better."

Soon Dr. Bob and I saw a sight which tens of thousands of us have since beheld, the sight of the man on the bed who does not yet know he can get well. We explained to the man on the bed the nature of his malady and told him our own stories of drinking and recovery. But the sick one shook his head, "Guess you've been through the mill boys, but you never were half as bad off as I am. For me it's too late. I don't dare go out of here. I'm a man of faith, too; used to be deacon in my church. I've still faith in God but I guess he hasn't got any in me. Alcohol has me, it's no use. Come and see me again, though. I'd like to talk with you more."

As we entered his room for our second visit a woman sitting at the foot of his bed was saying, "What has happened to you, husband? You seem so different. I feel so relieved." The new man turned to us. "Here they are," he cried. "They understand. After they left yesterday I couldn't get what they told me out of my mind, I lay awake all night. Then hope came. If they could find release, so might I. I became willing to get honest with myself, to square my wrongdoing, to help other alcoholics. The minute I did this I began to feel different. I knew I was going to be well." Continued the man on the bed, "Now, good wife, please fetch me my clothes. We are going to get up and out of here." Whereupon AA number three arose from his bed, never to drink again. The seed of AA had pushed another tendril up through the new soil. Though we knew it not, it had already flowered. Three of us were gathered together. Akron's Group One was a reality.

We three worked with scores of others. Many were called but mighty few chosen; failure was our daily companion. But when I left Akron in September 1935, two or three more sufferers had apparently linked themselves to us for good.

The next two years marked the "flying blind" period of our pioneering time. With the fine instinct of that good physician he was, Dr. Bob continued to medically treat and indoctrinate every new case, first at Akron City Hospital, then for the dozen years since at famed St. Thomas where thousands passed under his watchful eye and sure AA touch. Though not of his faith, the staff and sisters there did prodigies. Theirs is one of the most compelling examples of love and devotion we AAs have ever witnessed. Ask the thousands of AA visitors and patients who really know. Ask them what they think of Sister Ignatia, of St. Thomas. Or of Dr. Bob. But I'm getting ahead of my story.

Meanwhile a small group had taken shape in New York. The Akron meeting at T. Henry's home began to have a few Cleveland visitors. At this juncture I spent a week visiting Dr. Bob. We commenced to count noses. Out of hundreds of alcoholics, how many had stuck? How many were sober? And for how long? In that fall of 1937 Bob and I counted forty cases who had significant dry time — maybe sixty years for the whole lot of them! Our eyes glistened. Enough time had elapsed on enough cases to spell out something quite new, perhaps something great indeed. Suddenly the ceiling went up. We no longer flew blind. A beacon had been lighted. God had shown alcoholics how it might be passed from hand to hand. Never shall I forget that great and humbling hour of realization, shared with Dr. Bob.

But the new realization faced us with a great problem, a momentous decision. It had taken nearly three years to effect forty recoveries. The United States alone probably had a million alcoholics. How were we to get the story to them? Wouldn't we need paid workers, hospitals of our own, lots of money? Surely we must have some sort of a textbook. Dare we crawl at a snail's pace whilst our story got garbled and mayhap thousands would die? What a poser that was!

How we were spared from professionalism, wealth, and extensive property management; how we finally came up with the book *Alcoholics Anonymous* is a story by itself. But in this critical period it was Dr. Bob's prudent counsel which so often restrained us from rash ventures that might have retarded us for years, perhaps ruined us for good. Nor can we ever forget the devotion of Dr. Bob and Jim S. (who passed away last summer) as they gathered stories for the AA Book, three-fifths of them coming from Akron alone. Dr. Bob's special fortitude and wisdom were prime factors in that time so much characterized by doubt, and finally by grave decision.

How much we may rejoice that Anne and Dr. Bob both lived to see the lamp lit at Akron carried into every corner of the earth; that they doubtless realized millions might someday pass under the ever widening arch whose keystone they so gallantly helped carve. Yet, being so humble as they were, I'm sure they never quite guessed what a heritage they left us, nor how beautifully their appointed task had been completed. All they needed to do was finished. It was even reserved for Dr. Bob to see AA come of age as, for the last time, he spoke to 7,000 of us at Cleveland, July 1950.

I saw Dr. Bob the Sunday before he died. A bare month previous he had aided me in framing a proposal for the General Service Conference of Alcoholics Anonymous, AA's Third Legacy. This bequest, in pamphlet form, was actually at the printers when he took his final departure the following Thursday. As his last act and desire respecting AA, this document will be sure to carry a great and special meaning for us all.

With no other person have I ever experienced quite the same relation: The finest thing I know how to say is that in all the strenuous time of our association, he and I never had an uncomfortable difference of opinion. His capacity for brotherhood and love was often beyond my ken.

For a last word, may I leave with you a moving example of his simplicity and humility. Curiously enough, the story is about a monument — a monument proposed for him. A year ago, when Anne passed away, the thought of an imposing shaft came uppermost in the minds of many. People were insistent that something be done. Hearing rumors of this, Dr. Bob promptly declared against AAs erecting for Anne and himself any tangible memorial or monument. These usual symbols of personal distinction he brushed aside in a single devastating sentence. Said he, "Annie and I plan to be buried just like other folks."

At the alcoholic ward in St. Thomas his friends did, however, erect this simple plaque. It reads: "In Gratitude: The friends of Dr. Bob and Anne Smith affectionately dedicate this memorial to the sisters and staff of St. Thomas Hospital. At Akron, birthplace of Alcoholics Anonymous, St. Thomas Hospital became the first religious institution ever to open its door to our Society. May the loving devotion of those who labored here in our pioneering time be a bright and wondrous example of God's grace everlastingly set before us all."

He Kept the Faith

November 1954

Bill D., AA Number Three, died in Akron Friday night, September 17, 1954. That is, people say he died, but he really didn't. His spirit and works are today alive in the hearts of uncounted AAs, and who can doubt that Bill already dwells in one of those many mansions in the great beyond.

Nineteen years ago last summer, Dr. Bob and I saw him for the first time. Bill lay on his hospital bed and looked at us in wonder.

Two days before this, Dr. Bob had said to me, "If you and I are going to stay sober, we had better get busy." Straightaway, Bob called Akron's City Hospital and asked for the nurse on the receiving ward. He explained that he and a man from New York had a cure for alcoholism. Did she have an alcoholic customer on whom it could be tried? Knowing Bob of old, she jokingly replied, "Well, Doctor, I suppose you've already tried it yourself?"

Yes, she did have a customer — a dandy. He just arrived in DTs. Had blacked the eyes of two nurses, and now they had him strapped down tight. Would this one do! After prescribing medicines, Dr. Bob ordered, "Put him in a private room. We'll be down as soon as he clears up."

We found we had a tough customer in Bill. According to the nurse, he had been a well-known attorney in Akron and a city councilman. But he had landed in the Akron City Hospital four times in the last six months. Following each release, he got drunk even before he could get home.

So here we were, talking to Bill, the first "man on the bed." We told him about our drinking. We hammered it into him that alcoholism was an obsession of the mind, coupled to an allergy of the body. The obsession, we explained, condemned the alcoholic to drink against his will and the allergy, if he went on drinking, could positively guarantee his insanity or death. How to unhook that fatal compulsion, how to restore the alcoholic to sanity, was, of course, the problem.

Hearing this bad news, Bill's swollen eyes opened wide. Then we took the hopeful tack, we told what we had done: how we got honest with ourselves as never before, how we had talked our problems out with each other in confidence, how we tried to make amends for harm done others, how we had then been miraculously released from the desire to drink as soon as we had humbly asked God, as we understood him, for guidance and protection.

Bill didn't seem too impressed. Looking sadder than ever, he wearily ventured, "Well, this is wonderful for you fellows, but can't be for me. My case is so terrible that I'm scared to go out of this hospital at all. You don't have to sell me religion, either. I was at one time a deacon in the church and I still believe in God. But I guess he doesn't believe much in me."

Then Dr. Bob said, "Well, Bill, maybe you'll feel better tomorrow.

Wouldn't you like to see us again?''

"Sure I would," replied Bill, "Maybe it won't do any good. But I'd like to see you both, anyhow. You certainly know what you are talking about.''

Looking in next day, we found Bill with his wife, Henrietta. Eagerly he pointed to us saying, "These are the fellows I told you about, they are the ones who understand.''

Bill then related how he had lain awake nearly all night. Down in the pit of his depression, new hope had somehow been born. The thought flashed through his mind, "If they can do it, I can do it." Over and over he said this to himself. Finally, out of this hope, there burst conviction. Now he was sure. Then came a great joy. At length peace stole over him and he slept.

Before our visit was over, Bill suddenly turned to his wife and said, "Go fetch my clothes, dear. We're going to get up and get out of here.'' Bill D. walked out of that hospital a free man, never to drink again. AA's Number One Group dates from that very day.

The force of the great example that Bill set in our pioneering time will last as long as AA itself.

Bill kept the faith — what more could we say?

Dr. A. Weise Hammer

May 1957

T his simple account of the passing of one of America's finest surgeons stirs memories that will always be bright in the annals of Alcoholics Anonymous. Dr. A. Wiese Hammer was one of the best friends that AA will ever have.

Several of Philadelphia's old-time members have written up the full story of Dr. Hammer and his benefactions. And here is the substance of what they had to say:

It was February 1940. Jim, a New York AA, had just moved to Philadelphia and he was trying to get a local bookstore to carry the book *Alcoholics Anonymous*. The bookstore's manager protested that his customers could have no possible interest in the book *Alcoholics Anonymous*. As for himself, he couldn't care less.

Overhearing this turndown, a lady standing nearby got into the act. She said she had sent *Alcoholics Anonymous* to her alcoholic nephew in Los Angeles. To the astonishment of the whole family, the problem boy had sobered up instantly and he had stayed that way for some three months. This was unheard of. Nevertheless, the bookstore manager remained unimpressed.

But when Helen Hammer heard of Jim's attempt to start the group at Philadelphia, her delight was boundless. She immediately led Jim and one of his new prospects to her surgeon husband.

Dr. Hammer in all that he undertook was a huge enthusiast. This full-blooded, ruddy-faced man had a zest for living which poured out of him right around the clock. And this joyous contagion he could spread to just about everybody he met. The moment he heard Jim's story about AA his good work for our Society began at once. As we shall see, it was not confined to Philadelphia only; Dr. Hammer went to bat for us nationally at a time when AA had great need for this kind of good friend.

Here is what Dr. Hammer did: opened his home to all AA members; secured the Philadelphia Group its first meeting rooms; introduced us to Dr. Stouffer, another great friend-to-be, who was then chief psychiatrist at the Philadelphia General Hospital; secured us treatment and visiting privileges there; had AAs speak before the county medical society; along with his good wife, Helen, attended nearly every AA meeting for years; gave free medical and surgical aid to every AA who wanted it; visited other cities to talk about AA and paid the expenses of the Philadelphia members he took along; offered to buy the Philadelphia Group its first clubhouse (which had to be declined); saw that his friend, Judge Curtis Bok, owner of the *Saturday Evening Post,* became interested in AA; and finally induced the judge to assign Jack Alexander to do the famous article in 1941 that made our Fellowship a national institution.

This is only an abbreviated list of Dr. Hammer's good works for our Society. Doubtless hundreds of his benefactions will never be known, except to those individual sufferers to whom he was so notably kind.

Then, too, I find it impossible to write about Dr. Hammer without the happy recollection of Dr. Dudley Saul, another noted Philadelphia physician who constantly vied with Dr. Hammer in good works for us drunks.

To our intense astonishment *— and always to our great benefit —
these two great gentlemen fiercely competed with each other to figure
out something bigger and better they could do for Alcoholics Anonymous. This is a great story in itself which I'm going to tell one of these
days. How could AA in its infancy ever have survived without friends
such as these Philadelphia physicians who worked shoulder to shoulder
with Drs. Tiebout and Silkworth at New York?

To Helen Hammer I send AA's deepest sympathy and gratitude.
And I often wonder what her memories of our early days must be.

To Father Ed — Godspeed!

June 1960

E arly Sunday morning, April 3, Father Edward Dowling died peace-
fully in his sleep. The place was Memphis, Tennessee. Cheerfully
unmindful of his ebbing health, he had been visiting one of his "Cana"
groups. [A favorite undertaking which he founded, Father Ed's Cana
groups are dedicated, under church auspices, to the solution of difficult
family problems through the practice of AA's Twelve Steps.] Never was
there a gayer evening than in the hours before. He would have wanted to
take his leave of us in just that way. This was one of the most gentle souls
and finest friends we AAs may ever know. He left a heritage of inspiration and grace which will be with us always.

Father Ed had planned to be at our 1960 Long Beach Convention,
come July. This prospect, now to be unfulfilled, brings a moving recollection of his appearance at AA's St. Louis International Convention of
1955. It seems altogether fitting that I repeat the introduction I then
made of him, together with an account of the unforgettable impression
he left upon me the very first time we met — a fragment of history

recorded years afterward in *AA Comes of Age:*

"With deep joy, I present to you Father Ed Dowling who lives at the Jesuit House right here in St. Louis. Father Ed, knowing whence comes his strength, is definitely allergic to praise. Nonetheless I think that certain facts about him should be put into our record — facts that new generations of AAs ought to hear, read, and know.

"Father Ed helped to start the first AA group in this town; he was the first clergyman of his faith to note the surprising resemblance between the spiritual exercises of St. Ignatius (founder of the Jesuit order) and the Twelve Steps of Alcoholics Anonymous. As a result, he was quick to write in 1940 the first Catholic recommendation of AA of which we have any knowledge.

"Since then, his labor for us has been a prodigy. Not only have his recommendations been heard worldwide, but he has himself worked at AA and for AA. Travels, AA meetings, wise and tender counsel — these works of his can be measured in thousands of miles and thousands of hours.

"In my entire acquaintance, our friend Father Ed is the only one from whom I have never heard a resentful word and of whom I have never heard a single criticism. In my own life he has been a friend, adviser, great example, and the source of more inspiration than I can say.

"Father Ed is made of the stuff of the saints.'"...

"A great cheer of welcome greeted Father Ed Dowling as, indifferent to his grievous lameness, he made his way to the lectern. Father Dowling of the Jesuit order in St. Louis is intimately known to AAs for a thousand miles and more around. Many in the Convention audience remembered with gratitude his ministry to their spiritual needs. St. Louis old-timers recalled how he helped start their group; it had turned out to be largely Protestant, but this fazed him not a bit. Some of us could remember his first piece about us in *The Queen's Work,* the Sodality's magazine. He had been the first to note how closely in principle AA's Twelve Steps paralleled a part of the Exercises of St. Ignatius, a basic spiritual discipline of the Jesuit order. He had boldly written in effect to all alcoholics and especially to those of his own faith: 'Folks, AA is good. Come and get it.' And this they certainly had done. His first written words were the beginning of a wonderfully benign influence in favor of our Fellowship, the total of which no one will ever be able to compute.

"Father Ed's talk to us at the Convention that Sunday morning flashed with humor and deep insight. As he spoke, the memory of his first appearance in my own life came back to me as fresh as though it were yesterday: One wintry night in 1940, in AA's old Twenty-Fourth Street Club in New York, I had gone to bed at about ten o'clock with a severe dose of self-pity and my imaginary ulcer. Lois was out somewhere. Hail and sleet beat on the tin roof over my head; it was a wild night. The Club was deserted except for old Tom, the retired fireman, that diamond in the rough lately salvaged from Rockland asylum. The front doorbell clanged, and a moment later Tom pushed open my bedroom door. 'Some bum,' said he, 'from St. Louis is down there and wants to see you.' 'Oh, Lord!' I said. 'Not another one! And at this time of night. Oh, well, bring him up.'

"I heard labored steps on the stairs. Then, balanced precariously on his cane, he came into the room, carrying a battered black hat that was shapeless as a cabbage leaf and plastered with sleet. He lowered himself into my solitary chair, and when he opened his overcoat I saw his clerical collar. He brushed back a shock of white hair and looked at me through the most remarkable pair of eyes I have ever seen. We talked about a lot of things, and my spirits kept on rising, and presently I began to realize that this man radiated a grace that filled the room with a sense of presence. I felt this with great intensity; it was a moving and mysterious experience. In years since I have seen much of this great friend, and whether I was in joy or in pain he always brought to me the same sense of grace and the presence of God. My case is no exception. Many who meet Father Ed experience this touch of the eternal. It is no wonder that he was able to fill all of us there in the Kiel Auditorium with his inimitable spirit on that wonderful Sunday morning."

Everyone then present will remember this famous quote from Father Ed's St. Louis talk:

"There is a negative approach from agnosticism. This was the approach of Peter the Apostle. 'Lord, to whom shall we go?' I doubt if there is anybody in this hall who really ever sought sobriety. I think we were trying to get away from drunkenness. I don't think we should despise the negative. I have a feeling that if I ever find myself in Heaven, it will be from backing away from Hell."

In Remembrance of Ebby

June 1966

I n his seventieth year, and on the twenty-first of March, my friend and sponsor Ebby passed beyond our sight and hearing.

On a chill November afternoon in 1934 it was Ebby who had brought me the message that saved my life. Still more importantly, he was the bearer of the grace and of the principles that shortly afterward led to my spiritual awakening. This was truly a call to new life in the spirit. It was the kind of rebirth that has since become the most precious possession of each and all of us.

As I looked upon him where he lay in perfect repose, I was stirred by poignant memories of all the years I had known and loved him.

There were recollections of those joyous days in a Vermont boarding school. After the war years we were sometimes together, then drinking of course. Alcohol, we thought, was the solvent for all difficulties, a veritable elixir for good living.

Then there was that absurd episode of 1929. Ebby and I were on an all-night spree in Albany. Suddenly we remembered that a new airfield had been constructed in Vermont, on a pasture near my own home town. The opening day was close at hand. Then came the intoxicating thought: If only we could hire a plane we'd beat the opening by several days, thus making aviation history ourselves! Forthwith, Ebby routed a pilot friend out of bed, and for a stiff price we engaged him and his small craft. We sent the town fathers a wire announcing the time of our arrival. In mid-morning, we took to the air, greatly elated — and very tight.

Somehow our rather tipsy pilot set us down on the field. A large crowd, including the village band and a welcoming committee, lustily cheered his feat. The pilot then deplaned. But nothing else happened, nothing at all. The onlookers stood in puzzled silence. Where were Ebby and Bill? Then the horrible discovery was made — we were both slumped in the rear cockpit of the plane, completely passed out! Kind friends lifted us down and stood us upon the ground. Whereupon we history-makers fell flat on our faces. Ignominiously, we had to be carted away. The fiasco could not have been more appalling. We spent the next day shakily writing apologies.

Over the following five years, I seldom saw Ebby. But of course our drinking went on and on. In late 1934 I got a terrific jolt when I learned that Ebby was about to be locked up, this time in a state mental hospital.

Following a series of mad sprees, he had run his father's new Packard off the road and into the side of a dwelling, smashing right into its kitchen, and just missing a terrified housewife. Thinking to ease this rather awkward situation, Ebby summoned his brightest smile and said, "Well, my dear, how about a cup of coffee?"

Of course, Ebby's lighthearted humor was quite lost on everyone concerned. Their patience worn thin, the town fathers yanked him into court. To all appearances, Ebby's final destination was the insane asylum. To me, this marked the end of the line for us both. Only a short time before, my physician, Dr. Silkworth, had felt obliged to tell Lois there was no hope of my recovery; that I, too, would have to be confined, else risk insanity or death.

But Providence would have it otherwise. It was presently learned that Ebby had been paroled into the custody of friends who (for the time being) had achieved their sobriety in the Oxford Groups. They brought Ebby to New York where he fell under the benign influence of AA's great friend-to-be, Dr. Sam Shoemaker, the rector of Calvary Episcopal Church. Much affected by Sam and the "O.G.," Ebby promptly sobered up. Hearing of my serious condition, he had straightaway come to our house in Brooklyn.

As I continued to recollect, the vision of Ebby looking at me across our kitchen table became wonderfully vivid. As most AAs know, he spoke to me of the release from hopelessness that had come to him (through the Oxford Groups) as the result of self-survey, restitution, outgoing helpfulness to others, and prayer. In short, he was proposing the attitudes and principles that I used later in developing AA's Twelve Steps to recovery.

It had happened. One alcoholic had effectively carried the message to another. Ebby had been enabled to bring me the gift of grace because he could reach me at depth through the language of the heart. He had pushed ajar that great gate through which all in AA have since passed to find their freedom under God.

In Memory of Harry

July 1966

By the time this issue of the Grapevine reaches its readers, the whole world of AA will have heard of the passing of our well-beloved friend, Dr. Harry M. Tiebout, the first psychiatrist ever to hold up the hands of our Fellowship for all to see. His gifts of courageous example, deep perception of our needs, and constant labor in our behalf have been — and always will be — values quite beyond our reckoning.

It began like this: The year was early 1939, and the book *Alcoholics Anonymous* was about to hit the press. To help with the final edit of that volume we had made prepublication copies in multigraph form. One of them fell into Harry's hands. Though much of the content was then alien to his own views, he read our upcoming book with deep interest. Far more significantly, he at once resolved to show the new volume to a couple of his patients, since known to us as Marty and Grenny. These were the toughest kind of customers, and seemingly hopeless.

At first, the book made little impression on this pair. Indeed, its heavy larding with the word God so angered Marty that she threw it out her window, flounced off the grounds of the swank sanitarium where she was, and proceeded to tie on a big bender.

Grenny didn't carry a rebellion quite so far; he played it cool.

When Marty finally turned up, shaking badly, and asked Dr. Harry what next to do, he simply grinned and said, "You'd better read that book again!" Back in her quarters, Marty finally brought herself to leaf through its pages once more. A single phrase caught her eye and it read, "We cannot live with resentment." The moment she admitted this to herself, she was filled with a "transforming spiritual experience."

Forthwith she attended a meeting. It was at Clinton Street, Brooklyn, where Lois and I lived. Returning to Blythewood, she found Grenny intensely curious. Her first words to him were these: "Grenny, we are not alone anymore!"

This was the beginning of recovery for both — recoveries that have lasted until this day. Watching their unfoldment, Harry was electrified. Only a week before they had both presented stone walls of obstinate resistance to his every approach. Now they talked, and freely. To Harry these were the facts — and brand new facts. Scientist and man of

courage that he was, Harry did not for a moment look the other way.
Setting aside his own convictions about alcoholism and its neurotic
manifestations, he soon became convinced that AA had something, perhaps something big.

All the years afterward, and often at very considerable risk to his
professional standing, Harry continued to endorse AA. Considering
Harry's professional standing, this required courage of the highest order.

Let me share some concrete examples. In one of his early medical
papers, that noted one on "Surrender," he had declared this ego-reducing practice to be not only basic to AA, but also absolutely fundamental
to his own practice of psychiatry. This took humility as well as fortitude.
It will always be a bright example for us all.

Nevertheless this much was but a bare beginning. In 1944, helped by
Dr. Kirby Collier of Rochester and Dwight Anderson of New York,
Harry had persuaded the American Medical Society of the State of New
York to let me, a layman, read a paper about AA at their annual gathering. Five years later this same trio, again spearheaded by Harry,
persuaded the American Psychiatric Association to invite the reading of
another paper by me — this time in their 1949 Annual Meeting at Montreal. By then, AA had about 100,000 members, and many psychiatrists
had already seen at close range our impact on their patients.

For us of AA who were present at that gathering it was a breathtaking hour. My presentation would be "the spiritual experience," as we
AAs understood it. Surely we could never get away with this! To our
astonishment the paper was extremely well received — judging, at least,
from the sustained applause.

Immediately afterward, I was approached by a most distinguished
old gentleman. He introduced himself as an early president of the
American Psychiatric Association. Beaming, he said: "Mr. W., it is very
possible that I am the only one of my colleagues here today who really
believes in 'spiritual experience' as you do. Once upon a time, I myself
had an awakening much akin to your own, an experience that I shared in
common with two close friends, Bucke and Whitman."

Naturally I inquired, "But why did your colleagues seem to like the
paper?"

His reply went like this: "You see, we psychiatrists deeply know
what very difficult people you alcoholics really are. It was not the claims
of your paper that stirred my friends, it was the fact that AA can sober
up alcoholics wholesale."

Seen in this light, I was the more deeply moved by the generous and magnificent tribute that had been paid to us of AA. My paper was soon published in the *American Psychiatric Journal,* and our New York Headquarters was authorized by the association to make all the reprints we wished for distribution. By then the trek of AA overseas had well begun. Heaven only knows what this invaluable reprint accomplished when it was presented to psychiatrists in distant places by the fledgling AA groups. It vastly hastened the worldwide acceptance of AA.

I could go on and on about Harry, telling you of his activities in the general field of alcoholism, of his signal service on our AA board of trustees. I could tell stories of my own delightful friendship with him, especially remembering his great good humor and infectious laugh. But the space allotted me is too limited.

For Sister Ignatia

August 1966

S ister Mary Ignatia, one of the finest friends that we of AA shall ever know, went to her reward Friday morning, April 2, 1966. Next day, the Sisters of Charity of St. Augustine opened their Mother House to visitors. More than one thousand of them signed the guest book in the first two hours. These were the first of many who during the two days following came to pay their respects to Sister.

On Monday at high noon, the Cathedral at Cleveland could barely seat its congregation. Friends in the city and from afar attended the service. The Sisters of Charity themselves were seen to be seated in a body, radiant in their faith. Together with families and friends, we of AA had come there in expression of our gratitude for the life and works of our well-loved Sister. It was not really a time for mourning; it was instead a time to thank God for his great goodness to us all.

In its affirmation of the faith, the Mass was of singular beauty; the more so to many, since it was spoken in English. The eulogy, written and read by a close friend of Sister's, was a graphic and stirring portrayal of her character and of her deeds. There was a most special emphasis upon the merits of AA, and upon the part co-founder Dr. Bob had played in Sister's great adventure among us. We were assured as seldom before that those who dwell in the fellowship of the spirit need never be concerned with barriers or with boundaries.

For those thousands of men, women, and children whose lives had been directly touched and illumined by Sister, it would perhaps not be needful to write this account of her. Of Sister, and of the grace she brought to all these, they already know better than anyone else. But to the many others who have never felt her presence and her love, it is hoped this narrative may be something for their special inspiration.

Born in 1889 of devout and liberty-loving parents, Sister entered into this world at Shanvilly, County Mayo, of the Emerald Isle. The famed poet Yeats, born nearby, once remarked that the strange beauty of County Mayo had been specially designed to raise up poets, artists, heroes, and saints. We can little doubt that even when Ignatia was aged six, and her parents had emigrated from Ireland to Cleveland, she was already beginning to manifest many a sterling virtue.

Soon the child began to reveal unusual musical talents, both for piano and voice. A few years later she was seen giving lessons at the home of her parents. During 1914, she became possessed of a great desire to become a religious. In this year she joined the community that many of us AAs know so well — the Sisters of Charity of St. Augustine. There she continued her musical education and her teaching.

But even then, as ever since, Sister was frail, exceeding frail. By 1933 the rigors of her music teaching had become too great. She had a really serious physical breakdown. Her doctor put to her this choice: "You will have to take it easy. You can either be a dead music teacher or a live Sister. Which is it going to be?"

With great good cheer, so her community says, Mary Ignatia accepted a much quieter and less distinguished assignment. She became the registrar at St. Thomas Hospital in Akron, Ohio — an institution administered by her order. At the time it was wondered if she could manage even this much. That she would live to the age of seventy-seven was not believable; that she was destined to minister to 15,000 alcoholics and their families in the years to come was known only to God.

For a considerable time Sister serenely carried on at the admissions desk in St. Thomas. It was not then certain she had ever heard of AA.

Though Group One at Akron and Group Two in New York had been in slow and fitful growth since 1935, neither had come to public notice.

However, in 1939, the scene changed abruptly. In the spring of that year the AA Book was first printed, and *Liberty* magazine came up with an article about our Society in the early fall. This was quickly followed by a whole series of remarkable pieces which were carried by the Cleveland *Plain Dealer* on its editorial page. The newspaper and the mere two dozen AAs then in town were swamped by frantic pleas for help. Despite this rather chaotic situation, the Cleveland membership burgeoned into several hundreds in a few months.

Nevertheless, the implications of this AA population explosion were in some ways disturbing, especially the lack of proper hospital facilities. Though the Cleveland hospitals had rallied gallantly to this one emergency, their interest naturally waned when bills often went unpaid, and when ex-drunks trooped through the corridors to do what they called "Twelfth Step" work on sometimes noisy victims just arrived. Even the City Hospital at Akron, where Dr. Bob had attended numerous cases, was showing signs of weariness.

In New York we had temporarily got off to a better start. There we had dear old Dr. Silkworth and, after a while, his wonderful AA nurse Teddy. This pair were to "process" some 12,000 New York area drunks in the years ahead, and so they became, as it were, the "opposite numbers" to the partnership of co-founder Dr. Bob and Sister Ignatia at Akron.

Much concerned that, hospital-wise, his area might be caught quite unprepared to cope with a great new flood of publicity about AA, Dr. Bob in 1940 decided to visit St. Thomas and explain the great need for a hospital connection that could prove permanently effective. Since St. Thomas was a church institution, he thought the people there might vision a fine opportunity for service where the others had not. And how right he was!

But Bob knew no one in authority at the hospital. So he simply betook himself to Admissions and told the diminutive nun in charge the story of AA, including that of his own recovery. As this tale unfolded, the little sister glowed. Her compassion was deeply touched and perhaps her amazing intuition had already begun to say, "This is it." Of course Sister would try to help, but what could one small nun do? After all, there *were* certain attitudes and regulations. Alcoholism had not been reckoned as an illness; it was just a dire form of gluttony!

Dr. Bob then told Sister about an alcoholic who then was in a most serious condition. A bed would simply have to be found for him. Said Mary Ignatia, "I'm sure your friend must be very sick. You know, Doctor, this sounds to me like a terrible case of indigestion." Trying to keep a straight face, Dr. Bob replied, "How right you are — his indigestion *is* most terrible." Twinkling, Sister immediately said, "Why don't you bring him in right away?"

The two benign conspirators were soon faced with yet another dilemma. The victim proved to be distressingly intoxicated. It would soon be clear to all and sundry that his "indigestion" was quite incidental. Obviously a ward wouldn't do. There would have to be a private room. But all the single ones were filled. What on earth could they do? Sister pursed her lips and then broke into a broad smile. Forthwith she declared, "I'll have a bed moved into our flower room. In there he can't disturb anyone." This was hurriedly done, and the indigestion sufferer was already on his way to sobriety and health.

Of course the conspirators were conscience-stricken by their subterfuge of the flower room. And anyhow, the indigestion pretense simply couldn't last. Somebody in authority would have to be told, and that somebody was the hospital's Superior. With great trepidation, Sister and Dr. Bob waited upon this good lady, and explained themselves. To their immense delight she went along, and a little later she boldly unfolded the new project before the St. Thomas trustees. To their everlasting credit they went along too — so much so that it was not a great while before Dr. Bob himself was invited to become a staff physician at St. Thomas, a bright example indeed of the ecumenical spirit.

Presently a whole ward was devoted to the rehabilitation of alcoholics, and Sister Ignatia was of course placed in immediate charge. Dr. Bob sponsored the new cases into the hospital and medically treated each, never sending a bill to any. The hospital fees were very moderate and Sister often insisted on taking in patients on a "pay later" basis, sometimes to the mild consternation of the trustees.

Together Ignatia and Dr. Bob indoctrinated all who cared to listen to the AA approach as portrayed by the book *Alcoholics Anonymous,* lately come off the press. The ward was open to visiting AAs from surrounding groups who, morning to night, told their stories of drinking and of recovery. There were never any barriers of race or creed; neither was AA nor church teaching pressed upon anyone.

Since nearly all her strenuous hours were spent there, Sister became a central figure on the ward. She would alternately listen and talk, with infinite tenderness and understanding. The alcoholic's family and friends received the very same treatment. It was this most compassionate caring that was a chief ingredient of her unique grace; it magnetically drew everyone to her, even the most rough and obstinate. Yet she would not always stand still for arrant nonsense. When the occasion required, she could really put her foot down. Then to ease the hurt, she would turn on her delightful humor. Once, when a recalcitrant drunk boasted he'd never again be seen at the hospital, Sister shot back, "Well, let's hope *not*. But just in case you *do* show up, please remember that we already have your size of pajamas. They will be ready and waiting for you!"

As the fame of St. Thomas grew, alcoholics flocked in from distant places. After their hospitalization they often remained for a time in Akron to get more firsthand AA from Dr. Bob, and from Akron's Group Number One. On their return home, Sister would carry on an ever mounting correspondence with them.

We AAs are often heard to say that our Fellowship is founded upon resources that we have drawn from medicine, from religion, and from our own experience of drinking and of recovery. Never before nor since those Akron early days have we witnessed a more perfect synthesis of all these healing forces. Dr. Bob exemplified both medicine and AA; Ignatia and the Sisters of St. Augustine also practiced applied medicine, and their practice was supremely well animated by the wonderful spirit of their community. A more perfect blending of grace and talent cannot be imagined.

It should never be necessary to dwell, one by one, upon the virtues of these magnificent friends of AA's early time — Sister Ignatia and co-founder Dr. Bob. We need only recollect that "by their fruits we shall always know them."

Standing before the Cleveland International Convention of 1950, Dr. Bob looked upon us of AA for the last time. His good wife Anne had passed on before, and his own rendezvous with the new life to come was not many months away.

Ten years had slipped by since the day when he and Sister had bedded down that first sufferer in the St. Thomas flower room. In this marvelous decade, Sister and Dr. Bob had medically treated, and had spiritually infused, five thousand alcoholics. The greater part of these had found their freedom under God.

In thankful recollection of this great work, we of AA presented to the Sisters of Charity of St. Augustine and to the staff of the St. Thomas Hospital a bronze plaque, ever since to be seen in the ward where Sister and Dr. Bob had wrought their wonders. The plaque reads as follows:

"In Gratitude:
The friends of Dr. Bob and Anne S.
affectionately dedicate this memorial
to the Sisters and staff of
St. Thomas Hospital.
At Akron, birthplace of Alcoholics
Anonymous, St. Thomas Hospital became
the first religious institution ever
to open its door to our Society.
May the loving devotion of those who
labored here in our pioneering time
be a bright and wondrous example
of God's grace everlastingly set
before us all.

Visitors at St. Thomas today often wonder why this inscription says not a word about Sister Ignatia. Well, the fact was, she wouldn't allow her name to be used. She had flatly refused; it was one of those times when she had put her foot down! This was of course a glowing example of her innate and absolutely genuine humility. Sister truly believed that she deserved no particular notice; that such grace as she might have could only be credited to God and to the community of her sisters.

This was indeed the ultimate spirit of anonymity. We who had then seen this quality in her were deeply affected, especially Dr. Bob and myself. Hers came to be the influence that persuaded us both never to accept public honors of any sort. Sister's example taught that a mere observance of the form of AA anonymity should never become the slightest excuse for ignoring its spiritual substance.

Following Dr. Bob's death, there was great concern lest Sister might not be allowed to continue her work. As in other orders of the church, service assignments among the Sisters of Charity were rather frequently rotated. This was the ancient custom. However, nothing happened for a time. Assisted by surrounding AA groups, Sister continued to carry on at St. Thomas. Then suddenly in 1952, she was transferred to St. Vincent Charity Hospital at Cleveland, where, to the delight of us all, she was placed in charge of its alcoholic ward. At Akron a fine successor was named to succeed her; the work there would continue.

The ward at Charity occupied part of a dilapidated wing, and it was in great need of repair and rejuvenation. To those who knew and loved Sister, this opportunity proved a most stimulating challenge. The Charity trustees also agreed that something should be done. Substantial contributions flowed in. In their spare hours, AA carpenters, plumbers, and electricians set about redoing the old wing — no charge for their services. The beautiful result of these labors of love is now known as Rosary Hall.

Again the miracles of recovery from alcoholism commenced to multiply. During the following fourteen years, an astonishing 10,000 alcoholics passed through the portals of Rosary Hall, there to fall under the spell of Mary Ignatia and of AA. More than two-thirds of all these recovered from their dire malady, and again became citizens of the world. From dawn to dark Sister offered her unique grace to that endless procession of stricken sufferers. Moreover, she still found time to minister widely to their families and this very fruitful part of her work became a prime inspiration to the Al-Anon Family Groups of the whole region.

Notwithstanding her wonderful workers within the hospital, and help from AAs without, this must have been a most exacting and exhausting vocation for the increasingly frail Sister. That she was providentially enabled to be with us for so many years is something for our great wonder. To hundreds of friends it became worth a day's journey to witness her supreme and constant demonstration.

Toward the close of her long stewardship there were brushes with death. Sometimes I came to Cleveland and was allowed to sit by her bedside. Then I saw her at her best. Her perfect faith and her complete acceptance of whatever God might will were somehow implicit in all she said, be our conversation gay or serious. Fear and uncertainty seemed entire strangers to her. On my leave-taking, there was always that smiling radiance; always her prayerful hope that God might still allow her a bit more time at Rosary Hall. Then a few days later I would learn that she was back at her desk. This superb drama would be reenacted time after time. She was quite unconscious that there was anything at all unusual about it.

Realizing there would come the day which would be her last, it seemed right that we of AA should privately present Sister with some tangible token that could, even a little, communicate to her the depth of our love. Remembering her insistence, in respect of the Akron plaque, that she would not really like any public attention, I simply sent word that I'd like to come to Cleveland for a visit, and casually added that should her health permit, we might take supper together in the company of a few of her stalwart AA friends and co-workers. Besides, it was her fiftieth year of service in her community.

On the appointed evening, we foregathered in one of the small dining rooms at Charity Hospital. Plainly delighted, Sister arrived. She was barely able to walk. Since we were old-timers all, the dinner hour was spent in telling tales of other days. For her part, Sister regaled us with stories of St. Thomas and with cherished recollections of Anne and co-founder Dr. Bob. It was unforgettable.

Before Sister became too tired, we addressed ourselves to our main project. From New York, I had brought an illuminated scroll. Its word-ing was in the form of a letter addressed by me to Sister, and it was written on behalf of our AA Fellowship worldwide. I stood up, read the scroll aloud, and then held the parchment for her to see. She was taken by complete surprise and could scarcely speak for a time. In a low voice she finally said, "Oh, but this is too much — this is too good for me."

Our richest reward of the evening was of course Ignatia's delight; a joy unbounded the moment we assured her that our gift need not be publicized; that if she wished to stow it away in her trunk we would quite understand.

It then seemed that this most memorable and moving evening was over. But there was to be another inspiring experience. Making light of her great fatigue, Sister insisted that we all go up to Rosary Hall, there to make a late round of the AA ward. This we did, wondering if any of us would ever again see her at work in the divine vocation to which she had given her all. For each of us this was the end of an epoch; I could think only of her poignant and oft-repeated saying, "Eternity is now."

The scroll given to Sister may now be seen at Rosary Hall. This is the inscription:

In gratitude for Sister Mary Ignatia on the occasion of her golden jubilee:
Dear Sister,

We of Alcoholics Anonymous look upon you as the finest friend and the greatest spirit we may ever know.

We remember your tender ministrations to us in the days when AA was very young. Your partnership with Dr. Bob in that early time has created for us a spiritual heritage of incomparable worth.

In all the years since, we have watched you at the bedside of thou-sands. So watching, we have perceived ourselves to be the beneficiaries of that wondrous light which God has always sent through you to illu-mine our darkness. You have tirelessly tended our wounds; you have nourished us with your unique understanding and your matchless love. No greater gifts of grace than these shall we ever have.

Speaking for AA members throughout the world, I say: "May God abundantly reward you according to your blessed works — now and forever."

In devotion,
Bill W.

Sam Shoemaker

February 1967

D r. Sam Shoemaker was one of AA's indispensables. Had it not been for his ministry to us in our early time, our Fellowship would not be in existence today. Therefore the recent publication of his biography entitled *I Stand By the Door,* so well authored by his wife Helen, is a poignant reminder of our great debt and a welcome addition to our comprehension of this magnificent friend.

First let me acquaint our newer generations with the "Sam" we oldsters knew so well in the first days of AA, and in the years since. For this purpose I'd like to tell of Sam's appearance at our International Convention in 1955, held in St. Louis. I quote as follows from our book of history, *AA Comes of Age.*

"Dr. Sam looked scarcely a day older than he had almost twenty-one years earlier when I first met him and his dynamic group at Calvary's parish house in New York. As he began to speak, his impact fell upon us there in the Kiel Auditorium just as it had upon Lois and me years before. As always, he called a spade a spade, and his blazing eagerness, earnestness and crystal clarity drove home his message point by point. With all his vigor and power of speech, Sam nevertheless kept himself right down to size. Here was a man quite as willing to talk about *his* sins as about anybody else's. He made himself a witness of God's power and love just as any AA might have done.

"Sam's appearance before us was further evidence that many a channel had been used by Providence to create Alcoholics Anonymous. And none had been more vitally needed than the one opened through Sam Shoemaker and his Oxford Group, associates of a generation before. The early AA got its ideas of self-examination, acknowledgment of character defects, restitution for harm done, and working with others straight from the Oxford Group and directly from Sam Shoemaker, their onetime leader in America, and from nowhere else. He will always be found in our annals as the one whose inspired example and teaching did the most to show us how to create the spiritual climate in which we alcoholics may survive and then proceed to grow. AA owes a debt of timeless gratitude for all that God sent to us through Sam and his friends in the early days of AA's infancy.''

No one, I think, can read Helen Shoemaker's book, *I Stand By the Door,* without being the better for it This vivid and moving account of Sam at home, in his ministry, and in his public life is a portrait in breadth and in depth of one of the finest human beings of our time.

Bernard B. Smith

October 1970

I deeply regret that my health will not permit me to attend the services for my old friend Bern Smith. His death is a great personal loss to me, for I have leaned heavily upon him for many years. His wise counsel was always mine for the asking; the warmth of his friendship, mine from the beginning.

From the very beginning, Bern Smith understood the spiritual basis upon which the Society of Alcoholics Anonymous rests. Such an understanding is rare among outsiders. But Bern never was an outsider — not really. He not only understood our Fellowship, he believed in it as well.

Just one month ago today, Bern made a remarkable and inspiring talk to some 11,000 of our members gathered in Miami Beach to celebrate our Fellowship's thirty-fifth anniversary. The subject of his talk was Unity — truly an apt subject, for no man did more than he to assure unity within our Fellowship.

For that matter, he did much to assure our very survival, for he was one of the principal architects of our General Service Conference.

Bern Smith would not want, nor does he need, encomiums from me. What he has done for Alcoholics Anonymous speaks far louder than any words of mine could ever do. His wisdom and vision will be sorely missed by us all.

I can only add that I have lost an old and valued friend; AA, a great and devoted servant.

Articles About the Grapevine

Editorial: The Shape of Things to Come

June 1944

In the book *Alcoholics Anonymous* there is a chapter called "A Vision for You." Wandering through it recently, my eye was caught by this startling paragraph written a short five years ago. "Someday we hope that every alcoholic who journeys will find a Fellowship of Alcoholics Anonymous at his destination. To some extent this is already true. Some of us are salesmen and go about. Little clusters of twos and threes and fives of us have sprung up in other communities through contact with our two large centers...." Rubbing my eyes I looked again. A lump came into my throat. "Only five years," I thought. "Then but two large centers — little clusters of twos and threes — travelers who hoped one day to find us at every destination."

Could it be only yesterday that this was just a hope — those little clusters of twos and threes, those little beacons so anxiously watched as they flickered, but never went out.

And today, there are hundreds of centers shedding their warm illumination upon the lives of thousands, lighting the dark shoals where the stranded and hopeless lie breaking up — those fingers of light already stretching to our beachheads in other lands.

Now comes another lighted lamp — this little newspaper called the Grapevine. May its rays of hope and experience ever fall upon the current of our AA life and one day illumine every dark corner of this alcoholic world.

The aspirations of its editors, contributors, and readers could well be voiced in the last words of "A Vision for You": "Abandon yourself to God as you understand God. Admit your faults to him and your fellows. Clear away the wreckage of your past. Give freely of what you find, and join us. We shall be with you, in the Fellowship of the Spirit, and you will surely meet some of us as you trudge the Road of Happy Destiny. May God bless you and keep you — until then."

The Grapevine:
Past, Present, and Future

July 1945

The Grapevine has just completed the first year of its existence. Scores of enthusiastic letters are coming in. They are written from all parts of the United States and some from foreign countries. They congratulate the Grapevine staff and ask them to keep up their good work.

To these felicitations I'd like to add my own. A grand job has been done by the volunteer staff, who gave freely a vast amount of time and labor. And some gave money, too; you don't start a paper on hay. To the retiring volunteers, I want to say, along with every Grapevine subscriber, "Congratulations and thanks."

How did the Grapevine start, and where does it go from here?

Last summer several New York AAs decided it was about time the groups in our metropolitan area had a monthly publication. At first there was some discussion about getting it suitably endorsed by the local groups, the Alcoholic Foundation, or somebody. But no one could endorse a magazine that hadn't yet appeared. The Grapeviners went ahead anyway on the theory that if their sheet was good enough it would take on; if it proved too corny or dull it would flop automatically — and quickly! People could, the Grapeviners said, "take it or leave it alone."

In a burst of local pride the Grapevine staff mailed the first printing to all the groups in the United States. No pressure or soliciting. They just mailed it. Subscriptions began to filter in from everywhere. No longer a trickle, they are today a stream. The Grapevine now has subscribers in every one of the forty-eight states and even abroad.

Foreseeing a broader activity, members of the Grapevine staff were good enough to ask me a few months ago if I would take an interest in the venture for the coming year. They told me they thought the magazine might be enlarged to national dimensions; that ultimately it should be incorporated, and finally, perhaps, hooked up with the Alcoholic Foundation, which, as nearly every AA knows, is the sponsor of our Central Office and all our national undertakings.

This conversation made it abundantly plain that while rotating squads of volunteers might always continue to procure and edit pieces for the Grapevine and participate in setting its policy, there could be no doubt that continuous paid help and enlarged working facilities would soon be necessary. They asked if I would help with these arrangements and perhaps contribute a piece occasionally. These things, health permitting, I agreed to do.

Besides the volunteer staff, we now boast one part-time paid secretarial worker to help handle details. This work, however, continues to mount, as does the volume of potential editorial content. More paid help will probably become necessary and the size of the magazine may have to be expanded, all of which would require a slight increase in the subscription rate. The Grapevine is self-supporting now and should be kept that way always, rather than be dependent on subsidies or gratuities, to insure its continuity, quality, and service.

Though the Grapevine is young, it is commencing to have its own tradition. Every member of the staff aspires to make the paper a true voice of AA. All of us are very sensitive to the thought that it ought never to be sectional in its appeal nor should it take sides on any controversial question. While it must constantly talk of people, in its news and views, it ought never to glorify or belittle anyone, nor lend itself to a commercial undertaking, nor become a mere mouthpiece for any of us, even the Central Office or the Alcoholic Foundation. Of course, everybody will see pieces in the Grapevine now and then with which he or she will not agree. So it must always be understood that these pieces reflect the thoughts and feelings of their authors but not necessarily those of the Grapevine. To crystallize these traditions and principles we ask for more contributions from all parts of the country.

Meanwhile, please don't expect too much of us too quickly. We are still understaffed; we can't possibly answer all of your letters and inquiries. I am afraid that will have to go for me, too. I shall be unable to engage in personal correspondence. I can only write a piece to all of you now and then.

If agreeable to the subscribers I would like to discuss in coming issues such topics as anonymity, leadership, public relations, the use of money in AA, and the like. Upon matters such as these, our tradition and practice is by no means well settled. Like most older AAs, I have come to place great reliance on the ability of our groups to work out correct principles, once given sufficient experience. The purpose, therefore, of the forthcoming pieces will be to present the current thought, the pros and cons, on these moot questions. These articles will be suggestive only. Their object will be to promote further discussion rather than to announce any new principle.

We of the Grapevine once more affirm that this is your periodical. It will be the vehicle for your thoughts, your feelings, your experiences, and your aspirations — if you care to make it that. While we can only publish a fraction of the material which will come to hand you may be sure that we shall do our fairest and best in making the selections. Always wishing to reflect AA and nothing but AA, it will be the ideal of the Grapevine always to serve, never to dictate or command. Please help us make it a true voice.

What Is Our AA Grapevine?

December 1946

Hundreds of AAs have not yet seen or heard of the Grapevine. Others query, who is it? What is it? What are its ideals? So I have been asked to explain.

The Grapevine is our principal monthly journal. It is devoted to the interests of Alcoholics Anonymous — and to nothing else. It tries to publish the news and portray the views of AAs everywhere. It aims to reflect a cross section of our thought and action. Already reaching all parts of America, it is beginning to be read in foreign lands. Some of its 5,600 subscribers are nonalcoholics vitally interested in our progress and philosophy.

In short, the Grapevine is rapidly becoming "the collective voice of Alcoholics Anonymous." Like everything else that is good the Grapevine has been an evolution — not a promotion. Like Topsy, "it just grew." Now let me cut back into our past to let you see more of why and how the Grapevine came to be.

Ten years ago our Fellowship was a weak and wobbly infant — just a few alcoholics clinging desperately to an ideal and to each other. These early ones were the originators of the Alcoholics Anonymous movement. As our numbers swelled the newer members naturally looked to the older ones for help and example. They began to call us older ones leaders, and in the case of Dr. Bob and myself they coined for each of us the rather resounding title of founder. Since AA really had a score of founders he and I really wish that hadn't occurred. But it did — simply, we suppose, because we were the first in point of time and were therefore of the longest experience.

Thus it happened that we came to have, in the minds of our fellow AAs, a rather unique status. Never official, always informal, yet there it was. In matters of principle or policy AAs began to regard Bob and me as representing their collective conscience; they also began to think of us as a sort of heart to the movement which took in the constant stream of incoming problems and perplexities and then pumped out answers. Then as we went about among the growing groups, he and I were asked to stand on platforms and expound AA to ever larger audiences. So it was that we became the collective "voice of AA." As a friend put it, "That was a whale of a big order!''

Bob and I agree with him. It's too big an assignment for any two alcoholics. We're too fallible. And were we infallible we couldn't last forever anyhow. Hence he and I have been, for a long time now, in process of passing these functions of conscience, heart, and voice over to others.

Years ago we helped set up the Alcoholic Foundation whose trustees became guardians of your general AA funds, and who of late, by custom and general consent, are more and more regarded as the custodians of AA Tradition and general policy. The trustees are no body of authority. They simply act as a sort of general service committee to all AA. Primarily they are custodians and mediators. As such, they are beginning to be seen by the groups as representing our collective AA conscience. Bob and I hope that trend will continue. This seems likely as the trustees and their duties are becoming better understood.

A year after the creation of the Alcoholic Foundation, the book *Alcoholics Anonymous* was published in April 1939. This too was the enterprise of a group of AA members who thought our experience ought to be codified and set on paper. This group supplied funds, suggestions, and stories. Bob and I were given the task of deciding what should go into the book and I was assigned the writing of its text. The publication of the AA Book marked the point in our history where our early members, along with Bob and myself, transferred our experience through this new medium to an ever wider circle which now promises to be the wide world of alcoholism.

The AA Central Office at New York came into being simultaneously with the book. Here our staff nowadays answers thousands of inquiries, looks after our overall public relations, writes letters of encouragement to new and isolated groups, sees to the printing and distribution of group lists, pamphlets, literature and the book *Alcoholics Anonymous.* Several years ago the trustees of our Foundation acquired full ownership of the AA Book and at the same time assumed a custodial oversight of the Central Office whose financial support has gradually been taken over by the groups through their voluntary contributions to the Foundation. Thousands of new members have found their way to AA, hundreds of groups have been helped with their growing pains, and millions of people have heard of AA through the functioning of the Central Office. Little by little, our Central Office is becoming recognized as the heart of AA. It receives inquiries and problems, then pumps out information and the best answers it can. Thus one more function of the originators of AA is in process of transfer to the Central Office staff. The Central Office has almost become the central heart of AA.

"Now," you say, "what has all this got to do with the Grapevine?" Just this: Like the earlier groups which assembled the Foundation, the AA Book, and the Central Office, the Grapevine began two years ago among several newspaper-minded AAs who thought we needed a monthly periodical. They were willing to contribute a little money and boundless effort to make it a success. At the beginning, this group of AAs had no special authorization from anyone. They merely took off their coats and did a job, a job so well done that at the end of a year they found their paper in national distribution. There was no sponsoring, no promoting. Like the AA Book, the Central Office, and the Foundation, the Grapevine became a national institution on its own effort and merit.

Arrived at this point, members of the staff came to the trustees to discuss the future of the publication. They also asked me to write some pieces and requested me to ascertain if the groups would like to have this periodical as their principal AA publication. Hundreds of groups and individual subscribers came back with an enthusiastic "Yes." There was scarce a single dissent. Accordingly, the Grapevine was incorporated, its beneficial ownership transferred to the Foundation, and it is now being managed by a joint committee composed of two trustees of the Foundation, two members of the volunteer staff, and its editor. Not quite self-supporting yet, we hope it will presently become so. Consequently we are witnessing still another transference. The Grapevine is becoming the voice of Alcoholics Anonymous.

As one of the staff members recently put it, "We think that the Grapevine ought to become the 'voice of Alcoholics Anonymous,' bringing us news of each other across great distances, and always describing what can be freshly seen in that vast and life-giving pool we call 'AA experience.' Never taking part in the controversial issues of religion, reform, or politics, never seeking profit, never lending itself to commerce or propaganda, always mindful of our sole aim to carry the AA message to those who suffer alcoholism — such is our idea for the Grapevine."

With these sentiments Dr. Bob and I heartily concur. We hope that AAs everywhere will feel it to be their newspaper; that our able AA writers will contribute freely; that all groups will send in news of their doings which may be of general interest; that the Grapevine will presently take its place in the minds of all AAs as one of our essential central services close alongside the Foundation, the AA Book, and the Central Office.

You see, dear fellow members, Dr. Bob and I have a slightly ulterior motive! For, when the transfer of our original functions of conscience, heart, and voice is made complete to these newer, better, and more permanent agencies, then we old-timers can really take a walk!

Through the AA Looking Glass

November 1950

T his is a plug for the Grapeviners and all their works. May they live long and prosper.

One looks in one's mirror to powder, shave, or admire. But the good AA is apt to look deeper. Every morning he gives thanks for a sober countenance, he asks forgiveness for lingering resentment, he hopes for grace to live the coming day well. At nightfall he takes another look, saying, "Well, my friend, how did we do today? Thanks be to thee for the privilege of living."

Thus the AA's mirror reflects not rouge, but gratitude; not conceit, but humility; not froth, but reality. It reflects a priceless experience.

Reading the Grapevine is something kindred. But the Grapevine is a far bigger mirror. Here we get an inspiring glance over the other fellow's shoulder as he meditates. We're magically transported into the midst of our brothers and sisters everywhere. We feel at one with them. Alice in Wonderland was never like that. Through the AA looking glass we joyously roam the spacious mansion which Providence has provided us — that incredible freedom house called AA.

For the Grapevine is truly your magazine and mine. Its contents, month by month, are your thoughts, your ideas — about AA and anything else that may be on your mind. Each month more than two hundred of you, on an average, send in something to be printed. The Grapevine is not written by a bunch of high-domed ivory tower boys in New York. *You* write it.

With each issue, you see how ably the cream of your editorial contributions has been selected — and how skillfully presented in a publication which each one of us can be proud of. Perhaps you've wondered how this job is done so well each thirty days. Well, it's done as most everything else in AA is done — by AA members who pitch in and do it with no thought of reward other than to help. Unpaid, unsung, perhaps they've labored long enough in complete anonymity, even among their own fellows.

So, maybe, you'd like to meet the Grapeviners. They're the ones who capture those precious images for you. Each month they give you the freshest sights, sounds, and impressions of AA on the march. Grapevine is the magic carpet on which you can ride our circuit.

First off, here's Al, the editor. Al is supposed to be a hard-working feature writer for the newsreels. When he actually works for the pictures, nobody can say. Most of the time he's at the Grapevine office putting the paper to bed — or, maybe, getting it up in the morning. Whatever editors are supposed to do, Al really does. Read the Grapevine and you'll agree.

Now meet Clyde, Paul, Rod, and Sig. The first is a noted fiction editor; the second is a top rewrite man; the third is one of those advertising execs, and the fourth — well, he's somehow in public relations. All this brass probably checks Al up and surely backs him up. Now and then they dash off pieces themselves. Next come the art boys, Budd and Glen. Pretty keen, too. But they should be. They're top-hole art directors and illustrators on the outside. Have you seen the Grapevine art work lately? Better take a look. Or better still, subscribe.

At this point I present the Grapevine money experts. The fact it is running a deficit isn't their fault at all. In real life both of them, Mike and (another) Bud, are treasurers for publishing houses. Mike is also the Grapevine treasurer. He took over that bleak and thankless job from Dick S. (not the Cleveland Dick S.) a while back. Bud lingers on as a contributor and elder statesman for he is, you must know, one of the founders of our journal. To be dead sure everything is buttoned down tight, the Grapevine has two more money men — super money men. They're the Foundation trustees, Jonas and Leonard, who sit in with the Grapevine management.

The Grapevine and You and Me

June 1957

T he AA Grapevine has some plans which I would like to discuss with you and these plans include frequent articles by me. I shall try to write something to all of you each month during the next year.

Several considerations have prompted this resolve. The first is that Lois and I can no longer travel about to see you, face to face. We admit we are not quite so young as we used to be. If we go much of anywhere, then in fairness we ought to go everywhere. But "everywhere" in AA is now a lot of territory. It takes in North America, seventy overseas beachheads, and 200,000 AAs. If we journeyed out to see all of you, I guess we'd never get home! So this is a very good reason why I want to chat with you every month in the Grapevine. It can be the next best substitute for widespread travel.

Another reason is this. As AA grows in breadth and depth, so should the Grapevine, for this is the largest mirror we have of up-to-date AA thought, feeling, and activity. Thanks to its devoted workers and contributors of the past, our magazine has always managed to grow.

Periodically the Grapevine makes a special effort in this direction. One of these spurts is on right now. We want to catch up with worldwide AA in all of its new and fascinating facets and ramifications. We want to catch up with the old-timer who sometimes thinks, perhaps rightly, that our magazine is too much slanted to the problems of the newcomer.

So then, what can you and I do about it? First, we have to clear away a serious handicap. If a bigger and better journal is to be produced, its staff, paid and volunteer, will have to be enlarged — the paid people a little, the volunteers a lot. Both in subscription and editorial departments the magazine has long been understaffed.

The fact is that the Grapeviners have been waging a losing battle against inflation — a battle which has been going on a long time. At 25 cents, the price has stood unchanged for the last dozen or so years. It's about the only remaining article in the world that hasn't gone up, except perhaps "Life Savers" candies. Meantime the costs of putting out the periodical have soared, just like everything else. Even after the recent big push for subscriptions, the Grapevine still can't get by. This state of affairs is totally unsafe for the long run and it is a bar to any large improvement in size or quality, now or ever, under these conditions.

This spells it out that the price surely has to go up to 35 cents a copy or $3.50 a year. Of course, we know that everybody will be glad to give that extra dime for the Grapevine. A preliminary survey abundantly confirms that fact. This will take away the hurdle that our Grapeviners, for all of their dedication, can no longer surmount.

With this accomplished, you and I can still help a lot. The Grapevine wants to add sixteen more pages. It wants to add several departments: a news section, Al-Anon activities, and others. It wants more interest for our five- and ten-year members. It is looking hard for every promising new idea the staff can lay hands on.

Surely you and I could supply some of these much needed ideas.

So why don't you folks out there sit down and write me some "idea" letters? I don't mean pieces or full articles quite yet. What the Grapevine wants is your notion of what you would like to see printed in the magazine. This could include a vision of new departments, a topical list of new subject matter, or actual titles for new articles on which the staff could follow through. . .and what — most especially — you would like me to write about in the coming twelve months.

On your part this will have to be very much a labor of love, quite in the spirit of anonymity. I'm sure your mail will be far too large for me to answer. But you certainly can, and I know you will, give the Grapeviners and me a wonderful lot of excellent and usable ammunition.

Consider, readers, what a bargain you are getting. If we bought all this brass, at the full-time rates they soak folks on the outside, we'd be paying them about $10,000.00 a month. But for us AAs they sit up entire nights working on Grapevine for nothing but love. Can you beat that?

Let's not get the wrong idea! Let's have no illusion that it doesn't cost money to produce the Grapevine. When a magazine has a circulation of 23,000, there are problems that didn't exist when its readers could be counted in the hundreds. Even perspiring volunteers can't steal enough time from their breadwinning activities to do what needs to be done.

Offices are needed. Files, and plenty of filing space is called for. Records must be kept so that your subscription doesn't get lost. Expensive equipment must be bought. Correspondence must be answered. Phones must be answered. So the Grapevine *must* have full-time workers, too — a paid staff (of nonalcoholics) who do 90 percent of the job. The editor claims that these hard-working nonalkies do all the drudgery and then he and the drunks move in and take all the bows. So let's not patronize or underestimate these full-timers. Let's meet them:

First, there's our conscientious Kitty. She, aided by two young women and a young man, does her work in a downtown basement somewhere under Brooklyn Bridge. Going uptown you shake hands with the front office folks — two of them. In his cubicle you see John bending over the Vari-Typer. That's a lad who can't afford even one hangover. He has to be right all the time. They tell me he is, too.

Now here's Virginia. She's managing editor. On the Grapevine, that means a willing soul who'll do every job that the rest of the crew can't or won't. Four out of five Grapevine pieces come in from out of town. If that article of yours is pretty corny, she lets you down easy. She sends you a swell letter of thanks from the whole Grapevine staff and confides that your piece has been filed away in a precious receptacle she calls "the ice box." They may be able to use it later on — she hopes! Virginia has to cut and edit everybody. Drunks are so long winded, you know. So she has to trim our gush to fit the Grapevine space. Mine, too! She can usually make contributors hit a deadline or delay the printer without getting anybody very mad. (When the volunteers have proudly put the dear old Grapevine to bed — meaning they survived those anguished hours of polishing their final copy — Virginia sits back and smiles wryly.) It seems the volunteers can get away with boners. But not Virginia. If anything goes wrong, if the Grapevine falls out of bed again — well, Virginia done it! Yet she loves life on the Grapevine. Every Grapeviner will tell you the same thing. For them it's truly a labor of love. There's no other explanation for what these folks do for us twelve times a year.

What do you think the Grapeviners would like from you and me? Appreciation? Of course. Pieces contributed? Sure, send them in, they chorus. Subscriptions? Here they brighten way up, and say "Brother, now you're talking!"

Al, the editor, recently tipped me off. Said he: "The Grapevine is in a bad fix. Costs have been going sky high. Printing, postage, rent, payroll — everything. Can't help it. It means cutting the magazine in half or increasing the 25 cent price. This first is unthinkable, the second is bad news. The Foundation can't take up our deficit forever. Where do we go from here?"

"What about a lot more subscriptions," I asked. Al scratched his chin. "Another 10,000 by Christmas might turn the trick," he replied.

Maybe my last look into the Grapeviner's mirror was too much. I can't resist Al's blandishments anymore. Can you?

Let Us Read — and Thank God

October 1958

his is Grapevine's first international issue, and I'm mighty glad to see it going to press.

This event reminds me that the Grapevine's original charter was drawn by an AA lawyer, since gone to his reward. He was a fine lawyer, too. Therefore, his charter was a workmanlike and properly legalistic job. But our departed friend was much more than a good draftsman. He was an AA with a vision — a vision of what the AA of the future could be and what part the Grapevine could play to make that dream come true.

When he wrote the "general purpose" clause of the charter he quite forgot being the lawyer and launched into an extra-enthusiastic portrayal of the Grapevine's purposes and prospects — so much so that in the pioneering year of 1944 his vision seemed all too farfetched for most of us.

One of his phrases has always stuck by me. He pictured the Grapevine as AA's "magic carpet" which could instantly transport every reader to countless cities and hamlets and to those still lonesome outposts on distant shores where our Society would one day flourish.

Like no other, this international issue shows our friend's dream fulfilled. In the brief fourteen years since he penned that first charter, his early vision has been far surpassed by the glorious reality of what has actually taken place among us.

Let us read this issue from cover to cover — and thank God.

An Anniversary Letter

June 1959

T his issue of the Grapevine marks the anniversary of its founding exactly fifteen years ago.

The memory of some of those first editorial meetings will linger with me always. Seated around a table in a tiny cheerless room some place downtown, the founders pored over their freshly written copy for the first issues. In those days the enthusiastic founders did everything. Not only did they do the art work, write the bulk of the stories, they kept the books, they paid the printing bill, they typed the address on each copy, and finally licked all the stamps. So went the happy monthly paroxysm of creating what was to become the principal monthly journal of our whole Society.

Today, 35,000 readers see mirrored in each issue of the AA Grapevine a monthly vision of the worldwide thought, feeling, and activity of our whole Fellowship. It is our great means of intercommunication; a magic carpet on which each of you can ride to the more distant reaches and watch new brothers and sisters emerge from darkness into light.

On this happy occasion I send my warmest affection to Grapevine readers and staff alike. May God prosper the Grapevine always.

INDEX